# PRACTICAL GEOGRAPHY

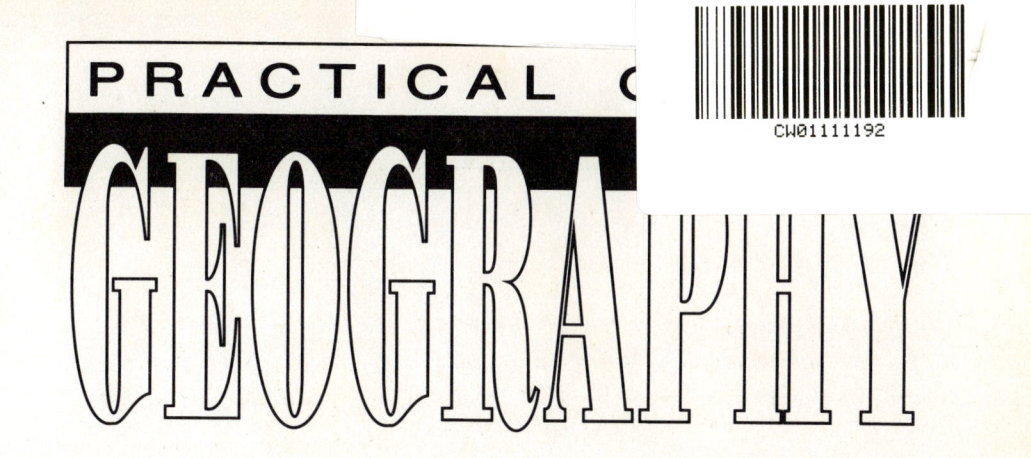

## TEACHING WITHIN THE NATIONAL CURRICULUM

**RACHEL BOWLES**

Published by Scholastic Ltd,
Villiers House, Clarendon Avenue,
Leamington Spa, Warwickshire, CV32 5PR

©1993 Scholastic Ltd
Reprinted 1993
2nd revised edition 1995

Written by Rachel Bowles
Edited by Christine Lee and Joanne Boden
Sub-edited by Jo Saxelby-Jennings
Designed by Keith Martin and Lois Sparling
Illustrated by Lynne Willey
Front cover designed by Sue Limb
Front cover illustration by Nancy Anderson
Tables prepared by Joanne Boden and Margaret Eaton
Photographs by Richard Butchins (pages 18 and 30), Isobel Butchinsky (page 148), Mike Howarth (pages 7, 13, 17, 21, 53, 77, 123, 137 and 153), Nicholas Spurling (page 177), Mike Turner (page 111), John Twinning (page 121) and Chris Tyrrell (page 163)
Extract from *Using IT Across the National Curriculum: a handbook for the primary classroom* by Sue Senior (1989, Owlet Books) (Chapter six, page 95) reproduced by permission of Sue Senior and Owlet Books.
Chapter eleven, figure 2 reproduced by permission of Curriculum Council for Wales.
Chapter five, figure 7 adapted from *Into Geography* (Book 1) by P and S Harrison/M Pearson (Nelson) pages 27, 29 and 30. Chapter five, figure 9 adapted from *Into Geography* (Book 2) by P and S Harrison/M Pearson (Nelson) pages 60 and 61.

Every effort has been made to trace and acknowledge the photographers and publishers whose material appears in this book. The publisher apologises for any omissions.

Material from the National Curriculum is Crown copyright and is reproduced by permission of the Controller of HMSO

Designed using Aldus Pagemaker
Printed in Great Britain by Ebenezer Baylis & Son, Worcester

**British Library Cataloguing in Publication Data**
A catalogue record for this book is available from the British Library.

ISBN 0-590-53521-8 2nd revised edition
(ISBN 0-590-53026-7 1st edition)

All rights reserved. This book is sold subject to the condition that it shall not, by way of trade or otherwise, be lent, hired out or otherwise circulated without the publisher's prior consent in any form of binding or cover other than that in which it is published and without a similar condition, including this condition, being imposed upon the subsequent purchaser.
  No part of this publication may be reproduced, stored in a retrieval system, or transmitted, in any form or by any means, electronic, mechanical, photocopying, recording or otherwise, without the prior permission of the publisher, except where photocopying for education purposes within a school or other educational establishment is expressly permitted in the text.

# Contents

**Introduction** 5

**Chapter one**
**What is geography?** 7
    Geography and the National Curriculum 9

**Chapter two**
**The enquiry approach** 13
    Stage one: how much is already known? 15
    Stage two: what information must be collected? 15
    Stage three: how is information to be recorded? 16
    Stage four: analysis 16
    Stage five: interpretation 16
    Tools of enquiry 17
    Special educational needs 19

**Chapter three**
**Fieldwork** 21
    Children's observations 21
    Fieldwork and the National Curriculum 22
    Fieldwork and other subjects 22
    Progression in fieldwork skills 24
    Incorporating fieldwork into the school curriculum 30
    Preparing for fieldwork 31
    Whole-school programme 33
    A fieldwork programme 36

**Chapter four**
**Maps and map-making** 53
    Map skills at Key Stage 1 54
    Map skills at Key Stage 2 65

**Chapter five**
**Other ways of learning** 77
    Visual communication 77
    Books and narratives 83
    Locality studies and stereotypes 84
    Museums 89

**Chapter six**
**Information technology** 95
    Information technology and graphicacy 95
    Communicating geographical ideas 96
    Handling information 97
    School-produced data files 101
    Measurement and control 104
    Overlay or concept keyboards 105
    Electronic mail 107
    Project HIT 107
    Using IT for mapwork 108
    Software selection 109

**Chapter seven**
**The classroom and resources** 111
    The ideal classroom 111
    Central reference 113
    Equipment for outdoor measurement 113
    Models and modelling needs 116
    Classroom approaches 116
    Human activity and the environment 119

**Chapter eight**
**Recording and assessing** 121
    National Curriculum requirements 121
    Assessment and the learning process 127
    Activity and assessment 135

**Chapter nine**
**Progression in practice** 137
    Progression in fieldwork 140
    Progression in looking at places 144
    Progression in looking at human features 148
    Progression in environmental geography 150

**Chapter ten**
**Programmes of study 153**
   The nature of the programmes 153
   The enquiry approach and topics 155
   The place of geography in the whole-school curriculum 155
   The planning schedule 156
   Geographical schemes of work 158
   Freedom of choice 160
   Lesson plans 161

**Chapter eleven**
**Topics, projects, places and themes: KS1 163**
   Starting points: stories and poems 164
   Schemes 167

**Chapter twelve**
**Topics, projects, places and themes: KS2 177**
   Role-play 177
   Landscape evaluation 181
   Schemes for Key Stage 2 182
   Cross-curricular topics 188

**Photocopiable pages 191**

**Resources 206**

The author wishes to thank the following schools for their assistance in the preparation of this book:
Balgowan Primary School, Beckenham, Kent;
St Mary's RC Primary School, Eltham, London;
and Fossdene Primary School, Charlton, London.

# Introduction

The aim of this book is to provide the non-geographer with a framework for teaching geography, based on the National Curriculum programmes of study, which is both rigorous and flexible. It is important that the all-round primary teacher realises that much of the knowledge needed for geography lesson planning is already known to them and their classes, but not from a geographical perspective. The teaching of geography is, therefore, about setting guidelines for understanding this information and enquiring further into the patterns observed. This book also aims to show the progression of knowledge and a sequence of techniques which will make for rewarding teaching and continuity within school. The book is intended to present criteria for selecting material suitable not just for the National Curriculum programme, but also for the individuals being taught. Teaching geography through the programme of study for each key stage makes this possible. The links between early work and later attainment are clearly revealed by using the level descriptions which constitute the single attainment target. All the quotes given in bold type in this book are taken from *Geography in the National Curriculum*, DES (1995, HMSO). The requirements of the National Curriculum are more than just a core of hard knowledge, and understanding is required in order to appreciate the knowledge. This understanding contributes to cross-curricular themes which have 'the ability to foster discussion of questions of value and belief; they add to knowledge and understanding and they rely on practical activities, decision making and the inter-relationship of the individual in the community.' (from 'Themes' in *Curriculum Guidance 3: The Whole Curriculum* NCC, 1990).

It is important to maintain among the staff an open approach to sharing their experience of geographical work. This will aid not only the selection of content and resources, but also the format for recording experience and achievement and thus helping to build up a worthwhile compendium of resources and experiences for the ever-varying needs of the children. This book aims to show how this approach can work in practice.

# Organisation of the book

This book is broadly divided into three themes. Chapters one to eight discuss the contribution of geography to general education and to learning within the curriculum framework. Learning through enquiry, fieldwork (enhanced by the use of information technology) and visual and narrative experience is examined, together with the development of spatial intelligence through graphicacy. Assessment of achievement and development is also considered.

Chapters nine to eleven expand upon the earlier part of the book by making connections between the National Curriculum programmes of study and the progression possible in each area of attainment in geographical education. Strategies for dealing with specific requirements are given by illustration and in tabular form, with an emphasis on developing a wider view of the environment and the world in general.

Finally, Chapters eleven and twelve examine topics, projects, places and themes at Key Stages 1 and 2 in both subject-specific and cross-curricular situations, using group work and whole-class approaches. These final chapters are intended to draw together the various strands considered throughout the rest of the book.

# Chapter one
# What is geography?

Geography is more than knowing where places are to be found, and everyone is a geographer to some extent. You know why your town is important to you. It can provide work, shelter and entertainment. It is located in your 'personal' geography, the extent of your spatial knowledge of the immediate world around you. This is knowledge which you have gathered and stored since birth. You know how to reach specific places by road, rail or some other means of communication. If you do not know, you use a rail timetable or a map. Any journey will involve addressing certain geographical questions. For example, suppose you were to plan a journey of several hundred miles to a town which had formerly been served by rail, but for which bus service information was now provided in the relevant timetable. This would prompt questions such as:
• Why had the rail communication stopped?
• Why should the town have retained its significance in an area which on the map looked totally isolated?
• What was it like there?
• How had the town come to be located in that precise spot?
• When had it achieved its importance?
• What was the weather like?
• Would you need warmer or cooler clothing?

Most people are familiar with their own locality and most are aware of places further afield, either through personal experience or through the media. Tourist offices provide helpful maps in their brochures, while newspaper and television reports often contain maps to help locate the newsworthy areas. Thus, knowledge of such places is not learned by rote. It takes more than rote knowledge to understand, for example, how one town can become more important than other towns of a similar size in the same country. The upheavals in Eastern Europe since the late 1980's have required even the casual television viewer to ask why towns other than the capitals have become the focus of attention. Very often the answer lies with a variety of geographical factors. A town might be the regional centre for a specific group of people, the centre for a special agricultural activity or industrial complex, the natural centre of communication within that region and so on.

Often a town or a region will become well-known by association with characteristics such as leisure, industry or cultural activity. Thus the Cairngorms might typify the leisure industry, the West Riding of Yorkshire might typify the wool trade and Oxford or Cambridge might typify cultural activity. This, of course, is over-simplistic. The fact that associated or even contrasting activities are to be found in these areas illustrates how complex the attributes of a region can become. Thus the slopes suitable for skiing in the Cairngorms are adjacent to slopes forested with coniferous plantations and other hills used by farmers, and are all served by the same roads. Thirty years ago the West Riding of Yorkshire provided lucrative careers for whole families in industrial concerns making carpets and cloths for suits and blankets, as well as jobs in road haulage and food production for the towns which had developed round these concerns. The West Riding could easily be used for topics such as 'Clothes', 'Homes', 'Energy', 'Farms' and 'Journeys'. Moreover, the fact that few of the same factories concerned with these industries exist today offers a potential area of enquiry by both historians and geographers working on the topic of 'Change'.

By contrast, Oxford and Cambridge were originally places of contemplative thought and learning. However, to allow the scholars sufficient time for these activities other people had to be employed to do the essential cleaning, gardening, shopping, cooking and other ancillary occupations. In time, the needs of such communities extended from self-sufficiency to providing lucrative craft industries, which later developed even further to become part of national industries producing cars, books and computers.

People who work in towns such as Cambridge or Oxford are drawn from a wide area, criss-crossed with a network of communications. When studied geographically, this network can be shown to have a pattern developed from a 'hierarchy' of places. Small villages look towards the nearest market town. The market towns look towards the nearest large town equipped with more facilities and the large towns look towards the regional centre to provide major administrative guidance. In this way recognisable regions, each with distinctive characters, have evolved.

So far we have looked at four different places with descriptions based upon common knowledge. To learn more about them we have to venture further into other realms of geographical knowledge. For example, the science of physical geography offers an understanding of the complexities of the slope and weather in the Cairngorms, as well as the primary advantages of plentiful soft water, supplied by many small, swift streams to drive the mill wheels of the Pennine region of Yorkshire for the woollen industry. Investigation into the way these places have developed also involves considering the effect of human activities. What political, economic and sociological considerations led some entrepreneur to think of building a hotel and ski-lift in the Cairngorms? Why did many woollen mills close and their buildings become smaller units making wares for the retail gift market? When did the cultural world allow industry to camp on its doorstep? How did

Cambridge become the regional centre to which many local roads lead? Where does Oxford send its products (people, as well as cars)? Geography examines the character of places; asks questions – where? what? how? why? and when? Geography looks at the spacing of places in relation to each other and to other physical features on the Earth's surface. For example, volcanoes are liable to erupt and be a danger to life, yet the volcanic 'ring of fire' round the Pacific encompasses some of the most highly populated places in the world. This forces the geographer to address a number of questions. Why have people come to live in these dangerous places? How have they prospered? What is it like to live there? Where are these areas? When are they dangerous?

Geography is the only subject to ask as its primary question 'where?' It is the only subject to consider the relative spacing of places and, consequently, is the only subject to focus closely on ways of communicating the idea of spatial relationships by means other than words and numbers. Graphicacy, the method of graphic communication which shows the plan of a house, the layout of a park, the route to the library or the shape of the landscape, was defined in 1972 by Professor W.G.V. Balchin as, 'the communication of spatial information that cannot be conveyed adequately by verbal or numerical means' ('Graphicacy' in *Geography* (No. 256), Vol. 57, Pt. 3).

Thus, the placing of the Cairngorm hotels in relation to the ski slopes and the roads, the location of water-mills down the Pennine streams and the situation of the colleges in the centre and the location of industries on the outskirts of Oxford and Cambridge can only be shown adequately by maps. The maps need not be beautifully drawn but should have understandable symbols, even picture symbols, in a linear framework and enough labels to illustrate whatever relationship is being shown. Figure 1 shows how a map can succinctly demonstrate the relationship between natural and man-made features.

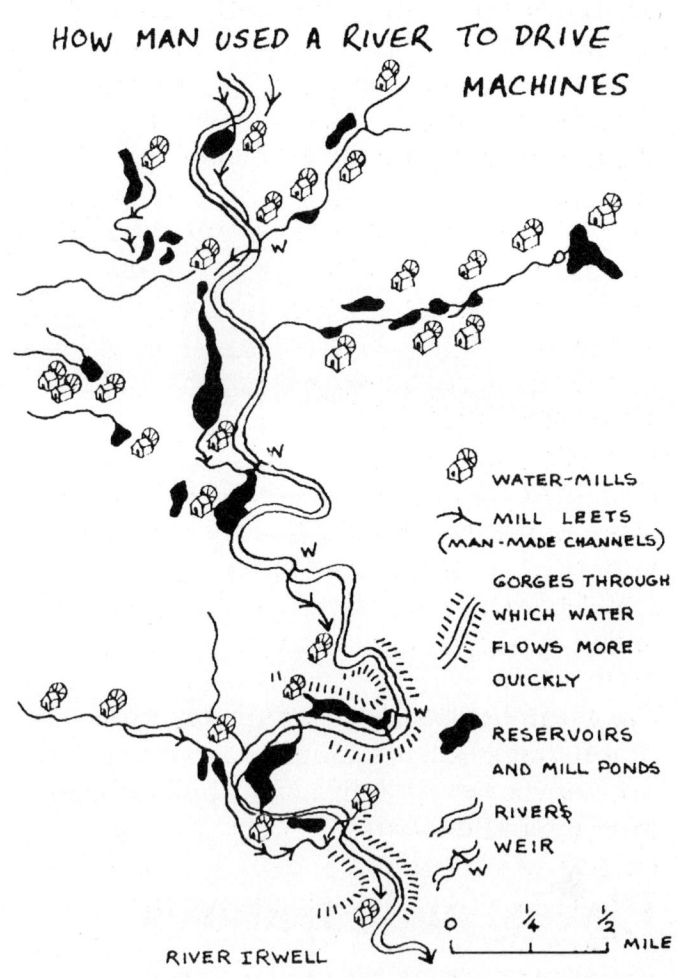

Figure 1

# Geography and the National Curriculum

So far we have looked at the various questions and skills which the study of geography entails. How are these questions and skills accommodated in the National Curriculum?

# Geographical skills

Geographical skills cover the use of maps and photographs and the means of collecting information for maps by direct observation in the locality. Observation forms the necessary groundwork for the development of graphicacy. As such, it is as important as the alphabet is in the development of literacy and numbers up to

100 are in the development of numeracy. Moreover, in talking about observations, not only is a geographical vocabulary being built up, but oracy is also being practised.

## Places: main features

Children are encouraged to use their geographical skills to address the following questions:
• What makes a place distinctive?
• Where is the place located?
• How does it compare with other places in local, regional, United Kingdom, European Union and international contexts?

## Places: physical features

Children are invited to consider the following questions about physical features:
• How are places affected by weather, weather patterns and conditions around the world?
• What kind of river, sea and landscape features are found in the places studied?
• How did they come to be so?

## Places: human features

Human features focus upon people's relationship with both the physical environment and with their neighbours.
• How many people are there?
• What kinds of settlements and communications are there?
• When did these features come about?
• What activities have developed?

## Places: environmental change

This area of geography considers the consequences of human activities in the localities studied.
• How have people changed the locality by their activities?
• How can different demands be managed?
• What changes will improvements bring about?

Figure 2 on page 11 indicates how some of these questions can be asked at each level in each of the target areas. It is not a suggested scheme of work, merely an indication of *how* geographical questions may be asked and answered. Figure 3 on page 12 places localities work in the context of themes and places

The subsequent chapters look at the work engendered by such planning.

# Using the locality: some aspects

| Level | Observation and recording | Investigation and communication | Physical features | Human features | Environmental change |
|---|---|---|---|---|---|
| 1 | Walk round school. Find school on a map. Make a model of some part of the school. | Describe what has been seen. What important building is there? What is its name? | Which way does the pavement or playground slope? Are we on a hill or in a valley? | Who else lives or works in the street or school? How do they travel home/to work? | What is good about the street or playground? What spoils it? |
| 2 | Find a street or area near school and observe in groups the details of contrasting buildings. | Talk about the contrasts. Look at old photographs and relate them to the present. Where else are such buildings and land found in the locality? | Where are the wet and dry places? Why? Where are the hills and valleys? What kind of weather do we have? | Where do people come from to this place? Where do they go to buy books? Food? How do they get there? Where do they work? | What could make the street/park better? What is changing? |
| 3 | Make a map showing the route home from school in the correct sequence. Select a place on the map to investigate. | Visit several places in the locality and use maps, photographs and archive material to find out more about them. How different are they from each other? From another locality? | Discover why the places are different in character (e.g. streams, lakes, ponds). Where is the highest hill? Where is the flattest ground? | Find out why the land is used differently. (e.g. Why are allotments here and not there?) Why is the land used for industry not houses? | Investigate local change. Think of some solutions to unsightly areas in the locality. What causes 'dumps'? What needs to be retained (e.g. the playing area)? |
| 4 | Use measuring equipment in the playground and the locality (e.g. as part of planning a garden). | Find out why certain buildings (e.g. library), land uses (e.g. park) and activities such as shopping are located at particular sites. | Investigate where the local streams start and finish. Measure changes in the stream during the year. When is the water level highest? Lowest? | Compare the size of different land uses and their location. How does this affect activities. | Find out about local recreational open space. How can it be increased? |
| 5 | Obtain information from the 1:25,000 and 1:50,000 OS maps. | Investigate the major influences in the home region and fit the locality into the region. What is it like? Where do we fit? | Investigate good local examples of weathering and erosion. Relate these to changes in stream or slope. | Investigate how places are linked in the area – why and how. Are there conflicts? | Consider the effect of a local activity and how it could be managed or sustained. |

Figure 2

# Chapter two
# The enquiry approach

An enquiry approach is expected by the programmes of study at all stages of the curriculum.

The programme of study for Key Stage 1 states that pupils should be given opportunities to:
**'a) investigate the physical and human features of their surroundings;
b) undertake studies that focus on geographical questions... and that are based on direct experience, practical activities and fieldwork in the locality of the school...'.**

It also states that, in investigating places and a theme, pupils should be given opportunities to **'observe, question and record, and to communicate ideas and information.'**

In addition, the programme of study for Key Stage 2 states that, in investigating places and themes, pupils should be given opportunities to:
**a) observe and ask questions about geographical features and issues;
b) collect and record evidence to answer the questions;
c) analyse the evidence, draw conclusions and communicate findings.'**

At all stages this enquiry is expected to involve the development of skills,

13

knowledge and understanding about places and themes.

The Geography Non-Statutory Guidance (1991) published by the NCC suggests under 'Teaching Methods' (6.3) that an enquiry may include:
• asking a question;
• collecting relevant data from primary and secondary sources;
• analysing and interpreting data;
• presenting findings;
• drawing conclusions;
• evaluating the enquiry.

The Non-Statutory Guidance for Teachers, Section F 'Aspects of teaching and learning in Geography', Part 1 'Enquiry', from the Curriculum Council for Wales, emphasises that:

'Enquiries become geographical when the questions are formulated to develop geographical ideas and concepts and to explore places and geographical themes. Effective questioning can enhance the quality of geographical education, developing attitudes of curiosity and interest and ensuring an active involvement in the learning process. Sound, relevant and well constructed teacher-led questions in the early stages will serve as a model for pupils' enquiries.'

Figure 1 shows the place of teacher-led enquiry in the development of the study of

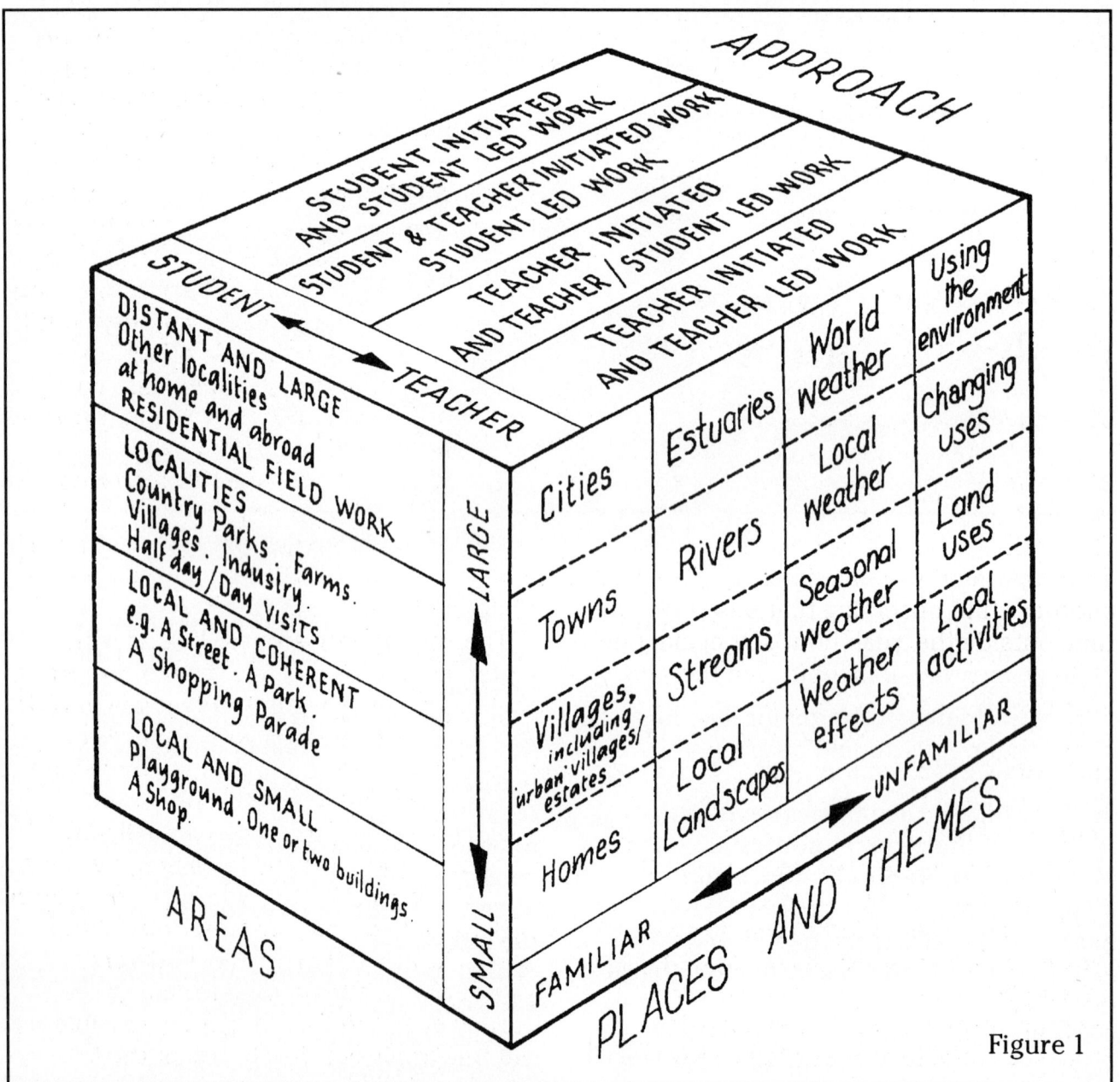

Figure 1

areas and themes. This does not mean the exclusion of child-inspired work, rather that the disparate ideas generated by the children are more easily fitted into a coherent unit if a well thought out framework has been prepared by the teacher. Conversely, as enquiry proceeds, so the children's body of knowledge and experience grows, enabling new lines of enquiry to be generated. The teacher's role is to ensure that the children select the most valuable line of enquiry to fulfil the requirements of the National Curriculum.

Both non-statutory documents emphasise that there is no fixed sequence to the enquiry approach. Children's understanding of the environment is built up slowly, using skills steadily acquired from babyhood. This understanding is consolidated with knowledge gained during the process of enquiry. Enquiry can take the form of individual explorations or directed group explorations. In practice enquiry falls into five stages.

## Stage one: how much is already known?

This stage uses earlier observations and interpretations. These may include some observations which would seem to be at variance with each other. For instance, one child declares that buses are always late. This statement is immediately qualified by another child observing that buses run on time outside the 'rush hour'. Or again, one child insists that all pebbles are the same, 'just stones'. Another child promptly enthuses about the various pinks, whites and blacks which can be seen. Not one of these statements is absolutely right, neither are they absolutely wrong. However, taken together each theme is worthy of further investigation.

The bus investigation would be suitable for Key Stage 2 enquiry, as it demands skills developed in mathematics and early geography map work. The enquiry into stones is suitable for Key Stage 1 work, as it requires the development of the skills and vocabulary of sorting and classifying.

These two themes will be followed as examples of the stages of procedure in the enquiry approach. Both enquiries will also develop the life skill of identifying ambiguities and grey areas.

## Stage two: what information must be collected?

The bus investigation would probably be undertaken by Y5 or Y6 children. These children might have already undertaken a traffic census and be conversant with the variable flow during the day. In this case the data would need to have a wider base.

The enquiry could be extended to consider whether factors such as the length of journey or the route could affect buses keeping to time. The bus route could be plotted on a map of the school locality, either a 1:10,000 Ordnance Survey map or a large scale A-Z map, and the enquiry could then be extended to include other bus travellers in the school and even to co-opting the help of other schools in the area, both primary and secondary. A questionnaire would have to be devised, providing information on the numbers travelling, how far they travel, where from and what problems they encountered (see Chapter six for use of IT).

The enquiry into stones (linking with materials work in science) would require that everyone brought in some hand-sized stones from as many different places as possible. (Initiate good practice by fixing labels indicating where the stones were found on each stone. Use clear nail varnish to adhere each location label and then varnish over them. This is effective for both porous and non-porous materials.) If the school is situated in an area of diverse geology, or in a town built from a great variety of materials, it might be possible to plot the origins of the stones on the local map. The children could then begin to examine the stones more closely and sort them. The criteria for sorting could include texture, colour, fizziness when put into a bowl of lemon juice or vinegar and the effect of light (does the stone sparkle, shine or remain dull?). The teacher would have to prepare for the sorting process by ensuring that scratching tools, vinegar or lemon juice, bowls, vocabulary cards, colour charts and record sheets on which to note observations (see Chapter three, page 24) were available to allow the children to start work immediately. Other criteria for sorting might be suggested by the children, depending upon what is available (for example, crystalline rocks lend themselves to sorting by crystal size).

# Stage three: how is information to be recorded?

The older children involved in the bus survey could find a suitable Ordnance Survey or road map to trace in order to make a location map. This would satisfy KS2, PoS, 3c, d. The results of the questionnaire could be entered on a database from which graphs, charts and flow diagrams of the number of travellers on each route and at what times could be generated.

Younger children could draw the various stones, make graphs of sets or build labelled miniature rock gardens.

# Stage four: analysis

The process of analysis often coincides with classifying the information and deciding how best to show the results. Again, if the framework has been prepared beforehand by the teacher, this process can develop into making a display (for example, a chart to show which rocks are the hardest).

# Stage five: interpretation

The whole investigation could bring to light several factors to be considered geographically. The older children would investigate how bus transport is affected by the distance travelled and how the time of arrival varies, not only with the time of day when the journey is made, but also the day of the week. Investigation would reveal how this in turn is influenced by the location of places of work and the times of starting and finishing work, not to mention the times at which the raw materials for the work are delivered. The children would realise that the weather could prove to be a factor, as could unforeseen hazards such as football matches or cows being moved from field to field.

The budding geologists could be heading towards technology in realising that hard and soft rocks have their uses (that sandstones feel like sandpaper, soft powdery rocks are reminiscent of blackboard chalks or talcum powder) or that colour can give rocks value (as for jewellery) and make them more than 'just stones'.

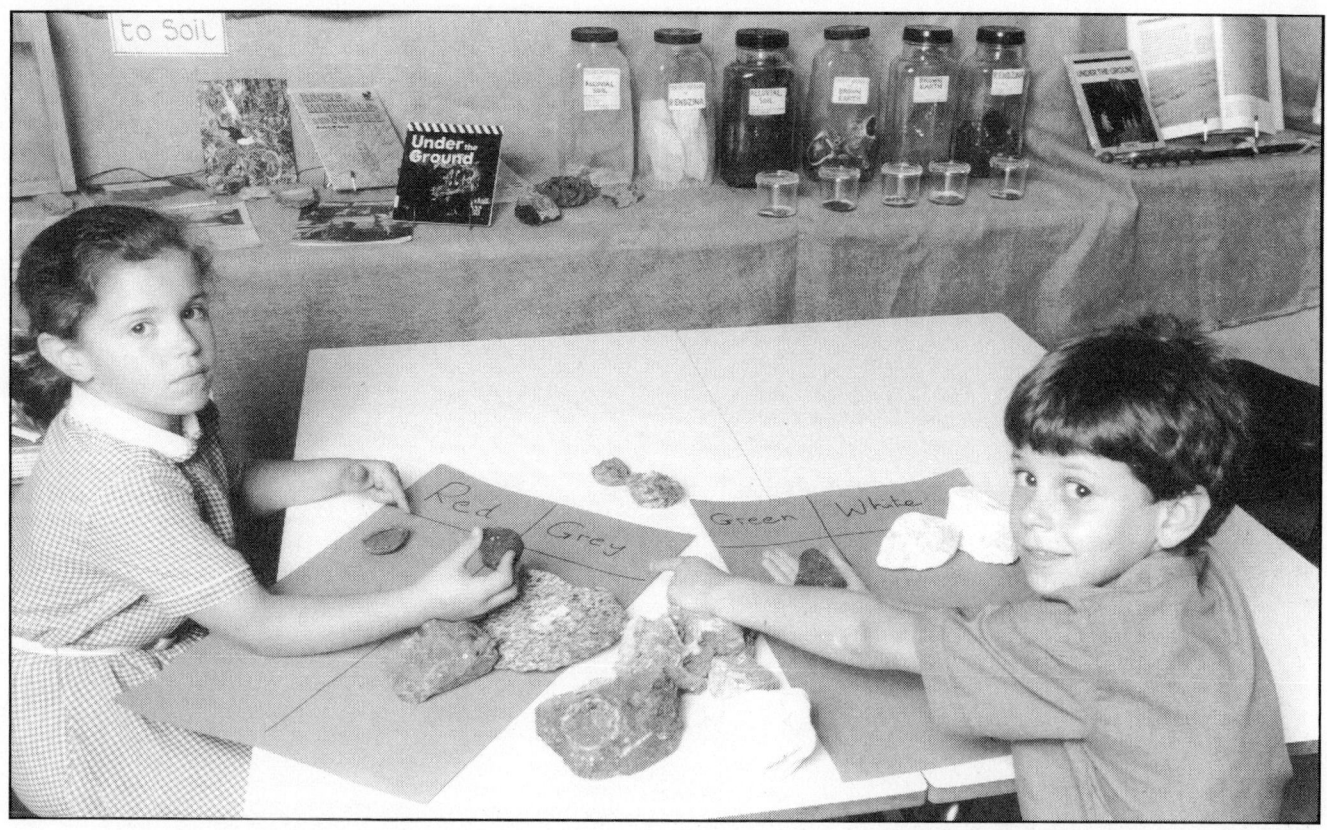

Interpretation is the most important stage of the enquiry. It can in turn become the starting point for another sequence of enquiry. For example, asking a question such as, 'Does a detour on a journey, because of few bridging points over a river, always mean a longer journey time?' would expand the topic to considering the quality of the road network, the influence of physical barriers such as slope and water, the pattern of the network and the factors which influence it. In the investigation about stones, recognising the features and qualities of different stones and relating these to where the rocks were found or where they are used, raises questions such as, 'Are hills made of the hardest rocks?' or 'What kind of rock is used to build our houses?'

Thus the enquiry sequence is really an endless loop which changes the complexity and features of its structure with the level and the needs of the children as well as contributing towards the completion of the National Curriculum, the foundation of which is made up of the five questions, where? what? why? how? and which way?

## Tools of enquiry

The tools of enquiry are wide-ranging and include the skills developed and used in the core subjects. The ways of using the tools are varied, covering individual research, collaborative learning, group work and class work. The basic tools are:

• Basic classroom skills are the most obvious tools. These include reading (descriptions from stories, poems, newspapers, magazines, books and letters), writing (summaries, personal reports, accounts and assessments) and talking and listening (describing journeys, landscapes and the activities of other people, as well as discussing the management of the enquiry).

• Maps and mapwork include the Ordnance Survey, commercial and pictorial maps, as well as maps made by the children themselves, based on gathered data.

• Work outside the classroom involves observing and recording the numerous elements of the environment created by physical and human factors.

- Visiting places of specific geographical interest could include farms, a building site, a factory or a leisure centre built on to an existing swimming pool. The children could find out the function of each of these places.
- Visitors could be invited in to the classroom as part of the investigation into specific places of geographical interest. This might include a follow-up visit by a farmer or factory manager as part of developing an ongoing relationship between the school and the working world. It could also include visitors with overseas connections, such as people with relatives living in a country which the children are investigating.
- Learning also occurs from material presented by the teacher, such as an explanation of thunderstorms or the movement of the sun. This may eventually be transformed into a practical activity carried out by the children.
- Audio-visual material such as slides, photographs, aerial photographs, tapes, videos and television can be used as an enquiry tool.
- Children should be encouraged to use quantitative data, such as fieldwork results (e.g. children's traffic census), other people's data (e.g. Planning Department traffic census returns), official averaged data (e.g. census enumeration data, recorded every ten years and available 100 years later) and data from a variety of sources further an enquiry. All the above examples could be used to record change in the environment.
- Develop role play and simulation games to recognise the interplay of several factors, such as the farmer's year or the planning of a housing estate.
- Play educational games to emphasise the various changes encountered along a specific route (such as the journey to school or the course of a river, played as a dice game with hazard squares).
- Use new technology, such as databases, word processors, computer simulations or concept keyboards to move data about and juxtapose several sets of data or to develop vocabulary by relating image to word.
- Use the products of new technology, such as satellite photographs and imagery,

to look at the spatial relationships of weather phenomena and other environments on the planet (such as tropical grasslands, or the Mississippi flood plain).
• Undertake practical activities using collected information. This could include making models of a street, farm or transport terminus to give reality to a map and photograph and draw attention to detail.
• Undertake laboratory-style experiments to collect information (such as testing soils for acidity, sieving and drying samples of sediment from different sites to discover the products of weathering or analysing stream samples to discover the full load transported by water). Note that these differ from scientific experiments in that the samples come from the different environmental areas being studied, to add comparative information on those places, rather than being experiments in their own right.

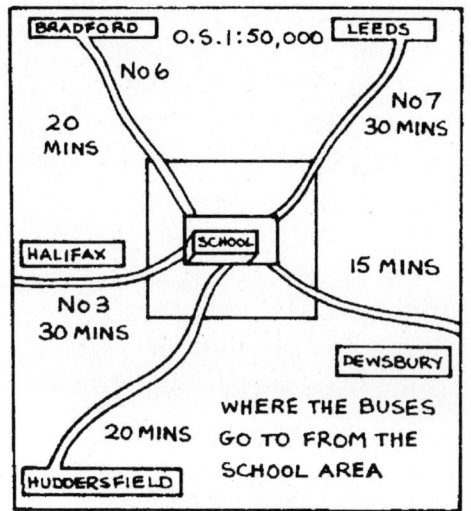

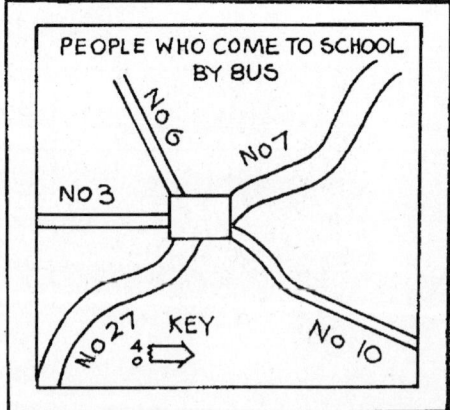

Figure 2

## Special educational needs

The child with special educational needs is greatly helped by the practical nature of the enquiry approach. Deaf and blind children can add an extra dimension to enquiry by the need to give greater attention to sensory information, such as textures and relief. The whole class can also gain from the need to emphasise variation in size by touch (for example, understanding changes in particle size). An example of applying tactile skills would be to create a sequence of crystals, starting with a group of quartz crystals, then the crystals in a cube of sugar, coarse sandpaper, fine sandpaper, fine sandstone, the rough feel of flagstone and finally the smooth feel of clay. A similar sequence could be made with volcanic rocks, from the fine but rough feel of pumice, through the fine crystals as in a roadstone and finally to the coarser crystals in a granite.

Sorting these into crystal size order to show the effect of erosion or the effect of volcanic cooling at different rates (the slower the rate of cooling, the larger the crystal size) would help develop classifying skills. The size of sample could be reduced down to three classes or up to as many classes as you can find examples for, to cover the range of ability and ensure successful outcomes.

There is a helpful section (Chapter 3.5) by Sarah Smith, concerning children with special needs, in *Geographical Work in Primary and Middle Schools* (1988), which also includes the gifted child.

## The gifted child

The gifted child can be a useful adjunct in helping extend experiments by more detailed work or by extending research which can provide material for other groups. The gifted child can present the results of his or her research in a form suitable for the other children to add to their own observations, such as investigating bus and rail connections with regional centres outside the school catchment area and putting these routes on a small scale map (Figure 2, page 19).

Tape recorders, word processors, databases and overlay or concept keyboards can be used by gifted children to input data to the computer to provide visual answers when the computer is 'questioned' by the less able child.

Geographical enquiry with a balance of open-ended and structured tasks can enable children with special needs to demonstrate what is known and what can be done. The severely handicapped child can benefit from structured tasks based on the visual and graphic materials used by geographers. (Figure 3, based on Non-Statutory Guidance, 1991, provides a model for this.)

| ENQUIRY FOR THE SLOW LEARNER | |
|---|---|
| **Enquiry:** | Do different vehicles make different journeys? |
| **Investigation:** | Watch a video of local traffic; talk about what has been seen. |
| **Classification:** | Sort photographs or models of large and small delivery vehicles (such as oil-tanker, cement-mixer, tipper truck, bus, milk-float, police vehicle, van, ambulance, fire-engine, family car). Further sorting activities can consider those which make regular journeys into local streets and those which make special journeys. |
| **Interpretation:** | Match the service vehicles to the people who use them using picture cards (such as postman and van, fire-fighter and engine). |
| **Presentation:** | Show on a large map where a small vehicle, such as post-van and milk-float, goes, then a contrasting vehicle, such as fire-engine or tractor. |
| **Conclusion:** | Some vehicles make similar journeys, others make special journeys. |
| **Next enquiry:** | Are special journeys long journeys? |
| **National Curriculum:** | Describe ways in which people make journeys, i.e., make links. |

Figure 3

# Chapter three
# Fieldwork

'Field time is your most precious time – how precious you will know only when its days are past,' Carl Sauer (1954) 'The education of a geographer', *Annals of the Association of American Geographers*, Vol.46, pp.287–99.

This was quoted by Professor Denis Brunsden in his Presidential address to the Geographical Association in 1987. There he pointed out that, 'Fieldwork has developed from many origins and must be regarded as a fundamental pedagogical device within the British Educational system.' *Geography* (No.316) Vol.72 Pt.3 p.193 (June 1987).

## Children's observations

A wealth of observation goes on within every school. Children notice their surroundings in minute detail without realising the importance of what they have observed. It is the teacher's job to help them to make sense of what has been observed and noticed. For example, one junior school headmaster took a friend and his daughter across the Pennines to Liverpool. A small notebook was made for the nine-year-old, complete with sketches of what should be noticed, ranging from the Royal Liver Building and its decoration to the shape of the columns holding up the Dockland Railway and the rounded corners of the warehouses. This proved to be an unforgettable day which, 20 years later, became her foundation for a fieldwork exercise for teachers in training.

From an early age that same girl repeatedly visited a stream in a bluebell wood. Over the years and seasons the changing flora was noticed between each visit. Flowers were pressed and the different ways to the favourite spot were remembered and recorded. Decades later, all this observation surfaced in her realisation, on reading lists of the flora and shrubs common to relict woodland, that the bluebell wood was a remnant of an ancient woodland. The young girl, if asked, would probably not have been able to put into words what she had noticed at the time other than the flowers. Even if they are able to transmit some of their observations, young children will tend to keep the greater part of what they have noticed to themselves until they can fit it into a logical pattern. The pattern, however, has to have all the component pieces which can then be arranged, therefore the opportunities for observation have to be maintained regularly.

At one school, a girl in Y6 asked what Y4 were doing at a particular stream (in fact, measuring how fast the water moved) and volunteered the information that the stream changed from season to season. This knowledge was based upon her own visits with her older brother that had gradually allowed her to see the pattern of changes to the stream. In the process of discussion, the connection between rainfall and high flow was confirmed.

When getting background material for work in the local environment, remember to ask the children where they go to play and what places they visit with their parents. This could all be part of developing mapping experiences. Even a picture map can reveal the 'roaming experience' of a child. It is a sad fact that nowadays roaming is not advisable, and therefore not allowed to the same extent as in the past. It is thus up to the school to ensure that the neighbourhood and locality is visited in a properly supervised, regular and wide-ranging observational fashion.

## Fieldwork and the National Curriculum

The statutory orders for geography outline the entitlement and expectation of fieldwork at all key stages. All pupils should be given opportunities to:

'Undertake studies... based on direct experience... and fieldwork in the locality of the school'.

They should also be taught to undertake fieldwork activities which, at Key Stage 1, should take place in the locality of the school and which, at Key Stage 2, should include **'the use of instruments to make measurements... and appropriate techniques'**.

Note that the fieldwork is not restricted to the school locality at Key Stage 2.

In considering curriculum content, the *Geography Non-Statutory Guidance* (1991) devotes a whole unit of work to 'Study of another locality' (Figure 1), where the pupil activities are wholly based upon on-site observation. It is expected that this work would be undertaken in Y6, but can only be undertaken with maximum benefit if similar work has previously been undertaken in the home locality.

The key question, 'What are the similarities and differences between the home area and the visited locality?' can only be answered by observing and recording in a systematic fashion. The skills of sketching, working in groups to measure and record, using compasses and clinometers, using cameras and taking meaningful samples cannot be taught in half an hour, standing on top of a cliff, in a blustery wind. These skills will have been initiated at Key Stage 1 and elaborated and revised at successive levels.

Also in the *Non-Statutory Guidance* (1991) under '6.0 Teaching methods' (Figure 2), it is significant that out of the nine methods listed only the enquiry approach and fieldwork are considered in detail

## Fieldwork and other subjects

Geography is not the only subject for which fieldwork is considered essential. Science and history both involve fieldwork – and whoever heard of landscape artists painting indoors!

The National Curriculum Council, in *Curriculum Guidance 7: Environmental Education* (1990), points out in 'Education

| UNIT OF WORK FOR A KS2 CLASS (YEAR 6) – STUDY OF ANOTHER LOCATION ||||||
|---|---|---|---|---|
| Key questions | Learning objectives | Pupil activities | Resources | Assessment objectives |
| What are the similarities and differences between the local area and visited locality? | Concepts:<br>Changing landscape<br>Land use<br>The protection of the environment | In the field:<br>Group/individual observation, sketching<br>Observation of flora, fauna and rocks | Ordnance Survey 1:50,000 maps<br>Large scale plans | Teacher assessment: Oral by listening to comments and asking questions |
| How is tourism important to that locality? | Skills:<br>Enquiry skills - data collection, observation, investigation<br>Map and atlas work<br>Use of primary and secondary sources | Simple group work to measure, record, sketch, photograph<br>Use of compass<br>Observation and sketching of a landscape<br>Discussion of land use<br>Orientate OS map on site; at viewpoint; at monument, e.g. castle keep<br>Draw sketch maps<br>Record temperature each day of visit to compare with Year 5's log book at school, recorded same time | AA/RAC atlases, information books, tourist brochures/maps, aerial photos<br>Teacher/pupils resources from locality<br>Photos, postcards, spreadsheet, data program | Pupils draw transect to scale |
| | Content:<br>Erosion of coast<br>Deposition<br>Protection of coasts<br>Use of coastal areas for leisure activities, hotels, retirement homes<br>Vegetation | | Clinometers<br>Compasses<br>Cameras<br>Hand lens<br>Sample jars and bags | Peer observation/ discussion<br>Teacher observation |
| | | | | Mount and label photos, comment on land use, etc. |
| | | | | Individual factual writing, drawing, folder production |
| Links with other subjects - mathematics, English, science<br>Cross-curricular themes - environmental education ||||||

Figure 1

IN or THROUGH the environment' that 'Firsthand experience is an essential part of helping pupils to develop a personal response to the environment and thus gain an awareness of environmental issues. This can start in the school itself, in its grounds and immediate locality, progressing to visits to more distant contrasting localities in the United Kingdom, and in other countries....Where residential experience, well-directed fieldwork and recreation can be combined, considerable progress can be made. Schools and LEAs should seek, wherever possible, to include this in the education of every pupil.'

It is clear that for each child to achieve the level of experience described above, a whole-school policy has to be agreed concerning the place and time of fieldwork in the curriculum, in order to accommodate the needs of each subject. Within the geography curriculum, there are certain statements of attainment which would be difficult to achieve without experience outside the classroom. Any work carried out beyond the everyday location of the class (including other areas within the school and grounds) is essentially 'fieldwork'.

---

The variety of teaching methods needed to match the abilities and interests of pupils is likely to include the following:

- knowledge given by teacher;
- fieldwork;
- creative activities, eg model making;
- questions and answers;
- individual and group enquiries;
- use of television, radio, tape, video and film;
- use of IT;
- use of books, leaflets, maps and atlases;
- role play and drama.

Figure 2

# Progression in fieldwork skills

As with mapping skills, the development of fieldwork skills can begin in the early years. Initially, the emphasis should be on collecting together a vocabulary to describe what has been seen, after which the children can begin to draw and make other representations of what has been seen. This can be followed by using simple record forms to classify the properties of samples collected from outside (Figure 3), slowly increasing the number of recordable features (Figure 4) until by Y6 the full-

SETS FROM SAMPLES

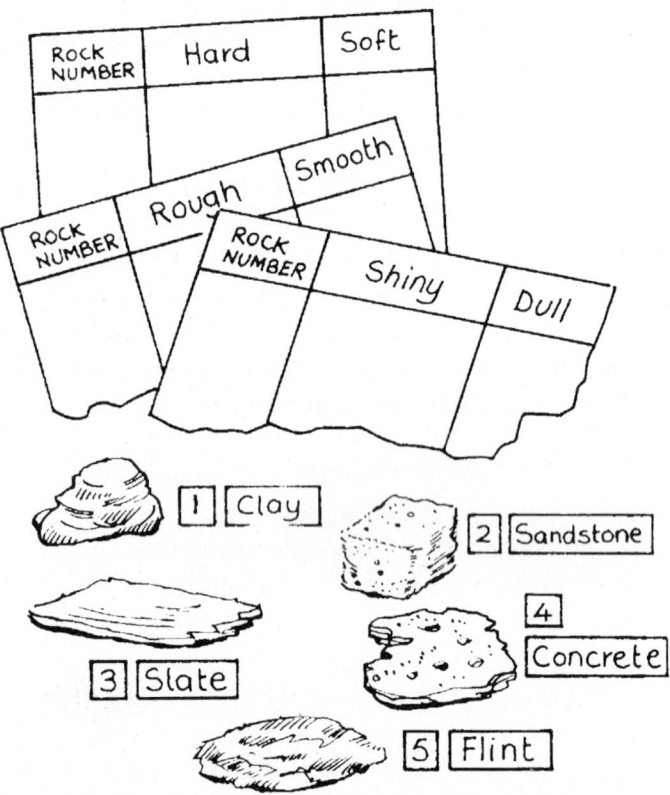

Figure 3

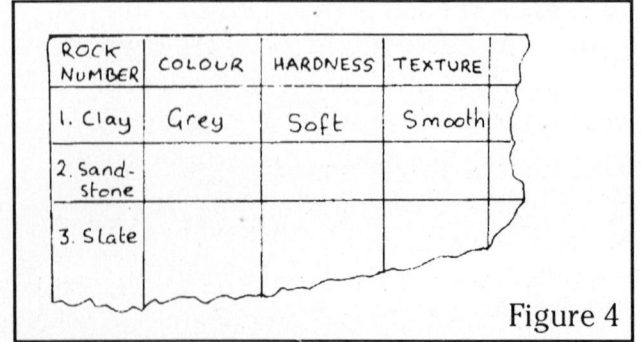

Figure 4

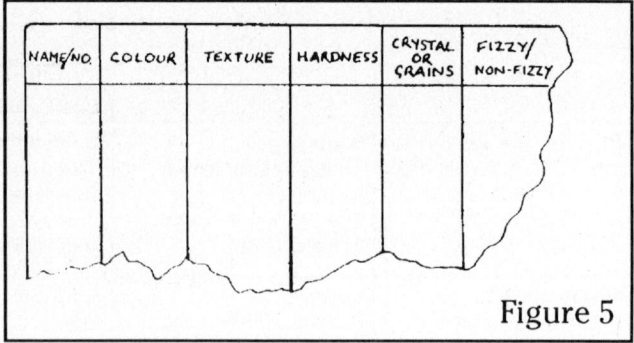

Figure 5

blown 'field form' (Figure 5) can be used by the children with confidence away from school in another locality, for example at the coast or on the moors or hills.

# Progression in field techniques: rivers

## Simulations

Not every school will be near a stream, but all the following simulations are possible with careful preparation.

To simulate the effects of water flow, a length of guttering partially filled at one end with sand, gravel and pebbles (ballast) can be used to represent the ground. The ballast should be damp and well patted down. A washing machine hose attached to a tap or a household watering can and spray can be used to represent the rain. Have a small bucket and a bailer to hand to remove water collected at the end of the guttering (Figure 6). Alternatively, drill a drainage hole at the end of the guttering and collect the water as it pours through.

Start by covering the 'hill' with a sheet of plastic and spray it to demonstrate water running over a surface protected with an impermeable layer. The water will not be able to sink or soak into the ground and so will model the action of water on tarmac and paved areas. Talk about or record the results in a drawing, showing what happens to the water, how its colour changes and where it goes to (this could be called a lake or the sea).

Remove the plastic. Is the sand wet or just damp? Leave the 'hill' uncovered and

Figure 6

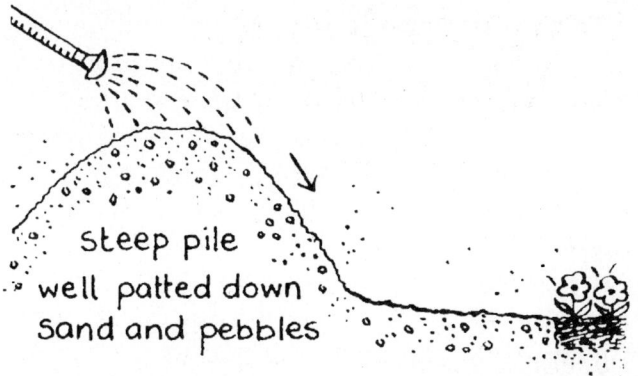

Figure 7

spray it again, gently at first, then more heavily. Talk about what happens first (the water should sink in) and then observe how the droplets collect then make a small channel and how the water which collects at the foot of the slope contains sand. This models the beginning of erosion, transport and deposition. Vary the flow and talk about the consequences.

Extend the activity to the playground to collect information for making a map to show the areas where water soaks in (permeable ground) and where it runs over the surface (impermeable ground). Younger children could be allowed to model the plan of the playground using thin plastic foam for the permeable areas and plastic sheet for the impermeable areas.

With older children the same experiment can be repeated in the playground using a hose and a 25kg bag of ballast containing a mix of sand, gravel and pebbles. Again the pile must be well patted down to form a firm hill (Figure 7). A gentle flow of water may well produce springs and certainly many small streams will collect into a river and the edge round the hill will become flooded and covered with washed out sand in the form of a flood plain.

With increased flow from the hose, the erosion will increase and larger parts of the hill will be moved away. Too sudden an increase in flow and the change will be disastrous (as happened with floods at Lynmouth in 1953, when a narrow valley became a roaring torrent, resulting in landslides blocking the streets and demolishing houses – look in newspaper archives for local examples).

A steady, slow increase of flow should make the channel deepen the valley within which it is flowing. The stages of change can be recorded with the aid of a stopwatch. Samples of dirty water from all the experiments can be collected into screw-top jars, shaken and left to settle. The particles will settle out into different layers over a period of time. Make a record and keep it to compare with samples taken from a local stream (Figure 8).

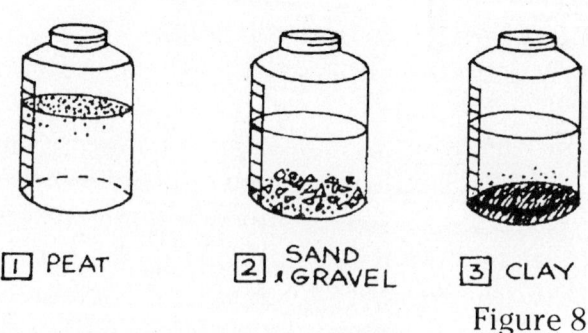

Figure 8

## Visiting a local stream

At Level 3 and Level 4, children have a wide and varied ability range. The chief difference age makes is in the range and number of observations possible. One would not expect children under the age of nine to spend time on more than one site. Repeated visits to the same site in different seasons make an in-depth study satisfactory to both teacher and child. Change and variation can be observed, leading to consideration of the effects of different climates and landscapes and the use of picture study. Working towards Level 5, however, can be enhanced with visits to several sites.

The original stream visited when developing observation, description and vocabulary could be used again for investigations with measuring equipment. The equipment should include the following:
- garden canes marked into 10cm units using coloured tape, thick string knotted into 30cm lengths or the more robust 3m ranging poles (marked in 0.5m units), plastic measuring tapes (30m) and metre rulers, at least one per group;
- freezer bags to contain samples of the sand, mud and pebbles from the stream bottom and banks (the bag labels can be marked in ball-point pen with the place name, grid reference, date and type of sample);
- plumb lines (or heavy screws on twine) to ensure that poles and canes are held vertically;
- floats (corks, orange peel, ping-pong balls, coloured lollipop sticks) and a shrimp-net to catch the floats at the end of a measured run;
- stop-watch to time the floats;
- notebooks, clipboards and record sheets, with polythene covers to keep them dry and clean.

Figure 9 shows a suggested layout for a record sheet. The captions are such as will fit on to a database screen (e.g. *Grass, Grass Plus, Our Facts*) or a similar child accessible database. Check the layout of your particular database and design the record form accordingly. This will make entering up the data easier and less liable to error, whether it is being undertaken by the children or by a helpful parent.

## Measuring river speed

The easiest place from which to measure river speed is a bridge. Otherwise it is necessary to throw the float forcefully towards the centre of the stream and have somebody positioned downstream ready to call out when the float passes.

Position one child on the bridge or river bank as Observer 1, then measure 30m (100ft) downstream from Observer 1 to Observer 2. Let another child stand by Observer 2 with a stop-watch or conventional watch with a second hand.

Drop anything which floats (orange peel is good) into the water, asking Observer 1 to call out as the float hits the water or when the float passes a pre-determined point. Ask the stop-watch operator to start the watch at the first call and stop it when Observer 2 calls out.

Let another child (Observer 3) catch the float with a net while someone else (Observer 4) records the stop-watch time.

Repeat the measurement process five times and discard any interrupted runs, then calculate the speed of each reading in metres per second. Take an average from the five readings.

Level 4 children could be allowed to repeat the exercise at three other places on the same stream/river system separated by at least 2km (5km makes for more significant readings). If the calculations are made within a short space of time on the same day, the children should come to understand that a river does not slow down going downstream despite the fact that the slope over which the river flows, which it has created with its own deposits, is less steep than higher up the valley. Many factors account for this, the most important being that the amount of water increases downstream as more tributaries are collected. The apparently slower movement of the water is connected with the fact that the water movement is much smoother, is carrying much smaller particles and is flowing in a smoother channel. All this leads to friction which increases overall speed downstream. The water authorities use these properties in their flood prevention tactics by keeping channels clear of vegetation and encased in smooth masonry. Should the speed of flow

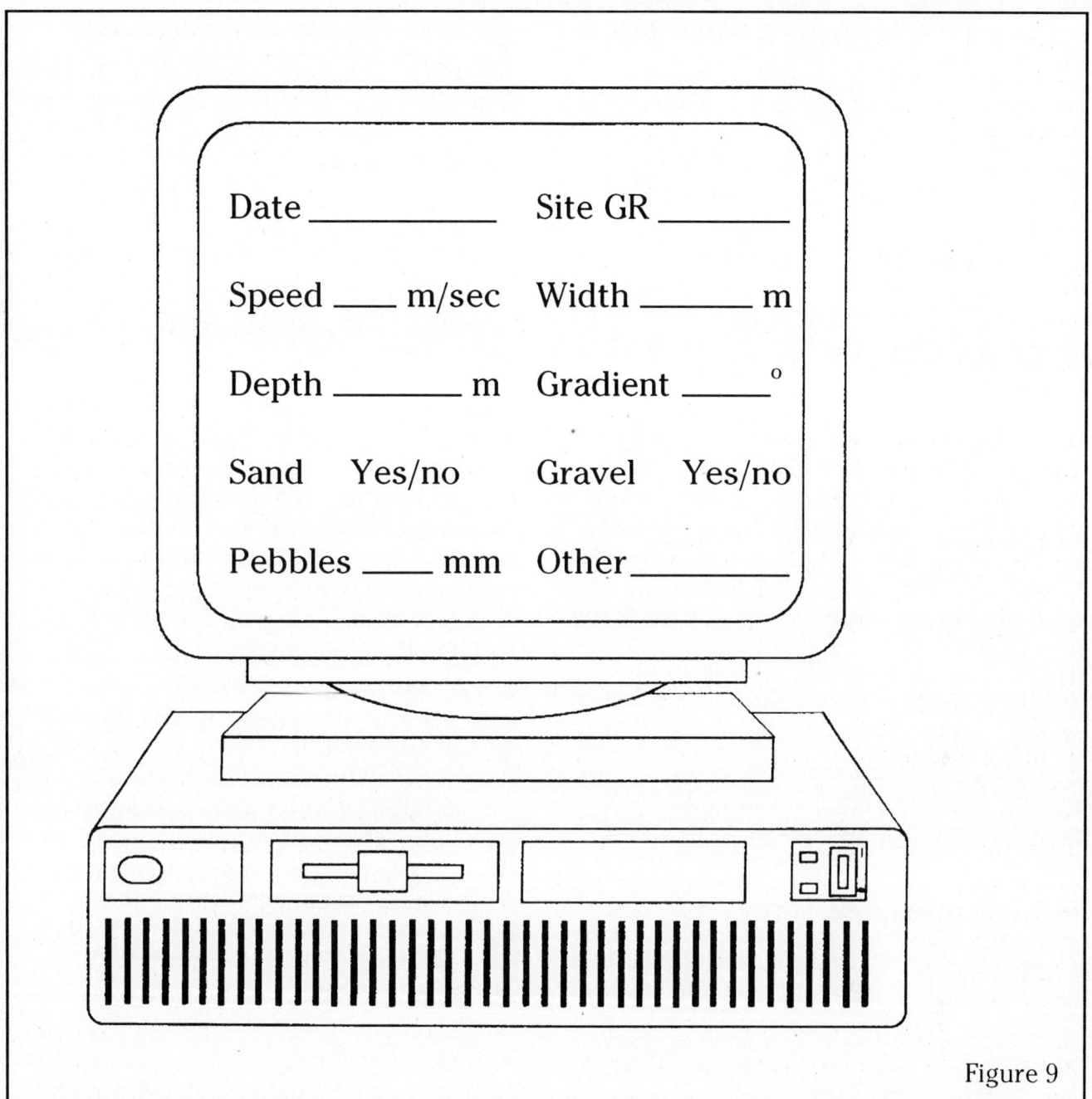

Figure 9

(velocity) in your observations drop significantly, ask the children to look at the industrial and other human features requiring water, such as a treatment works or a factory. Help them to understand that taking out water reduces the quantity and the rate of flow.

Point out that the material in the stream bottom seems to be sorted into large and small sediment particles with the larger pebbles collecting in similar places on the stream bed. This can also be seen in layers in the stream bank. Refer back to the experiments with guttering (page 24).

Many streams are small enough and have little enough water in summer to allow investigation by older children in wellingtons. A stretch of stream without tributaries (check on the 1:25,000 Ordnance Survey map) is often of paddling depth somewhere along its course.

At the chosen site measure depth by asking two children to hold a tape tight across the stream at water level, while another child uses a metre rule or a marked garden cane to measure up from the stream bottom to the tape at regular (0.5m) intervals across the width of the stream,

27

calling out the readings to a recorder on the bankside.

Depth can also be measured from a road or footpath bridge with a convenient rail which can be used as a datum line. Let one child (Observer 1) stand on bridge above the point where the water touches the bank and hold one end of the tape. Let another child (Observer 2) walk across to a similar point above the other bank and hold the other end of the tape. Ask a third child (Observer 3) to use a long pole, cane or a heavy, weighted line to measure at regular intervals (0.5m) the distance between the water surface and the rail of the bridge. Mark on the pole or string the point where it touches the bridge rail when the end or weight touches the water. Ask Observer 3 to continue lowering the pole or weight until the stream bottom is felt and mark the new position on the pole or string. The depth of water in the stream will be the distance between the two marks. Ask Observer 3 to call out this distance to allow a fourth child (Observer 4) to keep a record. Six to ten readings should be possible on a bridged stream in this way.

## Follow-up work

• Ask the children to draw up the channel depth and width measurements on squared paper using the same interval for the vertical and horizontal scales (for example, 1cm represents 1m).
• Ask the children to draw the profile of the channel measuring downwards from a horizontal line on the page representing the water surface. Extend the banks upwards above the water line if possible.

## Erosion, transport and deposition

The patterns of erosion, transport and deposition can be simulated using guttering and polystyrene coving. Set up a length of wide guttering raised at one end on a block, the other end blocked with an end-stop into which a 2.5cm (1") sized drainage hole has been made with a short length of hose stuck in with an epoxy adhesive such as Araldite. Position this end over a bucket (Figure 10).

Slowly pour in a steady trickle of water. After about a minute the water will start to flow in a curving pattern. The spiral (helical) flow of water goes some way to explaining why rivers form regular meanders in even the smallest streams.

Place a dry sponge in the top of the gutter and pour water on to it, observing what happens. This is the equivalent of rain falling on very dry ground. Compare this

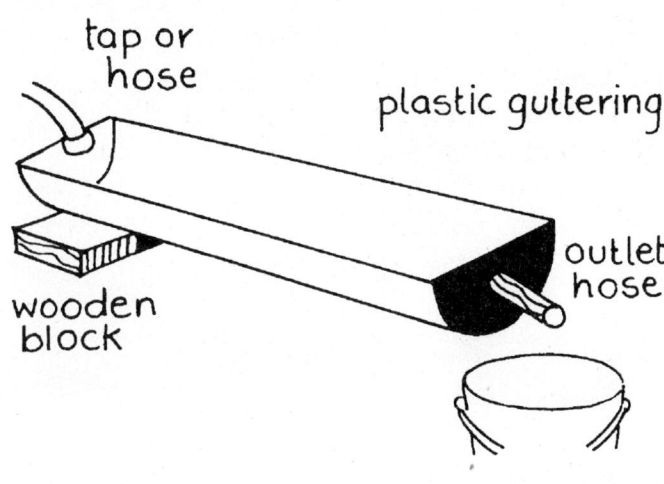

Figure 10

with the way in which water flowed in the previous experiment.

Repeat the activity using a damp sponge. What happens? Water should start to flow out of the sponge before it is completely soaked, demonstrating flow by gravity.

Next replace the sponge with a pile of sand and spray it with water. Encourage the children to look at what happens to the sand, making sure they watch the stopped end of the gutter and look at the water in the bucket. (The water in the bucket will now be dirty.) This is erosion, transport and deposition.

Replace the sand with ballast mixture and spray it again. Ask the children to observe what happens to the large particles and pebbles. Increase the flow of water steadily. (You may need to dredge out the end of the gutter at this stage.) This demonstrates selective erosion, variable transport and heavy deposition and can be used to introduce to children the concept of erosion, transport and deposition depending not only upon the amount of water available to work but also upon the kind of material available for erosion and transport.

## The enquiry process

During the above experiments, make sure that the children think what might happen before they begin (hypothesising), decide what needs to be observed and note what happens (observation), complete a record sheet (recording) then discuss what has been seen and recorded and decide what it means (interpretation). Does what actually happened agree with their predictions? Does this lead on to another hypothesis?

## Further channel work

Take a narrow length of polystyrene coving and split it lengthways in two using a central regular wavy line with broad curves, similar to the curving pattern that was made by the clean water down the gutter. Stick the two halves to a larger piece

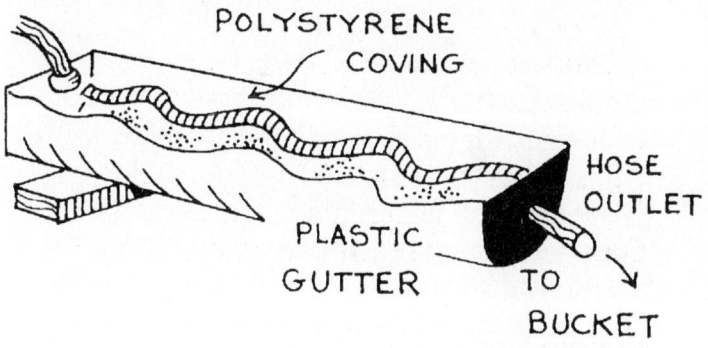

Figure 11

of polystyrene coving so that there is a central channel of about 4cm between them, as in Figure 11. Leave the model to set overnight using small blocks or masking tape to hold the edges together. When the model has dried thoroughly, fit it into the length of gutter.

Repeat the experiments as before and ask the children to sketch the distribution of the sand and gravel.

The model's sand and gravel banks, separated by a relatively bare channel, represent the riffles and pools seen on a real stream. Visit your local stream or use photographs and video to look for these riffles and pools. There may be a local fisherman who would be able to explain what happens to the riffles and pools over a year of changing flow conditions.

There are many variations possible with these experiments, such as increasing or reducing the water flow, increasing the slope of the channel or changing the sediment to all gravel or all clay, either in the plain gutter or with the polystyrene channel.

# Incorporating fieldwork into the school curriculum

Features of the locality cannot be left to daily 'observations' made by the children as they travel to and from school. Often familiar features are 'invisible' because they play no significant part in our lives. For example, one does not 'notice' the postman or milkman every time they pass by. Did you know that even in a modern housing estate windows and doors have enough variation to be classified and sorted?

Geography, of course, does not have the prerogative for noticing similarities and differences – only in showing where they occur, for example which doors in a street have a certain shape. The study of mathematics can just as easily benefit from looking for different shapes in the neighbourhood. One reception class in a multicultural school settled in by walking round in small groups to each other's homes. There each child was photographed by his or her own front door, much to the delight of everyone. The photographs were then mounted and became part of a topic on rectangles and triangles. A simple map was made of the route and displayed alongside a fictitious map, showing the houses built by the Three Little Pigs, to show the spacing of their homes and to compare them with the spacing and building materials of the children's homes. In this example, the teacher not only made sure that the class had had similar experiences to talk about and describe in their school work, but also had a very handy reference for learning the children's names and using material with which they were all familiar. Meanwhile a 'set' of geographical features had been collected.

# Preparing for fieldwork

## Practical considerations

Ideally, it would be useful if the teacher could go out with his or her class and do fieldwork in response to the demand 'Show me where...', but this in itself requires that the question is asked of a teacher already prepared with the answer. This may be the case with a teacher who has worked in the area for a long time, but even so only some areas of the environment will be understood in depth and the young or inexperienced teacher will have much preparation to do.

The following preparatory steps are crucial to successful out-of-class work.
• Visit the place to be studied, including the routes to it. Preparation for out-of-class work means actively finding out what is there, the contrasts, the similarities, the signs of change, the points which can be talked about before and after the visit and the material which can be used to help develop a skill (for example, the Victorian villa shown in Figure 12 was first photographed and later drawn to make an exercise in recording observation).

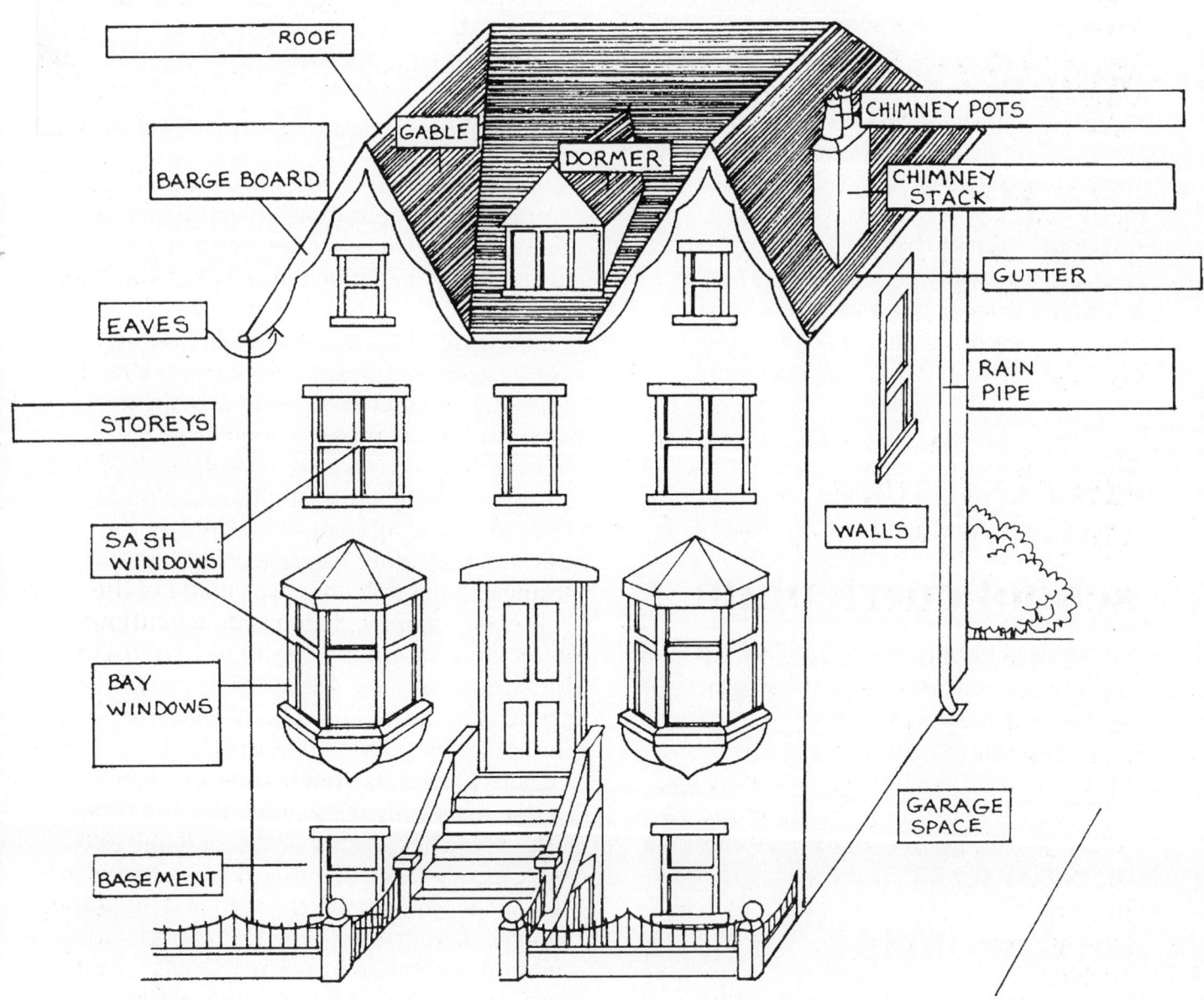

Figure 12

- Read the local authority guidelines for your school. These will vary from authority to authority. They will advise on minimum staff levels, group size, safety equipment, insurance requirements and so on. The school may already have a plan of action which satisfies the LEA requirements, but each teacher is expected to be aware of the guidelines.
- Match what you would like to do with what it is possible to do. This means having clear aims and a clear idea of the kind of activity which will be undertaken.
- Go to the headteacher and the rest of the staff with your proposed plan to see how it fits in with other people's requirements and the demands on extra help.
- Once you have established that the field trip is possible, prepare a detailed framework covering the preparation time needed in the classroom, as well as your own preparation necessary to achieve your aims and objectives. Remember to include the follow-up time needed to give full value to the work undertaken outside.
- Plan and prepare the necessary equipment. There may already be a basic kit for working outdoors, for example, clipboards and protective covers, but each excursion will have its own unique requirements.
- Prepare 'bad weather' plans or contingency plans in case of illness or other unforeseen circumstances.
- Inform the parents well in advance of the field trip and then send out reminder notes maybe two weeks beforehand. It may be school policy to enlist the parents' cooperation from the beginning of their children's schooling so that the purpose of out-of-classroom work is understood. You may already have a network of parents who are able to help. In this case, you will undoubtedly have circulated in advance a programme for the term. Nonetheless, each excursion requires a standard letter with a signed reply slip for insurance purposes.

## Ancillary help

Out-of-classroom work can take as little time as 20 minutes or as much as a whole day or more. Key Stage 1 children are probably not going to require more than a day for their longest field trip, but they will need to make many small, short visits, often in small groups.

For out-of-classroom work, most local authorities stipulate one adult for every 20 children. In reality, one adult per ten children is more practical. For an average class size, this allows for a leader, someone to 'bring up the rear' and a link person in the middle. This works if the party is going to a destination where extra help is at hand as a matter of course. However, it assumes you are moving about as a crocodile and it certainly does not allow for relaxed, informative conversation, whether about how to record observations or about the meaning of observations. Moreover, a crocodile is a cumbersome way of moving a class about.

The ideal group size for which to aim is very often five children per adult. For example, when measuring a stream, a group might require four investigators and one recorder. On the other hand, a group of six can be broken down into two groups of three, comprising two investigators and one recorder, for example when doing a street traverse. Groups of five or six are more manageable in terms of moving about busy streets or for keeping quiet when walking through a nature reserve. Moreover, the adult's attention can be given to the development of skills on the spot or for keeping conversation to the matter in hand.

When organising a class trip, two of the accompanying adults should be qualified teachers. That does not mean depleting the school staff, however – in one case a student teacher's tutor provided the necessary help. Retired teachers have also been known to provide much needed help. Both categories of staff are usually only too aware of the value of outdoor work not to supply a helping hand.

In the current economic and social situation, we cannot assume that all mothers will always be available to supply ancillary help. Many, of course, will have their own jobs. Bear in mind that some fathers may be available because of flexible work hours. Early retirement may also mean that friends or relatives are able to give a helping hand, while existing school ancillary workers may be able to spare an hour between jobs. Always let your needs be known loud and clear well in advance and make sure that your helpers know what is expected of them, that they are being more than just child-minders, and prepare them accordingly.

## Research and reconnaissance

Research and find out in advance as much as possible about the area and topic to be investigated. There is no substitute for firsthand knowledge of an area. Do not be lulled into assuming that the area will be the same as on your last visit. If you make your reconnaissance visit some time ahead of the planned visit then endeavour to make a further quick check over the route for potential difficulties. In towns, one-way systems and road works have a nasty habit of appearing over night. In the country, seasonal changes can make dramatic differences in the landscape – water levels change, crossing points can become impassable and hedgerows can increase in width thus obscuring viewpoints. One stream used regularly over two decades became part of a Site of Special Scientific Interest and, thereafter, to visit it required a licence. This was only revealed when a courtesy call was made by a teacher to the nearby field centre to make sure there would be no clashes with their fieldwork programme.

Preparation work not only covers collecting as many brochures, maps, information leaflets and books as possible, but also involves making contact with people who may be inconvenienced by your investigations. Farmers, forestry wardens, landowners, park keepers, caretakers, shopkeepers and many others appreciate being involved in your plans, even if it is only to be negative and say, 'Not that day'. They might well be able to suggest a time more appropriate for the work you wish to do, when they might be able to give you more attention themselves. If you are clear about what you wish to do and make your preparations in good time, the general public, whether the pensioner tending the allotment or the landowner and the farm manager, can become strong supports.

## Whole-school programme

School which have always included fieldwork, as a matter of course, in their curriculum have found that a policy of regularity and consistency pays dividends in the form of having more time for preparation. If you know there is the possibility of one whole-day or half-day visit per half-term for the infants, that in addition the lower juniors have the chance to have one long weekend away each year and that upper juniors have the chance of a full residential field course, it becomes feasible to investigate potential fieldwork locations at reasonable prices not just one term in advance but as far in advance as the year before the main excursions are to be undertaken. Reconnaissance work can thus be undertaken at leisure, rather than being pushed through at breakneck speed to meet someone else's schedule.

The time-scale need not be as long for the shorter excursions. For example, at the February/March half-term, one school asks its staff to begin thinking about topics and associated visits for their classes in the next academic year. By the beginning of the summer term, meetings have been held and feasibility enquiries are underway. By the beginning of the summer holiday, the pattern for the new academic year has been roughed out. New members of staff are included in a meeting held at the beginning of the holiday and preparation by both class teachers and subject co-ordinators is assigned. Before the autumn term begins, the final programme is published so that staff can see where their classwork fits in with the rest of the school.

Figure 13 shows a sample plan for topic areas and associated visits through which cross-curricular needs will be covered. The school in question has followed this programme of preparation for a period of several years, but the effect of the demands of the National Curriculum has brought with it an increased lack of room to manoeuvre. The plan, however, has always been adaptable in order to satisfy the needs of the classes and changing conditions – such as National Curriculum requirements.

## Season of visits

Two major considerations when planning outdoor work are the weather and the effects of the tourist season. The need to provide time for both preparation and follow-up preclude the use of the first and last weeks of a term or the holidays for field visits. The second half of the spring term is a possibility. Although some museums and places of interest do not open until after Easter, special arrangements can often be made. The first half of the summer term also has much in its favour, as admission charges are usually still low, the weather is

### TOPICS AND FIELDWORK/VISITS

**KS1 L1-3**

| | Autumn | | Spring | | Summer | |
|---|---|---|---|---|---|---|
| **R** | My home | | Toys | | New life | |
| | Colours | Family | | | Ourselves | Plant/animals |
| | Draw/paint a local feature | My address | Bethnal Green Museum of childhood | | A farm visit | |
| **1** | Shopping | | Push & pull | Keeping safe & healthy | Our school | Minibeasts |
| | Local visits to shops and supermarkets | | Transport museum | | Visit another school | Scadbury Park or ANO |
| **2** | North wind and sun | Party time | Under control | What is history? | Treasure Islands | |
| | Outward Mill | Visit a local church | Science Museum | | A river or canal trip | |

**KS2 L3-5**

| | Autumn | | Spring | | Summer | |
|---|---|---|---|---|---|---|
| **3** | Ground level | Is this music? | Victorians | | Ancient games | |
| | Visit locality maps/land use, buildings | Theatre, music | Bethnal Green Museum | Local walks | A tour round a sports stadium | |
| **4** | Invaders and settlers | Paper and print | Supermarket | | Up, up and away | Making light work |
| | | Papermill | Visit Sainsbury's, Safeways | | Visit Gatwick | |
| **5** | Hunter and hunted | Marooned | Tudors | Did you hear that? | Beyond Beckenham | |
| | Zoo or Natural History Museum | | Hampton Court | | School journey to Felden Lodge, Hemel Hempstead | |
| **6** | Moving image | New worlds | Heat and fire | | Ancient Egypt | |
| | MOMI, London | Walk to South Norwood Country Park | | | School journey to Skern Lodge, North Devon | |

Figure 13

## OUT OF CLASS WORK

**KS1 L1-3**

| | Autumn | | Spring | | Summer | |
|---|---|---|---|---|---|---|
| **R** | Draw and paint a local feature. | Make a photographic trail of homes, special buildings, woods, hills, streams, with a series of small group visits. | Collect building materials. | Visit a public building or community centre. | Follow a sensory trail. | |
| | Start weather observations. | | | | | |
| **1** | Orienteering in playground with picture cars. | Visit, observe and draw different kinds of homes. | Conduct a water/ice hunt. | Observe traffic movements including at the nearest shops. Draw, record different kinds. | Make a farm visit to see production of, e.g. lambs/wood, calves/milk, chicks/eggs, market garden/veg. | Follow a local, old path. Along the way, note differences in use now and in the past. |
| | Begin to record weather observations. | | | | | |
| **2** | Plan a trail to look at slope and follow it. Record land use. | Explore different surfaces for water. Include a stream. | Plan a trail for character buildings to show a nature of settlement. Follow, draw, research. | Visit homes in the neighbourhood - old, converted or new. | Investigate community goods and services. Visit people at work, e.g. fire station. | Return to stream. Share garden water rota. Visit allotments or market garden. |

**KS2 3-5**

| | Autumn | | Spring | | Summer | |
|---|---|---|---|---|---|---|
| **3** | Investigate play areas. Individual maps, class map. Visit one; walk. Improve? | Investigate another land use e.g. small firm, building site, swimming pool. | Contribute to school garden. Model stream work in playground. | Make a transect to relate to slope, water, vegetation, land use. | Visit farm to find out about land use. | Revisit firm or building site to compare with farm. |
| | | | | | Extend weather recording to mini-stations round school. | |
| **4** | Map wet and dry places in local area/street furniture/plan of 'adopted' environment. | Investigate wear and tear in the neighbourhood. Link with mini-weather observations. | Visit a local stream to look for evidence of erosion, transport and deposition. Link with soils (science). | Visit a new shopping mall or business centre to compare with local parade or high street, etc. | School day journey. Visit a contrasting locality, e.g. coast, hill, lowland. | Revisit stream. Measure for database at more than one site. |
| **5** | Follow the local stream if possible from source to confluence. | Investigate timed journeys in locality by foot, bike, bus, etc. | Revisit building site; assess landscape impact. | Investigate local soils on a soil trail. Apply to school garden (with science). | School journey-week. Another region. | Use school garden for conservation and irrigation experiments. |
| **6** | Visit local river at several places. | Visit local depots - bus, train, PO, freight. Research routes followed from actual way sheets. | Visit selected areas, e.g. housing estate, industry, agricultural, as preparation for a programme change. | Investigate selected landscape for impact of visitors. | Adopt a contrasting landscape (visited in 4 and 5) or heritage site and look at visitor impact. Day visit. | Make and research a trail for use by local visitors. |

Ongoing work through school and the whole year: Weather observations; school garden; rock collection; soil (with science).

Figure 14

improving, water levels are manageable, there is a great variety of plant life visible and rural locations are probably at their most rewarding. After the spring bank holiday, booking anything becomes more difficult because of the competition from tourists for transport and accommodation. In the autumn, decent weather is often possible up to the first week in November. Again, prices are reasonable and negotiable. Which group is taken will depend upon the ease of doing the advance administration in the previous summer, but fieldwork in the autumn term often results in good working relationships between teachers and peers for the rest of the year.

# A fieldwork programme

Figure 14 shows fieldwork undertaken by seven year groups over the course of six half-terms, working on the assumption that in each half-term there will be one day available for outdoor work with a geographical bias.

The suggestions below include preparation and follow-up work together with cross-curricular applications, based on the programme of study.

## Key Stage 1

### Reception

#### My favourite places (Early autumn)

Use opportunities at Key Stage 1 to **'observe... and to communicate'** to teach **'geographical terms'** such as *house* and *road*. In the classroom the children could be following a topic on colour or shape, learning the basic vocabulary and recognising the colours or shapes in the areas around them in the classroom, such as the home corner, in their clothes and in various places outside school. Drawings could be made of the different kinds of doors in the school, the different window shapes and so on. What are the children's favourite colours or shapes? Have they seen these colours or shapes on their way to school? Where? What are they like? Are they in a quiet place? Are they in a house? A shop? Can they draw the place?

Each day could start with looking at the weather and putting the appropriate symbols on a weather chart. The children could also look at the effects of weather in terms of colour and shape. Does the rain change the colours of the playground or the paths when they become wet? Where does the rain move from and to? Do places look different in the rain? In the sun? Do shadows and puddles change shape depending on the weather?

Eventually the discussion will focus on or can be led to consider a specific place which everyone agrees is special in some way and a visit can be arranged, to allow the children to observe and draw all or part of the feature, such as a window or a door, a gutter along which the rain runs down and out, or a window which reflects the sun. On return, a model can be made of the local feature using cardboard boxes, wallpaper and poster paint. Other local features can be discussed and identified on a large scale plan of the school area or ideally upon an oblique aerial photograph (see Chapter four, page 63). If the plan is covered with plastic, picture symbols can be stuck or drawn on to the surface representing the various favourite places.

#### More local features (Christmas/New Year)

While the weather is sufficiently good, prepare a photographic trail made up of the places mentioned most frequently by the children, as well as those places which you feel they should have noticed.

Over the next two half-terms, make an ongoing frieze display compiled from the children's discoveries during their visits. This could include photographs of the children standing by their own front doors (see page 30), interspersed with the photographs and their drawings of local features. These could include the town's Christmas decorations, showing where the tree and public decorations are to be found, how the street furniture is decorated and so on. The effect of wintery weather with frost and snow outlining trees and buildings in the locality can again be used to bring details into focus.

All these activities offer an excellent starting point for expressing children's feelings about the environment and how the weather can change the feel of a place.

#### Beginning a collection (Spring)

Take into school examples of different bricks, tiles, wood and other building materials. Start a materials table. Encourage the children to collect photographs or take photographs of buildings which are made from different materials. Mount, label and give them an address. Plot this place on a local map (PoS, 3d). Tell the Tale of the Three Little Pigs (p164).

A follow-up activity could be to sort the collection according to colour and texture and plot the origins of the samples on the area map (PoS, 3d). Conversation, while sorting the collection, could lead back to the colour of the local buildings and the materials which go to make them. In rural areas there may be quarries where the local rock can be seen.

Extend the activity by using photographs, pictures and videos of real or imaginary places that have buildings of similar materials. Discuss why similar materials have been used for similar features (glass for windows, wood for doors and so on). Now collect on a world-wide basis and use maps and globes to see the location of similar or different houses. Remember, the oldest buildings in any country use local materials, often wood and brick, while the newest buildings increasingly use concrete and glass.

If building is happening nearby, try to arrange a visit, if necessary taking a handful of children at a time.

## Special buildings (Late spring)

In the summer term, a visit to a public building or community centre could fit in with topics such as 'Ourselves' or 'People'. The programme of study requires an investigation of the uses made of buildings in the local area and further afield. Churches lend themselves to an extensive study, while the library, health centre, post office, fire and police stations all have a wealth of detail which can help reinforce the work on observation begun in the autumn term and the work touched on in the spring when looking at the materials in the environment. Again, on return to the classroom the location of the chosen building can be noted on a large scale map of the area, along with the location of other similar buildings (PoS, 3d).

## What I like best (Early summer)

Reinforcement and revision of the work begun in the autumn can be followed through with a sensory trail which also accommodates the programme of study requirement for the children to discuss and explain their likes and dislikes about features of their environment (PoS, 6a). Again, the weather observations can be used to highlight how different things look in the sunlight of summer and how this can influence feelings about a place; which will help the children to develop a broad, descriptive vocabulary and expand their concepts concerning places and seasons. Preparation could involve the children in pointing out on the large neighbourhood plan a route which would take in their favourite buildings and places in the locality. The follow-up could include drawing, writing and making models as well as discussion.

# Year one

## Route making and regular weather observations (Early autumn)

In Y1, children have to be taught to follow a route on a map, as well as follow directions and identify familiar features from maps and photographs. They should now be becoming familiar with location language (left, right, up, down, backwards, forwards) which eventually converts into north, south, east and west. Games such as 'Hunt the thimble' or finding the position of the 'treasure' on a map initiate the use of direction language and maps (PoS, 3c).

Outside the classroom, a trail around the school can be organised to find special features, such as a picture, an unusual door knob or a fire bucket or blanket. Some three-storey Victorian schools will need careful but stimulating thought. More modern schools with outlying classroom could involve taking the exercise outdoors.

Make a large scale plan of the school and mark each feature on the plan with a number. Make a set of cards with photographs or drawings of each feature, then cover them with clear adhesive plastic film. Let the children work in pairs, using a copy of the school plan, to move round the school locating the various features numbered on the map and giving each card the correct number. Alternatively, attach numbers to the objects around the school for two children to locate using the map (PoS, 3d).

When the children return to the classroom, ask them to put the cards in the correct sequence and point the route out on the map and talk about it. Reinforce the activity by letting the children use the numbered cards to go over the route in the correct order once more but this time seeing which pair can *walk* round in the shortest time. New routes can be devised by reordering and renumbering. This time the route shown on the map can connect partly completed puzzle pictures (such as the top view of a dustbin, Figure 15), with the missing part of the picture being covered over and their sequence following the numbered plan. On return to the classroom the name of the puzzle object shown in the completed picture can be written on the plan (PoS, 3b, c).

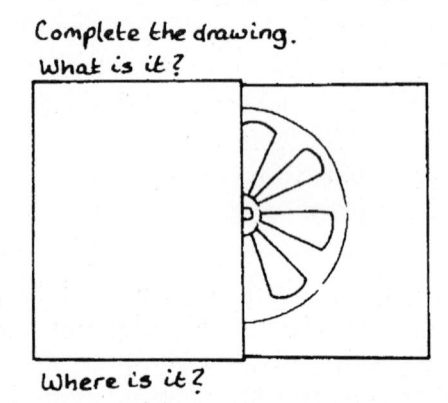

Figure 15

## Simple weather recording

In Y1, weather recording can begin in earnest with the selection of a specific site and the design and manufacture of simple instruments to show how much rain falls each day. Collect rain each day in a set of similar containers, such as milk bottles, and at the end of a week talk about the different levels. Discuss changes in the weather regarding rain, wind (observe the revolutions of a toy windmill) and sun (see Chapter nine, page 141). Try to keep the record going for two weeks in each month and maintain discussion about the weather (for example, how it affected playtime and whether coats were worn). With each month, changes will be significant enough to make comparisons with other parts of the world when they are read about in stories or seen in posters or pictures in books (PoS, 5c).

## Homes and communities (Late autumn)

In order to investigate features outside the area, the use of land and buildings in the locality has to be extended beyond the work begun in the Reception class. The topic of 'Homes' can lead to classifying the different kinds of homes in the neighbourhood, from flats to detached houses, from housing estates to accommodation over shops, from very old to very new.

A large scale plan can be made showing the various kinds of home in the locality and a route can be prepared using the children's suggestions. Observations in the local area can be recorded by drawing and labelling, and this can then be used to make comparisons with homes in other places worldwide, aided by the observations of the weather as an ongoing event. For example, compare the day's temperature with that in the Arctic, where children live in cabins or, with the coming of Christmas, compare how children in other lands decorate their homes (children in the Amazon Basin do not have Christmas fir trees, for example) to emphasise the difference in seasons between the northern and southern hemispheres (PoS, 1c; 5c).

## A water hunt (New Year)

The regular occurrence of rain or snow makes the winter a suitable time for observing water in different forms, by looking around the school grounds for puddles and seeing how the water drains away. Water can also be observed by going to a stream or a pond, or even by looking at bird baths. (Make a survey of who provides water for the birds, as well as food, in winter.)

Give the 'address' of each water location and put symbols for them on a large scale school plan (PoS, 3d). A study of water can be combined with indoor work on different gravels and composts to work out which materials are used most appropriately in the school garden, for example, gravel for paths or compost as a moist planting medium. Make a tactile map of the different areas around the school by covering a sheet of card with a layer of PVA adhesive and sprinkling on soil, sand or fine gravel, depending on the type of surface and sticking on plastic sheeting to represent puddles (PoS, 3a–d; 5a, c). Colour blue any areas of ground that become muddy. (Blue is always used on Ordnance Survey maps to represent water.)

## Shops and journeys (Early spring)

The last half of the spring term is most appropriate for investigating another land use in the locality, such as the shopping parade. Besides looking in detail at one particular shop, the children could consider it in context with the other shops in the area, as well as investigating how goods are delivered to the shops. Classwork in maths may have sorted out the different ways of moving goods. Observation with a simple checklist could be undertaken, at what are considered in the area to be 'safe spots' (see Chapter seven), to record how many kinds of vehicle pass by within a specific time, such as 15 minutes. Groups of three could be asked to record one particular kind of transport, such as small vans or large lorries. Surveys could also be undertaken at different times of the day.

## Settlements and transport

The survey material can be used in several topics, for example 'Homes', 'Shops', 'Moving' and 'Work', and goes some way to covering an investigation into how people make journeys, why different means of transport are used and needed and why people make journeys of different lengths.

The follow-up work could be undertaken on locating the places where vehicles come from, locating where people work and how they travel and where the children would go to get really special toys. Through this the children will begin to understand that most homes are part of a settlement, that settlements vary in size and that goods and services needed by the community are dependent on road transport.

With older children this could be extended by trying to record the place names on lorries or vans, and then trying to locate these places in an atlas. Schools near arterial roads will find that the follow-up atlas work quickly leads to investigations into Europe, as well as into other parts of the British Isles. This is relevant to PoS, 1c, 3e, f, 5a, 6a–c.

## The farm visit (Early summer)

A farm visit at the beginning of the summer term can be used to follow up the investigation into the provision of goods for the community, as well as teaching how land and buildings are used (PoS, 5d). The environmental theme can be investigated and discussed (PoS, 6a–c).

When making arrangements for farm visits, take care that the farmer understands what you need. Discuss with him:
- the purpose of the visit;
- the age and relevant experience of the children;
- specific activities you wish to undertake;
- precise details about dates, times, safety, discipline and wet weather arrangements;
- his own needs and requirements.

A phone call or a letter will not be sufficient – a preliminary visit must be arranged. A Geographical Association booklet expands on this area of investigation.

Initial work in the classroom before the visit should use stories and models to prepare the children for the vocabulary which will be used to describe the farm buildings, the farming year and the farm animals.

It is best to plan such a visit for the beginning of a half-term unit as the follow-up work will be very time-consuming. After such a visit to an educational farm, one class undertook follow-up work ranging from writing, model-making, weaving with paper and making thread from real wool combed from a fleece to presenting an assembly on 'Spring' and how lambs and lambing fit into farming life.

## The settlement – old paths (Summer walk)

The programme of study asks that the children are taught to identify activities which have changed the environment and to consider the ways in which they can improve their own environment.

Most settlements have expanded by developing over farm land. This expansion can be clearly seen by looking at old maps of the area and comparing them with a contemporary Ordnance Survey map. A combined history and geography exploration of a local path can reinforce route work, land use recognition and investigations into change of use, as well as encouraging the children to think of ways to improve the environment. Begin by asking the children to point out the location of the school and other familiar features on the historical map. If the school had not yet been built at the time of the map, ask the children what had been there before. Make a list of the differences between the old and the new maps. Explain how over the years property developers have often bought single fields or groups of fields and that the remnants of the hedgerows can often still be seen. Further investigations can be made via the local library or newspaper archive which may be able to provide old pictures and accounts of the past landscape.

Once this preparatory work has been done, make a reconnaissance visit along the route, taking with you a list of things to look for. Appropriate clues to locate could include place names, remnants of old woods and old houses.

Once the children have been out on their investigation, follow-up work can involve more map work, model-making, photograph labelling and discussion. This work is appropriate to PoS, 6a–c.

## Year two

The statutory orders expect that by Y2 some children will be working towards Level 3, vocabulary will be developed and children will be able to consider the relationship between two features of the landscape. So, at this stage observation and recording become more important.

## Slope and land use (Autumn)

The programme of study requires that the children should be able to identify and describe familiar landscape features, such as rivers, hills and ponds, and to explore different slopes which give character. This should not prove difficult in upland Britain with its mix of steep, moderate and gentle slopes, but might be more difficult in fenland, although in fenland any hill will stand out in profile and will very often be an old settlement site. Preparation in class could involve modelling hill and valley

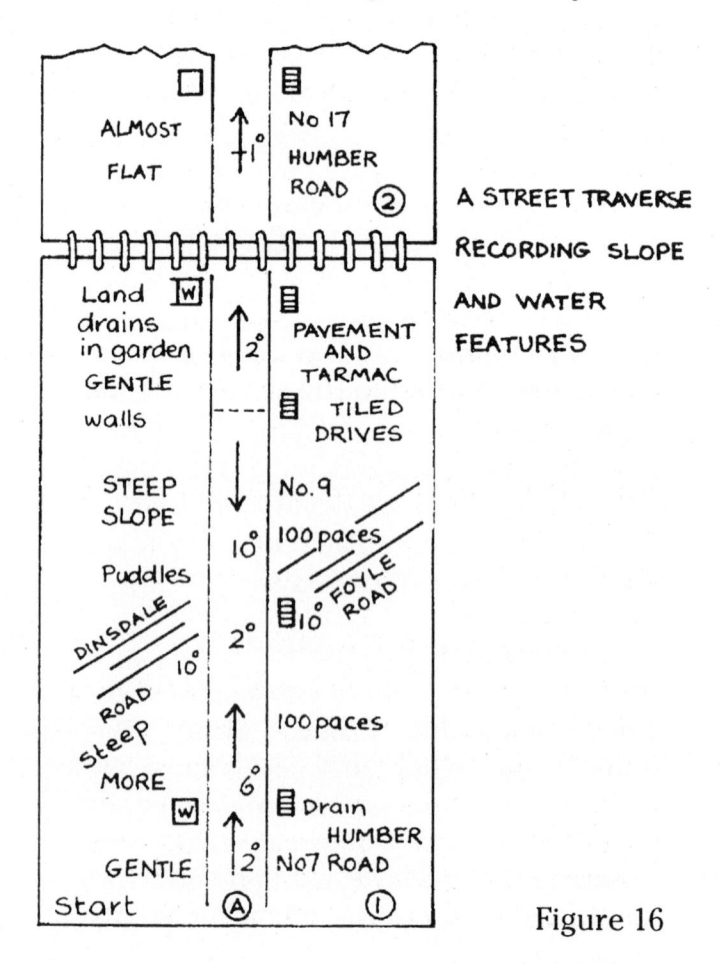

A STREET TRAVERSE RECORDING SLOPE AND WATER FEATURES

Figure 16

features with boxes and draping them with a cloth to smooth the outline. Taking a teddy bear or doll around this indoor hill-climb course will help to sort out 'up and down' vocabulary. Remember that to go down and then up involves crossing a valley and to go up and then down involves crossing a hill. Games such as 'The grand old Duke of York' can also help develop the relevant vocabulary.

Talk about the ups and downs of the neighbourhood. Use a large scale plan of the area and ask the children questions such as which streets are on a slope or which play area has good slopes for sliding on an icy day.

Plan a slope and land use trail, trying to include a route where the land use is specifically related to slope or lack of slope. For example, railways are usually built to follow the most level route, hence in most settlements with a railway (past or present) there is a slope up from the station to the town centre. Other old towns might have a castle on the hill and here could be an opportunity to combine history and geography along the route. In cities, developers may have physically cut land away, but watch which way the water flows in the gutter. Figure 16 offers a suggestion for recording field trip findings.

On returning to the classroom, the follow-up work could take the form of a three-dimensional frieze. This does not have to be to scale, but should show where the levels change and the way buildings have been adapted to the slope with, for example, steps.

## Running water (Late autumn/early winter)

Teaching children about the effect different surfaces and slopes have on rainwater when it reaches the ground calls for sand tray work with mounds of moist sand and ballast. Encourage the children to draw the patterns made by running water and the effect it has on the spread of the sand and gravel as it reaches the bottom of the mound.

Extend the work with gravels and composts begun in Y1 (see page 24ff) by having both moist and absolutely dry samples. In addition, work with different types of rocks soaked with water makes useful links with science. For example, if bubbles of air appear when the rock samples are immersed, they will soak up rain water. Alternatively, water will be repelled if the rock is impervious.

Include building materials with the rocks, because roofs and walls all intercept the rain on its way to the ground. If possible, make a short journey around the school grounds after a rainstorm to notice where the water runs away. More important, however, would be to get to the nearest stream to see how big it is and how much water there is, and to begin to introduce the river vocabulary (bank, flood, plain, bend, pool, deep, shallow, straight, sand, mud, gravel and so on). This work is relevant to PoS, 3a, b, c, d; 5a.

Back in the classroom, changes at the stream over the year can be discussed and connections made with the weather (PoS, 5c). Much writing and drawing work will be generated. Read the children extracts from Kenneth Grahame's *The Wind in the Willows* which gives good descriptions of seasonal changes in a river. The description of 'Pooh sticks' in A. A. Milne's *The House at Pooh Corner* can also be read to the children, and the game used to explore currents, if your local stream has a suitable bridge.

On the large scale plan, show in blue where the water runs down the gutter and compare this with the slope investigation.

## Our place (New Year)

Teaching children about the development of a place, why it is in a particular location and how it has grown or changed, requires detective work and cross-curricular links with history. Preparation can involve talking to local people who can remember significant changes, and finding out from old photographs and archive material which buildings have been there for a long time and what they have been used for. Buildings and other features can be located on a large scale plan or on a 1:25,000 Ordnance Survey map.

A possible route can then be planned with the objective of showing visitors to the town the essential features. This will include old buildings as well as new ones which may have the same function. For example, comparisons could be made between a modern hotel and an old coaching inn.

Follow-up work could use IT to make a brochure complete with reports, illustrations and the trail route. This work would be relevant to PoS, 3a, b, c, d, f; 5a, d; 6a, b.

## Heaps and holes (Early spring)

Every place has examples of holes caused by human excavation of one kind or another. They may now be used for rough play areas or entertainment or be regarded as dangerous places only fit for weekend anglers. There are often associated 'heaps', the old tips and spoil heaps comprised of the waste from mines or quarries. The Thematic Study requires the quality of the environment to be investigated. Depending on the area, the investigation can vary from a study of industrial archaeology to current industrial pollution. Time and the weather will have affected the oldest holes and may be an indication of the best way to incorporate a current 'eyesore' back into the environment.

Again, preparation will involve finding out what is already known and can easily be observed about the holes and heaps, then looking carefully at the 1:25,000 Ordnance Survey map for signs of past and present extraction. Make a plan with the help of the children, using coordinates to show the location of these features. Use the road network as a further framework by which to locate features. Plan how these features can best be investigated to fit in with other work. Encourage the children to consider the following questions.
- What was the landscape like before extraction (digging out)?
- What effect has extraction had?
- What is the current state of the landscape?

This will form the basis for classroom discussion about the need for extraction and the benefits or otherwise bestowed. This work is relevant to PoS, 3d, e, f; 5d; 6a–c.

## Work

In some areas, the work on heaps and holes described above may lead naturally into observations and suggesting reasons for the relationship between land use, buildings and human activity in the local area (PoS, 5d). If the children are already undertaking a topic which requires a visit to a workplace (for example, 'People who help us' might involve a visit to a fire station), they could easily incorporate geographical aspects. Other possibilities could include a building site, garden centre, a swimming pool or a small firm occupying a large site, comparing all large operations to the number of people employed. Before going on such a visit, decide on the kind of information which the children will be trying to find out, then make a personal reconnaissance visit to sort out the specific requirements of each site.

On returning from the visit, develop role play on the management of the workplace or set up a 'production line' to work out the difficulties of the work involved and the reasons for its location in the area.

## Using water (Summer)

As part of improving the environment, a project involving the school garden may have been undertaken and by the summer months a watering rota will be needed. One way to show the children why water is needed and why hose pipe bans are in place in some parts of the country, would be to make a return to the stream visited in the autumn (see page 41). This should prove an interesting exercise in recording similarities and differences, especially if the same activities are repeated. The water level will probably be much lower, and the stream flowing more slowly with weeds growing further down the bank. Encourage the children to find a reason for this by looking at weather records for the previous months, if necessary using records made by older children and put on the school database.

The investigation can be extended by asking gardeners what measures can be taken to save water. Further extension can be made to other warmer, drier climates and finding out what happens there when the streams dry up. This work applies to PoS, 3b, f; 5b, c; 6a, c.

# Key Stage 2

## Year 3

At Key Stage 1, outdoor experiences were designed to develop vocabulary so that the children could describe in geographical terms the world they see around them. Parts of the landscape were looked at in detail and other areas will have been looked at in the same detail for similarities and differences. Relationships between certain features will have already been recognised and commented on.

Work with lower juniors will extend this process. More vocabulary will be learned and more observations will be made in a more rigorous fashion. Recording will be more systematic and can be regarded as contributing to the body of knowledge collected by the school as a whole as well as to personal knowledge.

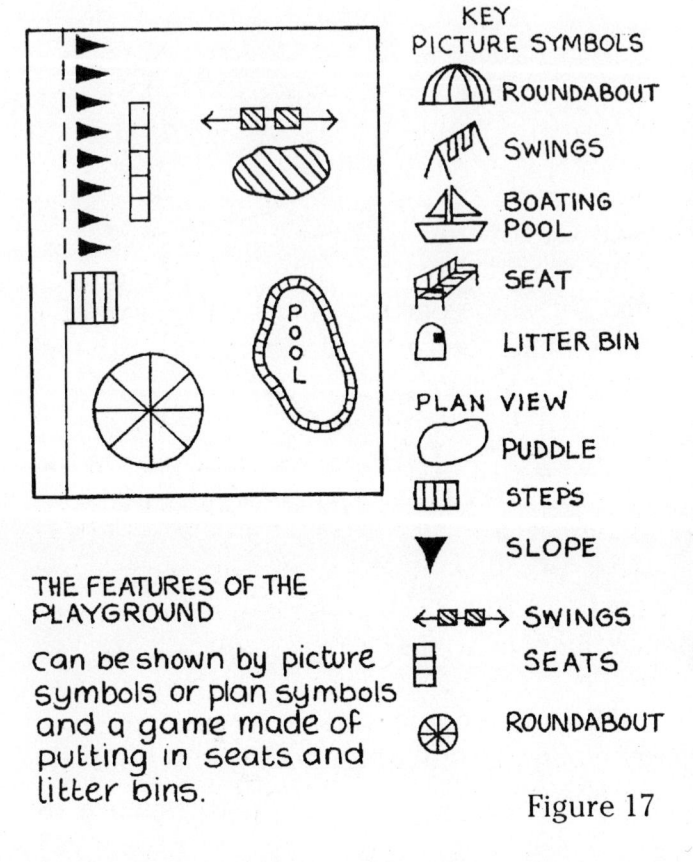

### Play areas (Early autumn)

Children frequently have a 'consumer's knowledge' of good and not so good places for play around their neighbourhood. Using a large scale plan of the area and the 1:25,000 Ordnance Survey Pathfinder map, first locate and then plot on a base map where children go to play. There does seem to be a gender difference these days which was less marked in the past. Various research investigations have revealed that once children reach an age to be allowed to move about unaccompanied, girls are less likely to be allowed to roam now than in the past. They tend to go to friends' homes and, indeed, have chaperones longer than boys. Also the car is used to take and carry equipment such as bicycles to nearby safe areas. A class map would, therefore, be a useful exercise, after each child has demonstrated their map-drawing ability, to show information about where they play. Use this information to choose a play area to visit and study in detail. Figure 17 suggests the kind of recording which could be used.

On returning from the visit, part of the follow-up work could involve making a map showing the route to the play area illustrating, in the right order, the features encountered on the way. This could be checked against the Ordnance Survey map or plan or used as a model for drawing other maps of routes, such as to relatives' houses, shops and so on. This would be relevant to PoS, 9b and 10a.

### Places of work (Late autumn/early winter)

The programme of study for Key Stage 2 requires that an investigation is made of the use of land and buildings in the local area and that correct geographical language is used to identify types of landscape features and industrial and leisure activities which the children have *observed* in the local area. At Key Stage 1,

THE FEATURES OF THE PLAYGROUND
can be shown by picture symbols or plan symbols and a game made of putting in seats and litter bins.

Figure 17

commercial and public uses of land by shops and services such as the fire brigade will already have been noted. These land uses should be added to the map showing play areas. This leaves two large categories – industrial land and farm land – to be investigated. On an Ordnance Survey map industrial buildings can be distinguished from houses by their shape – rectangular, large, with smaller shapes nearby and maybe light-railway lines. Links may already have been made with local firms in pursuit of the cross-curricular theme of economic and industrial understanding awareness. This could have been done through the LEA Education Business Partnership or via a SCIP/MESP coordinator or through parents or the local Chamber of Commerce, work shadowing on a teacher's own initiative, or following through an enquiry begun by the children in another part of the curriculum, such as technology (see Chapter nine). Firms can include building sites and the leisure industry – all process materials in some way and need land to spread out to accommodate the processing.

As with other visits, begin planning well in advance and ensure timing, safety precautions, learning objectives and intended outcomes are fully understood by both the children and the firm to be visited. Objectives could include seeing how much land the firm occupies, what type of buildings are there and whether or not it is part of a larger industrial area. Make a large outline plan of the buildings on the site and ask the children to colour it in, using different colours for different firms. This requires a great deal of observation.

Ask groups of children to carry out investigations into where materials for work are found and how they reach the firm, how the materials are processed and where the end products are sent. Encourage the groups to look for evidence of such activity. These observations will in turn raise questions which can be investigated in class with maps, atlases and a follow-up visit from a member of the firm – suitably briefed. This work would be applicable to PoS, 1b; 2; 3a, c, e; 5c.

## Work in the school grounds (New Year)

The programme of study combines teaching how site conditions can influence surface temperatures and affect wind speed

Figure 18

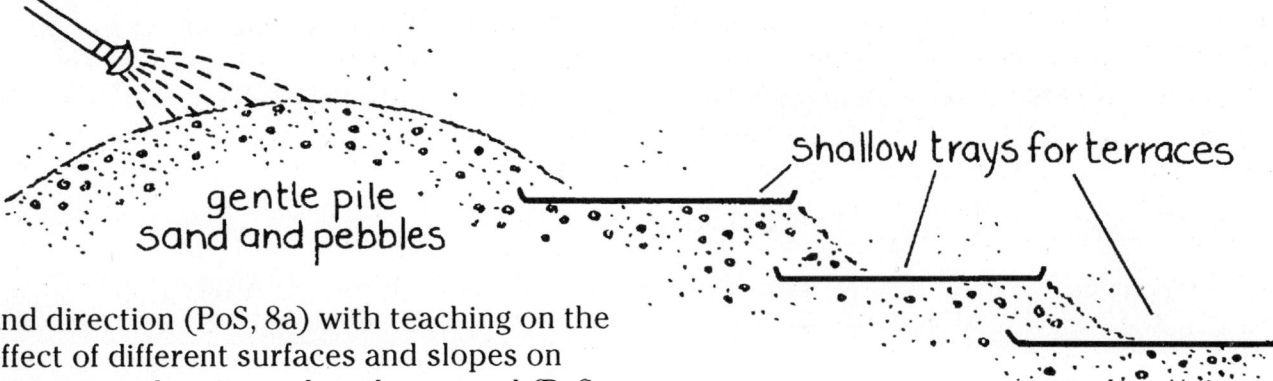

*Figure 19: gentle pile sand and pebbles; shallow trays for terraces*

and direction (PoS, 8a) with teaching on the effect of different surfaces and slopes on rainwater when it reaches the ground (PoS, 7a). The latter has already been touched on in Y2. Considering where to put plants in the school garden, especially plants with different needs, requires knowledge not only of the different soils but also of the different weather conditions. This would, therefore, be a suitable enterprise for the first spring of the junior school, especially if the garden were to be run on a whole school basis in order to utilise and investigate all the possible sites. The location of the plants can be agreed by staff and pupils together and the project can still be undertaken even if the only space available is in grow-bags and tubs. Figure 18 offers a suggestion for a 'chequerboard' design for a school garden.

Making simple weather measuring equipment and deciding how to record the information can be part of the enquiry and has cross-curricular applications. For example, information technology can be incorporated by fitting the record form to the format required by the school database package (see Chapter six). The weather recording equipment could be designed and made in technology, while the calibration of the measurements can be part of mathematical work.

The work on running water (see page 41) can also be extended with work in the school grounds. The stream visits made in Y2 need to be put in context and appropriate river vocabulary should be introduced. The children should now be beginning to understand that rivers have sources, channels, tributaries and mouths and should be shown that rivers erode, transport and deposit materials (PoS, 7a).

This can be demonstrated using the simulations described on page 24ff. Point out how the water makes a channel which has a beginning (source), a middle (the river channel) and an end (mouth). The mouth may develop as a funnel, like an estuary. The material washed down (eroded and transported) will probably accumulate and spread out (deposition), forming a fan-shaped mound (delta).

The mound of washed down material will gradually assume a more gentle slope. The enquiry can be extended to investigate how the process can be stopped. For example, terraces can be added to the simulation using small trays such as swiss roll tins, for the steps (see Figure 19). This effect can be seen in Asian rice paddy terraces. Alternatively, stones can be placed in a garland pattern, a successful technique used in the Sudan where water conservation is at a premium. This work is relevant to PoS, 4; 5c; 7b.

## A locality transect (Spring)

In the local area, investigations should include identification of familiar landscape features described with the correct geographical vocabulary. One way to achieve this is to consider a route which has a variety of landscape features related to slope, vegetation, water and overall land use. Unlike the earlier trails, several features will now be observed at once and related to each other. This lends itself to group work, as different children can be given specific jobs to be undertaken in

# SLOPE, SOIL, VEGETATION, LANDUSE

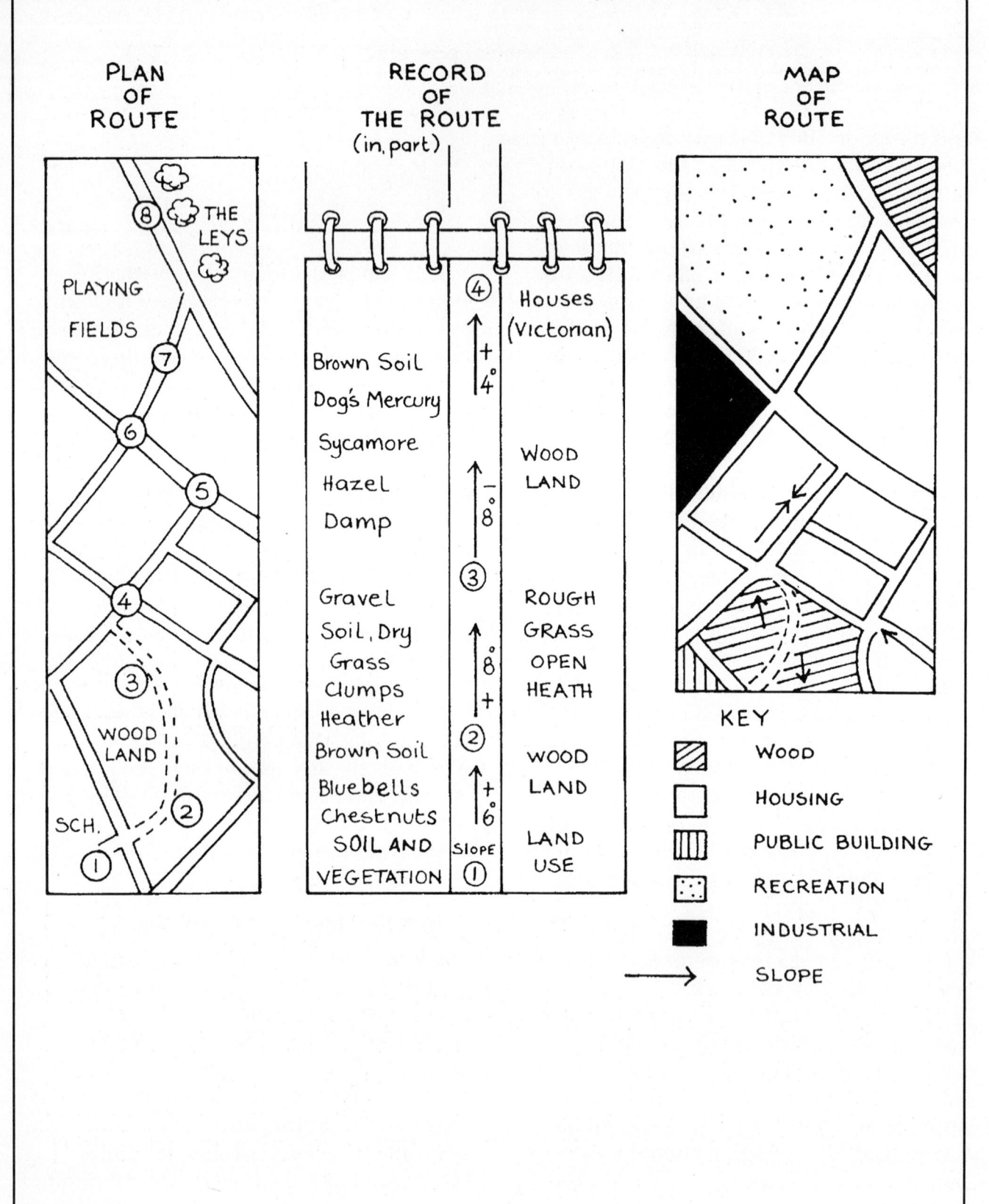

## PLAN OF ROUTE

THE LEYS
PLAYING FIELDS
⑧ ⑦ ⑥ ⑤ ④ ③ ② ①
WOODLAND
SCH.

## RECORD OF THE ROUTE (in part)

| SOIL AND VEGETATION | SLOPE | LAND USE |
|---|---|---|
| | ④ | Houses (Victorian) |
| Brown Soil | ↑ +4° | |
| Dog's Mercury | | |
| Sycamore | | WOOD LAND |
| Hazel | ↑ −8° | |
| Damp | | |
| | ③ | |
| Gravel | | ROUGH GRASS |
| Soil, Dry | ↑ 8° | |
| Grass | + | OPEN HEATH |
| Clumps | | |
| Heather | | |
| Brown Soil | ② | WOOD LAND |
| Bluebells | ↑ +6° | |
| Chestnuts | | LAND USE |
| | ① | |

## MAP OF ROUTE

### KEY

- ▨ WOOD
- ☐ HOUSING
- ⦀ PUBLIC BUILDING
- ⋮⋮ RECREATION
- ■ INDUSTRIAL
- → SLOPE

Figure 20

# CHART TO SHOW THE RELATIONSHIPS OF LANDSCAPE FEATURES ALONG A TRANSECT ROUTE

| ENVIRONMENT | SCORE 8 | 10 | 7 | 2 | 0 | 3 | 4 | 6 | 8 | 10 |
|---|---|---|---|---|---|---|---|---|---|---|
| LAND USE | RESIDENTIAL + OPEN SPACES | | COMMERCIAL PUBLIC RESIDENTIAL | | | INDUSTRIAL & TRANSPORT | | | AGRICULTURAL & OPEN SPACE | |
| OTHER BUILDINGS | SCHOOL | CHURCH | LIBRARY HEALTH CLINIC | | | TRANSPORT GARAGES AND WAREHOUSES | | | BARN | |
| RECREATION | PLAYING FIELD | WOODLAND WALKS OPEN SPACE | NONE | | | NONE | | | FOOTPATH WALKS | |
| INDUSTRY | NONE | | SMALL SHOPS | | | ENGINEERING & GAS | | | | |
| ROADS | MANY SMALL | Private & Public | MAJOR ROADS & RAILWAY | | | | | | MINOR ROADS FOOTPATHS | |
| HOUSES | DETACHED | SEMI-DETACHED | FLATS | TERRACES | | | | | | |
| WATER | DRY | | | | | STANDING, RIVER, WELL DRAINED | | | | |
| VEGETATION | School Grassland | Woodland | Gardens Rough Grass | | | Marsh & Rough Grass | | | Wood Pasture | |
| SOIL | Thin Sandy | Variable Loam | Sandy Brown | Thin Loam | | Clay & Clay Loams | | | Thin Pebbly | |
| ROCK | SANDSTONE | | | | | CLAY AND ALLUVIUM | | | GRAVELS | |
| SLOPE | Gentle | Moderate 3°–8° | | Steep 8° | | Moderate 3° | | Flat 1°–2° | Steep 10° | |

PROFILE (based on 1:25,000 or Clinometer readings)

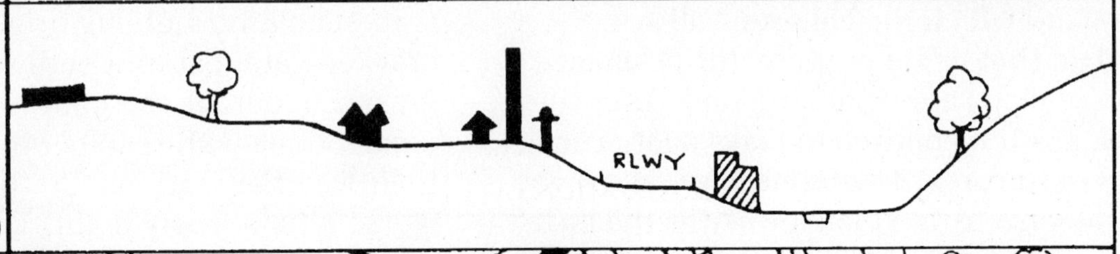

MAP (based on 1:25,000)

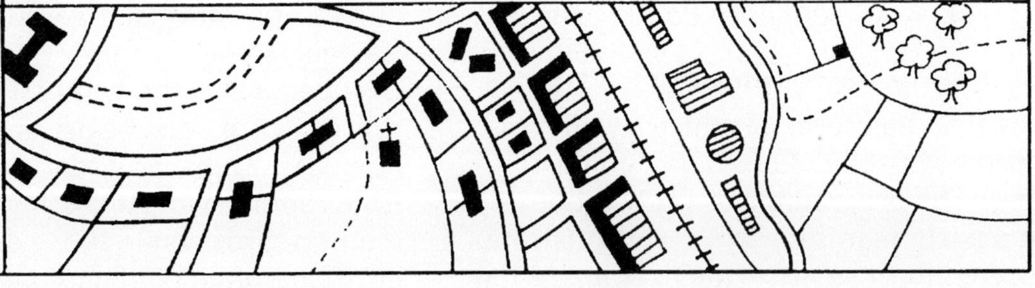

NB This can be built up by group work and plotting one or two features on several visits

Figure 21

detail at one particular section of the route (see Chapter nine). Observations can be recorded in a similar fashion to the earlier water hunt trail (Figure 20). On return to the classroom, the information can be recorded in the form of a chart (Figure 21). This work is relevant to PoS, 1b, c; 2a–c; 3a–c; 5a, c.

## The use of farmland (Early summer)

Two aspects of human geography are investigating how and why land is used in different ways, and why different amounts of land are required for different purposes. For example, a farm may comprise woodland, arable land, grassland, wasteland and land covered with farm buildings.

The farm which was investigated in Key Stage 1 may still be suitable for this investigation, but a new farm which provides a contrast may be better. The preparation required will be the same and should be repeated before each visit. The visit can be part of appreciating the markets and produce of the home region as well as being a contrasting locality in terms of its physical features.

Preparation should include mapwork in the classroom. Use a 1:25,000 Ordnance Survey map of the area, showing any slopes, water, wood, wasteland and farmland which the children will see. Explain that white areas on the Ordnance Survey map represent farmland. After the visit, ask the children to make a large scale plan of the area. The farmer may allow you to copy his estate plan for use as the base map. This work applies to PoS, 3a; 5a; 9b.

## Other land uses (Summer)

In the final half-term, organise a visit to a location whose land use raises conflicting issues. The programme of study requires that a particular issue which demonstrates how conflicts can arise due to competition over the use of land is looked at. This could be a project for widening a street involving building over gardens, or farmland being sold for development. Investigating a change in the use of land involves skills of mapwork, sketching, interviewing and research into past uses as seen on old maps and as shown in archive material. This work is applicable to PoS, 9c and 10a.

# Year 4

## Sketch maps (Autumn)

The programme of study requires representations to be made of real or imaginary places. Encourage the children to make sketch maps of small areas showing the main features and using symbols with keys, thus building on earlier map-making experience. More complicated maps can be made showing more than one feature, for example wet and dry places, street furniture in a new development or a plan of an adopted environment showing the extent of pollution or dereliction or the distribution of a species of plant.

## Wear and tear (Early winter)

Link weather site observations (PoS, 8a) with science work on materials and its application to everyday life in the local environment. A starting point may be the imminent refurbishment of the school exterior, reinforcing location of wear and tear (cracking paint, moss and damp) with compass direction (KS1, PoS, 3c).

Collect together examples of wear and tear, such as crumbling brickwork, a cracked gatepost or a path worn across the grass. Encourage the children to look for connections with results obtained from their weather stations. Do the cracks get worse after a frosty night? Do the bricks and mortar make a larger pile of debris at the foot of the wall after rain? Where does dust come from on windy days? Determine the aspect of specific areas using a compass. Those areas facing south suffer from rapid drying and being raised to high temperatures, while those areas facing north are often cold and damp areas. Make connections between debris which collects at the foot of walls, blocked gutters and drains and work on running water (p25) (PoS, 2a–c). Sort out why particles are of different size, experimenting with crushing a brick (between paper) and/or a piece of sandstone. This is a good time to make the point that this is the beginning of making real soil. (Compare with soil in the school grounds and then with a compost, made-up soil, from the garden centre.) Keep the samples, labelled (see below).

## Running water: 2 (New Year)

Take the children back to the local stream visited at Key Stage 1 and look for evidence that rivers erode, transport and deposit materials (PoS, 7b). Let the children take samples from the bed and banks of the stream and from adjacent land. Use these samples in further experiments such as sieving, drying and weighing, concentrating on their origin rather than their scientific properties. Compare with the debris and soil samples from the school grounds. Write about a particle going from a crumbling wall, into the gutter, then the river and so on.

## Contrasts in the locality (Spring)

In order to recognise similarities and differences between their local area and other localities, the study of the layout and functions (for example services provided, the work carried out there and the social centres and so on) of a small settlement or part of a larger settlement is required. In addition, it is necessary to evaluate the impact of any recent or current change.

Visit a new shopping precinct or business centre and compare it with similar developments in your neighbourhood. Encourage the children to use different recording techniques such as completing questionnaires, tape recording their observations or interviews and annotating maps to prepare for activities on residential school journeys. This work is applicable to PoS, 3b; 5b; 9b.

## School day journey (Early summer)

Organise a whole day out to visit a contrasting locality. For example, if your school is inland, organise a visit to the coast to allow the children to compare it with a river and to look for signs of erosion, transport and deposition (PoS, 7a, b). If your school is in a city, visit a small market town and encourage the children to investigate its character and function as a settlement (see Chapter nine) (PoS, 9a).

## Running water: 3 (Late summer)

Revisit the local stream, but let the children look at more than one site to allow them to see changes that take place along the course of the stream and to take a series of precise measurements (see page 26).

Showing the children that rivers receive water from a wide area can be achieved by visiting one site above a confluence and one below. Collect samples of soil and water at both sites for making comparisons with other samples. The sites will probably be at least 1.5km (1 mile) apart so you will need to address the problem of transport well in advance.

Back in the classroom, let the children enter their observations on a database. This work is applicable to PoS, 3b, f.

# Year 5

## The river (Autumn)

The programme of study requirement to recognise that rivers have sources, channels, tributaries and mouths, that they receive water from a wide area and that most eventually flow into a lake or the sea, can be achieved by a combination of map and fieldwork.

Let the children follow a local stream from its source to its confluence with a river. This might be a route of as much as 15–30km, in which case transport and stopping points should be planned well in advance. The route can be studied in terms of both physical attributes (such as bends and speed of flow) and human responses to it (as indicated by the buildings along the banks). Classwork beforehand could involve tracing the course first on an Ordnance Survey map and locating the land-use features and items of special interest. A historical dimension can be added by investigating the age and original purpose of buildings such as water-mills, thus encouraging the children to consider change and to look at this in an environmental context. This work applies to PoS, 7a, b; 3a–d; 10a.

## Journeys (Early winter)

To help put the locality in a broader geographical context and show how it is linked to other places (PoS, 5e), investigate travelling between points in the locality on a small scale, using different means of transport. Compare walking, cycling and using a wheelchair, as well as travelling by car, bus and rail. Time each mode of transport and plot the route on a large scale plan of the area. Extend this to places visited for everyday things, such as shopping, special treats and leisure activities. The work may be undertaken as individual or group projects using well known local routes.

This investigation lends itself to group work focusing on children from the same estate or road and can be spread over several weeks if necessary. It could also be planned to coincide with other out of school trips, for example, to the swimming baths. This work is applicable to PoS, 5e.

## Landscape impact assessment (New Year)

The programme of study expects investigations into how the environment changes. The construction of bridges, reservoirs, motorways and the associated quarrying for building materials probably has occurred recently in your area (PoS, 10a).

Take the children to visit, or revisit, a local building site with this section of the programme of study in mind, and let them record, sketch, photograph and generally collect material for considering the issue in class. Use IT (PoS, 3f) to make a balance sheet of advantages and disadvantages. Then consider the steps which are needed to manage and sustain the affected environment (PoS, 10b).

## Soils (Late spring)

Build on the children's science work involving describing soils (Sc, Materials, 1c) by collecting several samples from different parts of the locality – for example, the children's gardens, hedge bottoms, ditch sides. Use local geology and OS maps to devise a 'soil trail'. If there is a hill in the vicinity, the soil at the top of the slope will be different to that at the bottom, even if the land use is the same. Make your own map to show the locations. Link with the plants and creatures found at the same spot and consider if this influences the quality of the environment (PoS, 6a and 10a). Those schools in urban areas, where soils are built over except in parks, can develop this aspect using old maps to chart the environmental change. There may be chance to discuss improvements (PoS, 10b).

If the district is not suitable for collecting a variety of soil samples, this investigation could be combined with the land use study of the farm by taking soil samples from different parts of the farm.

## The residential school journey (Early summer)

Try to organise a whole week in a contrasting environment during which the children can ask questions and investigate in familiar ways new patterns and distributions in the locality. The out-of-doors activities developed over the previous five years will have led to competence in observing, recording and interpreting (PoS, 2a–c).

Some local education authorities still maintain residential centres with a warden and staff who can help organise a field week in all its aspects. As with other extensive visits a preliminary visit to sort out details, both academic and social, is essential and should be allowed for in the school planning policy.

Many schools already have firm links with a centre from which fieldwork can be undertaken. If such a venture is new to your school then your local education authority geography/humanities inspector/advisor should be able to put you in touch with a more experienced school to help answer your questions. *Explorations: A Guide to Fieldwork in the Primary School* by Stephen Wass (*Primary Bookshelf* series, Hodder & Stoughton, 1990) is a clear guide.

## The wider world (Summer)

The requirement that a contrasting locality be in a country such as those found in the tropics raises questions about ways of living with different weather conditions. This requirement can be given practical application by using the school garden for experimenting with ideas for conservation of water and soil, and different methods of irrigation. How long does it take to carry a bucket of water from the tap to the garden without spilling any? Can the children imagine watering a whole farm like this?

This work applies to PoS, 4; 5a, b.

# Year 6

## Running water: 4 (Early autumn)

A visit to the local gauging station or waterworks, combined with mapwork based on information from the local water authority covers several areas of the programme of study, such as showing that river measurements are needed to enable the water board to provide a reliable supply of water, learning where the fresh water supply is to be found in the region, recognising the methods used to reduce flood risk and finding out the dates of significant floods. This provides information for further research using local archive material and maps. This research, following on from the children's own stream measurements and weather records completed the previous summer, will show that their work, on a small scale, is just the same as that of the water authority. This would be applicable to PoS, 5a, c; 7a; 10b.

## Goods and services (Late autumn)

Visit local bus, train, Post Office and freight depots to find out how goods and services, needed by the community, are provided (PoS, 5e). This can be accomplished by group work, with each group reporting back to the class. Objectives should include looking at the way different means of transport are used for different purposes and how goods are transferred from one means of transport to another such as parcels from containers to trains to Post Office vans.

Preparation will involve the group thinking of suitable questions, based on their existing knowledge of the locality. Previous preparation on the part of the teacher will have involved liaising with the depots to ensure that the visits go smoothly. Old way sheets, giving lists of goods transported per journey, and work time sheets may be made available in advance by the depot to help develop role play and management games. This work applies to PoS, 2a–c; 3a–f; 5e; 9a–c.

## Settlements and land use (New Year)

Evaluate the impact of any recent or current change in land use. Look for the reasons for the location of various commercial developments and investigate the conflicts which arise due to competition. The topic of 'Change' can be a stimulus for looking at housing development, industrial location (light industry in place of heavy industry) and agricultural change or other types of economic activity. The research could be undertaken as part of planning and presenting a video on economic activity in the local area. The out-of-class work completed previously in the areas, for example visits to building sites, industrial firms and depots, and the contacts made will determine the precise details. This work applies to PoS, 2a–c; 3a–f; 9c; 10a.

### Environmental management (Early spring)

The programme of study requires that **'pupils should be taught how people affect the environment...'** and **'why people seek to manage and sustain their environment'** (PoS, 10a, b). Help the children to select a part of the local environment which could be developed to attract visitors, then encourage them to investigate the current pedestrian and vehicular use of the chosen area. Are the roads wide and safe enough and the footpaths adequate to provide for the impact of increased use? This may involve contacting the local planning department. Ask the children to evaluate the current landscape and use maps and diagrams to help them present a case for or against a proposed change to the environment, such as the increased number of visitors to their chosen area. This work applies to PoS, 9c; 10a, b and is developed further in Chapter nine.

### Pollution (Early summer)

The programme of study requires that pupils should be taught about matters affecting the environment and the management of such (PoS, 10a, b). 'Adopt' the nearest example of such pollution. This may involve arranging a visit to the local sewage works and then investigating the adopted environment for a detailed survey of pollution as a cross-curricular venture. Examples and expansion are given in Chapter seven. Use this work for PoS, 5a; 9c; 10a, b.

### The locality (Summer)

Encourage the children to research and make a trail, for use by visitors, which will show the geographical elements in a meaningful and logical fashion (PoS, 5a, e). If possible, extend this trail in the region around the school. Children could work in groups and report back to the class. Process the information as part of a cross-curricular activity so that history, art, technology, English and maths are all included.

## Conclusion

These ideas, of course, only offer a few possibilities. Geographers, as a matter of course, make a habit of walking round the school locality with a map, collect the Chamber of Commerce handbook and free newspapers. These give the flavour of the area and indicate past and present areas of local concern; starting points, if you like. If you have lived in the area for some time you will no doubt already be aware of local concerns, but may not think of them as geography, but as the 'news'. Information about a place adds up into a body of geographical knowledge, which can be expanded by asking why? where? what for? and enquiring further. A whole-school meeting, where everybody pools their geographical knowledge, should help develop a tailor-made programme using the best points of the locality and bringing in new developments to satisfy the National Curriculum requirements.

# Chapter four
# Maps and map-making

If someone asks you for directions, do you gesticulate to left and right while loudly giving instructions? Or do you hunt for a scrap of paper and draw a rough map with arrows and labels? Almost certainly you will have done your best to show the way, but will somehow feel dissatisfied. Perhaps you missed out a vital landmark or the scale went wrong and the last bit of the route had to be squashed on to a tiny bit of paper. You knew you could have done better because all the necessary information was there in your head and you could easily have physically guided the enquirer. How often does a child give up explaining and take your hand and lead you to the place they were trying to describe?

We all have cognitive maps in our heads complete with landmarks and blank areas for the places about which we have no information. It is no accident that the geography of London's streets is referred to by taxi drivers as 'The Knowledge', built up over time by repeatedly going over routes with a map.

Children's geographical knowledge is built up in the same way. From babyhood they build up knowledge about their surroundings by repeatedly moving along specific routes towards food, warmth, comfort, toys or attractive sounds and, from there, to explore unfamiliar areas. Spatial awareness is developed to a high degree by this discovery process. At the same time children learn to express themselves by talking (oracy), by recognising signs and eventually words (literacy) and by recognising the difference between the concepts of none, one, a few and many (numeracy).

The development of this spatial ability is known as graphicacy. The teacher of geography is responsible for continuing to develop this discovery process by using direct experience, enquiry skills and practical activities, both outside and inside the classroom. As with the development of literacy and numeracy, the development of graphicacy has to take place gradually, with variety in the way of working and with much repetition.

# Map skills at Key Stage 1

The programme of study at Key Stage 1 lists the map use and map-making skills which can be grouped in the following ways.

# Orientation

This skill involves position and direction and is concerned with knowing where you are and where you are going. The demands of the programme of study are that children **'should be taught to:**
**• follow directions, including the terms up, down, on, under, behind, in front of, near, far, left, right, north, south, east, west.'** (3c)
This covers children talking about their own maps as well as other maps and is a *minimum* requirement allowing the use of eight compass points to be developed and the use of letter and number coordinates to locate features on maps. This will enable more to be made of:
**'• use globes, maps and plans at a variety of scales; the work should include identifying major geographical features, locating and naming on a map..., marking on a map approximately where they live and following a route.'** (3e)

# Drawing maps

Children are also required to:
**'• make maps and plans of real and imaginary places using pictures and symbols.'** (3d)
Another *minimum* requirement. This should not preclude a child drawing around objects to make a plan, drawing a pictorial map to illustrate a story and showing his/her ability by making a map of a short route showing the main features in the correct order.

Children also need to develop the ability to:
**'• use secondary sources, e.g., *pictures, photographs (including aerial photographs).'*** (3f)
This allows features to be identified from both ground and oblique aerial views and the knowledge to be used to develop symbols. Symbols are merely stylised forms to represent common features of the landscape.

Some understanding of the concept of scale can also be begun by recognising and naming things in relation to each other. Sorting out proportional size before using units of measurement is as important in map drawing as in mathematics.

# Developing spatial awareness

The development of a child's spatial awareness is known as 'cognitive mapping ability'. In the early years it is possible to discern all stages of development of this ability. The earliest stages are wholly egocentric and the 'landmarks' of the child's mental map are those places which are visited frequently. Initially, these are restricted to the home and garden, then go on to include landmarks such as trees, churches, playgrounds, friends' houses, shops and various features seen on the way to school. These can be discussed and drawn and a first map can be produced. The essence of this map will be that the sequence of landmarks is right but the specific location, distance and direction will be somewhat vague. Indeed, depending upon the child, the map area might cover one corner of an A4 sheet or the whole of four A4 sheets.

With repeated journeys and experiences, particularly if discussed with other people, the mental map gradually becomes more objective. The child will recognise that certain features – a park, a church, a school or traffic lights – are always in the same place and related to each other in the same sequence. These features can be used as reference points to which further objective points can be linked. As more places are visited and more observations are made, the child gradually realises that the whole area contains a multitude of landmarks which can be related to each other and to other features beyond the area. This requires a degree of abstract thinking which not every child can attain without help from the teacher. It is this attainment which is aimed for by the end of Key Stage 2.

## Location vocabulary

Location vocabulary is fundamental to understanding map work. To know where you are and to be able to give and receive directions is usually achieved by noting landmarks with a location word (for example, 'Fetch Teddy, it is behind the sofa, under the window, beside the television').

An older child might describe the way to grandmother's house as, 'I go along the road, past the field on the right with the horses in, past the cottages with an arch in to the yard, to the shop on the corner. Turn right at the corner and then cross the road to the Co-op supermarket. Go past the supermarket, past the chestnut tree at the painter's house, past Cox's Bakery and up the hill. Grandma's house is number 25, it is in the middle of a terrace of houses and has a brown door.'

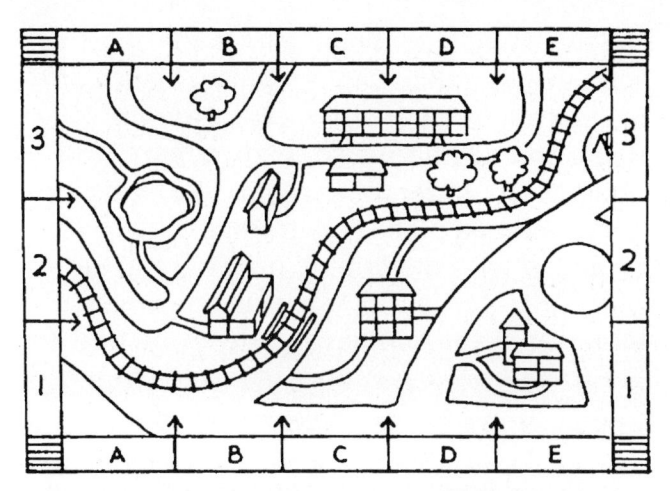

BORDER FOR MAKING GRID ON MODEL OR PICTURE MAP TO REDUCE OR ENLARGE SQUARE BY SQUARE ON TO A4 PAPER

Figure 1

This description of a route might be geographically correct but it still does not give all the landmarks on the route. For example, the shoe and hat shops might have been left out, together with the police station and the Liberal Club, landmarks which might prove more helpful for an adult.

When formally asked, a child might give only the minimum information ('past the field, right at the shop, up the hill to number 25') and volunteer the rest when more relaxed and chatting informally. Open, informal conversation is, therefore, most important with young children. It gives clues as to their interests and offers ways into starting and continuing locational activities.

Children can be encouraged to build up maps when they play. For example, a railway track can be drawn around on to a large sheet of paper and the layout used to develop a town plan with houses, shops and other features, as in Figure 1. This simple base map, with recognisable locations, will help you to assess spatial ability and can be used for comparable development over a period of time. Another map could be made using a rural location, such as Postman Pat's village or Winnie the Pooh's Hundred Acre Wood.

The use of such maps allows for pointing out a route, talking about where places are in relation to each other and generally using an imaginative context to help children to understand reality. Pointing to and naming a place can gradually be replaced with describing how to reach a place. Reinforce this by devising games in which the children have to describe how to get to another classroom, a feature in the playground or a building nearby. Games can also be used to reinforce the use of locational language (to the side of, through, over, round, under, behind, in front of), as can books describing journeys such as Pat Hutchin's *Rosie's Walk*. Make board games illustrated with places which might be seen during a journey by the class, the child's favourite animal or an imaginary character. (For example, the cat goes through a garden, over the wall, under the fence, down the steps, beside the pool, round the bin, up the tree, along the branch – and back again.)

PE activities can also be used to reinforce these words. Make a route with clue cards to take the children round an obstacle course of mats and boxes. Devise warm-up routines for emphasising left and right, forward and back.

## Location and compass direction

The convention for published maps is that north is at the top edge. Ordnance Survey maps show the deviation from magnetic north for the relevant latitude. Other maps only show north if the map is not orientated conventionally. This can be used to develop children's understanding of the points of the compass.

Introducing the children to compass direction is most easily accomplished by encouraging them to consider the sun and its changing position through the day. Shadow sticks can be used to show the apparent movement of the sun and, if observed on several consecutive days, will reveal the fact that the same pattern occurs on each day. In the classroom, plot the apparent movement of the sun by marking its position every hour with masking tape crosses on the window. If your room faces south the plot will show a curve with the highest point reached at midday (or 1pm BST). If your classroom does not face south then sunny mornings and sunny afternoons can be related to facing east or facing west.

Ask the children questions to heighten their awareness of the apparent movement of the sun.
- Who wakes up to a sunny bedroom in the morning?
- Who finds it difficult to go to sleep on sunny evenings?
- Where is the sun at lunch time?
- Which side of the house stays in shadow all day?
- Who lives on the sunny (north) side of the street? Who lives on the shaded (south) side?
- Is the back of the house sunny (south side) or shaded (north side)?
- Which bits of the garden are sunny all day?
- Which bits are sunny for part of the day? When?

In the northern hemisphere shadows always point north at noon and all other means of assessing north work on this principle.

Next, use a magnetic compass to find out the position of true north in the classroom. Mark the relevant wall or let the children paint a floor compass.

Figure 2 shows how a chart can be made to find out which part of the school grounds is most suitable for making a garden area. At this point it would be useful to introduce the children to the Ordnance Survey map and show them that north always lies along the top edge. Explain how, with the sun at your back at lunch time, east is always right and left always west. Some children are naturally aware of both map north and north as it relates to themselves so that they automatically mentally orientate the map information for working out where they need to go. Others have to turn the map consciously, as is

## WARMTH AND SHADE IN THE GARDEN / SCHOOL GROUNDS

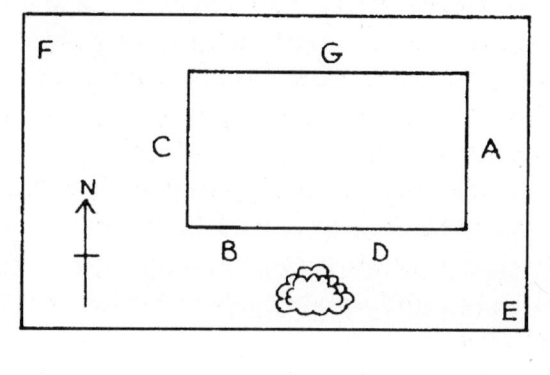

| ● SHADE ○ SUN TIME | SITES A | B | C | D | E | F |
|---|---|---|---|---|---|---|
| 8-30 – 9-30 | ○ | ○ | ● | ○ | ● |  |
| 9-30 – 10-30 | ○ | ○ | ● | ○ | ● |  |
| 10-30 – 11-30 | ● | ○ | ● | ○ | ● |  |
| 3-30 – 4-30 | ● | ○ | ○ | ● | ● |  |
| 4-30 – 5-30 | ● | ○ | ○ | ● | ○ |  |
| 5-30 – 6-30 |  |  |  |  |  |  |

Figure 2

required in orienteering, in order to align the top of the map with the direction of north on the ground. This work can be begun in the classroom or outside in the school grounds.

## Using maps in the classroom

Maps can be used to describe various subjects, such as the shapes of the continents, the places where certain animals are found, fictional lands and underground railway systems. This can be used as a basis for classroom discussion about the appearance of maps. The way maps look can be linked in with art and technology.

Show the children that maps don't just show the landscape, but also the distribution of playgrounds, post offices, homes, places of work and so on. Routes between places can be worked out logically from a map and then compared with the actual route. An exercise can be set up to see which landmarks from the map are as clearly noticeable on the ground (for example, the symbol PO for post office as opposed to the building itself).

## Reference map collection

In addition to the floor map, provide a large scale plan of the neighbourhood. If possible, use a plan which shows where all the children live. Usually this can be covered using the 1:10,000 Ordnance Survey map but be warned, the sheets are contiguous so it is quite possible that the area to be investigated may not lie within one sheet! As each class should have its own large scale plan of the locality, buy one map and use your local authority's reproduction facility on licence from the Ordnance Survey.

Mount the base map on strong card or hardboard, then cover it with clear adhesive plastic film so that water-based pens can be used on it. With younger children, especially Reception classes, a similar map at the larger scale of 1:2,500 (25") is valuable for allowing little fingers to point and shaky routes to be drawn. This map can be used as a floor map, although this might involve using several sheets. Enquire at your local authority's architects and surveyors department for copies.

For some schools, the 1:25,000 Pathfinder map might be appropriate. The value of this map is that it is colour printed and is the ideal resource for finding out where the water flows in the neighbourhood. Water is shown in blue, woods in green, contours in brown and rock features in black. House and field boundaries are shown to scale but paths and roads are slightly exaggerated. This map is photographically reduced from the 1:10,000 sheets and contains no less information. However, water and boundaries on the 1:10,000 sheet are both in black, making it difficult to trace the route of water especially in built-up areas. If you do not have the facilities for making colour copies of the Pathfinder map, it may be worth investing in one for each class.

The 1:50,000 Landranger maps have replaced the old Seventh Series One Inch maps (which incidentally are useful historic documents which provide references for change in the area). Even very young children can use these small scale plans to follow journeys to nearby towns and villages. It is not unknown for six-year-olds to be able to read 1:50,000 maps and pick out the holiday places they wish to visit. (Places to visit, such as castles and historic houses, are emphasised with blue labels, in special script.) A six-year-old will generally have no understanding of distance or of reasons for location but relationships will be noticed, even if only to observe there is, for example, a car park.

There are many more maps which could be collected, but these Ordnance Survey maps are the essential core, to be used as regularly as dictionaries are in language work.

## Developing your map collection

Although expensive to manufacture, maps are very often available free of charge or at a low price. The A-Z Geographia are the most common street maps but many others are available. Petrol stations usually stock maps and route guides of various scales, such as those produced by the AA and RAC. These maps are constantly being updated, but remember that locations as such do not change, so old editions can still be a good, free source of location information, especially those, such as the AA and Readers Digest maps, which are based upon Ordnance Survey records. These can sometimes be obtained from garages.

Other thematic route maps are produced by airlines, British Waterways, London Transport, British Rail, local tourist boards, holiday resorts and theme parks. Have a map-collecting session, then use the collection to find out what is being shown – and what you would have liked to have been shown!

## Introducing coordinates

On a group outing, the most common interruption is, 'Where are we?' To this end, an understanding of the principle of coordinates has to be taught from an early age. This does not have to be taught in a mathematical context. For example, you could develop a coordinate board game as shown in Figure 3.

The simplest grid system uses letters along top or bottom and numbers up the sides (Figure 4). More able children could be introduced to a simple numerical grid system (Figure 5) before proceeding on to the Ordnance Survey system of coordinates whereby each square is divided into ten parts each way, thus giving a number for any point within the square (Figure 6). This work is closely linked with mathematics, so stages of development can be linked and reinforcement can be mutually advantageous. Practise finding and giving locations.

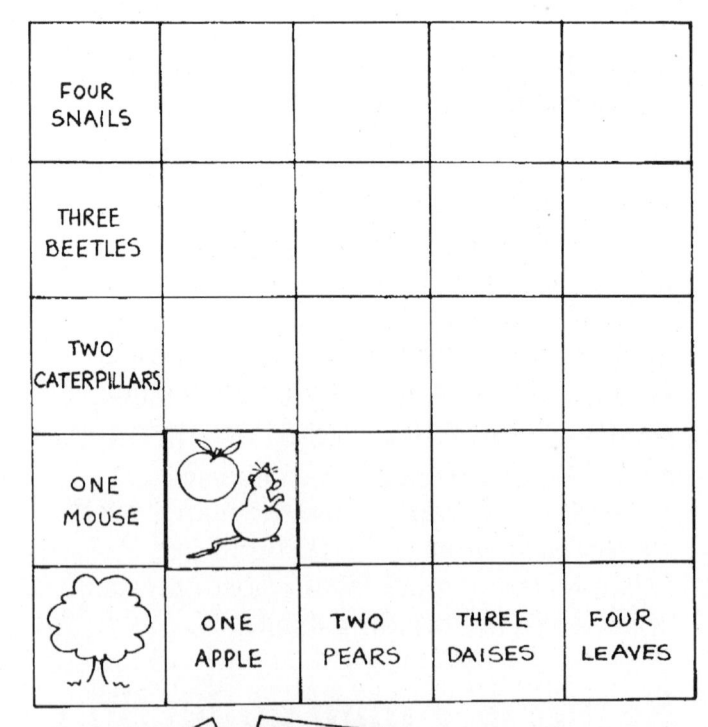

Figure 3

LETTER/NUMBER GRID SYSTEM    NUMERICAL GRID SYSTEM

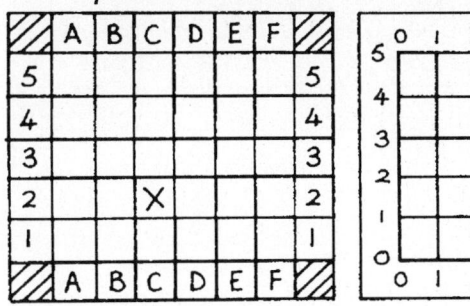

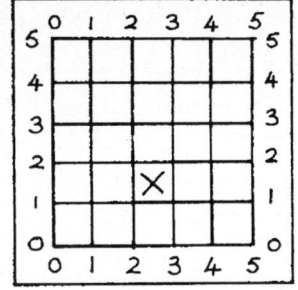

X = C2            X = 21 or 2515

Figure 4          Figure 5

NATIONAL GRID SYSTEM

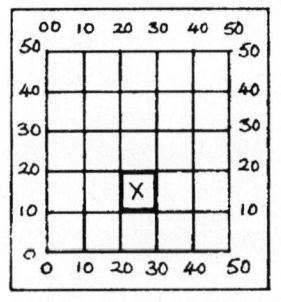

☐ = 2010
X = 205105        Figure 6

## Routes

The concept of routes can be introduced with location language in games and PE work or with a floor play mat upon which a village has been built, complete with traffic signs and places of significance. Make cue cards with the name of each place, then order them in a particular sequence and ask the children to follow the route on the map. Devise races between groups of children, timing them to see who can follow the sequence in the shortest amount of time.

Develop this by using photographs of the locality and asking the children to put them in sequence as they would encounter the places shown on a walk in the neighbourhood. This will enable the children to begin to form mental links between reality and maps. The table overleaf shows how work in the other attainment areas can be incorporated.

By the time a child is in the top infants there is usually no difficulty with pointing to their own position on the 1:10,000 Ordnance Survey map. By this age reading ability should be such that features can often be identified by the fact they are labelled on the large scale plans. However, structured work on drawing maps and using symbols will also contribute towards this part of the programme.

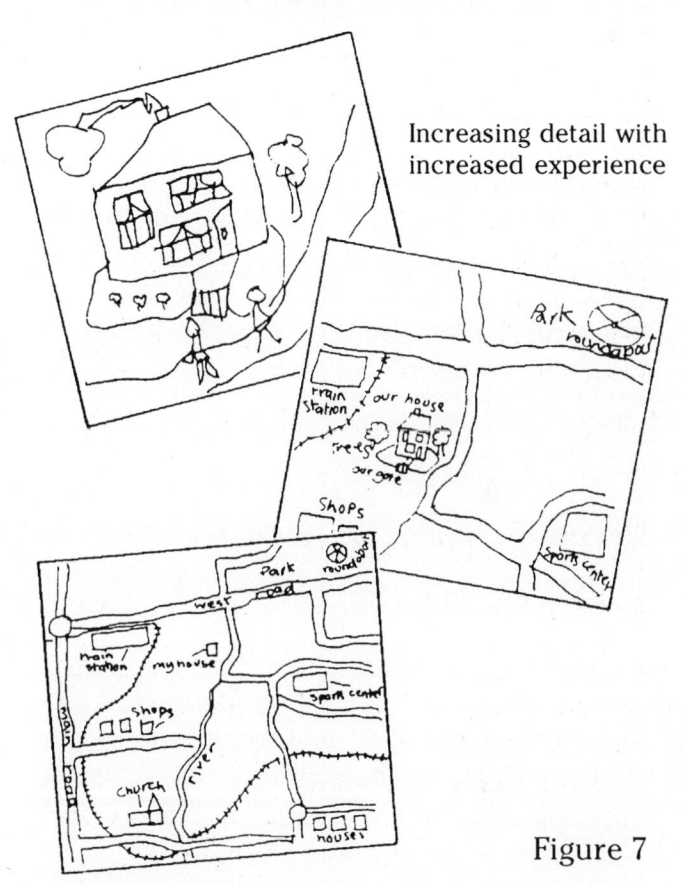

Increasing detail with increased experience

Figure 7

## Drawing maps and using symbols

Figure 7 is based on a diagram in 'Cognitive mapping' in *Teaching Geography* where Simon Catling describes how children's work can be used in the classroom to promote and assess their mapping ability. Other unpublished work with groups of children at all levels in a particular junior school, with a comprehensive mapping programme, showed that with each year the proportion of children at each stage changed in a regular fashion with maturation (see Figure 8, page 61). As maturation varied, however, there was still

# ROUTE DRAWING AND THE PROGRAMME OF STUDY

| Place | Physical features | Human features | Environment |
|---|---|---|---|
| **Level 1: Follow directions** | | | |
| • To a friend's house (address). | • To a pond (water feature); a viewpoint (top of a hill). | • To a shop, library (recognise buildings); the bus station (describe journey from school, how people travel); the post box (people and work). | • To a quiet place (sensory route for likes and dislikes). |
| **Level 2: Follow a route using a plan** | | | |
| • Around the classroom, school, park, home to collect specific items; a shop with a shopping list; a model farm with an animal or vegetable/fruit list; a model village with a bus.<br>• Of an imaginary place, e.g. Postman Pat's village, and describe the people; a plan sent by a linked school.<br>• Of a contrasting locality. | • Around a park linking different water places or in the locality visiting different places with water. Use the 1:25,000 OS map. | • Of a model between different buildings; of a picture plan or model of a village elsewhere.<br>• On an atlas to talk about long and short journeys; on the 1:10,000 OS map to the nearest toy shop; on the 1:50,000 OS map to a large toyshop in the nearest town.<br>• The journey of a banana from shop to home; from the tree to the shop. | • The journey of a box of fish.<br>• The local route to a recycling depot. |
| **Level 3: Make a map of a short route** | | | |
| • The way home.<br>• The way to the shops, library or park.<br>• The way to water features, green places or shops selling a special toy. | • The route of the local stream or a route to visit the stream or viewpoint. Use the 1:25,000 or 1:50,000 sheet. | • A journey to a relative or friend locally.<br>• Show lengths of different journeys.<br>• How to get to an important part of town. | • How to get to a favourite spot.<br>• The way to school.<br>• The way to a bottle bank.<br>• The way to the nearest green place. |
| **Level 4: Identify features on both a large scale map and an aerial photograph of the same place** | | | |
| All the above ways in each place and theme plus:<br>• Identify landscape features in the locality.<br>• Identify features in the home region. | • Identify parts of a river system.<br>• Locate sample sites. | • Make a trail linking different features.<br>• Make a trail across different parts of the settlement. | • Locate changes in the locality.<br>• Make a trail to show places needing protection. |
| **Level 5: Follow a route on maps of various scales and describe the features which would be seen** | | | |
| All the above ways in each place and theme plus:<br>• Make traverses along main roads, green link routes. | • Locate and follow causes of river floods and protection routines. | • Locate hypermarket or similar and follow the routes to it in the home region. | • Locate and make trail of pollution points. |

a proportion using the link-picture map regularly even at the age of ten (as we do when in a hurry, but not when given time to think and plan).

The first steps towards drawing maps are:
- being able to recognise and match, plan and picture;
- understanding the differences between front, side and plan view, and between elevation, oblique and vertical views;
- realising that shapes can be simplified.

These steps can be achieved by developing games where the children have to guess and match pictures and plan shapes, guess and match wrapped shapes with pictures or twin unwrapped shapes. Sort pictures into pictograms and symbols. Pelmanism using pictures and symbols is another short activity with a reinforcing element. Figure 9 suggests appropriate pictures and symbols to be linked.

The concept of plans can also be introduced by letting the children draw round their hands and feet, thus making 1:1 plans, then asking them to compare their plans with those of their friends, sorting them according to size and making comparisons.

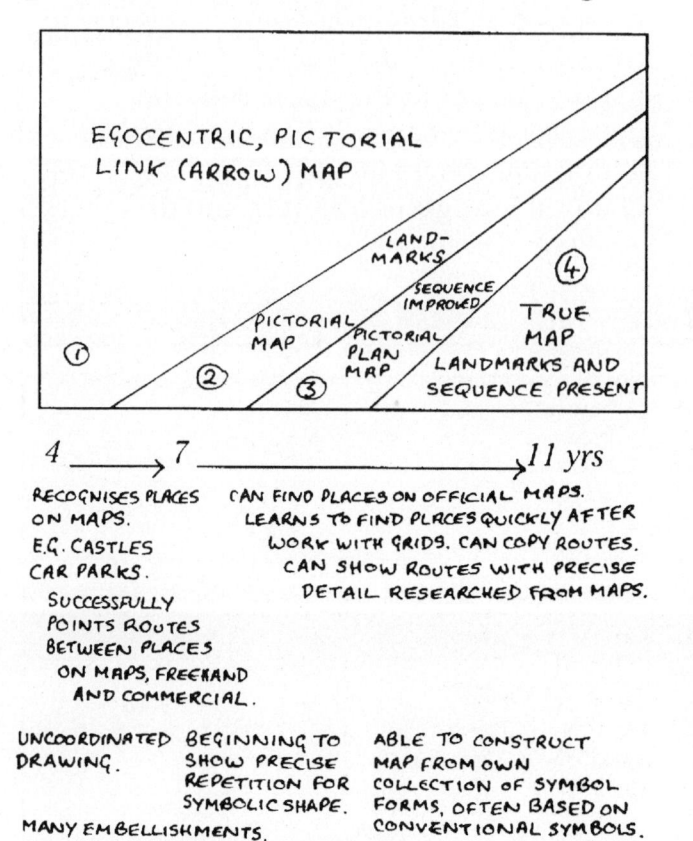

Reinforce this by using geometrical shapes such as cubes and linking them together to form different shapes, then asking the children to draw the appropriate plans.

To help the children realise that plans only show the area occupied by the object and not its height, use an overhead projector with tall objects, such as bottles and food packets, toy cars and lorries, doll's house furniture and other small objects. This technique can be used to suggest to the children what can be used to represent such items when drawing plans.

Another useful activity would be to ask a small group of children to sit round a collection of objects so that they each have different side views, then to ask them each to draw a picture of what they can see. When they have completed their drawings, ask them to compare them. What differences can they see? Ask them to swap positions and repeat the exercise. How different is the view now? Point out to the

Figure 9

Figure 8

children that they have been drawing exactly what they see and that in drawing a plan they have to do the same thing as though they were looking down at the object on the floor.

This can be followed by a group discussion on which shapes would be easiest to show on a plan.

## Firsthand maps

Many children, when shown a large scale plan of their school and its environs, exclaim, 'Just think, I'm in there, looking at this map which shows school in which I am looking at...' This is usually followed by the realisation that everything 'has shrunk to fit the space'.

To introduce the concept of a scaled down plan, put several objects together on a tray or a small table. Give each child a piece of A4 paper and ask them to 'shrink' the tray and its contents and draw them on the paper. This should be within the capabilities of the infant child. Do not mention scale at this stage. That will be covered later, when measuring is being mastered in fine detail. Simply ensure that a bird's-eye view of the group of objects is possible. Do not expect precise locations or accurate plan shapes but do ask the children to add labels. Even if poorly spelled, labels will begin to show that plan symbols can be named.

The next stage is to draw a plan of something the children can see in its entirety, but which is too large for them to stand above, for example the classroom, the corridor, the street or the playground. There are several approaches to this. One solution would be to ask the children to make a model of the chosen feature and convert it to a 1:1 plan (see page 61) and then redraw it at a smaller scale on to an A4 sheet. Another solution would be to give the children a prepared map of a familiar area, putting in features such as doors and windows, gates and changes in wall direction yourself, and then asking the children to add finer details by physically moving about and exploring the area to be mapped. Allow for several attempts. If the children have visited a building site, let them role play surveyors moving to different spots with their tripods to get different views and fixes. This technique may help the children to get the position of objects more accurate, although for many reasons furniture often seems to cluster in the middle or to one side of children's plans. Talk about the maps with the children. Why have certain objects been left off and others included? Explain to the children how cartographers and designers

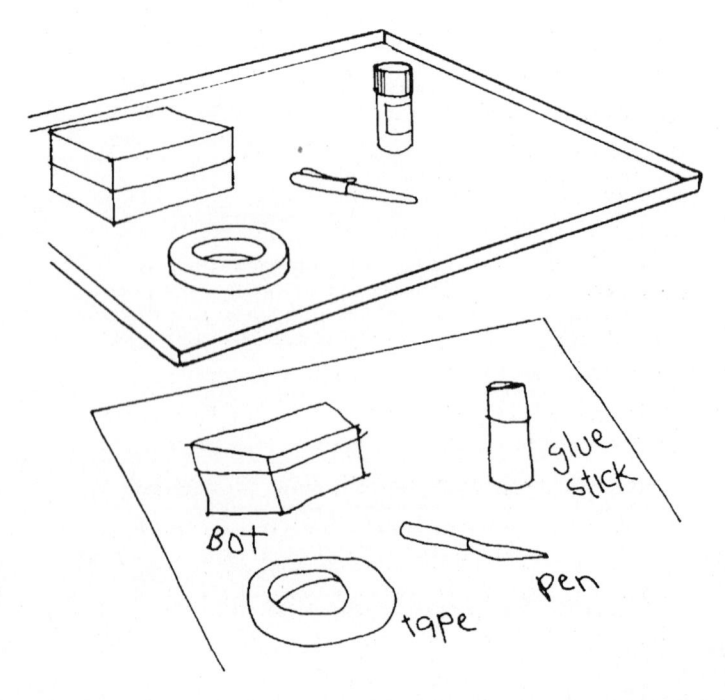

ELEVATION VIEW    TOP VIEW    SYMBOL

Figure 10

make many drafts before completing their finished work. Have a class discussion about which are the important features to be included in the plan. Allow plenty of time for redrafting. If the children have used an elevation view anywhere, a useful discussion can be held. Elevation view is not necessarily wrong, but can it be made more simple? Explain how trees, bushes and grasses are conventionally shown in elevation view but greatly simplified (Figure 10).

Maps may have been drawn as stimulus for a conversation to draw attention to the different landmarks in the locality. Let the children make similar cognitive maps and use them as a 'note book' over a period of time, adding further information to them as they explore the neighbourhood. This form of note-taking can coincide with looking at the different aspects of the environment. Where are the post boxes? Who passes the most shops? What kind of shops are they? How many houses have bay windows? How can they be shown? Are they in groups? All the while, make comparisons with the large scale Ordnance Survey plan to check that the sequence is right.

As other maps and plan shapes are used, the children will often use symbolic shapes which do not quite represent the item they are drawing. For example, they might draw symbols for detached houses with extensions to represent terraced houses. However, this will be rectified as field experience and more discussion adds knowledge to reality.

The table overleaf shows where there are other places in the programme of study for drawing maps.

# Scale

At Key Stage 1 scale, in the sense of precise representation, is neither required nor desirable. However, the language of scale (larger than, smaller than, middle size) should be developed alongside that of location. The story of *Goldilocks and the Three Bears* could be used to introduce the appropriate language. Let the children make models of the Bears' house and its three sizes of furniture. Encourage the children to ask questions relating to scale. 'How long should the beds be – three bricks, two bricks or one brick?' Links with maths should be made. The 1:1 plans of feet (see page 61) can be used to make a frieze which can then be used to emphasise 'back two paces', 'forward three paces' and so on. Show the children maps of different scales which depict the same building. This will not only help to show what is meant by large plan and small scale but will also show how the more an area of land is 'shrunk down' on to a small piece of paper, the more detail has to be left out. The boundaries of gardens and fields go first, then fewer trees are depicted, buildings show less detail and roads are wider, rather than to scale. Looking at photographs of the same object taken at various distances also emphasises this point.

# Pictures and photographs

Photographs taken from an oblique viewpoint give a high-up side-on view of spatial arrangements. As such, with the increased detail, more can be seen than on the ground. This, therefore, is a useful transition between photographs taken on the ground and the vertical aerial photographs used in Key Stage 2. However, photographs are, by nature, unselective and give everything the same emphasis. When looking at an aerial photograph it could be useful to have an acetate overlay, or several overlays, to help the children pick out different elements in the landscape

# MAP DRAWING AND THE PROGRAMME OF STUDY

| Place | Physical features | Human features | Environment |
|---|---|---|---|
| **Level 2: Make a representation** | | | |
| • Where they like to play and visit.<br>• Where they meet different people.<br>• Where home is in relation to other places.<br>• Places visited or heard stories about.<br>• Show England, Scotland, Wales and Northern Ireland.<br>• The different parts of the classroom, school, home, a farm.<br>• The features of a locality real or imaginary. | • Rocky, sandy, watery places in the locality.<br>• Wet places in the playground, on the school field.<br>• The British Isles. | • Buildings used for different purposes; make a route map to show special buildings.<br>• How parents/relatives get to work.<br>• Draw different work places and a route map. Make an imaginary map of the 7 Dwarfs and their work. | • Make a plan of the school garden; of their own garden growing area. |
| **Level 2: Identify familiar features on photographs and pictures** | | | |
| • Local landmarks e.g. church.<br>• Local activities e.g. fair.<br>• Own home, street, town centre.<br>• National monuments and place on a map.<br>• A local farm/industry (group of activities).<br>• A market, industry, etc., elsewhere.<br>• A picture map of two farms, etc. compare. | • Identify rock features e.g. tors, rocky mountains; rivers and waterfalls.<br>• Put rivers and lakes of different size in order; look at an atlas and put European seas in size order and country name; put hills, mountains, valleys and gorges in size order. | • Recognise public buildings, commercial buildings, different churches.<br>• Recognise groups of different homes. | • Bring in photographs of favourite places and describe them.<br>• Recognise on a photograph a recent change, e.g. a new development. |
| Locate all photographs and features on an appropriate map. | | | |
| **Level 3: Use a large scale map to locate own position and features outside. This can be used with fieldwork.** | | | |
| • Their homes on a 1:10,000 OS map; Public buildings and playing areas on a 1:10,000 and 1:25,000 OS map.<br>• Landscape features; use a picture map and letter/number coordinates.<br>• Community features; explain position in terms of need. | • On a 1:25,000 OS map of school grounds or blown up plan where soils were found.<br>• On a 1:25,000 OS map water features after using letter/number grid.<br>• On 1:10,000 or 1:25,000 OS maps familiar features. | • School, bus stops, places passed, on 1:10,000 OS map.<br>• Sources of supply of toys, etc. on 1:10,000 OS map.<br>• Distinctive features, on OS 1:10,000. | • Places liked/disliked after using letter/number grid.<br>• Quarries etc.<br>• Changes.<br>• Areas for improvement. |
| **Level 4: Draw a sketch map using symbols and a key** | | | |
| • Show where they play or can find flowers. Use own symbol.<br>• A garden plan; give a title and key (rudimentary).<br>• Show how they think people live in another locality.<br>• Show familiar features. Discuss symbols and key.<br>• Features of another locality.<br>• Land use of part of the local area e.g. shopping parade.<br>• Location of a change in the environment.<br>• Land use plan of a developing village, complete with symbols and a key. | • A water feature visited; use two agreed symbols.<br>• Where water soaks in, runs over or makes a channel. Discuss symbols.<br>• Location of the weather stations.<br>• Field site used to illustrate erosion, transport and deposition.<br>• Location of soil samples. | • Houses on each side of home.<br>• Postman's route and stops, or milkman etc.<br>• Part of the farm. Discuss the symbols and use a key.<br>• Layout and function of a settlement using symbols.<br>• Locational features affecting farm or factory. | • Sketch the location of the major features discussed in the locality. |
| **Level 5: Map evidence to help investigate places and themes** | | | |
| • Homes in class.<br>• Land uses, public buildings, industrial buildings, play places, shops, farms, transport depots.<br>• Hills, rivers, house types, types of work place, types of leisure, places of entertainment.<br>• Settlement and industry in the home region. | • Rock, soil and water in the neighbourhood.<br>• Wet and dry places.<br>• World distribution of hot and cold lands.<br>• Stream patterns in the locality.<br>• Physical pictorial map.<br>• Sunny, shady, windy sites.<br>• Drainage basin showing rivers and streams from atlas or 1:50,000 OS map. | • Homes, shops and churches.<br>• Post offices, newsagents, hospitals etc.<br>• Transport.<br>• Features of settlements, places for holidays, castles, houses etc. | • Distribution of protected areas at local and national scale. |

seen from above. Features to be highlighted could include the main street names to aid orientation, public buildings and hills and streams. With older infants, tracings could be made of patterns they wish to investigate. When the tracing is lifted it will soon become apparent that labelling on the tracing is essential. Going back to the large scale plan to aid identification reinforces the development of observational skills.

Once the possibilities of aerial views have been appreciated, photographs taken both at ground level and obliquely from above become a valuable resource, especially if they show places around the world taken at different seasons. Further benefit can be gained if such photographs are used alongside maps of the area. A link school in the area would prove a valuable source of information (see Chapter five).

# Map skills at Key Stage 2

The programme of study at Key Stage 2 lists the map use and map-making skills which can be grouped under the same headings as at Key Stage 1 (see page 54). Indeed if mapwork has not begun until Key Stage 2, learning about plan shape, direction, route following and relating picture to reality and the map must all be gone through in sequence, starting with talking with the children about their perceptions of their locality. Missing out these early stages very often leads to later confusion.

The initial work with a new class should be to find out what they have in common regarding understanding of their local environment. If you yourself are new to the district, this could bring to your attention local features about which you should find out more. Even if you are already familiar with the area, the variations in knowledge will give you an insight into the different emphasis each family gives to the locality and will guide your selection of areas for outdoor work.

Unlike the younger children, Key Stage 2 children will not draw maps from a purely egocentric viewpoint with lots of talking on a one-to-one basis. One-to-one teaching is not always practical with older children, but it can pay dividends if it is at all possible, especially with the introvert child. To encourage the children, give their maps a purpose; such as being used by tourists, visiting relatives, television documentary makers or school children visiting from another country.

## Photographs and pictures

Once the children's local knowledge has been established in this way, the needs of the National Curriculum can be addressed. Overall at Key Stage 2, the pupil has to select relevant information from a variety of sources, for example, photographs, maps, atlases and globes.

Photographs and pictures should be used to identify features such as homes, railways, rivers and hills, and to help children find out about places so that they can develop an ability to describe what they see in geographical terms. In mapwork, photographs and pictures are used to make links between plan views and reality, and to show and emphasise the juxtaposition of features of the landscape, for example, the bus station and car park next to the railway station. A photograph of a copse, a pond and a hedge meadow beside a timber-framed cottage is represented on the map by a triangle enclosing tree symbols, a round blue spot in a white patch bound by an irregular line beside a single black square on a narrow yellow road.

## General mapwork skills

Other overall requirements are that children should be able to '**develop the ability to recognise patterns... and to apply their knowledge and understanding to explain them**' (PoS, 1c).

These are important skills which can be developed in outdoor work, especially in the context of investigation in the local area. For example, asking the children to find out the many ways water occurs in the environment would involve interpreting different map symbols as well as investigating where water moves to and from, and how it moves. This in turn would involve measuring distance and direction, searching for elusive contour markings on maps and following the route of the stream. Features alongside the stream bank will of course be shown on the map, whether a mill complete with storage pond or a town placed at the head of tidal navigation and a bridging point on a river (for example Chester on the River Dee).

## Drawing maps

Children should also be taught to **'make plans and maps at a variety of scales, using symbols and keys'** (PoS, 3c).

Again, these skills can be developed with outdoor work. Sketch maps can be made to show puddles, muddy areas and dry places in the playground. Maps of routes to wet and dry places in the neighbourhood can be made and used by groups in the class. Discussion on the children's use of symbols and keys for these maps will enable comparisons with the official symbols to be made. Figure 11 shows a table of correspondence between picture symbols and Ordnance Survey symbols for different types of rock. Map-drawing activities in other areas of the curriculum are shown in the chart on page 64.

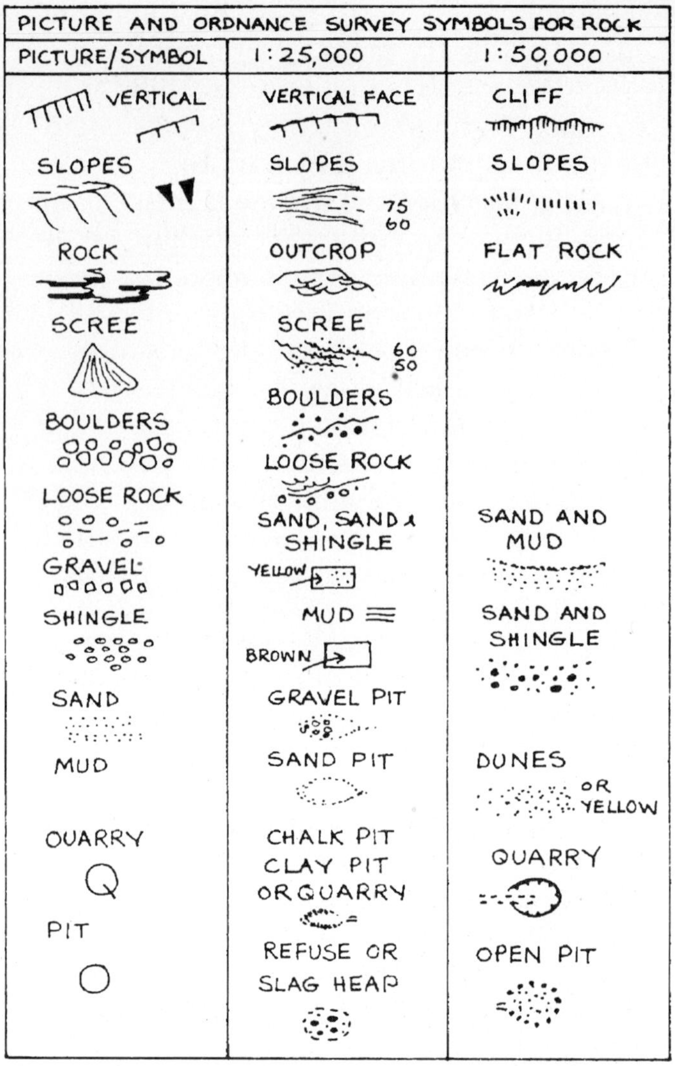

## Position and direction

More precisely, specific work concentrates upon children **'measuring direction and distance, following routes...'** (PoS, 3d), see the charts on pages 60 and 70.

Once the four cardinal points have been established, the addition of north-east, south-east, south-west and north-west makes description much easier. This may initially be introduced by asking the children to describe where the wind is blowing from and where it is going to. A wind vane should be in regular use for observation over a fortnight period. During that time, making a wind rose will help the children to form links between what is happening and the compass (Figure 12). Ask the children to shade a square on the appropriate area each day to show the direction of the wind.

Direction skills can be enhanced by using an arrow map, for example showing where features are in the classroom in relation to a pupil's desk, then relating them to the cardinal points of the compass. This can be extended to other places in school and finally to other places in the neighbourhood.

Older children will have no difficulty in recognising that places have fixed locations

Figure 11

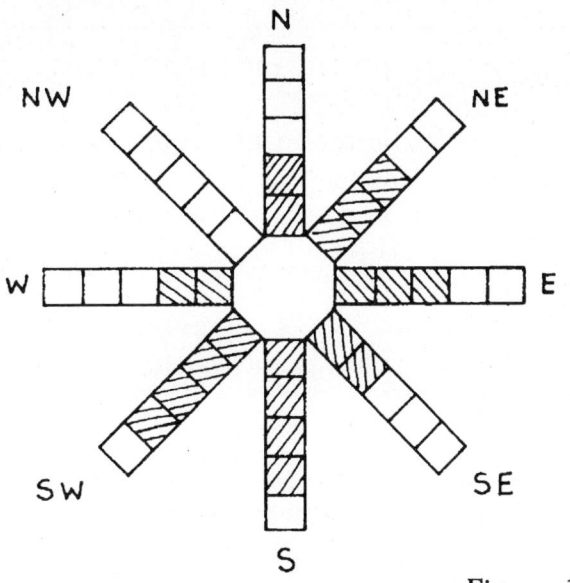

Figure 12

and can be related to each other in a similar fashion (for example, 'The church is situated north-east of the cricket field, up the hill. The view from the church porch is southwards across the valley.)

The importance of aspect, that is, whether a place has lots of sun or is in shade, is given greater precision when eight of the compass points are used. Thus, 'The north side of the school is in shade all the day, but the north-east corner gets some sun in the morning which helps to melt the frost and snow. Classroom 8 faces south and can be sunny all day, which makes it very hot some days.'

These observations can then be extended if you asked children to consider why in upland areas the main dwellings and cultivated land seem to be located more on one side of the valley than the other, and so on.

## Coordinates

The programme of study for Key Stage 2 requires that **'the work should include using coordinates and four-figure grid references...'** (PoS, 3d).

Constant use of grid references when talking about features shown on a plan or a map will help the children to understand the use of coordinates. When making plans for general use, incorporate a border of letters and numbers (see page 59) and eventually just numbers.

This would be an appropriate moment to introduce the children to the grid system as a means of enlarging and reducing maps and models. If the children have made a scale model of, for example, the local park, the allotments, a site of historic interest or a farm, show them how a record can be made using a string grid over the model and transferring the detail square by square to a similar grid drawn on A4 paper. This will be no easy task and there will need to be discussion about the symbols to be used, where the key will be put on the finished map and how slope, different surfaces and different land uses will be indicated.

## Large scale maps

Children should be able to use large scale maps to find out their position and identify features nearby. This is part and parcel of the general instruction: **'Studies should involve the development of skills and the development of knowledge and understanding about places and themes'** (PoS, 1b).

This skill is an important part of fieldwork and is a necessary tool for ensuring that small groups know where they are and which map symbol relates to the part of the environment they are observing. Preparation in the classroom should involve looking closely at the proposed route on a map, paying close attention to the grid references. This will go some way towards developing the habit of giving eastings (figures along the bottom and top row) followed by northings (figures up the side) for every location mentioned. When the children make sketch plans, encourage them to number the relevant lines according to the Ordnance Survey map for the area, even if only the border lines enclosing the map are numbered. If photographs are used to give a feel of a place to be visited, be sure to help the children locate with a grid reference the viewpoint from which the photograph was taken with a grid reference and to plot features in the photograph with their own grid references (four- or six-figure, if possible). If an outline sketch is given for completion in the field (see Chapter five), include the grid references in a similar way. This all aids orientation.

## Aerial photographs

Children should be taught to **'use secondary sources of evidence – pictures, photographs (including aerial photographs)...'** (PoS, 3e).

The aerial photograph is a detailed, unselective plan showing much which cannot be seen on the ground. Using vertical views makes the transition from ground view to map plan much easier. It is often helpful to have the aerial view blown up to the appropriate map scale. Most aerial views supplied are at the 1:10,000 scale (see Resources, page 206). They can be supplied to suit your exact requirements provided that you give at least a four-figure, preferably a six-figure, grid reference for your location.

Use a tracing, as described on page 65, to note the important points of the photograph. This should make it easier to match the points to a map. However, limitations will become apparent as soon as the tracing is lifted away from the photograph and is seen on its own without labels or reference numbers. Although the tracing can be of any features a child wishes to show, it should be completed with the addition of nominal labels using information from the map. The tracing will initially look a mess as the children try to reproduce features exactly in picture form. Orientate the map and photograph into alignment with each other using prominent features such as rivers and public buildings. Show the boundary of the photograph on the map.

All aerial photographs go out of scale at the edges but this should be no hindrance to recognising features and their representation on the map. Of course, the photograph edges will not coincide with the edges of the maps nor is north always at the 'top' of the photograph.

Discussion of what is shown on all three plans will develop an understanding of the importance of simplification and the use of symbols on a sketch map. A concentration upon boundaries and ways in which they can be shown, together with the use of different patterns to show different textures, has satisfying overlaps with art and the aesthetics of map drawing and depiction.

## Using maps

Children should be able to **'use and interpret globes and maps and plans at a variety of scales...'** (PoS, 3d).

The Ordnance Survey map has a wealth of detail stored on it, but this detail has to be separated out in order to understand the patterns of distribution. Ask the children to look for the locations of features such as farms, woods, orchards and public buildings.

The chart overleaf shows activities at different levels to develop these skills. There is no instruction as to the kind of map to be used although there may be thematic maps relevant to the topic in hand. For example, if you are looking at ports and car ferries, it might be best to look at an atlas or tourist brochure for the locality. However, the Ordnance Survey maps are the best investment (see page 57) and, if used as often as they should be, are worth protecting by some means. Simple edging with tape used to be a standard chore before laminating and clear plastic became widespread. Remember, maps get tatty at the edges and at the corners of folds. The Ordnance Survey supply special Outdoor Leisure maps which are ready laminated, and useful if your residential outdoor work is located in an area covered by one of these maps, such as South Devon.

If there is regular use of Ordnance Survey maps from the beginning of Key Stage 1 there should be no difficulty in helping children towards Level 5. The maps can be used, starting with the largest plans, first to explore, then to 'read', in order to choose places for investigation. This can be followed by a 'detective search' for clues to explain phenomena seen outdoors, for example, the sloping of streets towards each other revealing the course of a river valley, the stream channel of which is now hidden underground. This would be indicated on the map by a blue line suddenly stopping where the stream goes into a culvert.

## Further map work

There should be no need to isolate map work into special lessons if there has been a regular input of map usage and drawing into locality work from Key Stage 1. If a habit is made of completing each piece of work on the locality, stimulated by photograph and fieldwork, with a description, a sketch map and a piece of IT input, the innate personal geography of a child will be developed. This in turn will reinforce and develop habits of observation and deduction. Should, for whatever reason, a class of ten-year-olds find themselves in the position of not having used Ordnance Survey maps, the same sequence of exploration, reading and deduction should be used, together with ensuring the understanding of plan view and the use of symbols.

At this stage, teacher-drawn maps complete with grid, key, symbols and route can be a useful form of assessment before testing with a real route on an Ordnance Survey map, such as the 1:25,000. Above all, the use of maps should be seen to be part of the normal approach to an investigation. As with reading, numeracy and oracy, facility with maps and map-reading cannot be rushed. Time has to be given for much applied and repeated use. There should be no rushing on the part of the teacher.

## Relief maps

Little has been said about hills and valleys at the preceding levels, other than that they should be recognised features and named using the correct geographical vocabulary. Slope has already been brought to the attention of the infants and will have been frequently considered if outdoor work has been regularly undertaken. Modelling streams and using piles of sand have formed a crucial part of looking at water in the landscape (see Chapter three). At this point, it would be appropriate to examine landforms created on a plane surface. The sequence should be the same as with investigating other landscape elements – vocabulary related to reality, then to models, then to ways of showing features in as simple a way as possible. Let the children look at old maps of your area to see how hills were shown and then encourage them to relate these to modern symbols and to the aesthetics of map-drawing (Figure 13). Compare the hills

## USING MAPS FOR POSITION AND DISTANCE

| Place | Physical features | Human features | Environment |
|---|---|---|---|
| **Level 3: Use letter/number coordinates to locate features on a map** | | | |
| • Locate place on classroom/school plan.<br>• A fire station, etc., on local area plan.<br>• Home on area plan.<br>• Do a similar exercise with an overseas village/town.<br>• Groups of buildings.<br>• Home area on a plan of the UK.<br>• Name local landscape features.<br>• Do the same in other localities. | • Sites of soil and rock samples in the locality.<br>• Weather stations.<br>• Weather features, e.g. ponds.<br>• Coldest, hottest places on world map.<br>• Steep and gentle slopes, tarmac, grass, soil surfaces and drains.<br>• Physical features; photos on map. | • Match vehicles to people and then journeys on neighbourhood map.<br>• Picture map of the children's homes; talk about where they are.<br>• Journeys on sketch map of local area to locate shops, depots, etc.<br>• Countries with famine and refugees.<br>• Ports, resorts, holiday areas in the UK.<br>• Large and small scale sites in local area. | • Quarries and farms, etc.<br>• Likes/dislikes.<br>• Quarries, mines, plantations, fishing ports in UK.<br>• Changes in local area.<br>• Places in need of care.<br>• Heaps and holes, spoil tips, major constructions.<br>• Local refurbishments. |
| **Level 4: Use four-figure coordinates to locate features on a map** | | | |
| • Locate specific areas of land use on the 1:10,000 or 1:25,000 OS map or similar maps for other localities.<br>• Quiz for local features.<br>• Know where several similar sites are found.<br>• Landscape features in the region at 1:50,000 scale.<br>• Landscape changed by farming, industry, quarrying, mining and settlements at 1:25,000 or 1:50,000 scale. | • Water features on the 1:25,000 OS sheet.<br>• Steep/gentle slopes, grass/tarmac areas on 1:10,000 scale.<br>• Use as reference on a nature trail.<br>• Weather stations on 1:10,000 map.<br>• Parts of a river system on 1:25,000 OS map.<br>• Soil types on 1:10,000 scale. | • Homes of different types at 1:10,000 scale.<br>• Distinctive features at 1:10,000 scale.<br>• Large and small scale sites; make base map.<br>• Show contrasting areas at 1:25,000 scale.<br>• Different parts of a settlement on 1:10,000 or 1:25,000 OS maps.<br>• Changes on 1:10,000 or 1:25,000 OS maps.<br>• Factories, etc. | • Show specific changes on the 1:25,000 scale.<br>• Locate specific conservation sites, e.g. reserves. |
| **Level 4: Measure the straight line distances between two points on a plan** | | | |
| • Use string for journeys to school.<br>• See how far away countries are on the globe.<br>• Distances between capital cities.<br>• Distance from home or school to shops.<br>• As above for another locality.<br>• As above for school link area.<br>• Use rulers to measure local distances.<br>• Use a quiz game and measuring.<br>• Comparisons for distance to watch football, go swimming, etc.<br>• Measure site sizes.<br>• Compare distances.<br>• Measure and convert to scale.<br>• Distance between settlements. | • Length of ponds for size ordering.<br>• Distances to drains in base maps.<br>• Distances between contrasting weather stations.<br>• Straight length and full length of river. | • Compare journeys on large scale plan.<br>• Compare journeys on small scale plan.<br>• Distances travelled by birds and migrants.<br>• Different routes (air, sea, rail).<br>• Measure two ways to show site size.<br>• Compare straight line distances between settlements, to school, to water. Convert scales.<br>• Overall width of settlements at the same scale.<br>• Main transport links.<br>• Industry/farm to factory/market. | • Use to compare route lengths for conflicting road issues.<br>• Use with maths to determine area in land use issues. |

as shown on maps with the tracing paper exercise on the aerial photograph (page 68), then ask the children how the length of a slope can be shown. The progression is covered in greater detail in Chapter nine.

One habit that should be developed

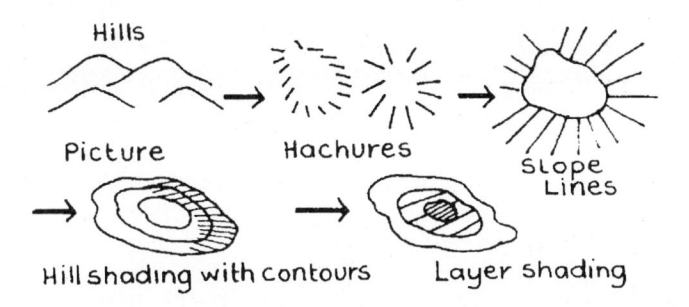

Figure 13

early, in order to prevent frustration later, is that of finding out the number for every thick contour crossed by, for example, a stream or a main road. These numbers will be in tens or hundreds so the children will find them easy to locate and comprehend. Ask the children to find out how far their school is above sea level. If you have a link school, ask the children to find out how high that is above sea level. Ask them to find out which are the highest and lowest places in the locality, then extend this investigation to the region, the country and the world. Draw their attention to the different ways of showing height using layer colouring, spots, triangles and lines. Encourage the children to consider whether the ring of contours is increasing upwards (hill) or downwards (hollow).

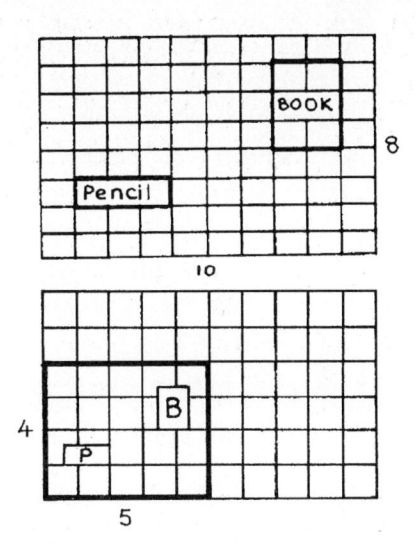

Figure 14

# Scale

Children **'should become aware of how places fit into a wider geographical context...'** (PoS, 1d).

At Key Stage 1, maps would have been drawn freehand, and size and scale would have been relative. There may have been a chance to measure with centicubes or similar small units to show differences in length and height. Squared paper will have been used to construct bar graphs on a 1:1 basis. A similar tactic can be used with map scales.

## Half scale plans

The group of objects on a tray or desk drawn on to a smaller piece of paper (see page 62) is a good beginning for going on to draw the same objects at half their real size. Give the children 2cm squared or 1cm squared paper, and ask them to draw around a pencil box on the graph paper, making sure that two adjacent edges of the box are aligned with lines on the paper. Ask the children to remove the box, then explain that they now have a 1:1 plan. Ask them to count the squares on two adjacent sides, divide the numbers by two and draw the resulting number of squares on a second sheet, placing it in the bottom left hand corner to represent its position on the 1:1 plan (Figure 14). This drawing will be at a scale of 1:2 (that is, one unit on a map represents two actual units). Repeat this technique with other objects. Label and cut out the shapes and stick them on to a 1:2 map of the tray or the desk, measuring the position of the objects from the edge of the tray or desk to ensure correct positioning on the 1:2 map. This exercise can be repeated where 1:1 plans are made of models and the model is 'stored' at a 1:2 scale. Once half scale has been recognised, ask the children to reduce the plans to quarter scale (1:4) and so on.

## Plans and maps of different scales

The relationship of plans to maps can be demonstrated by using the grid system on the local maps. The straight line distance between two known places on each map should be shown as well as the bar scale:

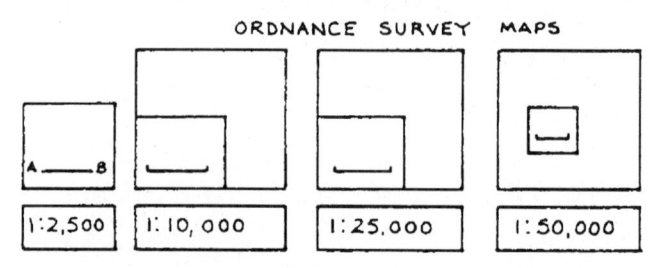

Figure 15

Ask the children to make a 'nest' of maps, starting with the classroom plan bordered in red; the school plan bordered in red and the classroom shown in solid red; the position of the school grounds on the neighbourhood plan outlined in red and the school buildings shown in red. Let them continue with the neighbourhood located in the town area, then the local authority/borough area, county, country, continent and the world, each time showing the last outlined area as solid red. For each map, have a scale bar which uses a basic centimetre unit representing a larger metric measurement with each new map (Figure 16). Explain to the children that they should never say that 1cm equals 2km, but rather than 1cm represents 2km, 1cm to 2km or 1cm:2km.

Exercises on the nest of maps will involve not only measurement but also a recognition of changing shape with changing size (see page 63).

Scale Bars

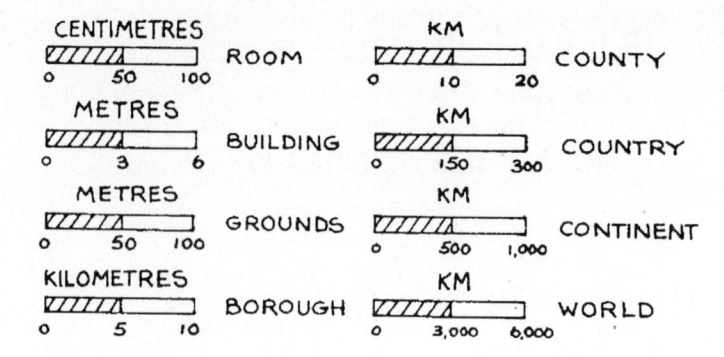

Figure 16

## Scale and reality

'Our Bodies' is a popular classroom topic which often involves drawing round a volunteer on to sugar paper. Let the children estimate the dimensions of the outline, then ask them to measure the outline and make a scale drawing. Obviously, drawing thirty 1:1 bodies will be highly impractical, but if the children work in pairs, estimating and measuring each other and then deciding on a scale, this will add a mathematical and geographical aspect to the science topic.

Planning a school garden also involves estimating, measuring and drawing to scale. The plant beds should be drawn to scale on squared paper in order to plan the rows of vegetables or flower patches. Incorporate a border of letters and numbers to give coordinate practice.

Encourage the children to draw a linear scale on all the maps made and use this for measuring, even when working on a traced map. By Y6, this should be automatic, together with adding a title and key, as the children should be aware that maps will be read by other people.

Once the children have understood the process of measuring straight line distances between points, show them how to measure along curved routes, using the process shown in Figure 17. This will be necessary in order to understand the difference between long and short routes between settlements and the children should be encouraged to measure actual distances along roads, railways and rivers.

measuring rivers

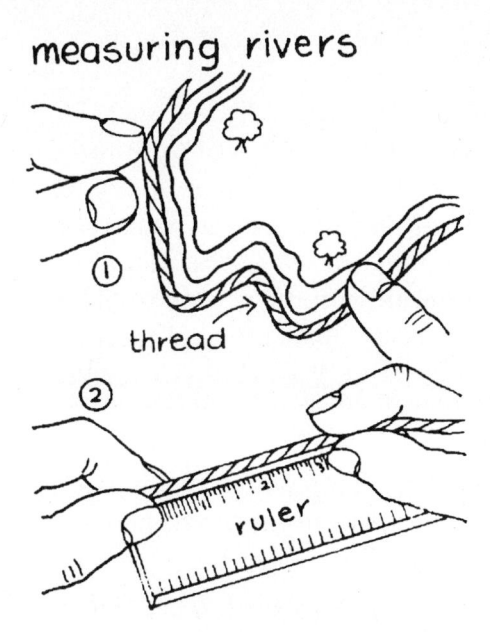

① thread

② ruler

String can be used to measure the length of streams and rivers

Figure 17

## Atlases and globes

Atlases and globes should be used by the children from an early age. Five-year-olds can be quite blasé about the world as depicted on an inflatable globe, especially in a multicultural class. However, this does not necessarily mean that they understand what a globe really represents. They will nevertheless be 'reading' it at its face value, in much the same way as they read any map. They should become aware of facts such as Australia being on the opposite side of the world to Britain. Similarly, children will pore over atlas maps to find places they know about or to see which country the animals come from whose pictures can be seen on the map border. The use of map, atlas and globe has to be continuous and concurrent if meaning is to be developed.

Each classroom should have several atlases stored alongside the globe. Whenever a place outside Britain, that is new to the children, is discussed, ask them whether they can find it in the atlas and on the globe. Can the children locate it on the globe when it is only marked on the atlas map? Again use the atlas as a 'place dictionary'.

Gradually, impatience and an increasing need to locate overseas places will dictate the need in the Key Stage 2 classrooms for a good reference atlas with a clear index and contents page. There will be distribution maps in these larger atlases, although these can also be found in some of the smaller junior atlases. Again, use these on a 'let's find out' basis. Every map has a scale and key which can be used to reinforce the work begun on the Ordnance Survey maps and which should be used alongside the 1:50,000 maps of both the UK and overseas countries (1:50,000 is an international scale; the Ordnance Survey publish many maps of developing countries). The marginal information on both the 1:25,000 and 1:50,000 Ordnance Survey maps includes latitude and longitude in degrees and minutes.

## Latitude and longitude

The Equator and the tropics of Cancer and Capricorn will have been used regularly to show where the countries with tropical climates are to be found. Similarly, the Arctic and Antarctic circles will have been used to show the location of polar climates. The use of the parallel lines of latitude which run north and south of the Equator and which cross with the vertical lines of longitude which pass through the poles gives an international grid system. This can be introduced after the children have become familiar with using the grid reference system. Every reliable school reference atlas uses this system (sometimes alongside a letter-number system) which takes the guesswork out of finding the location of places, the names of which the children might find on imported food, for example.

Explain to the children how the latitude is always given first (N or S). The longitude comes second with W or E after. For example:
Greenwich, London – 51.29 N 00.00
Manhattan, New York – 40.48 N 73.58W
Latitude is an angle between the Equator and the poles. Longitude measures the

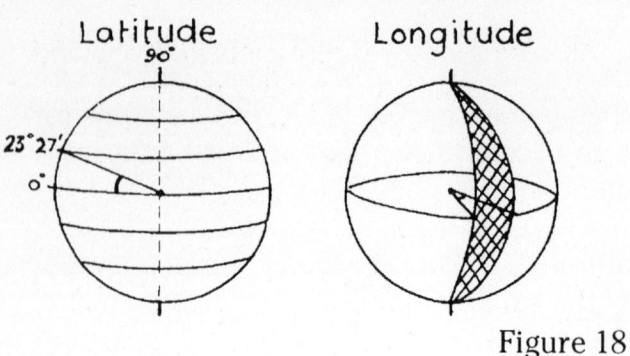

Figure 18

circumference of the earth from 0 to 180 degrees east and west of the Greenwich Meridian (Figure 18). Longitude and latitude references are given in degrees and minutes. Each degree is divided into 60 minutes and each minute is divided into 60 seconds. This links in with time zones (which are equivalent to 15 divisions of the earth's circumference and the movements of the earth). The named latitudes, the Tropics of Cancer and Capricorn for example, are connected with the seasons and the apparent movement of the sun. The earth's axis is not 'vertical'. During the earth's rotation, when the North Pole is tilted towards the sun, it is summer in the northern hemisphere. The longest day (21 June) occurs when the sun is directly over the Tropic of Cancer, the northern limit of the apparent movement of the sun. As can be seen from Figure 19, winter occurs in the northern hemisphere when the sun is apparently furthest away, when the North Pole is tilted away from the sun. The shortest day (21 December) occurs when the sun's rays are perpendicular to the Tropic of Capricorn.

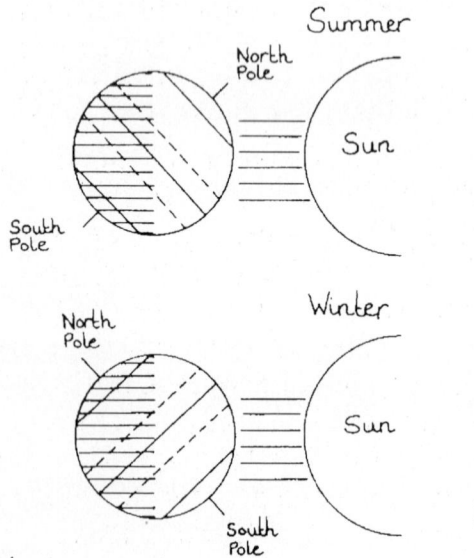

Work on understanding latitude and longitude can be linked with work in maths, as there is much overlap with geometry and mathematical language as well as with science and the mechanics of the solar system. Get the children used to using the grid system in a truly international fashion. It is part of the everyday working language of airline pilots and sailors the world over, so devise a role play about diverting routes due to bad weather. This will involve use of the grid system if authenticity is to be maintained.

## Flat earth and round earth

Figure 20 shows four projections. Mercator's projection is designed for navigators, based on the principle that any straight line is a line of constant compass bearing. It basically comprises a cylinder of paper curved round the globe. Were the globe translucent, with a source of light inside and latitude and longitude lines enclosing it, the shadows of the lines projected on the paper cylinder would be straight. The fact that the Mercator projection has over the years been abused as a political map (due to its apparent overemphasis of the size of European countries in relation to, for example, Africa) would no doubt cause the inventor great distress were he alive today.

Peters' projection, quite rightly, set out to counteract the misconception, brought about by Mercator's projection, that the lands in the temperate and polar latitudes were of greater extent than the tropical lands. Greenland is therefore cut down to size and the vastness of India and the southern continents is more easily appreciated. However, while the land masses are the correct size in relation to each other, the shapes are distorted. Nonetheless, the changed shape has usefully highlighted the plight of the sheer vastness of the developing countries of the south compared with the developed countries of the north.

Figure 19

MERCATOR 1569

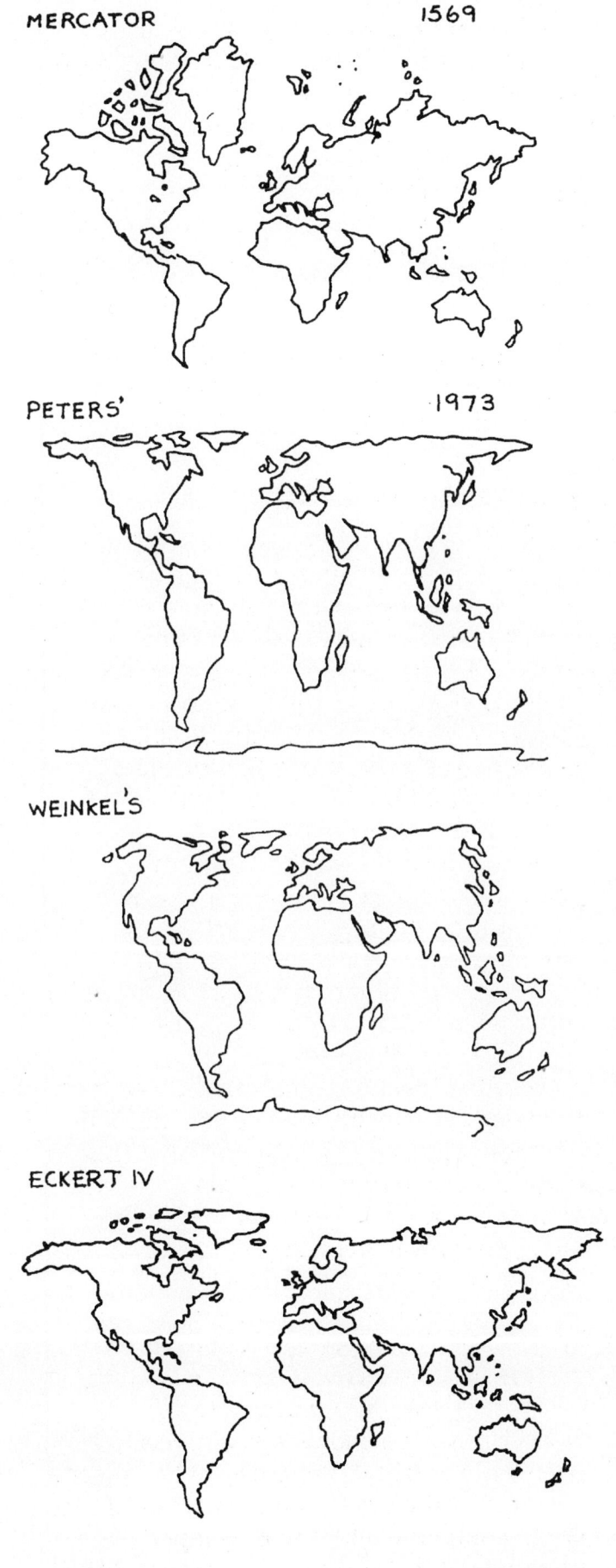

PETERS' 1973

WEINKEL'S

ECKERT IV

Figure 20

The difficulties of representing a curved surface on a flat surface are easily modelled. Suggestions range from peeling an orange in strips, to opening up the covering of a 'Chocolate Orange' to reveal the extra paper squashed round the segments. Mollweide made the point by leaving his projection in segments (Figure 21 overleaf). Other cartographers have experimented and compromised. On some, for example, Weinkel's, the distortion at the edges is clear, thus reminding the observer that the world is round.

The Eckhert IV is similar and now used by the National Curriculum instead of Gall's as before.

Experiment with putting A4 sheets of paper round the globe starting in the centre of each continent. This should emphasise that projection distortion always occurs towards the edges of the paper and that to show neighbouring relationships accurately the focus should start with the countries concerned. We are very familiar with maps centred upon the Greenwich meridian which show both sides of the Atlantic. Try showing the Pacific from an Australian point of view. Look at the top and bottom of the globe. What shape is Antarctica? Who faces whom across the North Pole?

Ask the children to make their own globes using the technique shown in Figure 21. The globe can be represented as a flat surface but mathematical adjustment will be required to ensure accuracy at any one point. Ask the children to find the longest and shortest established air or sea routes between countries around the world using the string technique as shown on page 73. Measure the distance first on the globe, then on the atlas map. Explain to the children that in geography they have to be sure of using the right map for the right purpose, for example using polar projections for showing aerial routes in the northern hemisphere. Encourage them to collect the projection names from the border information on atlas maps. The great variety is astonishing (see, for example, *The New Oxford School Atlas*).

## Make your own globe

1. Coat a tennis ball with contact adhesive. Allow it to dry.
2. Coat the back of the segments with adhesive.
3. Cut round the segments, making sure to keep the centre join intact.
4. Wrap the segments round the ball pressing the pointed ends at the top and bottom so that they meet at the poles. (It is best to do this with alternate segments first, then the rest.)

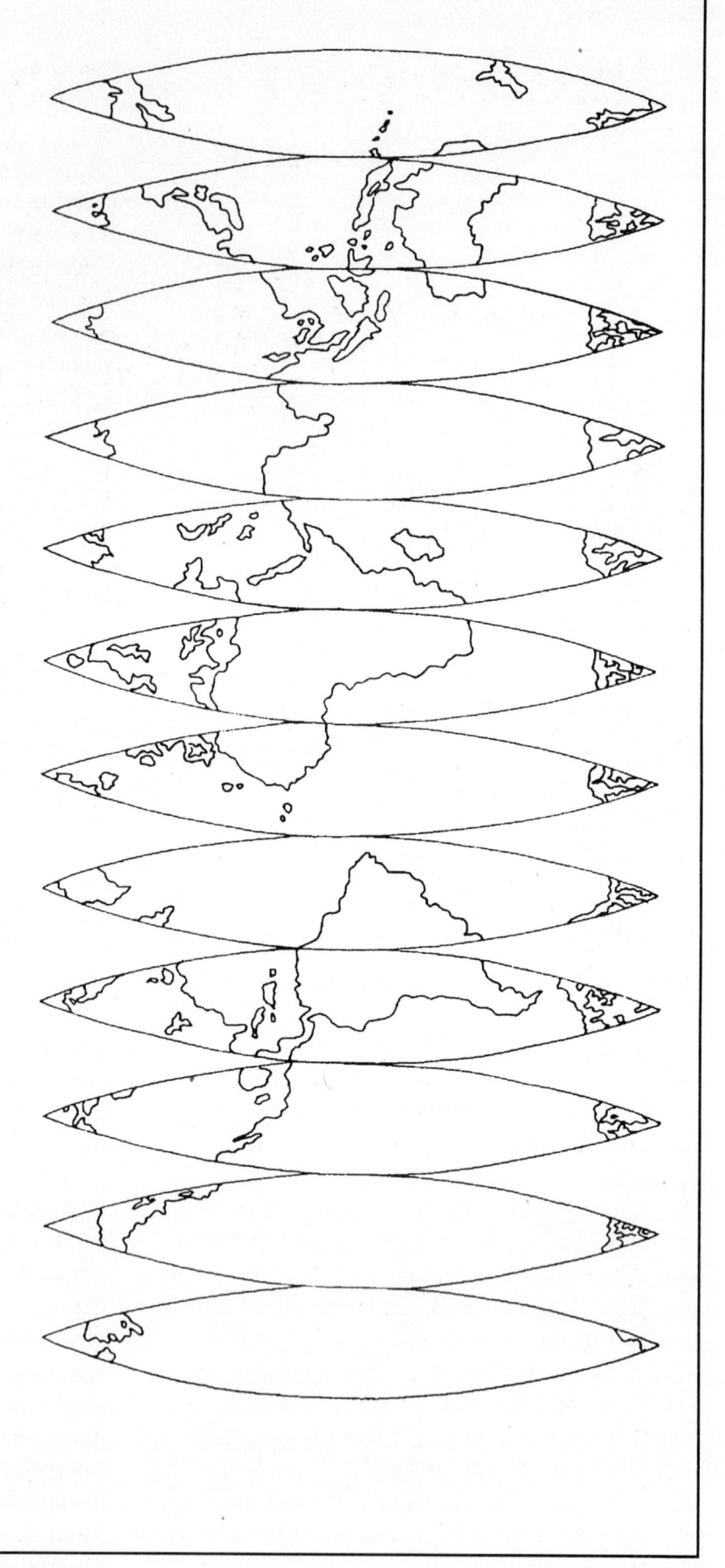

Adapted from the *Jacaranda Junior World Atlas* (1971)

Figure 21

# Chapter five
# Other ways of learning

## Visual communication

'Did you see?' is possibly the most common daily question, whether it refers to something interesting on television, something unusual in the street or to a particularly striking addition – whether natural or man-made – to the world about us. How often is the response, 'No, where?'? Sometimes it is easy to guide the unobservant directly to the item in question. At other times it needs conscious effort. Nonetheless, visual communication is an important way of teaching and deserves structured attention beyond the instruction in the programme of study that at Key Stage 1,
'1. Pupils should be given opportunities to:
b)... focus on geographical questions, *e.g., What is it like?...*
2. to observe... and communicate.
3. Pupils should be taught to:
a) use geographical terms, *e.g., hill, river, road...*
...f) use secondary sources, *e.g., pictures, photographs... books, videos, CD-ROM encyclopaedia,* to obtain geographical information.'

By the time Key Stage 2 is reached, the vocabulary and skill of observation is extended to:
'a) use appropriate geographical vocabulary, *e.g., temperature, transport, industry, agriculture,* to describe and interpret their surroundings;
e)... and other sources, *e.g., television and radio programmes, books, newspapers, visitors to school* – to inform their studies;
f) use IT to gain access to additional information sources..., *e.g.,.... using newspapers on CD-ROM, using word-processing and mapping packages.*'

77

## Teaching observation

Observation skills can be introduced by playing 'Kim's game', where the children study a tray of miscellaneous objects for a while, after which the tray is removed and the children are challenged to remember all the objects. The game can be adapted by using photographs of separate objects in sets, such as a vegetable or fruit set, a wheels set, a buildings set, a furniture set and a wet places set. Show the children the photographs one at a time, then show them a set with one removed and ask the children which one is missing. Repeat this with the other sets of photographs.

'Pelmanism' takes this activity one stage further by using photographs of parts of a larger object or pairs of objects (for example, knife/fork, apple/orange, boat/oars, car/steering wheel, walls/roof, postman/postbag). The photographs should be mounted on to card and covered with adhesive plastic film. To play the game, place all the cards face down then ask the children to take turns to choose a card, look at it carefully, then put it back. Encourage the children to look out for cards that form pairs with previous cards. If they think they have found a pair, ask them to turn over both cards and put the pair to one side, if they have remembered the location of the cards correctly. 'Snap' can also be played with these cards.

## Observation in the locality

Get into the habit of taking photographs while on walks about the neighbourhood. These can be used for various modes of enquiry. An oblique view of the neighbourhood, taken from a highrise building (such as flats or offices) or a tower (such as a church, water tower or monument), can be used to trace a route via various features (see page 65). Photocopy or enlarge the picture and laminate it to enable labelling with water-based pens. Number the features and use them as the basis for a discussion about a walk and what would be seen along the way. Label the features and ask the children to put them in order for a route to be followed on the ground.

Next, use photographs of the features shown on the neighbourhood map for conversation and planning. Make a sequence of features, missing out a few, then take the children for a walk along the route and ask them what features were missed out of the photograph sequence (PoS, 1a; 5a).

Make photographic sets of physical features (rivers, ponds, steep hills and so on) and places of work or special buildings (PoS, 5d). Photographic sets could also be made showing the children's favourite and least favourite places.

When more than one feature is to be considered at any one time, large detailed pictures and photographs should be used. These could include street scenes, markets, a landscape at different seasons of the year and a landscape before and after changes caused by man (linking with history). Show the children the particular picture and ask them to look at it carefully for one minute. Turn the picture over and ask the children to recall what has been seen. In this way assessment of personal observational skills is possible.

There has been very little organised research on picture observation but what has been done (Long, 1961) suggests that adults look at the main, large elements in the picture while children pick out the fine detail, such as the small candlestick on the edge of the table or the dog eating behind a stall in the bottom corner of the picture.

Another challenge to observational skills would be to remove an obvious element in the picture, such as a local landscape feature like a pond or public building. This could be done by providing the children with a photograph or picture of an area, together with a sketch of the same place with a feature omitted and asking them to 'spot the mistake'.

## Photographs and the enquiry approach

Enquiry skills can be developed alongside observation by using a photograph showing, for example, everyday life in another part of the world, and encouraging the children to ask questions such as 'How?', 'Why?', 'Where?' and 'What?'

Children could be encouraged to work individually, then in groups of four, to think of questions they would like to ask the people in the photograph. This will lead them on to finding out more information using atlases, books and other photographs. Once their research is completed, give a caption to the photograph and let pairs of children undertake further work on another photograph, again raising questions, finding answers and devising a caption.

The skills of observation and accurate description come together in writing captions for illustrations. The work described above could form the starting point for work on a new locality in the UK or in the wider world (PoS, 4; 5), culminating in a large display about characterising the area studied. Part of the display could be sketches made by tracing features from the original photograph and giving pertinent labels. Many physical features can only be understood if the fine detail of the characteristics is accompanied by a geological or physical history description. A labelled photograph and sketch help to create understanding (Figures 1 and 2).

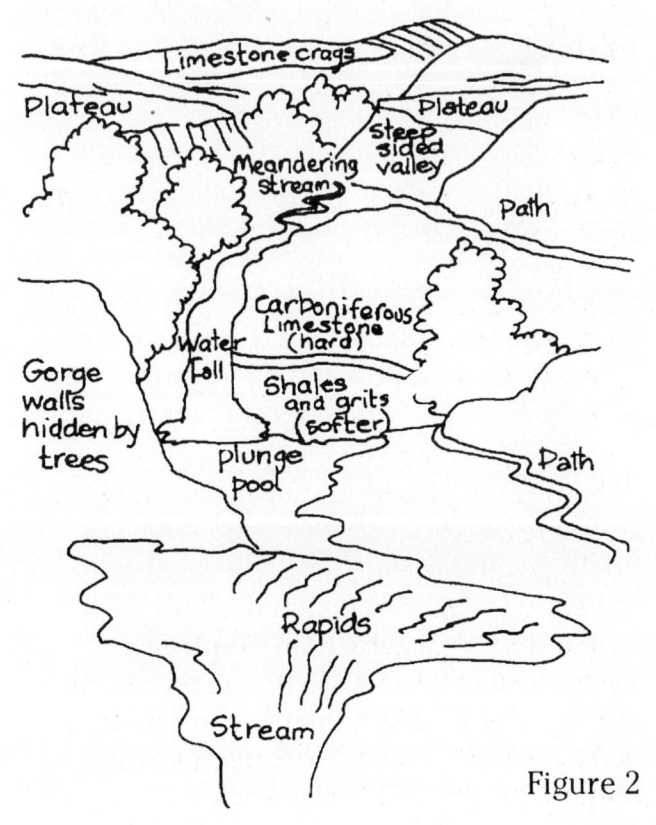

Figure 1

Figure 2

Figure 3

Sets of photographs can illustrate the process of erosion, transport and deposition (for example, a corrie, a glacier, a moraine and a U-shaped valley or a spring, stream, gorge, flood plain and delta for ice and water respectively).

## Photographs as working plans

One way to link reality with map work is to model elements of the environment. Photographs can help to act as a template or guideline. For example, the photograph the child is holding in Figure 3 would be a useful reference for making a floor plan and LEGO airport, complete with planes, freight and passengers. This activity would not only give practice in observing detail, but would also help develop the idea of scale.

## Similarities and differences

In Y2 to Y4, the sets of pictures used to develop observation and description should grow to sufficient numbers to allow comparison between localities. Make a collection of mounted photographs from tourist brochures covering general localities and countries. It would also be useful to make a collection of photographs of the school locality to send to an exchange school. Remember that seasonal variations are important in all spheres of activity. These collections deserve staff discussion and the delegation of a photographer/picture archivist to be responsible for building up the collection. Some schools have a centrally organised collection of photographs. The Geographical Association supplies packs of colour photographs of overseas places suitable for all Key Stages (see Resources on page 206).

The photograph sets can be used for assessing similarities and differences between localities. Place the photographs face down on the table, and ask the children to take turns to choose two photographs at random. Any two which seem to be linked (for example, modern urban buildings, railway stations, Marks & Spencers, Macdonalds and so on) can be kept by the child. Other similarities to look for could include lowland areas, or European and North American urban areas. At the conclusion of the game, a study of the detail of the photographs could stimulate the children to look for the differences which show more precisely where the localities are to be found.

Differences can be tackled first with photographs on themes (for example, animals around the world) and by mapping the localities on a globe or an atlas map. Topics such as 'Plants', 'Clothes' and 'Homes' all lend themselves to recognising similarities, but also to clarifying the fact that differences are often due to very basic reasons such as weather (PoS, 5c).

As the ability to cope with more than one factor develops, comparison between a distant locality and the home area can be extended to comparisons between two distant localities. These sets of localities could be related to different places, objects or people, and used in order to stimulate empathy and evaluation. Ask the children to rank the pictures in order of size, similarity and like/dislike. This latter criterion will encourage prejudices to be aired and stimulate enquiry into reasons for the differences and similarities. Other criteria for selection could include the cleanest, brightest or muddiest, the one with the most space or the one with the most greenery (both in urban and rural situations!).

Figure 4

## Selection

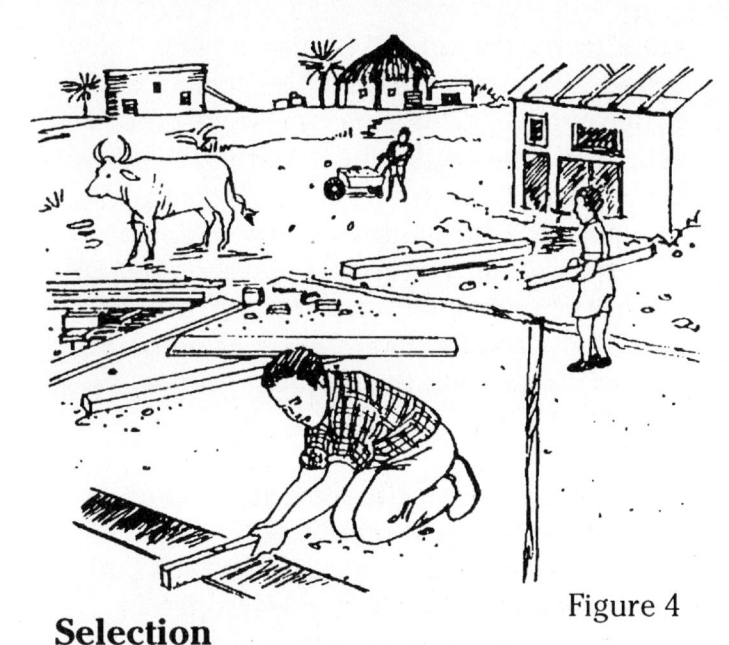

Ask the children to make selections of groups of photographs showing similar features such as water, hills, woods, work or play. The children should become aware of more than one possibility for selection as a photograph might contain several layers of information. For example, a photograph of an Alpine valley could be used, with various captions, to show the beauty of Alpine scenery (PoS, 5a; 6a), the way roads and other routeways cope with the steep slopes (PoS, 5b; 6b), the erosion, transport and deposition of a river (PoS, 7b) and the fact that some areas are very sparsely populated (PoS, 9b). Not only are observation skills required here, but also language skills for the use of geographical, descriptive and emotive terms.

It never fails to intrigue the children when they discover that 'cropping' a photograph can completely alter the viewer's perception of what is shown. The camera can trick the eye into supplementing information. Ask the children to form pairs and give each pair a simple card frame with which they can cover parts of a picture. Ask each pair to decide the content of their mini-picture and note the new meaning compared to the original. For example, by careful framing, Figure 4 could be perceived as being a picture of an English building site. The same picture could be used on a whole-class basis by framing the lower half of the photograph and asking the children for clues to indicate what is happening outside the area shown.

## Photographs, sketches and cartoons

Photographs are a useful resource for making sketches for labelling (see page 79). Slides are invaluable for projecting on to a small clear wall space and allowing small groups of children to work on investigating a new locality. The same slides can also be used in preparation for an activity by projecting the image on to an A4 sheet and drawing a simplified diagram. The same diagram or series of diagrams can be traced on to acetate and used to pull the evidence together, by superimposing acetates on top of each other until a final diagram can be built up.

# Resource sheets

The advent of the photocopier has meant that much up-to-date information from newspapers, comics and travel brochures can be used, together with questions to guide enquiry work in the classroom. Combined with the different fonts and layouts possible with a word processor, a variety of activity sheets can be made.

When designing activity sheets, remember that 'white space' can be valuable. Avoid long lines of text and keep instructions short, varied and in sequence. Break up the text with illustrative material, both humorous and instructional. Type your resource sheets, or at the very least use a printed script, never longhand. Remember that bold headlines and boxes guide both the eye and the hand.

Resource sheets are useful when a topic requires some quiet collection of data and allow attention to be given to more complicated practical exercises, especially when working on a 'carousel' or 'circus' basis of groups circulating round a range of activities. Resource sheets also allow work to be done on visual material such as maps, posters and large pictures pinned up on a display.

## Picture packs

Picture packs, whether home-made or commercially produced, can be used to introduce a new topic on a city, a country or a local attraction. Include illustrations of tourist attractions, street names, products and annual events. Top junior children could be encouraged to write a tourist brochure using captioned illustrations and a map showing how to reach the destinations by various means of transport.

## Videos, television and radio programmes

Both the BBC and independent television companies produce programmes aimed at the geographical requirements of the primary school. There is regular information available so ensure your school is on the mailing list. Better still would be to have several members of staff on the mailing lists to enable resources to be pooled and also to allow for perusal of the schedules in one's own time. There is also a tremendously wide range of excellent videos now available aimed at the educational market.

There are often printed support materials to accompany television and radio programmes. In many cases these stand on their own as resources or fit in with a geographical series already published. However, no programme-maker expects their work to be used as a child-minding device. They are meant to stimulate and support work already taking place in the classroom. To this end, recording programmes for use at a time suitable for the school is allowed and 'back issues' are also available. This means that programmes and videos can be viewed by teachers sufficiently ahead of time to allow the content to be reviewed and its impact maximised. For example, a (BBC) *Zig Zag* programme on 'Water' was watched by one school as part of a topic on water which included a school trip on a canal, a visit to a local stream and the beginnings of investigating a local drainage basin, as well as the bulk of the science work which was the ultimate aim of the topic unit.

Previewing a programme enables clue cards for vocabulary, mapwork cards and other activity sheets to be developed in advance. The series are often shown more than once in a week, thus allowing a routine to be established for recording regularly. The transmission schedules are usually available two terms in advance of the succeeding academic year.

There may be within the school community, families, staff and ancillary staff who own camcorders. There may be untapped enthusiasm just waiting to be asked to help record change in the environment (PoS, 6b; 10a). Again, assess your needs early and send out the requests well in advance (Chapter seven).

## Aerial photographs

Aerial photographs are not available with sufficient detail for all parts of the country at a scale suitable for use with maps (Chapter four). There may well be a scheme in your area involving Aerofilms Ltd, the Ordnance Survey or a smaller concern with a group of schools clubbing together to produce a set of photographs. Try the Yellow Pages to find out whether there is a local company who would be able to fly a sortie. Cost will be determined by the number of participants. As well as using the views as an aid to making the link between reality and the map, a recent aerial photograph will also show any changes which have taken place since the last map survey (PoS, 6b; 10a). Further use of aerial photographs is explored in Chapter four.

# Books and narratives

## Key Stage 2

There are some magical geographical descriptions written by regional authors. Nobody has bettered Kipling's description of the iron-rich Central Weald in *Rewards and Fairies*. This description, however, is spread throughout the book and so is best read as an individual curled up in a comfortable niche.

## Regional descriptions

The author Hammond Innes describes landscapes with great accuracy, while Thomas Hardy's Wessex is so clearly described that it is still possible to recognise certain features. Look out for particularly striking descriptions of landscapes by these authors and read them aloud to the children. Ask the children to draw their own impressions of the places, then to locate places with similar features with the aid of the Pathfinder or Landranger series.

## Travel descriptions

Each Sunday, we are assailed with a wealth of descriptive writing in the travel sections of the colour supplements. Much of this writing is by prize-winning authors who are Fellows of the Royal Geographical Society. Introduce the children to any of the works of Eric Newby, Gavin Young, Bruce Chatwin, Eric Shipton and Robin Hanbury-Tennison, and add the writings and television programmes of David Attenborough and Gerald Durrell. All these will help to give the children the feel of other countries and cultures. The list is endless and constantly being expanded. As with photographs, start collecting and make your own anthologies.

## Children's fiction

*Stig of the Dump* by Clive King contains such a clear description of a chalk quarry that it seems possible to locate it on the North Downs. There are many children's books which contain vivid regional descriptions. Many local libraries keep a list of authors who have written about their own area. Remember to locate the places mentioned on an Ordnance Survey map. Extend the investigation to a wider region and ask the children to locate the appropriate areas in an atlas. Children's literature is so rich in good descriptive, environmental writing that the overlap between English and geography can be well served by using information technology and editing skills to make a class anthology of examples which the children encounter. The anthology should include excerpts at various reading levels.

## Non-fiction

Factual books should have a Flesch score of more than 80 to be accessible. (This is based on the average values from 10 random samples of 100 words. The Flesch score = $206.835 - (0.846 \times wl) - (1.051 \times sl)$, where $wl$ = average number of syllables per 100 words and $sl$ = average number of words per sentence.) The most recent series from such publishers as Wayland and Franklin Watts are published at two reading levels. These series, beautifully illustrated in colour, are usually factually and methodologically up to date. Beware, however, of the reissue of older series in new covers which might not have kept abreast of the new economic developments and changes in the developed and developing world. Graphics have also improved considerably with the advance of computerisation, so there is now no excuse for cluttered and inaccurate maps. Look for books with clear colour photographs, a glossary and suggestions for further reading. With such books it is likely that equal care has been taken over accuracy of content. Remember also to assess their suitability both for you and your class.

The Resources section on page 206 lists the main geography series, both new and well-established. Their styles vary, though all follow similar concepts and methodology. One class of top primary children considered two such series and did not hesitate to recognise that one suited those who could cope with a content-rich text followed by a series of exercises, while the other was more suited to less able class members because the text was broken up into short extracts with simple questions requiring short answers. The answers in both of the above cases covered the same material and definition of concepts.

The material used in all the texts mentioned in this book has been gathered painstakingly from original sources and has often been tested in the classroom. It is worth having a set of each series in the staff resource area. One of the best ways of seeing what is available is to visit a book exhibition where it is possible to evaluate resources provided by publishers and other school suppliers.

## Key Stage 1

At Key Stage 1, picture books and favourite stories can act as starting points (see page 83). Anne Gadsden's booklet, published jointly by the Geographical Association and Cheshire County Council, shows how to appraise a story and develop its potential along several routes, and is especially applicable to 'the thematic study on the quality of the environment...'

## Locality studies and stereotypes

The programme of study for Key Stage 1 specifies that **'Pupils should... become aware that the world extends beyond their own locality, both within and outside the United Kingdom...'**.

At Key Stage 1 the locality of the school is defined as **'...its immediate vicinity; it includes the school buildings and grounds and the surrounding area within easy access. The contrasting locality should be an area of similar size'**.

Remember that even for small children at Key Stage 1, the size of locality is much greater for rural children than urban children. Distinctive features such as important buildings, shops, playing areas and homes spread out the further away one moves from a town centre, a cause for distinction in itself.

A case study is a useful way of introducing the characteristics of a region to be studied. For example, we are aware that parts of Canada and the northern United States are very cold. We can ascertain how cold these places are by looking at the climatic statistics given in atlases or better still in the worldwide weather reports given in daily papers. How the cold weather affects the way people live is less easy to find out. Descriptions based on personal experience are necessary to provide details about travel, dress and the routine of the day, for example making time to check that the snow tyres are safe, that snow fences are firm and that there is enough food in the house should the snow get too deep for travel.

Newspaper and magazine reports containing such descriptions should be collected and television documentaries and holiday programmes should be recorded. Links with children in other parts of the world can be developed by organising a penfriend scheme. Multicultural schools and schools with a mobile population (for example, the children of diplomatic, forces, overseas professionals and clergy families who have travelled about because of their parents' jobs) are in an enviable position, with many possibilities for obtaining information about other places. A visiting parent or grandparent who grew up in another country might be able to show the children photographs and answer the sort of queries which often only arise on the spur of the moment.

## A day in the life of...

An investigation into a day in the life of someone from another country should include items on activities, descriptions of meals taken and when, clothes worn, journeys made (with distances and mode of transport), how supplies of food are obtained and stored, precautions taken because of the weather, times of sunrise and sunset, entertainment (not everyone has a television) and times of starting school or starting work.

There should ideally be more than one day described as most parts of the world have some kind of variation in day-to-day life, such as seasonal changes or festival activities. All these reflect in some way the human response to the environment.

The following categories of objects are worth collecting as resources for 'A day in the life of...' investigation, both for the home region as well as the wider world.

**Everyday objects:**
- a TV guide;
- a local newspaper;
- a shopping list;
- stamps;
- food wrappers;
- local industry merchandise labels;
- recipes;
- games;
- bus and rail timetables;
- postcards.

**Maps and plans:**
- photographs and plans of a home, showing the room(s) and the garden;
- photographs and plans of a school, showing classroom(s) and playground;
- maps of the local area, showing the location of the houses and school;
- maps of the region, showing the location of the area under consideration;
- maps of the country showing the location of the region, and the major routes and cities, giving a clue as to how long it takes to reach the cities from the locality.

**Photographs:**
- everyday activities in the case study area, including shopping, travelling, entertainment, work and services (How does the post come? Is there an ambulance service?);
- activities in the region and in the rest of the country, illustrating both the similarities and the differences (for example, if you are looking at a Normandy village in a dairy farming area, photographs of other regional activities may offer information about Normandy cider-making, coastal fishing towns and the regional town, Rouen);
- families (How big are they? Where do they live? What do they do?);
- buildings including homes, schools, shops, places of worship, public buildings, follies, and workshops (their interiors as well as their exterior views);
- the production processes of common objects (such as making bricks, baskets, pots and pans), recycling (such as sandals from tyres or glass-bead necklaces from old bottles for the tourist trade) and more traditional processes such as gathering rubber latex, collecting bananas, harvesting sugar cane, making muslins and silks for saris, making maple syrup, and so on, which all take place with varying degrees of mechanisation;
- features you would be shown if you were visiting, including beauty spots but also more everyday features such as the nearest hill for a view, the local stream, the nearest wood or open space and other features in the region and the country.

## School links

The various collections mentioned above comprise all those elements of the environment which you are required to study for Key Stages 1 and 2. It is an awesome list but it should be possible to make a similar collection of things for your own locality, ready to send in exchange for similar material from a contrasting locality from your link school. You may already have a collection of appropriate material if you have been encouraging the children to observe, enquire and become interested in the area in which they live.

Hunt round for your contacts and evidence of previous visitors to the school. See if a pack can be put together and then use the checklist overleaf to see what needs to be added. The Commonwealth Institute (see Resources, page 206) is not only worth a visit, but will also supply artefacts, books and other materials to schools anywhere in the country. They also have a list of contacts of Commonwealth nationals who are able to visit schools and help with investigations. Similarly, the Schools Unit of the Central Bureau for Educational Visits and Exchanges (see Resources, page 206) can help set up links with schools in other European countries.

The whole investigation can be recorded in small units, such as 'Places we like to show visitors', combining photographs or a video, maps to show a visitors' trail, descriptions of the features (geography) and other interesting information (English) accompanied with illustrations (art). The benefits of this kind of investigation are as follows:
- the detailed information which is collected will present real farms, factories, valleys, hills, villages and homes in a variety of ways;
- the studies will raise the factors which are of significance to the development of that particular environment, for example the sequence of crop rotation which is dictated by the climate and water supply, the different functions of a village as part of a regional community or the reasons for siting a factory, which help to give a balanced understanding of similarities and differences between places;
- there is more opportunity for the class to identify with the situation and the people involved and the difficulties that are encountered in different parts of the world;
- second-hand material from someone you know who lives in a specific location encourages working from the particular to the general, and offsets making gross generalisations (for example, your contact may be a dairy farmer, but may not be from an exclusively dairy farming region, as further investigations would reveal);
- by looking at a place in depth, and considering one particular group of people, the children can investigate the way they live and the way they are affected by matters external to their everyday lives, which will help to avoid stereotyping and, by giving examples showing as many locations as possible, will help promote a balanced view of the world.

# Other sources for studies in detail

Although collecting information for a link school is enjoyable, it is also time-consuming. Remember that your link school may not be able to come up with all the information required at the right moment – they too have pressures and stresses! Other useful sources of information are the various aid agencies which produce some excellent up-to-date, detailed material. Print runs tend to be short, so not all studies remain available for a great length of time, but a list of the more recent ones is in the Resources section on page 206. Through its journals *Primary Geographer, Teaching Geography* and *Geography*, the Geographical Association provides detailed material including photopacks which can be adapted to a class's needs.

*Geographical* magazine, the Royal Geographical Society's monthly journal for the layman, contains a wealth of detail on all matters relating to the different environments and peoples around the world, as does the *National Geographic Magazine*. Many commercial enterprises such as BP and Shell offer educational materials as part of their promotional activities which, used judiciously and selectively, can be of great value.

Whatever resources you use, the aim should be to show as many locations as possible, and to balance the 'disaster' view (often provided by the media) with the 'official' view (often provided by the embassy or trade bureau material) and the view of travellers (*Geographical* magazine), aided by relatives, school links and straight statistics from the atlas and year books.

# Simulations and games

One way of appreciating the lives of people in other parts of the world is to simulate a situation and work through the problems that arise during the simulation (for example, how to get between two points). Figure 5 simulates the possible difficulties which can arise when going from home to an ice-cream van across the park. The problems are the various barriers which have to be negotiated, both dangerous (the road) and pleasant.

With older children a similar game can be devised using a village as the starting point and a town as the finishing point. Colour the intervening squares to represent possible barriers and difficulties, such as mountains, hills, a river, nature reserves and railways. Give each square a value according to the nature of the item to be crossed and explain to the children that the objective is to make the journey in the most economical way possible. Use the lowest values to encourage or discourage use (for example, bridges could be worth one point, while rivers and railways could be worth eight). Hills should be fairly expensive to cross, but not as much as boggy ground. Let the children play the game from each departure point and see which route is the most expensive.

One of the earliest geographical games, *The Railway Game*, devised by Rex Walford, followed the fortunes of the railway builders across the continent of North America. Using dice and chance cards detailing hazards such as snow, lack of supplies and lack of money, the rival railways creep across the continent. Several commercial games follow the same principle. Figure 6 overleaf offers a suggestion for a snakes and ladders game on a theme of tropical farming (adapted from *Starting Geography: Food*, Scholastic). Simulations can also be done with computer models (Chapter six).

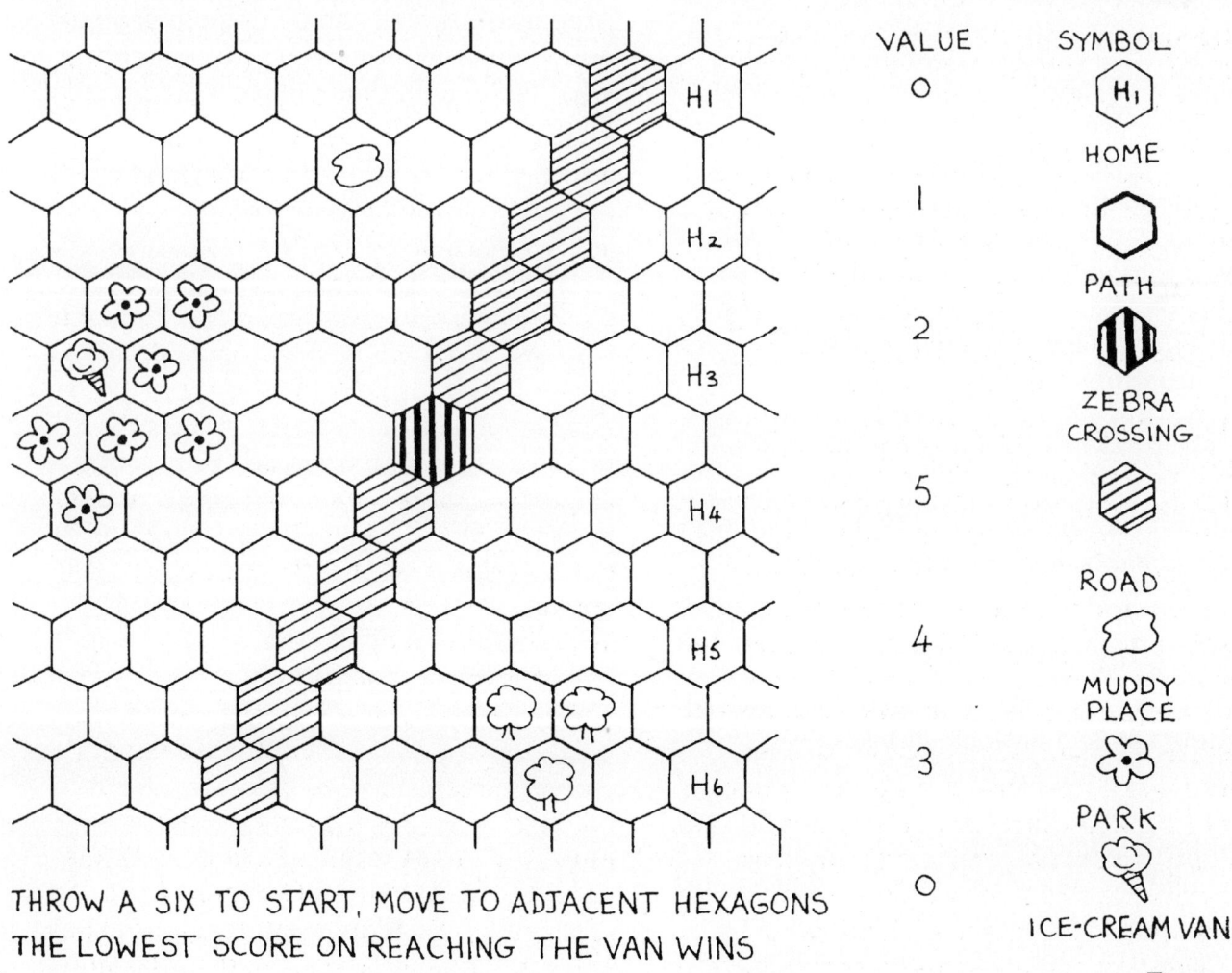

| VALUE | SYMBOL | |
|---|---|---|
| 0 | $H_1$ | HOME |
| 1 | ⬡ | PATH |
| 2 | ▥ | ZEBRA CROSSING |
| 5 | ▨ | ROAD |
| 4 | ☁ | MUDDY PLACE |
| 3 | ✿ | PARK |
| 0 | 🍦 | ICE-CREAM VAN |

THROW A SIX TO START, MOVE TO ADJACENT HEXAGONS
THE LOWEST SCORE ON REACHING THE VAN WINS

Figure 5

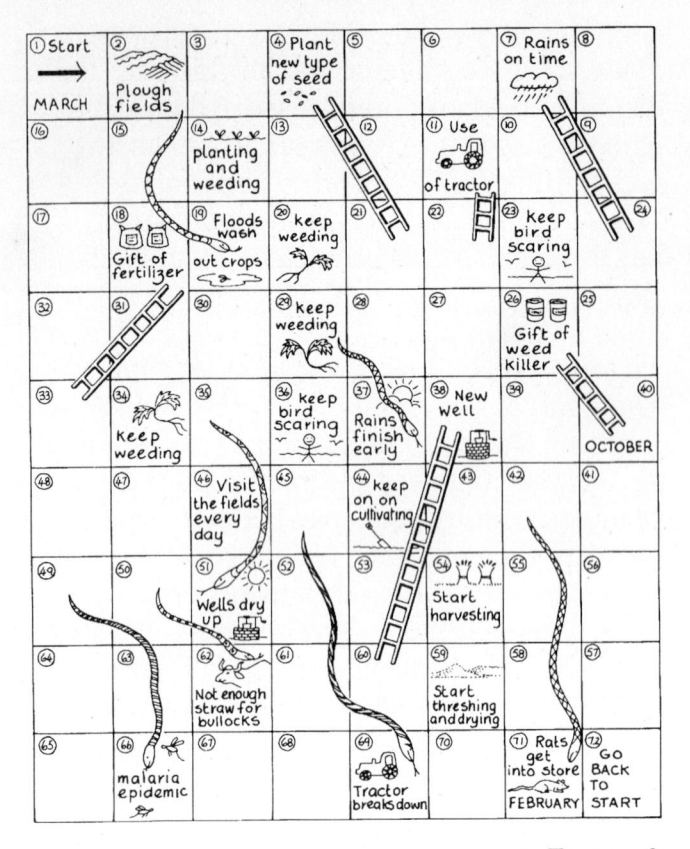

Figure 6

There are various advantages in using games and simulations in this way. Group activities are encouraged along with social skills, decision skills are practised and the situations and problems have to be considered frequently. The children will begin to understand the workings of the decision process and the sequencing of work processes. The complex nature of real life situations will be highlighted and finally motivation will be enhanced for learning about other places. Rex Walford outlines the rationale of using games and gives examples in *Geographical Work in Primary and Middle Schools* (1988).

## Role-play and gender

Role-play offers the same geographical benefits as simulations and games. However, being by definition dramatic, role-play offers more variations and allows similarities and differences to be highlighted, as well as issues and problems.

Figure 7 uses material adapted from *Into Geography* (Book 1) (Arnold Wheaton). Let the children form groups to translate these illustrations into playlets depicting the school day. Encourage them to expand the ancillary roles of family, schoolfriends and other people. Use as many props as are required to show differences in climate, the amount of daylight and the food the children eat. At the end of each trilogy, let the audience outline the similarities and differences, then ask the players to point out the finer details. Encourage the whole class to discuss the contrasts with their own lives.

Role-play also allows different issues and values to be considered. Ask the class to role-play a day in the life of a woman and her family living in an Indian village and the decisions they may have to make about lighting, heating, water supply, food and tilling the fields, first in the dry season and then in the wet season. Individual needs of the family from the young to the old should be considered, as should the position of women in the rural life of India. The preparation work can be done in groups and should include each group deciding what life in an Indian village would be like. Figure 8 gives information on rural life in South India. In India, families are extensive

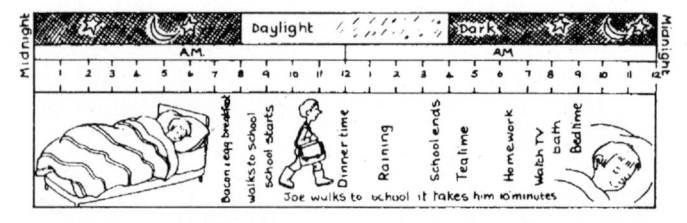

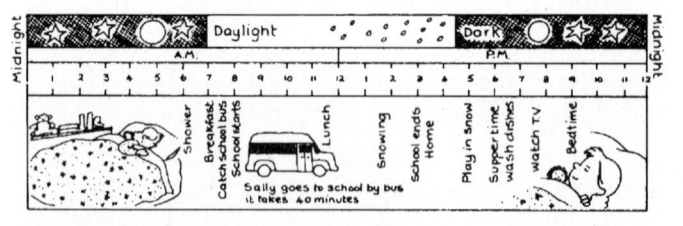

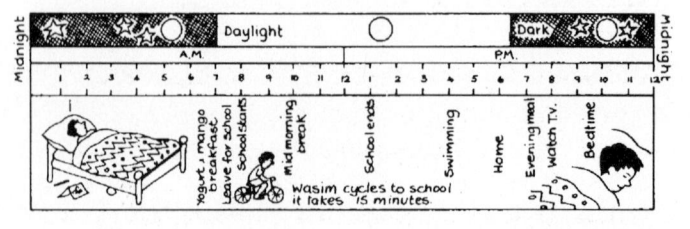

Figure 7

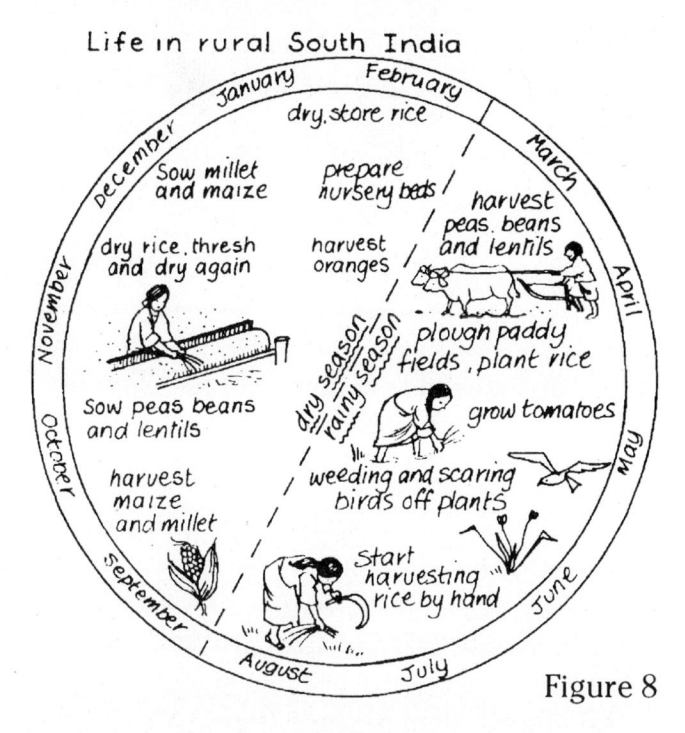

**Figure 8**: Life in rural South India — a circular calendar showing monthly activities:
- January/February: dry, store rice
- December: Sow millet and maize
- November: dry rice, thresh and dry again
- February/March: prepare nursery beds
- March: harvest oranges
- March/April: harvest peas, beans and lentils
- October: Sow peas beans and lentils
- April/May: plough paddy fields, plant rice (rainy season / dry season)
- May: grow tomatoes
- September: harvest maize and millet
- June: weeding and scaring birds off plants
- July/August: Start harvesting rice by hand

and villages are close-knit and confer about major decisions. The Action Aid pack, *Chembakolli: a Village in India* (1991) provides photographs and further details.

## Other issues and values

Issues much closer to home can also be considered through role-play. Planners, local inhabitants, government officials and visitors can clash over a proposed bypass. A local newspaper headline could provide the necessary stimulus. Preparation should involve collecting information about the proposed site using mapwork and photographs.

Decide upon the characters of the participants and the perspective of their involvement (for example, a 50-year-old garage owner, a 22-year-old secretary working in a nearby town, a landowner, and so on). Let the children work in pairs to develop the personalities and prepare a case for each person, then ask one of each pair to present the viewpoint at an enquiry. Different perceptions will emerge and your role should be to maintain a balance and act as chairperson or even arbitrator.

A similar activity could encompass the issue of tourist access to hitherto remote and relatively under-used environments, such as the Burran in Ireland (subject of an EEC grant for new roads and 'interpretation centre'), the Cairngorms in Scotland or the National Parks. Whatever subject is chosen, there should be clear follow-up. The children's initial research might have resulted in a display for use in the enquiry to which could be added the final conclusions including any geographical points about protection of the environment (PoS, 10b), the economics of making decisions (PoS, 9c), the effect upon features in the locality (PoS, 5a), the physical constraints and disruptions (PoS, 5c) and, of course, mapwork (PoS, 3c).

# Museums

Museums about people such as the Museum of Mankind or the Commonwealth Institute in London, or your local metropolitan museum, can be invaluable for geographical investigations. New approaches in the museum world encompass much more the techniques of role-play, simulations and games. Vast photograph and video presentations are often available, as well as simulation models, such as the volcanic eruptions and earthquake simulations at the Natural History Museum in London. As with other visits, involving other people at an early stage and developing a clear mutual understanding of what is wanted and what can be provided is a good route to success.

Museums are a specialised resource often complete with classroom, teaching staff and prepared materials. Many have their own packs which can be used in preparation and many have work sheets which may or may not be suitable, but which may provide you with ideas for activities for the children. Museums' guides are useful resources giving details of facilities of museums throughout the country, together with contact names and the range of special programmes available. Nevertheless, a preliminary visit and an appointment with the education officer is still *essential* in order to pre-arrange your visit and to find out the material most suited for different age groups. The museum staff may already have a programme of study which suits your needs or you may prefer to tailor your own schedule, particularly as the majority of museum visits are most beneficial in mid-topic, after preliminary work has raised questions and potential outcomes have been identified. Remember to book early – the popular museums fill their Education Service diary months in advance and late booking, at the very least, could mean having to accept an inconvenient time. Use the following procedure when arranging a museum visit.

• Having identified a suitable topic or locality, the study of which could be enriched by a museum visit, arrange the visit to fit in with the school schedule for topics and other out-of-school work, as part of your overall term or even whole-school planning. This should be done at least one term ahead.

• In the same term, or at the very latest in the first week of the term of the visit, ring the museum's Education Service to arrange a date and time and enquire about any special programmes which might merit adjusting the original schedule. Find out the museum requirements for staff/pupil ratio and if there are facilities for eating packed lunches. Arrange a meeting to consider preliminary requirements for the content of the visit. Confirm all this in writing.

• At the same time, provisionally arrange for supervision and book transport. Again, confirm in writing. If the visit is to be part of a whole-day excursion, avoid the temptation to organise too many activities. Usually there will be sufficient experience for the children with the journey and the museum. The coach company would probably appreciate a post-rush hour start. This would allow sufficient time for a brief pre-visit focus meeting. Returning to school in time for a brief concluding session, before the end of the school day, will set the scene for work to continue using the museum experience.

• Make a preliminary visit yourself to the museum well in advance to discuss with them your chosen topic or locality, to look at the resources available and to book or collect slides, artefacts, posters and books from the School Loan Collection for preliminary work in class. Discuss with the museum staff activities which will suit the class.

• Write a letter to the parents with details of the proposed visit and a tear-off slip for payment/insurance requirements according to your school/local authority practice.

• Begin work in class on the chosen locality and use the material from the museum to set the scene. A display of resources, carefully mounted and well captioned, will arouse curiosity. Help the children to locate the area on the globe and in the atlas and encourage them to compare its size, physical features and climate with those of Britain. Encourage them to look for similarities and differences in farming, historical development, size of towns, animals and plants. Begin a wall display of maps showing how to get there in as many different ways as possible, looking at both different routes and different modes of transport.

• Devise a set of questions which the children will be able to answer during the museum visit.

• Make a final check on transport arrangements a few days before the visit. Give a checklist to the children to take home so that clothing, food and any other arrangements are confirmed with the parents.

• On the day of the visit, start the school routine as usual if possible and give the children a rundown on what to expect and how they are expected to behave. Once everyone is on the coach, do a quick head count before departure.

• On arrival at the museum, leave the children on the coach with adequate supervision, then check in at reception and collect your instructions from the museum staff. Return to the coach and remind the children of the programme, where to go if they get lost and where to meet for departure and at what time. Ask the children to disembark from the coach and get them to leave their coats and packed lunches in the cloakroom.

• Move on to organise the activities room. For example, at the Commonwealth Institute clothes can be tried on, artefacts can be handled, musical instruments can be played and nationals from the country to be studied can be asked to share their specialist knowledge on different aspects of their country. Many other museums around the country can offer similar activities. All the questions thought of in class have to be well considered if they are to be asked at this point.

• The children can then be allowed to work in groups to investigate further in the museum. Alternatively, they could have lunch before going on to other activities. Worksheets could be used or the class could follow their own programme of work. For example, they could collect details for making a model back at school to show traditional and modern housing or collect information to design a tourist poster and brochure. Encourage them to look for the answers to their questions.

Allow an hour for the activities and half an hour for eating. Through all this activity, supervision is vital, not just for maintaining order but also so that a teacher is on hand to direct attention, answer queries and give support in asking the museum staff questions. Carefully observe the children's reactions to each element of the visit so that you can build on the experience back in the classroom. Some areas of the museum may not come up to expectation, whereas other areas may exceed all anticipated reaction and merit more time and attention back in the classroom.

• Round off the visit by allowing time in the museum shop. Postcards and miniatures all help to focus the experience back in the classroom. Collect further material for classroom investigation (such as slides or a film).

• Re-embark on the coach at the agreed time. Do another head count – don't go down in school history for leaving someone behind!

• Follow-up work could include an exhibition showing the products of the country and the kind of houses and buildings. The children could make a brochure enticing visitors to the country and make investigations into the difficulties the farmers encounter. Investigations into cooking, music, clothes, art and religion could all be developed. Further material could be obtained from agencies such as Oxfam and Christian Aid (see Resources, page 206) to widen the children's interest and to encourage them to consider both the viewpoints of the visitor and the native inhabitant regarding the country's development and history.

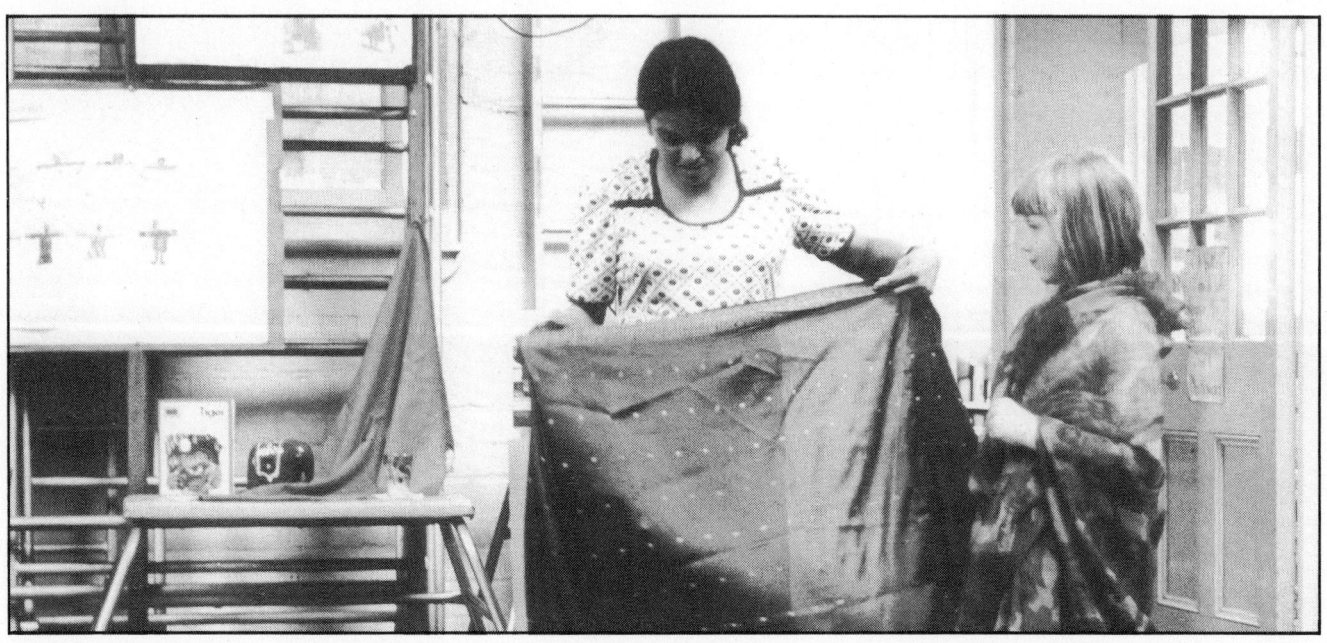

# Wider horizons

The idea that a child's sense of place develops from birth has been mentioned earlier. The need to know where different places are in relation to each other is part of making sense of the world about us. This soon develops into a sense of territory, whether imagined or real. This territory might be just a bedroom, but it will be a special bit of space from which to explore and return to, and a yardstick by which other places can be measured. This will expand to include the whole home, the home area, the home town, the home region and eventually identification with the home country.

Other people's previous experiences can help us to locate a new place in our personal geography. Knowledge of other people's activities in a place help to give it its distinct characteristics. Often children gather information by associating places with enjoyment, for example, Denmark with Legoland, or with dramatic events, such as the 'bombing' of a lava flow to save farmland and lives in Italy. This information can be developed, on the one hand that Legoland can be easily reached by car and ferry, on the other that given an advantageous climate people will risk the volcanic hazards in order to grow profitable crops on the fertile soils of past eruptions. The most important association, however, is by comparison with their own life styles and how they feel about their own places.

Feelings aroused by a place will inevitably colour a child's attitude to that place. On moving to a new place a child's response may often be, 'I feel at home here' or 'Let's leave, there's nothing to do'. It is only a short step from these feelings to feelings of concern or indifference about an environment, to recognising the need for conservation or developing a hatred that can only be expressed in vandalism. Feelings are usually not extreme, just an acceptance that not every place is perfect and that adjustment to a new place may be necessary. Such feelings may also affect how other, more foreign, parts of the world are viewed.

Using photographs, simulations, games, visits and audio-visual programmes all help us to make sense of the world about us.

The sooner a child can accumulate accurate balanced images, the greater will be the chance for him or her to grow up with the ability to see both the positive and negative aspects of a place.

Open-mindedness is of great importance when looking at similarities and differences between places. Urban areas are now, in the developing world, a yardstick for speed of development and standard of facilities. This has led to a great move from the countryside to the town to share in these improved conditions. Unfortunately, this has led to the growth of 'shanty towns' on the outskirts of many cities, as the demand for shelter has outstripped the provision of houses. These are not to be regarded as 'slums' in the developed world's sense of grinding poverty. The shanties can be transformed once a plan is undertaken to put in an infrastructure of roads, drains and piped water. It can, however, take 20 years to move up, on a self-help basis, from a one-roomed shanty home to a two-storey concrete house with tiled roof and enough room for the family to each have their own space. Yet it has happened. The fact that during these improvements the place looks to be in a turmoil should not be taken as a negative fact, but rather a positive sign for the future.

Empathy needs to be encouraged and children should learn to enquire beyond the surface evidence. They need to understand the reasons for differences

## TICK THE PICTURE YOU THINK IS TRUE FOR TODAY

INDIANS HUNT FOR FOOD. HOW?

WHAT DO INDIAN AIRLINE PILOTS SLEEP ON?

HOW DO WELSH GIRLS DRESS TO GO DANCING?

WHICH BUILDING IS HOME TO AN INUIT FAMILY?

HOW DO ARAB BUSINESSMEN TRAVEL TO THE OFFICE?

Adapted from *Into Geography* (Book 2) by P. and S. Harrison/M. Pearson (Nelson) pp. 60 and 61

Figure 9

which, in their limited knowledge, often are used as status symbols but which, elsewhere, are valueless, as everyone is affected by the same condition.

The realisation that rural life has its own speed has to be appreciated not deplored. The grief of a mother returning home to her parents' rural abode, be it on the western fringes of northern Europe, a Mediterranean village or a rural Caribbean community, on coping with her own children's rejection of the good things of rural living because the trappings of piped water, Tarmac roads and speedy transport were missing, is very tangible and, in these days of comparatively easy travel, not unusual. Yet her children would have been helped if they had been led to expect that all rural areas, in all parts of the world, were similarly 'disadvantaged' and that this was no reflection upon the communities in those areas, rather upon the difficulties of providing facilities owing to geographical factors such as slope, distance, economics and so on.

Empathy is also required to appreciate that the discrepancy between rural and urban life in one culture could have roots in the demands made upon it by another culture. This understanding can happen in a haphazard fashion or it can be approached systematically, considering the geography of places from the viewpoint of the life styles and cultures of the people living in that place. Figure 9 demonstrates stereotypes and the real-life situation. Use this type of comparison as a discussion starter about a new place, to see what the class have gleaned so far from conversations and pictures. A complex picture may be built up, with contradictions becoming evident. Stereotyping begins early through attempting to simplify without clarification. For example, Inuit did and still do build igloos, but they were an essential part of the Inuit's nomadic, hunting lifestyle, and are now often replaced with portable tents. Their permanent houses were built of wood, stone and turf. Today they are still built of wood, but with modern modifications to accommodate the polar climate. Always clarify the children's feelings and knowledge about the wider world by at least giving a rounded picture of each environment.

Similarities and differences need to be understood from a positive point of view. Geography developed from exploration. Exploration led to a desire to make sense of the location and distribution of the world's climate, surface features and resources and a realisation that the distributions are a response to natural processes and, later, the effects of man upon the world. For example, once most parts of the world were covered in woodland. As can be seen now in the equatorial forest, the clearing of the world's forests for fuel and agriculture was slow until new technology and agricultural practices increased the rate of clearance, and natural replacement of the woodland was hindered by erosion or the encroachment of another, less useful vegetation as, for example, in the Mediterranean lands. Gradually, man has learned to counterbalance these mistakes by initiating good practice.

It is the geographer's prerogative to show what is good practice in each part of the world. To show that one country's way of farming, for example nomadic grazing, is compatible with the natural constraints of the country's climate and that to impose a new way of farming is not always the way to improve matters. There are many examples from the tropical dry-lands, where nomadic grazing is the traditional way of managing the environment, of land spoiled by over-enthusiastic irrigation which has briefly brought rich returns through the export of cash crops such as maize or cotton and encouraged the nomads to settle, and then ended in disaster through overgrazing and lack of provision of food in times of severe drought. The facts and sequence of these events can be simulated, but the understanding comes with empathy and consideration of a 'what if...' line of enquiry.

A geography teacher should aim to develop within children an ability to look for evidence, and be aware of bias in the reporting of any situation. They should look first for the things they know and are familiar with – the similarities. The differences can then be investigated and accounted for in terms of space, time, climate, biological response, economics and the sheer human variety of ways of doing any activity. Moreover, having made a survey of these influences, you should draw attention to the fact that there is no simple explanation and that all the factors can be considered in reasonable discussion. This, in turn, reflects upon the initial view of similarities, highlighting the, perhaps surprising, agreement of so many elements in so diverse a world.

There is no clear prescription for creating understanding of the wider world. A variety of ways of learning have been described above. These, in all cases, should be accompanied with a sensitivity and insight towards the development of a balanced way of looking at the world, without losing the sense of fascination and curiosity that children get from the exploration of the world about them.

# Chapter six
# Information technology

## Information technology and graphicacy

*Geography in the National Curriculum* (1991) non-statutory guidance for teachers in Wales warns: 'Although an aspect of IT may be delivered in geography it should not be presumed that any particular aspect is exclusively delivered in geography.'

This statement came to mind when reading the following extract from a book by Sue Senior:

'A tape recorded map is another interesting way of introducing direction and screenings. If the children are taken for a walk within or outside the school grounds with the intention of reaching a certain place such as the local shop or the school gate, the route can be recorded. Several children could take turns to announce the next part of the journey (English Attainment Target 1, Levels 2 and 3). The children will, of course, need to specify where they are starting from, for example, "With your back to the classroom door, turn left, go forward until you reach the glass doors ..."

'A natural progression from this would be to photograph or draw the landmarks, write the instructions down and make guide books of the school or local area (English Attainment Target 1, Levels 1, 2 and 3). The instructions could be entered

95

into a word processor, and the children could be encouraged to choose a most suitable style of print for their intended audience (English programmes of study 7–11, Attainment Targets 3, 4 and 5).

'The document for Mathematics says that 'None.... object to being put, with the face exposed, inside a gaily painted large cardboard box which meant to resemble a robot. They love being instructed to go forward, turn left or right.... (Maths Attainment Target 11 Levels 1 and 2).

'These are all games and experiences which provide children with the requisite background experience to understand the concepts behind Logo and to be successful at the outset.' From *Using IT across the National Curriculum: a handbook for the primary classroom* Sue Senior (1989, Owlet Books)

These are also all games and experiences which provide children with the requisite background experience for developing the concepts behind mapping and understanding the space about and beyond themselves. They are part of developing spatial intelligence and of graphicacy. All National Curriculum subjects are required to develop and apply IT capability in their curriculum area.

Figure 1 integrates the programmes of study for both geography and technology. There are five IT areas or 'strands' of capability, as defined by the National Council for Educational Technology in *Focus of IT* (NCET, 1991), where the child should show competence.

The areas are:
- communicating ideas;
- handling information;
- modelling;
- measurement and control;
- applications and effects.

These are now contained in two IT themes. Electronic equipment should include video and tape recorders, telephones, calculators, word processors, computers and music equipment. The following suggestions are not exhaustive and probably echo work already being practised in other areas.

# Communicating geographical ideas

Geographical ideas can be communicated through the use of word processors, electronic mail systems, graphics and mapping software, desktop publishing software and newsdata systems, using words, numbers or pictures. IT allows the easy and rapid development, revision and refinement of ideas before communicating them to individuals, the class, school or neighbourhood.

There is no doubt that IT can enhance the quality of pupils' geographical experiences. A child who is not very good

| Geography PoS 'Pupils should be given opportunities... to develop and apply their information technology (IT) capability... .' | | |
|---|---|---|
| | **IT themes** | **Geographical programmes** |
| **Communicating and handling information** | • Generate and communicate their ideas in different forms using text, tables, pictures and sound.<br>• Enter and store information.<br>• Retrieve, process and display information that has been stored. | • Use geographical terms in investigating places.<br>• Make maps and plans using pictures and symbols.<br>• Undertake fieldwork activities.<br>• Use secondary sources, e.g. video, CD-ROM encyclopaedia.<br>• Use IT to assist in handling, classifying and presenting evidence. |
| **Controlling and modelling** | • Create, test, modify and store sequences of directions.<br>• Use IT equipment and software to monitor external events.<br>• Explore the effects of changing variables. 'What would happen if?'<br>• Recognise patterns and relationships from models and simulations. | • Follow directions; make plans and maps at a variety of scales.<br>• Undertake fieldwork, including the use of instruments to make measurements.<br>• Develop the ability to recognise patterns and ask: 'How and why is it changing?' |

Figure 1

with words could well master a painting program or make a drawing for the touch or concept keyboard to show what has been observed on a visit to a farm. The concept keyboard could then be programmed to show the appropriate words on screen and this could then be elaborated upon by the teacher or other children, using either words or drawings.

## The range of information technology

Nowadays, IT covers a wide range of electronic equipment. Tape recorders can be used to great effect, not just for recording interviews and sounds on site, such as on a farm visit or in a shop, but also for continuation reports. You may have visited a farm in the spring. What happened to the lambs? Did the hay get cut in time? What help came for the harvest? These and other questions can later be answered on tape by arrangement with the farmer. A quarterly tape has been known to help provide an ongoing relationship, backed up by photographs and videos. The same process could be used with the shopkeeper at different seasons of the year, for example to record the orders for Christmas and Easter or, in a multicultural community, at various other festival times.

The concept keyboard and the tape recorder could be used in conjunction with a desktop publishing package to produce an article on the visit. The newspaper need not be produced by the class making the visit, but could be compiled by another class who need to practise editing skills.

Desktop publishing can be used to a greater extent when considering environmental issues, when different points of view might need to be presented. For example, the question of pollution by nitrates versus the sole use of organic fertilisers, and the relationship of both to the movement of water through the soil could provide top juniors with a formidable but multifaceted view of the problems associated with agribusiness and conservation. They could use photographs and accounts given by farmers and could interview, on tape, a representative from the local rivers authority.

Issues could be presented as documentaries by using video recorders for collecting evidence. At both key stages, reorganising the collected material into a visual 'news' presentation acts as a useful means of reinforcing the knowledge gained. It is clear that for IT to have the greatest effect, there needs to be a whole-school plan in order to make the most of visits, visitors and the collection and processing of information and data. Figure 2 overleaf, based on 'Geography and IT?' by C. Parker in *Micro-scope* 32 (MAPE), shows what could be done at each level for each attainment target.

## Handling information

Introduce the children to software which can handle data, spreadsheets and allow information retrieval in various forms. This includes video text systems and branching databases.

Using these systems allows the children to store, retrieve, modify, process and present the material they have collected. They also enable children to examine patterns and relationships from this to form and test hypotheses. Finally, they can select information from a range of sources and apply it to a range of problem-solving exercises.

Interviews, for example with a farmer or a river authority representative, should be prepared beforehand on a word processor, paying particular attention to the sequence of questions, but should also be scrutinised to check that the range of information collected provides a balanced view. This information will inevitably include numerical and classifiable data.

Other questionnaires could be undertaken with a link school and could be concerned with services in the community and individuals' ability to use them. For example, in an urban locality, the

# GEOGRAPHY AND IT CAPABILITIES

| GEOGRAPHY | ACTIVITIES | TECHNOLOGY |
|---|---|---|
| Follow directions. | Use a programmable toy to follow directions around obstacles in the classroom. Follow a tape-recorded route. | Talk about ways in which equipment such as toys and domestic appliances respond to symbols or commands. |
| Make a plan of a real or an imaginary place. | Use a graphics program to create a plan of an island from pictures or symbols already created. | Use computer generated pictures, symbols, words or phrases to communicate meaning. |
| Follow a route using a plan. | Use a concept keyboard to create a route. | |
| Record weather observation made over a short period of time. | Use a word processor to write about the weather, store and retrieve text to add each subsequent day's observation. | Use information technology for the storage and retrieval of information copy. |
| | Use a concept keyboard to add symbols to text. | Work with a computer. |
| Make a map of a short route showing features in correct order. | Use a concept keyboard and word processor to produce a map with labels. | Use information technology to make, amend and present information. |
| Identify features on aerial photographs. | Use a concept keyboard and word processor to produce a labelled diagram. | Use information technology to make, amend and present information. |
| Use four-figure coordinates to locate features on map. | Use *List Explorer* and concept keyboard. | Use information technology to retrieve, develop, organise and present work. |
| Measure and record weather using direct observations and simple equipment. | Use data logger and sensors and data handling package to analyse and display information. | Use information technology to retrieve, develop, organise and present work. |
| Follow a route and describe it. | Write description for a tourist on a word processor. Record route directions and commentary. | Use information technology to retrieve, develop, organise and present work. |
| Identify activities carried out by people in the local area. | Use a concept keyboard and a word processor to find out information about people in the local community. | Work with a computer. |
| Identify the features of a locality outside the local area. | Use a concept keyboard with a photograph of people in a distant place to retrieve information about people in the community. Exchange information on tape and video. Use e-mail. | Use information technology for the storage and retrieval of information copy. |
| Explain the relationships between land use, buildings and human activities in the local area. | Collect information about buildings in the local area, enter it into a database and sort and retrieve information to identify the different activities within each building. | Collect information and enter it into a database (whose structure may have been prepared in advance) and to select and retrieve information from the database. |
| Explain why some activities in the area are located where they are. | Use a concept keyboard at different levels to map different elements, e.g. communications, land use, rivers and water features. | |

| | | |
|---|---|---|
| Give an account of an issue that has arisen from the recent or proposed changes in the locality. Compare viewpoints arising from the issue studied above and present their own conclusions. Explain how conflicts can arise over the use of land in the locality. | Produce a newspaper front page giving an account of a current, local issue, e.g. the construction of a by-pass. Present a variety of views and editorial comment obtained from CD-ROM, encyclopaedia and newspapers. | Use information technology to retrieve, develop, organise and present work. |
| Recognise seasonal weather patterns. | Use the concept keyboard or graphics programme to complete a description. Use a simple database to sort. | Use computer to generate pictures. Use computer generated pictures, symbols, words or phrases to communicate meaning. |
| Identify and describe a familiar landscape. | Use photographs of local features on the concept keyboard with word processor or symbols. | Collect information and enter it into a database (whose structure may have been prepared in advance) and to select and retrieve information from the database. |
| Explain how site conditions can influence surface temperature and local wind speed and direction. | Use a data logging device to identify differences in temperature in a small area of the playground over a period of time, e.g. *Weather Reporter*. Also use the concept keyboard to create a temperature map from the data of the school and its surroundings. Enter evidence from river or beach work on to data handling package, e.g. *Junior Ecosoft*. | Amend and add information in an existing database to check plausibility and interrogate it. Use a computer model to detect patterns and relationships. Amend and add to information in an existing database. |
| Demonstrate an understanding that most homes are part of a settlement, and that settlements vary in size. | Use photographs and a word processor on a concept keyboard to describe the sequence of settlements. | Use computer generated pictures, symbols, words or phrases to communicate meaning. |
| Explain why different forms of transport are used. | Enter up traffic and journey surveys on a database and use to make graphs of different forms. | Collect information and enter it in a database (whose structure may have been prepared in advance) and select and retrieve information from the database. |
| Identify and name materials obtained from natural sources. | Use an overlay keyboard, pictures and word processor. | Work with a computer. |
| Express personal likes and dislikes about features of the local environment. | Use a painting programme with a word processor. | |
| Suggest how they could improve the quality of their own environment. | Use a simple art package to create a poster urging other children to save waste paper for recycling. | Use computer generated pictures symbols, words or phrases to communicate meaning. |
| Give an account of an activity designed to improve the local environment. | Use a word processor to create an information sheet on an environmental improvement activity for circulation to parents. | Use information technology to make, amend and present information. |
| Describe the restoration of a local 'damaged' landscape. | Create a presentation of words and pictures for the school entrance following a visit to a land reclamation scheme. | Use information technology to retrieve, develop, organise and present work. |

Figure 2

inhabitants would generally be used to being within easy reach of a doctor or dentist, probably within walking distance (regardless of choice). However, a rural area would have a very different experience, while a tropical community would not be able to provide answers to many of the questions. However, so that similarities and differences are made clear, make sure that your link schools all use the same questionnaire. Figure 3 gives some idea of the sort of questions which could be asked.

Questionnaires could be prepared using a word processing packages, such as *Prompt*, *Writer*, *Folio* or *PenDown*. The data collected could then be entered into a simple database such as *Our Facts* or *First Facts*, *Grass* or *Grasshopper*. (This latter is a spreadsheet which allows data from several sites to be entered and then compared.)

Entering and processing the locality services on a database or a spreadsheet saves considerable time which would otherwise have been spent on diagram construction before the similarities and differences could have been recognised. The information thus collected from several sources, whether about villages

| YOUR LOCALITY: WHERE TO GO ||||
| Service/Goods | Person 1 | Person 2 | Person 3 |
| --- | --- | --- | --- |
| Bread and milk | Supermarket[1] | Minimarket[2] | Milkman[3] |
| Fresh food | Supermarket | Parade[2] | M & S |
| Groceries | Supermarket | Minimarket | Supermarket |
| Clothes | Thurrock | Bexley Heath | Dartford |
| Shoes | Welling | Bexley Heath | Dartford |
| Chemist | Welling | Bexley Heath | Welling |
| Toys | Thurrock | Welling | Dartford |
| Sports | Welling | Eltham | Dartford |
| Household | Welling | Welling | Welling |
| DIY[4] | Sidcup | Welling | Dartford |
| Books/gifts | Thurrock | Bexley Heath | Dartford |
| Dentist | Welling | Eltham | Welling |
| Optician | Bexley Heath | Bexley Heath | Welling |
| Hospital | The Brook | The Brook | The Brook |
| Bank | Welling | Welling | Welling |
| Museum | London | Greenwich | Dartford |
| Theatre/Cinema | Thurrock | Eltham | Dartford |
| Swimming[3] | Bexley Heath | Bexley Heath | Bexley Heath |
| 1. Plot the different stores, by name, on a map.<br>2. Plot the housing estate and community shops around the minimarket on a map.<br>3. Plot the location of the different dairies and leisure facilities.<br>4. These, when mapped, often show the presence of industrial estates. ||||
| Evidence from a suburban junior school in SE London. ||||

Figure 3

from work done on a residential field course or by exchange with link schools in different localities, could be processed further. If the material can be printed out it can form part of a display of maps showing the distances involved in using various transport services.

## Commercial datafiles

Information for geography teachers is available from many sources. The Centre for World Development Education issues a 40 track disk (BBC) *What do we eat?* which provides information about foods and diets around the world. Children are expected to keep a 24 hour diary of their own food intake in order to make comparisons with diets in other countries. The children's original food diaries can be entered in to the database and graphs abstracted for comparison with similar graphs abstracted from the CWDE data.

Another way of gathering information is to use teletext. For example, a route-planning exercise for getting a lorry from Dover to a town in Scotland could involve using a road atlas to choose the most appropriate roads, then calling up Ceefax or Oracle for up-to-date travel and weather information. There is also travel information available on Prestel but this requires modem access via a telephone.

Older children could use the more sophisticated viewdata services, such as Prestel or Neris, which can be accessed by telephone using the Campus 2000 network. CD-ROM encyclopaedias and newspapers supported with atlas, photograph and clipart software brings a new dimension to locality work. Initially expensive, their cross-curricular contribution helps to maintain wide horizons. Children could create their own pages of information and decide upon ways of linking them together. For example, a whole-school project on a particular country could be enhanced by Y6 children collecting up-to-date information which younger children could then access for projects on, for example, 'Food', 'Clothing' or 'Weather'.

## School-produced data files

Schools are in a superb position for making their own contribution to science by recording weather observations as required by the National Curriculum. The fine detail obtainable by Y6 children can be entered on a database such as *Our Facts, Grass* or the RESOURCE *Weather Studies* database which would allow them to design their own files. The details could then be accessed by the younger children using a graphics package to find out just how cold 'cold' can be and what a really 'wet' day can be like, looking at both seasonal and daily contrasts. The beauty of keeping a database over a long period of time is that other areas of the geography curriculum can be serviced, for example comparing seasons in different years as part of an investigation into farming. Also, the pride in knowing that useful information has been gathered is a great motivational tool. The fact that it can be stored and accessed repeatedly makes it even more useful.

Weather recording can also be supported by the media. Weather satellite images on the screen, in conjunction with the shipping forecast on radio, can aid the recognition of extreme weather events as they unfold. A weather satellite image of the mid-Atlantic (including the British Isles) is shown daily on Ceefax and can be accessed and stored with a modem and BBC micro. One south-east London school used the computer to log the degree of damage created in the locality by the great storm of October 1987 which also involved the use of the local Ordnance Survey plans.

Other geographical applications for databases could include investigations into the way in which water erodes, transports and deposits material. Top juniors could make a field trip to a suitable stream with a bridge, from which they could take depth and flow readings at different seasons. This information could then be related to the rainfall records for the same period. The changes evident between seasons should then begin to make sense. Locked into a well designed database, the results of this team effort will be there for use by future years. In effect, it will be an archive as well as a database.

Other useful applications for databases include investigations into:
- modes of travel to school;
- ages and types of local houses;
- numbers of pupils living in different types of house;
- birds/insects/animals/flowers/trees seen on a transect or in a park;
- shops and places of entertainment;
- numbers of different shop types;
- types of goods sold in specific shopping areas;
- number of cars, lorries, etc., passing selected observation points;
- number of pedestrians at selected parts of a shopping parade.

# Modelling

The software which can be used for geographical modelling includes adventure programmes which can be highly structured (*Granny's Garden*), clearly explained but demanding more self-reliance (*Flowers of Crystal*), or unstructured so that the children have to make their own deductions and decisions based upon their experiences within the game.

Simulations, on the other hand, are set in 'real' situations. Variables can be altered and their effects observed. Outcomes of changes, which in reality would take place over a long period of time, can also be observed. The *Water Game* is a simulation in which the users go to a waterless country cottage and have to find water for humans, animals and crops from a variety of sources with several interruptions to the supply. However, it should be noted that in *Curriculum Matters 15: Information Technology from 5 to 16* (DES) it is asked that children should 'understand that computer simulations are not complete and accurate representations of reality.'

Modelling packages allow information collected in fieldwork to be entered and used to replicate a situation or to supplement information. For example, *Paper Round*, where the pupil creates the best route between a series of addresses. The route is then compared with the shortest route generated by the computer.

Modelling can also be achieved, using a spreadsheet such as *Grasshopper*. Data can be collected from several sites or from one site at different times. Comparisons can then be made between different graphs, and hypotheses can be tested by manipulating the data. Official data can also be entered. For example, the nearest river gauging station could provide both discharge (amount of water passing down the river channel at any one time) and rainfall measurements for selected months on a daily basis.

Entered upon a spreadsheet, the relationship between rainfall and river flow can be recognised. This can then be extended to asking questions such as, 'What if it didn't rain for a whole week in February?' This would involve completely eliminating the rainfall figures for one week and redrawing the adjusted discharge figures.

'*Water/Excel*' guides groups of students through spreadsheet work on data collected from water/soil experiments. This is developed using collected data on how water is used in homes.

These activities need not be restricted to one area or to one level. A computer can be used in several ways to set up a model of a place visited. For example, younger children could make a record of a farm visit using *Old MacDonald's Farm* that allows pictures and text to be combined into a book. This would also allow the layout and description of an actual farm visit to be made by younger children. *Old MacDonald's Farm* would be good preparation for using a simulation such as *Farming Pack: Farm game*, where an imaginary farm can be planted with different crops over a period of four years. The aim is to make a profit, but the weather changes from year to year. By taking account of the weather patterns and past profits, the crops can be changed to achieve better profits. Once the principle has been acquired, the farm can be relocated in different regions of Britain. Not only does this allow the discovery that good crop combinations in one area are not necessarily profitable elsewhere, but it also provides material for considering a contrasting locality.

This in turn can be followed by collecting data from different farms visited and entering it on a spreadsheet such as *Grasshopper*. The data required would be field names and sizes, crops and crop yields. Other factors could be entered such as soil type, slope and the aspect of each field. The field names are entered across the top row of the sheet. (However, giving each field a number rather than using a name would take up less room and thus allow data from more than one farm to be entered.) Other information is then entered for each field on separate rows (Figure 4).

Comparisons can then be made to reveal the factors most likely to influence yield. For example, are the fields with the poorest yields those with stony soils and facing north? Could yield be improved by sowing a different crop? With younger children, keep the factors simple as the farm topic will be returned to in greater detail at Key Stages 3 and 4. However, a similar use of the spreadsheet can be made by incorporating information from the mini weather stations round the school grounds related to plant growth. Again, the sites can be numbered and soil, aspect, rain, temperature and sunlight can be recorded and entered. The crop yield could be the height of plants (for example, of sunflowers), the number of successful germinations (for example, of lettuce) or the percentage of survival (where snails could be an added factor). Alternatively, the crops could be outdoor tomato plants with a straight yield in kilograms.

Computer simulation is a way of helping children gain some understanding of the way human decisions can influence the location of buildings. *The Windmill Game*, (part of the *Industrial Pack*) for example, involves children in the choosing of new sites for windmills at the lowest cost. This can be used with both younger and older children and has strong links with mathematics, as well as graphics. It is appropriate to PoS, 5c and d.

| File: (Farms) | Abbey Farm | Woodlands Farm | Own Farm |
|---|---|---|---|
| Fields: (Names/No.) | | | |
| Size: (Hectares) | | | |
| Soil:<br>Clay=0<br>Loam=1<br>Sand=2<br>Other=3 | | | |
| Stones:<br>None=0<br>Few=1<br>Many=2 | | | |
| Rain mm/ann:<br>Winter<br>Summer | | | |
| Temperature 0°:<br>Winter<br>Summer | | | |
| Crops: | | | |
| Crop yield: (K) | | | |
| Slope: (Degrees) | | | |
| Aspect:<br>NE<br>SW | | | |
| Other | | | |

Figure 4

# Measurement and control

IT equipment which can be used to investigate measurement includes programmable toys (such as Roamer), data logging devices such as light sensors and temperature probes which can record change over time and information from satellites and remote sensing equipment.

Investigating IT measurement and control can be introduced early in the classroom with the use of programmable toys. Once the children can realise that, given precise instructions in the correct sequence, a route can be followed or a set of actions can be undertaken, electronic control can be utilised to aid map skill development with both verbal instructions (left, right, backwards, forwards) and compass bearings (north two places, turn 270 degrees, go west four paces).

While properly working models are the domain of design and technology, links can be made in the design stage when considering using light switches with a control package. The recognition that the apparent movement of the sun corresponds with the lengthening or shortening day during the year will be reinforced by the regular changing of the instruction for turning the light on and off. Similarly, adapting the model for a house in the tropics will emphasise the even length of day and night.

This leads naturally to considering the use of IT control in the environment, with the switching on and off of street lights, the regulating of traffic signals, automatic heating systems, railway signals, motorway warning signals and so on.

Using electronic probes to measure soil, water and air temperature to obtain data which is then fed into a database allows further applications of IT to be considered. Using sensors (the probe), a processor (the database) and noting outcomes (graph of changes) is another way of demonstrating how systems work. By allowing continuous recording over a short period, sensors also allow differences to be demonstrated within a small area, for example aspect, shelter, light and temperature in the school playground can all be considered. Careful placing of sensors on a frosty spring or autumn morning can allow the sudden rise in temperature on south and east facing walls to be contrasted, over the period of time between assembly and break, with the slight change on north and west facing sites. If it is possible to arrange safe recording sites for sensing over a whole day, data explaining the much greater seasonal differences between the sites will be revealed. (More than one school has resorted to the roof top for external readings; similar experiments can be set up internally with 'safe' window sills.)

# Evaluating applications and effects

From using electronic equipment to measure or control small events, it is only a small step to recognising the influence of IT on the world outside, from automatic ovens to automatic smoke sensors and in the wider world, the use of satellites to transmit information about weather, stock exchanges or sport. Meanwhile, on the largest scale of all, there are satellite photographs of the earth's changing physical systems, which were instrumental in revealing the holes in the ozone layer and the outcome of which has been to make not only governments but also individuals conscious of pollutant (if invisible) gases.

Examples of how IT could be used can be added to by discussion and building up a chart. The top row of the chart could consist of as many electronic and information technology devices as the class can think of (this should increase with age and familiarity). Down the side could be listed categories such as children in school, children at home, the family at home, the family at work, the community at work, the community at play, national concerns such as the weather bureau, national rail and bus services, airlines, newspapers, other media and so on. The children could then fill in the chart by deciding which category of IT would be used by each group.

The advantages and disadvantages of IT can be similarly listed including the accuracy and accessibility of personal information. When revising addresses, ask the children to collect envelopes from home and school and sort them into typed, handwritten and computer-printed. Making a graph will reveal how much personal information is stored on computers, how few letters are handwritten, and how much we rely on IT.

# Overlay or concept keyboards

The concept keyboard is a touch-sensitive pad originally developed for children with special educational needs. It is increasingly being used in primary schools as a means of combining graphics and data analysis, for self-checking and as a means of building concepts from collected evidence. Pads come in two sizes (A3 and A4) and plug into the user port of the computer. The pads are divided into a maximum of 128 cells (Figure 5) which correspond to the computer cell system in such a way that when a picture or word is pressed on the keyboard the appropriate word or picture comes up on the screen. Thus the concept keyboard can be used for creative writing, report making, data analysis, picture exploration, map-making, Logo turtle instructions and so on. The software to enable this is called *Touch Explorer Plus*. (The teacher or pupil is

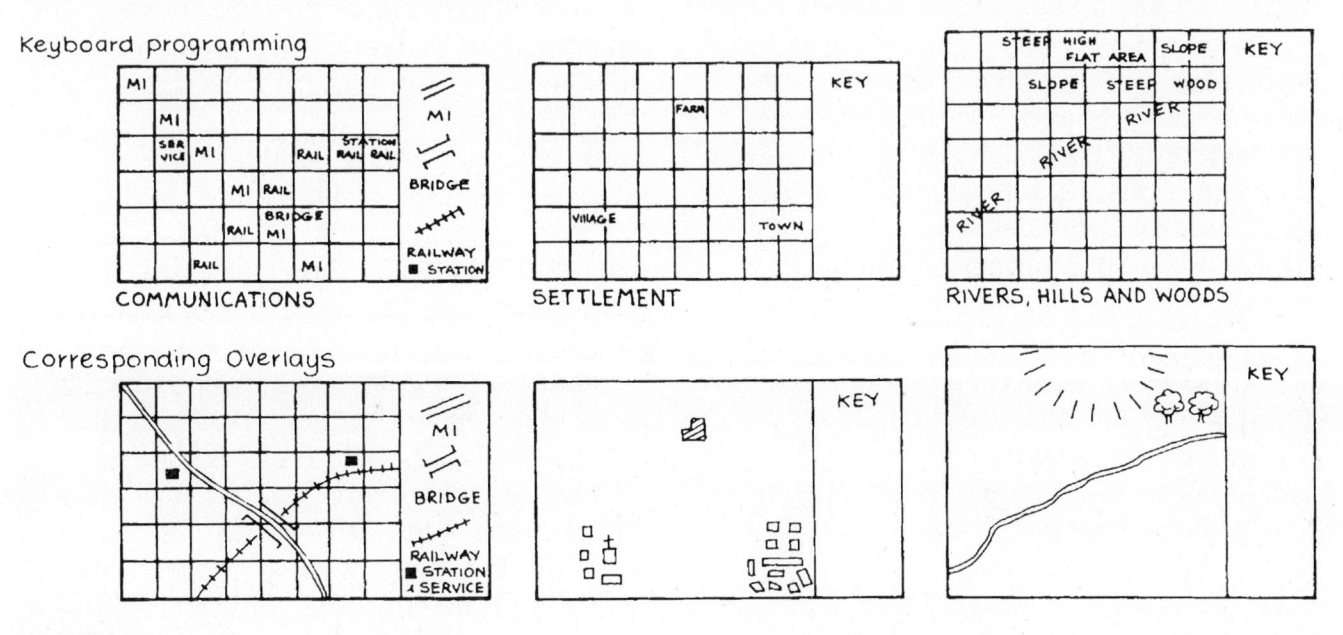

Figure 5

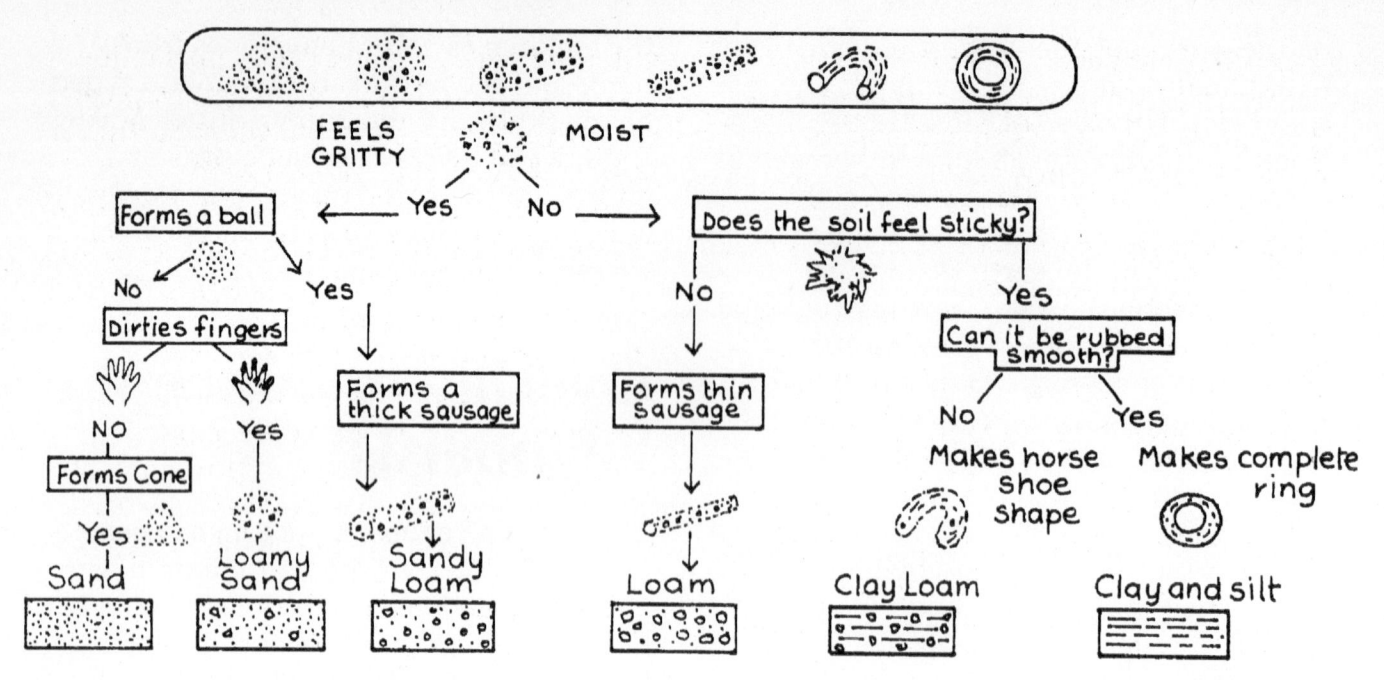

Figure 6

required to input words, pictures or instructions or there are packs and utility programs, such as *Concept* (NCET) which gives access to BBC programs, and *List Explorer*, a database which can be used at all levels of ability.)

Pictures and photographs can be stuck on to the pad, which can be programmed so that when different parts are touched, questions, labels or other prompts can come up on screen and copies of the pictures or sketches can be annotated.

It is possible for work to be undertaken on information input at different computer levels. For example, for each square pressed at one level, information about land shape can be given, (Figure 5, page 105) information about water, settlement and vegetation can be stored at three other separate levels, enabling a map to be built up, just as an Ordnance Survey map is built up. Each level of information will be accompanied by a keyboard overlay made using tracing paper or acetate sheets and water-based pens. As each overlay is added and the information accessed, so the children will be able to discover relationships and the reason for locations. This will give practice in map drawing and also in the use of symbols.

The concept keyboard is a useful means of storing information about your local area. For example, one south London school made a study of a street near the school. Drawings of the faces of the different inhabitants were places on the touch pad map, and when pressed they brought up information on address, house type, age, materials and changes that had been made to the building. To this could have been added historical information from the enumeration returns.

Maps can be reduced for the keypad, to be used as a stimulus for discussion and exploration. Using a map such as the 1:10,000 Ordnance Survey as an overlay, a land use map could be created showing, for example, offices, factories, shops and building sites. The patterns observed could then be discussed. With older children, the question of suitability of site for the factories or shops could lead to making a new map showing preferred sites. A *Touch Explorer Plus* file could be made with the advantages and disadvantages of each site noted.

Identification guides can be constructed using pictures on the touch pad with the criteria obtained and the classification coming up on screen. Figure 6 shows how different soil types can be identified by texture using the concept keyboard. The words are typed into the computer and come up when the picture is pressed. The possibilities are endless, both for open-ended work and program-supported work. Many ideas and details of use can be found in *Micro-scope*, the journal of Microcomputers and Primary Education (MAPE). The main criteria, however, is that if it can be drawn and labelled it can be used on the touch pad.

# Electronic mail

One of the recurrent needs in geography is to collect information about a geographical feature, such as a mountain or a place. With their emphasis upon localities, contrasting localities and the character of the wider world, the National Curriculum requirements have given renewed impetus to the publication of photopacks and the development of links between schools. This has led to an exchange of materials between schools (see Chapter five). Electronic mail or e-mail is a form of information technology which enables communication between computers via a standard telephone line with the addition of a modem which converts text from digits to analogue form for transmission. The information communicated is prepared using a word processor and stored upon a computer disk before being transmitted. The facility for transmission is called Campus 2000 and is used by many schools, not just in the UK but around the world. The cost of transmission is that of a local telephone call and there are facilities for compressing data should the message or text become too long/expensive. Subscribing to Campus 2000 allows you to have a mailbox (pigeon-hole) to which only you have the password but to which anyone can send a message. Children around the world are now able to exchange information about school life and home life, weather patterns, local industry, local social life, local current affairs, and so on. In the northern hemisphere it is comparatively easy to get newspaper reports about the weather in other countries, especially European countries, but more difficult to get such information for the southern hemisphere and tropical countries. Using electronic mail to form links with Australia, Africa and the Caribbean would not only provide seasonal contrasts but also information about the ways in which lifestyles are influenced by different climates. The links could run alongside information received over a longer time by surface mail. Using electronic mail in this way gives the advantage of immediacy and precise detail compared with the disadvantages of brief, edited descriptions in out-of-date reference books.

# Project HIT

Project HIT (Humanities and Information Technology) was started in 1988 and funded by the National Council for Educational Technology (NCET) to develop the use of IT in history and geography, and is based at the Institute of Education, University of London. There are a number of teaching packs published by Longman which are the outcome of groups of teachers, advisory teachers and teacher trainers working together to develop curriculum ideas and resources. The first packs established the use of databases, word processing, desk top publishing and modelling. The Key Stage 2 project run by the Sheffield HIT group, *Home Sweet Home*, was completely cross-curricular, used all the IT elements and produced questionnaires on homes which could be used in any locality. It also included a plan for a new housing estate, designs for sales brochures and operated an 'estate agency'. Key Stage 1 projects looked at children's understanding of time and sequencing (as important in geography as in history) and local environments and microworlds. Other Key Stage 2 projects examined physical geography in the local environment and transport systems. New HIT projects are looking at recent developments in IT but it is worth exploring material already published.

# Using IT for mapwork

Logo and programmable toys can be used to introduce the concept of direction and thus play an important part in learning about measurement and control.

## Programmable toys

The programmable robot 'Bigtrak' was a very popular floor robot which could follow instructions to move around a floor model or a large-scale map drawing of a maze. It has since been superseded by the Valiant 'Roamer' and Swallow Systems' 'Pip' turtles. Both are based upon a 360 degree circle so that, for example, a right angle turn is given as 90 degrees and the direction is given in terms of compass points. Both can be instructed to move in centimetre steps or larger units, thus allowing exact plans to be drawn on centimetre graph paper. If, for example, you wanted to show the shape and size of the quiet corner using footprints as units, the footprint could be drawn on to a piece of paper, the number of squares taken in its length rounded up or down and the final agreed number used in the instructions to the turtle. This undoubtedly involves mathematical skills but the end result involves graphics which is a part of both information technology and geography.

The turtle is a useful reinforcement for the development of locational vocabulary and for converting that vocabulary into cardinal points. To understand the relationship of north, south, east and west to each other necessitates understanding quarter, half and full turns. One way of doing this is by physically arranging a group of children so that one stands in the middle as the 'turner' and has to follow instructions and give answers, while another four stand at the cardinal points. The class teacher can call the turns such as 'a quarter turn', 'half turn' or 'full circle' and the 'turner' can be asked to say the direction at which he or she arrives. A program can then be written for the turtle based on this work and a group of children can take turns to operate the turtle, finishing at the cardinal point required.

Concepts of plan and scale can also be clarified by programming the turtle to accept actual measurements of the classroom and then drawing the classroom plan to scale. This can be extended to the school and playground plans, 'shrinking' the plan each time. Plans of the locality can be drawn with a screen turtle and Logo can be used to design new estates. Again, this can form a useful overlap with mathematics.

The development of skills in using grid references and compass orientation is often reduced to structured reinforcement. For example, there is commercial software available with straightforward structured programs such as *Maps and Landscapes 1 & 2* and *Micro Map 1 & 2*. *Introducing Mapskills 2* is similar but includes a yacht race game using compass bearings. These are all for the upper juniors. Adventures such as *Dinosaur Discovery*, often give mapping practice, where at the beginning of each quest there is a map. The skills in *Mapventure*, however, are achieved through the vehicle of a hot air balloon flight. Reinforcement takes the form of an adventure but with instructions very similar to those used in orienteering. Moreover, there are many ideas suggested in *Mapventure* which show how mapwork can be part of everyday learning with other topics rather than taken in isolation.

# Software selection

Choosing software for children is very like choosing books for them. Certain questions have to be asked.
- Is it user-friendly?
- Will it complement rather than duplicate other teaching strategies?
- Is it suitable for the level of teaching required?
- Are the illustrations effective?
- Does it teach in a structured way or by problem solving?
- Will it require considerable teacher-input either to incorporate it into a topic or to work with the children while they are using the program?
- Is teacher-input justified by giving the children experience or providing them with data which would be difficult to obtain in any other way?
- Does it meet with the National Curriculum requirements by developing facilities in storing, processing and presenting information and by showing the computer's potential for controlling and modelling?

Figure 7 offers suggestions for meeting the five strands of IT, according to level and geography attainment target. Open-ended software, games/simulations and CD-ROM are considered. Figure 8 overleaf shows where IT can be incorporated into a local enquiry involving out door observation and collection of data. Here simple GIS systems such as *Aegis 2* (see Resources) allow the import of OS maps at different scales to give reality to environmental surveys and other fieldwork and allow accurate mapping and measuring. A special pack for Years 5 and 6 has been produced with ITV *Geography in Place*.

| \multicolumn{6}{c}{SOFTWARE AND APPLICATIONS FOR IT IN GEOGRAPHY} |
|---|---|---|---|---|---|
| Level | Skills | Places | Physical features | Human features | Environment |
| 1 | LOGO Turtles<br>Programmable toys<br>Albert's House<br>Home Mapper | Concept keyboard<br>Touch Explorer Plus<br>Word processors<br>Prompt | Concept keyboard<br>Touch Explorer Plus<br>Datashow | Concept keyboard<br>Touch Explorer Plus<br>Busy Town | Concept keyboard<br>Touch Explorer Plus<br>Paintbox/Spa |
| 2 | LOGO<br>Prompt<br>Granny's Garden<br>Walk | Concept keyboard<br>Picture Builder<br>Touch Explorer Plus | Our Facts<br>Concept keyboard<br>List Explorer<br>Weather Mapper | Concept keyboard<br>The Farm<br>More About Me | Art package<br>Concept keyboard<br>Touch Explorer Plus |
| 3 | Concept keyboard<br>Adventure and simulations<br>LOGO<br>Sheepdog<br>Dinosaur Discovery<br>Mapventure | Databases<br>Datashow<br>Frontpage Extra<br>Desktop publishing<br>Encarta (CD)<br>School | Databases<br>Junior Pinpoint<br>Our Facts<br>Weather Reporter<br>Aegis 2 (GIS) | Simulations<br>Sim City<br>Farming Pack<br>First Facts<br>Distant Places (CD) | Adventure<br>The Forest<br>Front Page Extra<br>Crystal Rainforest<br>Badger Trails |
| 4 | LOGO<br>Maps and Landscapes<br>Cunning Running<br>Map Maker | Campus 2000<br>Pagemaker<br>Sand Harvest<br>Windmill<br>Discover York (CD)<br>Video Atlas | Campus 2000<br>Grasshopper<br>Junior Ecosoft<br>Introducing Geography<br>Water/Excel Landscapes | Campus 2000<br>Grass<br>Urban Settlements<br>The Commonwealth (CD)<br>Global Explorer | Campus 2000<br>Flowers of Crystal<br>The Water Game<br>Suburban Fox<br>Topographer |

Figure 7

# Planning a local enquiry on change supported by IT

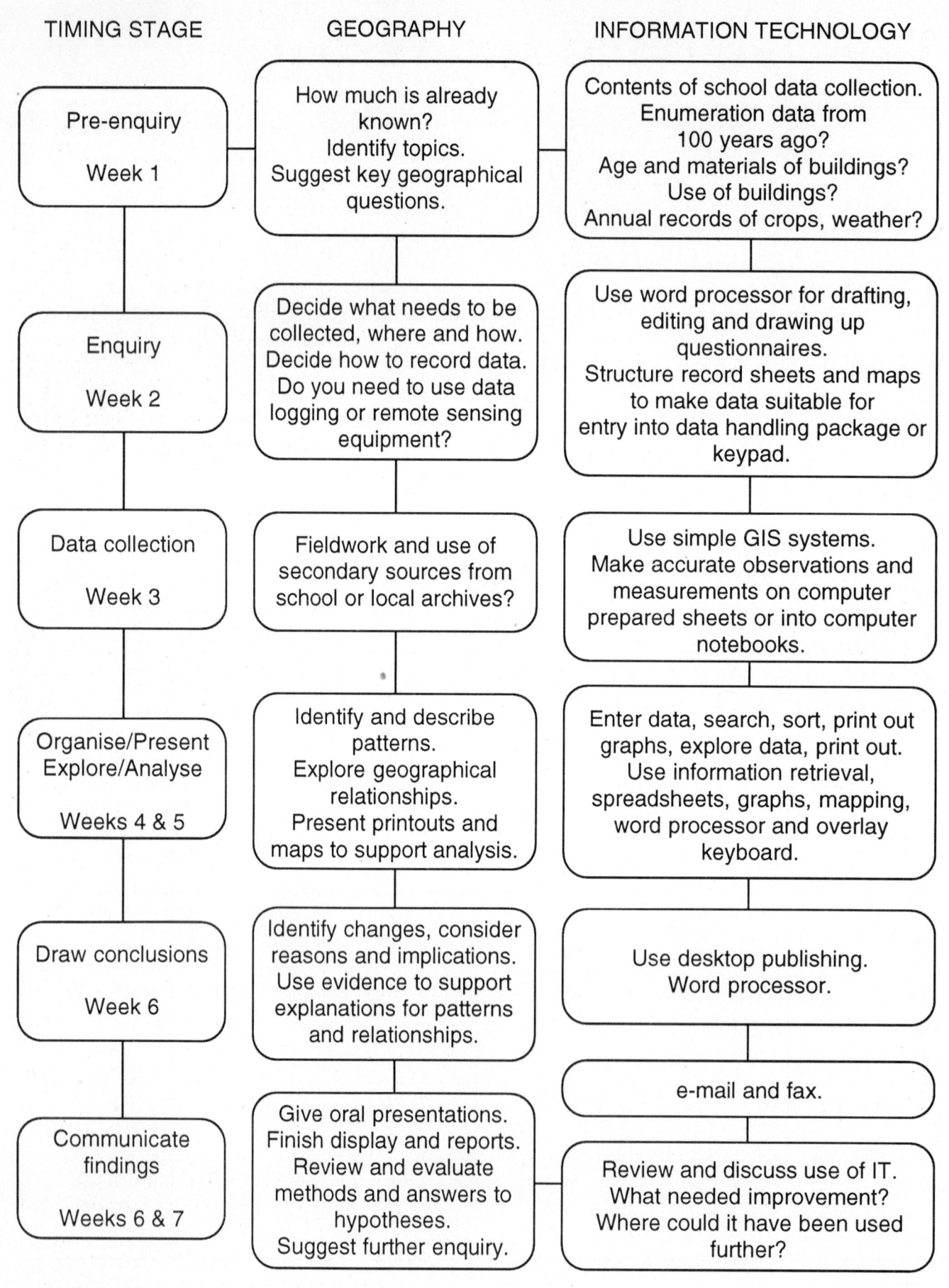

| TIMING STAGE | GEOGRAPHY | INFORMATION TECHNOLOGY |
|---|---|---|
| **Pre-enquiry**<br>Week 1 | How much is already known?<br>Identify topics.<br>Suggest key geographical questions. | Contents of school data collection.<br>Enumeration data from 100 years ago?<br>Age and materials of buildings?<br>Use of buildings?<br>Annual records of crops, weather? |
| **Enquiry**<br>Week 2 | Decide what needs to be collected, where and how.<br>Decide how to record data.<br>Do you need to use data logging or remote sensing equipment? | Use word processor for drafting, editing and drawing up questionnaires.<br>Structure record sheets and maps to make data suitable for entry into data handling package or keypad. |
| **Data collection**<br>Week 3 | Fieldwork and use of secondary sources from school or local archives? | Use simple GIS systems.<br>Make accurate observations and measurements on computer prepared sheets or into computer notebooks. |
| **Organise/Present Explore/Analyse**<br>Weeks 4 & 5 | Identify and describe patterns.<br>Explore geographical relationships.<br>Present printouts and maps to support analysis. | Enter data, search, sort, print out graphs, explore data, print out.<br>Use information retrieval, spreadsheets, graphs, mapping, word processor and overlay keyboard. |
| **Draw conclusions**<br>Week 6 | Identify changes, consider reasons and implications.<br>Use evidence to support explanations for patterns and relationships. | Use desktop publishing.<br>Word processor. |
| **Communicate findings**<br>Weeks 6 & 7 | Give oral presentations.<br>Finish display and reports.<br>Review and evaluate methods and answers to hypotheses.<br>Suggest further enquiry. | e-mail and fax.<br><br>Review and discuss use of IT.<br>What needed improvement?<br>Where could it have been used further? |

Figure 8

# Chapter seven
# The classroom and resources

Many primary children are fortunate in having a permanent base for their activities, rather than having to move between subject-based rooms as do children in later stages of their educational careers. Nonetheless, this does cause difficulties for practical subjects such as science, technology, geography and art. These subjects lend themselves to group work, which in turn requires an open-ended approach to the use of materials and the presentation of work.

## The ideal classroom

The ideal classroom includes the following features.
• A permanent water point (running water is required in many physical modelling situations and a jerry can is not always the best solution).
• An area for projecting pictures and diagrams for analysis work, as well as showing videos and films. Blinds, curtains or screens to reduce the light on the viewing area are essential. If you are going to copy photographs on to acetate, a good strong light for the overhead projector is an asset as it will enable press and brochure photographs to be shown clearly. Slides can be stored on carousel cassettes by topic/theme, thus enabling quick retrieval without losing a particularly useful sequence.
• A computer station complete with storage sections for disks, printer, paper and reminders to the children to make frequent 'saves' of their work, not to leave disks out of their paper sleeves and to handle the computer equipment carefully. Also have available 'help' cards for the particular program in use. The computer station does not have to be fixed – there are stations on

**CLASSROOM LAYOUT**

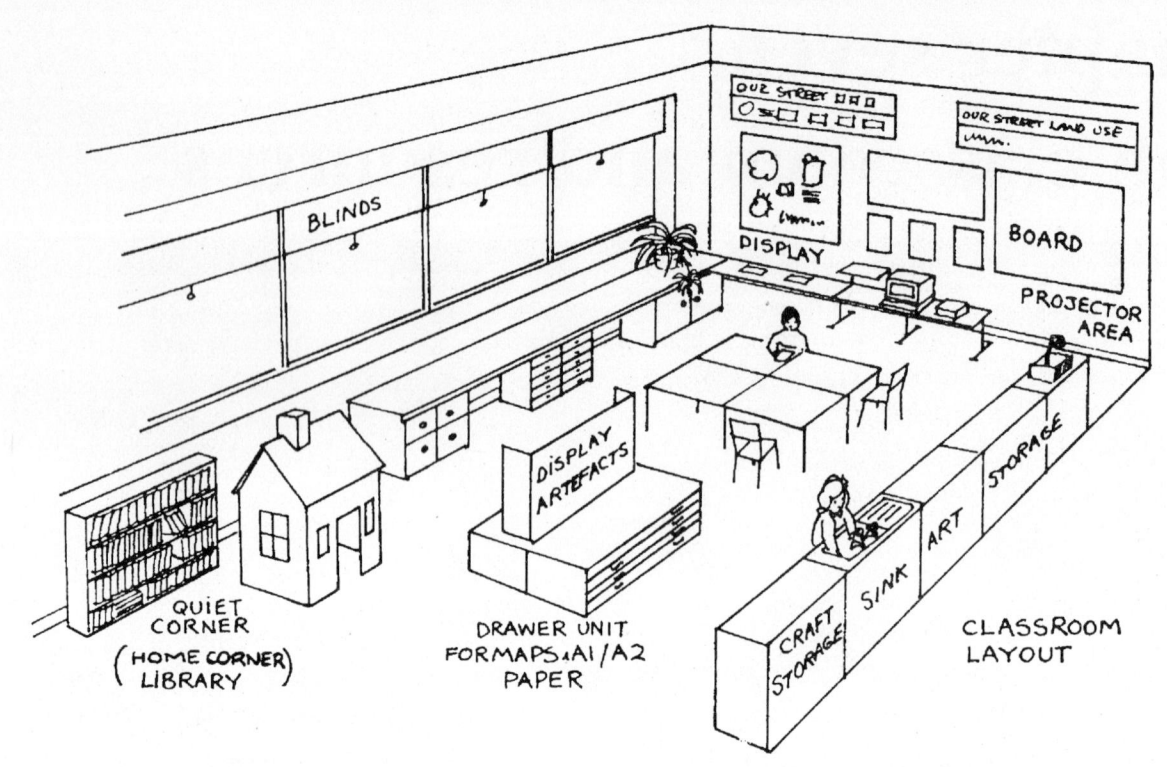

castors or suitable trolleys are also available.
- Flat storage for large maps and plans, no less than A2 size. Vertical plan files which can sit out in the corridor are not suitable as they are not easy for children to use.
- A filing system, which the children will find easy to use, for activity and evaluation sheets, as well as pictures and pamphlet resources. Other useful resources to file away include case studies, census findings, diaries, photocopies of documents, maps of excursion routes, both sketch and Ordnance survey map extracts, cue cards, snap and Pelmanism games for symbol work and vocabulary, flow charts, interview transcripts, jigsaw-puzzle maps, letters from link schools, journey logs, newsletters, newspaper cuttings, excerpts of good geographical description from adult and children's fiction and non-fiction, OHP transparencies, poetry, prints of landscape and domestic paintings, questionnaires, recipes, reports, statistics, stencils, surveys, time-lines, trail guides, work books, children's personal files, spare copies of keypad overlays and instruction sheets for information technology equipment.
- A lockable unit in which to keep back-up disks, spare function key strips, teacher notes, spare tapes, records and so on.

- An area for mounting display work. Remember that an essential part of communication is by visual display. Setting aside an area in which to compile a presentation of graphs, drawings, pictures, maps and word processed text lends efficiency to a piece of research on any topic or theme, whether by a group or an individual. It will confine the inevitable clutter and save you time when putting together displays.
- Display areas wherever possible. At least one display area should be situated above a table in order to link items of interest (soils and vegetation, clothes, toys, food and so on) to a map.
- A collection for map-making. At Key Stage 1, this should include a classroom plan, a basic school plan (obtainable from your LEA) and Ordnance Survey maps (1:1,250 [50"], 1:2,500 [25"], 1:10,000 [6"], 1:25,000 [2½"] and 1:50,000 [1"]). The school area plan or a plan of the area should be enlarged as far as possible (to at least 1:2,500 scale), mounted on plastic or card and covered with clear plastic.

Other useful map-making items at Key Stage 1 would include playmats (obtainable from educational suppliers), farmyard sets, LEGO or other building sets for modelling, sets of toy furniture, jigsaw maps, floormaps of the UK, Europe and the World (also available from educational suppliers) and wall maps of the UK, Europe and the World. It is useful to have blank maps as well as those with reference details and remember that the latter should not be overcrowded or garishly coloured. Also try to include a section of oblique aerial photographs. These can be obtained through Aerofilms, Ordnance Survey, Photoair and the National Remote Sensing Centre Ltd (NRSC) (see Resources, page 206). Other photographs could be obtained from local clubs or libraries.

At Key Stage 2, the map-making collection should also include vertical aerial photographs. NRSC can provide local area vertical photographs on disk for WINDOWS environments. Make a collection of maps from as many different sources as possible (for example, tourist guides, motoring associations, advertisements, posters, postcards, travel agencies, British Rail, bus companies, estate agents and local street plans). Ensure a supply of 2cm and 1cm squared graph paper, tracing paper and water based felt-tipped pens for marking.
- Other map sources should include atlases and globes. Globes should be free-standing, or hanging, either solid or inflatable. Plain globes could be made available for the children to mark on details for themselves (see *Primary Geographer*, No. 11, October 1992).

# Central reference

There are other items of equipment which it may be preferable to keep centrally in the staffroom. These might include the following:
- reference sets of geography book series;
- reference sets of teachers' handbooks;
- reference atlases such as the Reader's Digest or Times atlases;
- national and international timetables for surface, sea and air transport (ask the local reference library for the out-of-date copies);
- project packs;
- anthologies;
- picture sets;
- archives;
- audio tapes;
- case studies;
- cassettes of interviews;
- census returns;
- film, video, software and slide catalogues (commercial and loan services);
- copies of *Primary Geographer* and *Teaching Geography*;
- computer programs and packages;
- recordings;
- role-play packages;
- computer simulations and games;
- slide collections;
- television and radio timetables to help determine a recording routine;
- video collection.

This central organisation allows for collaboration between teachers and discussion on the usefulness of items as they are used. A signing-out system for each collection will enable lists to be generated at the end of the year showing who has used the various items and thus will indicate the previous experience of each class before they start with a new teacher in the autumn. Hopefully, this will cut back on the psychologically depressing comment, 'We've done this, Miss!'

It may also be worth advertising in your local paper or in teaching magazines for old collections of journals such as the *National Geographic* and *Geographical Magazine*. Someone may be looking for a 'good home' for a collection for which they no longer have room.

# Equipment for outdoor measurement

## Rocks and soils

Storage space for bulky collections of rock and soil samples needs careful consideration. Such collections can be displayed, but collections which are to be handled benefit from small-scale storage. For example, hand-sized specimens will just fit into the thin drawers for the storage of A4 handouts or multi-tray letter racks or a stack of tomato trays. Labels can be securely stuck on to rock samples with nail varnish. To do this, an impermeable base of successive layers of clear nail varnish should be built up on the most porous rocks, before finally varnishing over a label giving the geological name, rock type and, if possible, the site of collection (complete with grid reference!). Schools in urban areas may have to rely upon building up a collection gathered from waste material from the local stonemason, decorative stone merchant or supplier to landscape gardeners. Some commercial firms supply decent-sized examples of the most common rocks (see Resources, page 206). Wherever you collect, be sure to collect hand-sized specimens – nothing is learned by squinting at a small nugget.

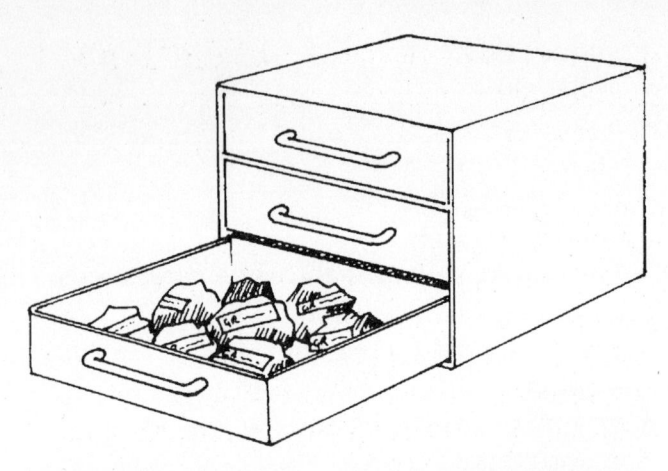

Lots of newspapers will be needed to protect surfaces when dealing with anything connected with the earth. Keep a heavy hammer and tools for scratching, such as a file, coins, oval nail and tiles of unglazed white pottery (streak plates) with the pile of newspapers. Grain size can be investigated initially with a series of domestic sieves (for example a fine tea strainer, a standard flour sieve and a coarse vegetable sieve).

Used with dividers and rulers in lieu of callipers, this will facilitate sediment analysis to look for evidence of erosion, transport and deposition. Jam or coffee jars make good settling jars – again, aim for uniformity of container to make calibration easy.

Although the precise study of rocks and soils has moved to science, the results of this study only has meaning when considering the geographical effect upon landscape – for example, 'Why is this hill here? Why are there heaths and open spaces here?' (often because of sandstones and gravels). Vegetation on limestone is very different from that on sands and clays – a contrast often found between localities, for example, Mendips, Peak District (limestone) Thetford Chase (sands).

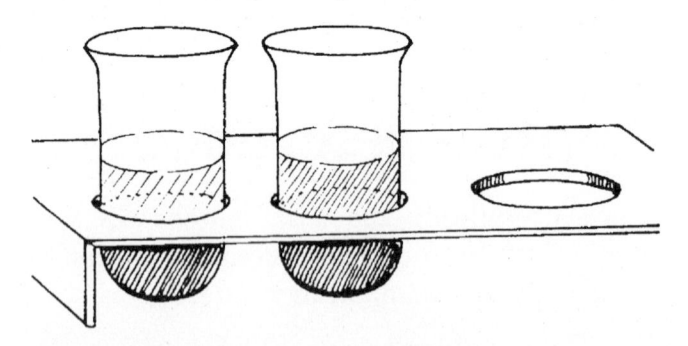

## Weather recording

Weather equipment for regular, detailed measurement can be expensive. Young observers need to be able to see for themselves the amount of rain that has fallen. In order to collect enough rain for a record, stick a wide funnel firmly in a jar, or cut off the top of a flat-bottomed plastic drinks bottle and wedge it upside down into the body of the bottle. This can be made readable by decanting the contents into a tall narrow bottle such as a milk bottle. Using an identical bottle each day and adding some food colouring makes a quickly calibrated and easily read record. Once the rain water has been collected, keep the bottles together. At the same time, catch rain in a wide shallow container with a ruler stuck inside to indicate how much water disappears by evaporation. Provide a greenhouse thermometer and ask the children to observe temperatures over a period of time, noting the maximum and minimum readings. All this will give plenty of data to use with comparative vocabulary. Similarly, simple equipment can be made for wind speed and direction measurement (Figure 1).

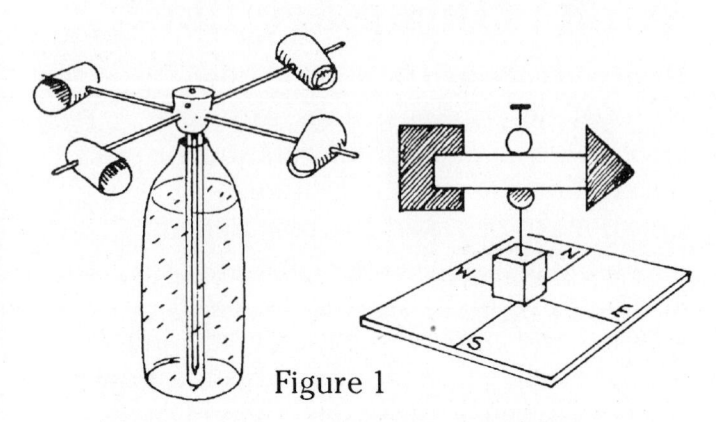

Figure 1

Older children can use IT to ensure that the equipment is more scientifically calibrated. Supply catalogues will be useful sources of information in this area and it is worth looking at several to find which pieces of equipment seem the most efficient. This makes for accurate records which, over the years, can be sampled with confidence. For example, using ventimeters (direct reading wind gauges) in a variety of locations and comparing results can reveal the importance of microclimates, which in turn can lay the foundation for understanding climates at a higher level.

## Slope

Understanding slope and what happens to the water once it reaches the ground helps children to recognise the variations in transport and erosion on beaches, river beds and slopes. Recording such variations requires the use of tapes, ranging poles and clinometers. Only one measuring tape need be purchased to enable you to mark a plastic clothesline into 0.5m lengths. Masking tape numbered using waterproof ink can be used to mark the divisions. 2m lengths of garden cane can be simlarly marked off in 0.5m divisions, then painted in bands of black, white and red like surveying poles. Gradient guns can be purchased, but the same principle can be achieved with a protractor and weighted fuse wire, fixed to a piece of plywood with thin screws (Figure 2). The only other equipment necessary are metre rules, which give fine divisions of measurement where needed, and quadrants of one metre squared which can be constructed out of wire coat hangers, untwisted then joined together and bent into a square shape.

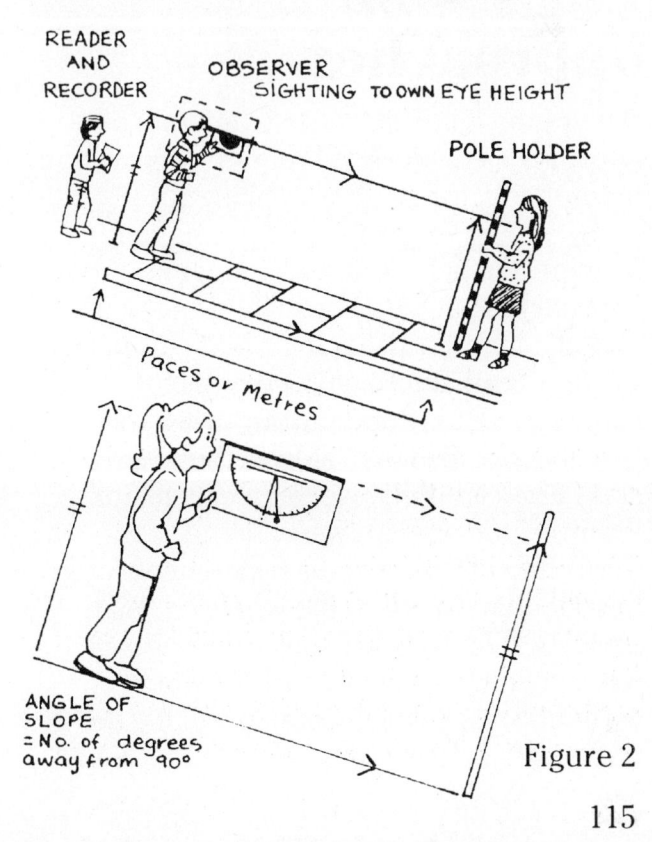

Figure 2

# Models and modelling needs

In the early years, junk materials will usually satisfy all modelling needs. However, once the children begin to investigate the use of sand, rock and water to show the different hill and valley shapes, modelling activities will require something more substantial than newspaper to protect the table top. It is worth investing in the large gravel trays used by gardeners; a large square tray accommodates enough sand to model eroding a hillside with a toy watering can or spray bottle. Longer narrow trays are useful for resting plastic gutters on when demonstrating the way water works in a channel. With both activities, a bucket is required to catch the overflow. Measuring beakers can be used for making fair tests on the speed of flow through or over different soils and vegetation cover. Lengths of hose are ideal for use with the rain gutter channel and for doing irrigation experiments in the school garden or for modelling the wearing down of a hill into a plain and for making a river basin with tributaries, mouth and delta.

# Classroom approaches

Geography lends itself to the full range of approaches to work. All require preparation beforehand, for example making sure activity and record sheets are clear and provide correct vocabulary. A whole-class approach is often needed when an open-ended computer program is being used for the first time. Routine procedures for starting, finishing and putting away are usually best demonstrated to the whole class first. Similarly, when looking at, for example, the work of water in the environment, the various experiments are best demonstrated to the whole or half the class as the pupils will have quite enough work making systematic observations without being instrumental in making the water move slowly or quickly. In this case, the teacher will literally be the facilitator. The follow-up work to the demonstration could be a pupil-led discussion, with further work on photographs undertaken on an individual basis.

However, whether the topic or theme is covered by groups rotating, so that all complete the same activity and practise the same skills, or as individuals following programmes of work using a prescribed, structured content, the same five questions must be asked to promote good geographical teaching.

- What is this place like?
- Where is this place?
- Why is this place as it is?
- How is this place changing?
- What would it feel like to be a person living in this locality or environment?

These questions were first put forward by Michael Storm in 'Geographical work in Primary and Middle School' (1988) and have been repeated since more recently in *Primary Geographer* (Autumn 1989). Subsequently, they have been taken as a general guide to promoting progress in geographical teaching and learning.

# What is this place like?

Have you collected together enough pictures, descriptions, maps, artefacts, slides, videos, weather information, product descriptions, music and art to enable questions to be asked and researched? Could the children set up a 'travel agency' to give information to the 'clients' about weather and climate, vegetation and animal life, landscape, lowlands and uplands, how the people live, eat, work and play? Could this be researched by individuals as well as groups? Could the information be presented from the material verbally and graphically as well as orally?

# Where is this place?

Are there enough maps and atlases, as well as a globe, which show not just the layout of the place but also the relationship of the chosen place to others. How far is it to the nearest big town, city, the capital, the coast, the mountains and hills? How can messages be transmitted there? (For example, it is no good using electronic mail if the country has no satellite connections and the telephone network is merely skeletal.) How long would it take to reach the place by road, rail, air and sea? These questions apply whether you are considering a distant place or the home locality. There should be local transport timetables in the class collection and the international ones in the central reference collection.

The programmes of study for Key Stages 1 and 2 imply that any classroom map collection should have a suite of Ordnance Survey maps for the locality, together with an atlas detailed enough to show places frequently in the news, both at home and abroad. In addition, you should have an Ordnance Survey map of any areas visited by the school. The central reference collection should include maps of at least two other contrasting localities, for example an urban area and a rural area or a lowland area and an upland area. A suite of maps is taken to mean at least one plan (1:2,500 or 1:10,000), one medium scale map (1:25,000 or 1:50,000) and one small scale map (1:100,000).

The Ordnance Survey also publish a Worldmaps series which comprises maps at varying scales covering, at the moment Barbados, Mount Kenya, Kilimanjaro, Praslin and Mahe in the Seychelles, the Cayman Islands, Ambergris Cay in Belize, the British Virgin Islands, St Vincent and Dominica. They include information on local history, produce, population and climate as well as the addresses of the Tourist Information Offices.

It should be noted that the places marked on the maps, A, B and C of the National Curriculum document are the minimum requirement. Both Key Stage 1 and Key Stage 2 children can study a locality 'overseas' either as a place or as part of a thematic study, and European maps are reasonably accessible. For example, you might choose the Grampians as a contrasting locality in the UK with its variety of landforms, water (rivers, snow, ice) and the impact of leisure and work activities. However, similar localities are to be found in the Alps. Both France and Italy (see map B of the National Curriculum document) have ski resorts. The French have most informative 1:50,000 maps, available from the National Map Centre (see Resources, page 206). The Himalayas could provide another suitable locality and information could be obtained from travel agencies catering for the specialist adventure holidays in Nepal.

Again, when comparing types of farm in Britain, ask whether any of the children have been on holiday to stay in a *gîte* in France. This could provide a focus for comparing the similar farms of Normandy and Brittany with those of southern England. Indeed, transport costs are such that it may be cheaper for some schools to cross the Channel for fieldwork in a contrasting locality than to move northwards.

## Why is this place as it is?

Answering this question will involve consideration of all the features which go to give a place its character. During the process of discussion and comparison with known places, similarities and differences will become apparent. A hilly place needs to be understood by first exploring slope in the home locality and in a modelling situation where the relationship between hard and soft rocks and scenery can be demonstrated. The modelling situation is especially important if the home locality is in lowland Britain. Again, reference has to be made to thematic maps, for example relief, rainfall, temperature, vegetation, population and geology. These maps are to be found in atlases, usually at a very small scale. Transferring this information to larger blank outlines is all part of map-making and developing skills in graphicacy. Photocopiable pages 191 to 193 provide blank outlines similar to those in the National Curriculum document. These can be used on an overlay keyboard linked to a word processor to help children make reasoned explanations, for example as to why a place is wet, hot and full of vegetation but with few people.

## How is this place changing?

This question involves research, whether looking at a redevelopment scheme down the high street, studying photographs showing the way new homes are being built in Nigeria, looking at old maps of the school area to see where the changes are taking place or comparing press photographs of the drought areas in Zambia with standard textbook photographs of dry grasslands.

Keep a 'window open to the world' through the local free press, the daily papers and the educational media. Good newspapers will give the previous day's weather and the next day's forecast, so a run of days can be collected at the end of each week to compare with the readings taken that week at school. The task of culling the weather news can be given to the children who are recording the weather at school. Other areas of news can perhaps be shared out, provided a steady supply of reportage is brought into school, including information by travel writers, foreign correspondents and home affairs correspondents.

## What would it feel like to be a person living in this locality or environment?

This question is the culmination of all the work previously undertaken in answering the earlier questions. If a link with another school has been established, the children can be set a series of assignments which involve putting themselves in the place of their counterparts and writing letters to the class. A newspaper account can be compiled with the aid of a desktop publishing package using pictures, maps, graphs and text culled from reference books, picture packs and media information. A gallery of pictures depicting different environments can be made, drawn from descriptive accounts, poetry and fiction. Role-play activities can be devised with the dialogue based on case study material, for example concerning transporting bananas from the plantation to the table. Posters and canvassing leaflets supporting local, national or international environmental issues, can also be designed.

Resourcing all these activities efficiently will depend upon supplying not only the maps and statistical information but also the human detail. In order to ensure that everyone has a chance to use and digest what will, over the time, become a rich database, the work will inevitably rely very much upon a topic approach, whether for area (for example, in the Caribbean) or theme (for example, dry grasslands). A whole-class 'talk and chalk' approach could not make use of a fifth of the materials required for a thorough study of place. By working individually or in pairs, in friendship groups or in structured activities, practice is being given which will reinforce core subject skills within a geographical context. Understanding is also the aim of the individual and, where this proves difficult, there is more chance that the teacher will be able to sit down and work the material into a more suitable form, whether by reinforcing jargon words, increasing comprehension by simplified cloze work or devising direct questions on implied information.

## Human activity and the environment

One of the most difficult areas to resource geographically is the area of human activity and its relationship with the environment. Yet in many ways this can be the most accessible resource. The geographer is interested in the concept of distance and the time taken to cover that distance, for example the journey to work. Within the school there is already a potential database, using information about the children's teachers' and ancillary staff's journeys to school. Information should be collected by devising a questionnaire suitable for database processing. The questionnaire could be adapted in order to collect information from classes in adjacent secondary schools and further education colleges. Meanwhile the routes to school taken by children and staff could be plotted on to the local base map. As the catchment area increases with each higher stage, so the regional map will come into use. Unusual routes, or routes which seem to take rather a long time to cover, will start to emerge, in which case you could ask someone to talk about the difficulties of their journey to find out something of transport problems. Once the project has begun to be extended to other schools and colleges, it could be useful to arrange for the local bus depot manager to make a visit to explain the difficulties he faces both in accommodating the community needs and taking into account the restrictions imposed by the environment and settlement layout. The project could be extended to the local business community through considering parents' journeys to work, to the shopping community through research into free transport services, to the welfare community via the ambulance service and by arranging a visit from the planners department. The possibilities are almost limitless and certainly worthy of considering as a school rather than a class investigation. Business contacts, sponsorship and professional bodies can all be used by the teacher of geography to form links with the community through visits by the children and guest speakers visiting school. Closer contacts can be established through the Schools Curriculum Industry Partnership/Mini-enterprise in Schools Projects and work placements in local enterprises are arranged for teachers by the Teacher Placement Service (see Resources, page 206) so that they can have some element of industrial or business experience. There is evidence that through these contacts the associated schools benefited from the closer links with the business community.

Similarly, the multicultural school has a valuable source of support materials for learning about clothes, food and climate in different countries. Parents, or those children who still have strong links with relatives in the home country, can add to geographical and historical knowledge, bringing in artefacts, sharing musical traditions and providing links with a school or schools overseas. Those children who have visited relatives in the home country are usually happy to share their experience. Adult members of the community sometimes need sensitive encouragement before they perceive that what they think of as ordinary is of extraordinary value to helping other people understand their country. One such account, given reluctantly, gave the precious insight, 'It is sad to think that the rural child, because of the need for every bit of land to be used for growing food, has even fewer places to play than the urban child' – the place being described was the northern part of the Ganges Delta in Bangladesh.

Ideally, resourcing schemes should be in place for the whole year to allow progression and continuity to be catered for in a relaxed fashion. However, common sense and experience suggests that this is not really possible nor, in many cases, desirable. However, if there has been a whole-school policy worked out for topics and outdoor work it should be possible to plan other resources around this framework.

This kind of organisation allows for forward planning and for tentative arrangements to be made with visitors from the community, who have their own commitments around which to work. It also allows for decisions to be made about hiring or buying audio-visual aids and for buying additional resources.

In the course of this preparation, the geography co-ordinator should have provided support with sample schemes, have collected together those resources already held by the school which are particularly useful for geography (and which may have lain unused in the back of a cupboard), discovered the gaps in resources and kept abreast of the new material being produced for Key Stage 1 and later for Key Stage 2. She or he will have provided support and guidance for background knowledge, such as mapwork and information technology, and above all, will have provided a curriculum plan and guidelines to be considered in INSET time. Other INSET considerations will include evaluation, assessment and means of recording in line with that already in place for other subjects. This will involve linking with other coordinators and advisory teachers to ensure that the Key Stage 2 children arrive at the secondary or middle schools with complementary skills and knowledge which will enhance, rather than be repeated, at Key Stage 3.

# Chapter eight
# Recording and assessing

## National Curriculum requirements

Although there is to be no formal assessment of geography at Key Stage 1, nonetheless anxious parents always like to be satisfied that their children are achieving in all areas. Furthermore, for the sake of good practice, each class teacher should know how much learning has taken place, in order to provide more realistic teaching tailored to the children's needs, while their next teacher needs to know the stages of progression which have been achieved, before embarking upon a new topic or further developing a skill. The National Curriculum Council's *Geography Non-Statutory Guidance* (1991) regards obtaining evidence of pupils' attainment as 'an integral part of teaching' because it allows a teacher to meet the following criteria.
• 'Identify what has been learnt.' The statements of attainment, with the non-statutory examples printed alongside, are meant to clarify the sort of evidence which will help with such identification.
• 'Monitor pupils' progress in each attainment target.' The evidence of attainment given alongside each statement, for each level in the non-statutory guidance, is meant to define the progress possible.
• 'Monitor pupils' progress in cross-curricular elements.'

- 'Diagnose and identify ways of overcoming particular learning difficulties.'

The collection of evidence upon which informed judgements can be made for determining a child's individual achievement can take several forms. It can be done through:
- observing children at work (for example, talking to each other when involved in developing an investigation. Are they able to describe or explain a situation, give information or instructions and justify a decision in a clear manner?);
- questioning and listening to pupils (for example, when working on a mapping exercise on the computer. Can the children explain why they have followed a particular strategy in order to solve a problem?);
- assessing written work, which could range from a simple record of observations laid out on a prepared form to a detailed description of a photograph or a place visited;
- testing, which could range from a fun quiz at the end of a week to serious tests with inbuilt difficulties to sort out the levels in a mixed ability class.

The guidelines also suggest involving children in assessing their own work as a useful way for them to find out their own strengths and needs.

# Formative assessment

Assessment evaluates both formatively and diagnostically. A sketch map for which a description has to be written can be used to see how far understanding of the use of symbols and scale has been achieved. This in turn will determine the next stage in the learning programme, will aid the setting of goals for individuals and will give overall feedback. When taken at several points, such assessment helps monitor achievement on a continuous basis, enabling the children to be involved in their own progress and generally helping the teaching/learning process.

# Summative assessment

Assessment can also summarise the achievements of a whole class at the end of a project which has involved different skills and concepts, and in so doing has covered a large body of knowledge, for example studying a locality in the developing world. Although the activities may have been regularly evaluated, the whole project also needs an overview. Do the class really know which are the major settlements? Try a map completion exercise. What are the stages of production of an important crop? What is the sequence of a farming year? Let the children put cartoon diagrams in order. Ask them to write an imaginary letter from a schoolchild in the area being studied, telling of a special event (unspecified so that the significance of cultural differences and similarities can be tested), together with associated details about the weather and physical features. Alongside this could be used more straightforward tests, such as matching statements or completing sentences.

Great care should be taken in the actual formulation of assessments. There is already within the school body a great deal of expertise on assessment which can be immediately applied to the newly structured courses. The general techniques already used to assess skills, concepts and knowledge in the core subjects are equally applicable to the foundation subjects. Geography involves skills common to both the sciences and the arts. Geography has one attainment target which sets the range of standards in pupils' performance in eight level descriptions. Key Stage 1 expects the range to be up to Level 3. Key Stage 2 ranges between Level 2 and Level 5. Teachers are required to make their own judgement as to which description best fits the pupils' performance. They are expected to consider the descriptions in conjunction with the descriptions for adjacent levels. This presumes that formative assessment is available to provide evidence for progression between the levels. The levels themselves are described in a systematic order which agrees with the order of statements in the programmes of study. In *Geography in the National Curriculum* (1991) the Curriculum Council for Wales, provided some helpful guidelines for appreciating the different kinds of attainment.

## Generic attainment

Generic attainment covers those skills which are used in many geographical activities. For example, coordinates and grid references (KS2, PoS, 3d) can be used to locate features in the classroom, to 'find the buried treasure' on a computer-generated map, to build a route on an imaginary map or indicate a route round a plan of the school grounds which has been given a letter/number grid. Similarly, at Key Stage 1, pupils should use secondary sources to obtain geographical information (PoS, 3f). This can be pictures, photographs including aerial photographs, books, videos, CD-ROM and can be related to the immediate locality, a locality elsewhere in the UK or overseas. The difference in attainment is that, at Level 1, children use the resource provided and respond to questions. At Level 2, they select information from the resources and use it to ask, as well as respond to, questions about the places. At Level 3, they use 'sources of evidence to respond to a range of geographical questions'. So, by Level 3, children can be expected to go away, select and bring back appropriate evidence, be it from information books, CD-ROM or holiday mementoes, to answer questions about the different features within a locality.

## Specific attainment

Some statements in the programme of study require a specific task to be set in order to test understanding. For example at KS1 3e it is expected that they should be able to name the countries of the United Kingdom. This knowledge could well have already been reinforced through model-making, route-planning and quizzes in the course of formative assessment. However, their very nature also requires a formal test. This need not always be a question-and-answer test. For example, one of the first essentials with Reception and Year 1 children is to ensure that they know their own address, what an address means and how to find the place of that address on a local map. The level of attainment can be sorted by the scale of map used: Level 1 – a local, large scale plan; Level 2 – an Ordnance Survey map where only the town area is named; Level 3 – using Map A to mark the approximate place of the home town in the country in which they live.

## Progressive attainment

Some statements in the programme of study permit open-ended assessment exercises which allow progression to be revealed. This kind of exercise will already be familiar to those teaching mixed ability classes, culturally mixed classes where poor literacy clouds comprehension and classes of vertical age grouping.

At Key Stage 1, the programme of study requires, under 'Places', that pupils should be taught:

• **'about the effects of weather on people and their surroundings'** (5c). A Level 1 child will be able to **'recognise and make observations'** about the kinds of clothes people wear for wet and dry weather, hot and cold conditions. At Level 2, children can describe the weather characteristics of places, including seasonal changes and differences between seasons in places beyond their locality. By Level 3, simple measurements of rain, temperature and wind enable descriptive comparisons to be made between different localities. In addition, pupils notice that different places have

similar weather features but the rain, wind and temperature have different characteristics. Through these levels the children's vocabulary is becoming more precise and descriptive.
• This leads into the more precise Key Stage 2 thematic work on 'Weather' (8) where studies show **'how weather varies between places and over time'** and reveals **'seasonal weather patterns'** (8b) such as the monsoon season (rather than wet season), the tropical storm season when hurricanes and typhoons are expected and the variations in snowfall between north and south, hill and lowland in a UK winter. Using instruments to make regular precise measures of rain, temperature and wind (KS2, 3b) provides evidence is comparable to daily newspaper and weather data. This enables studies **'about weather conditions in different parts of the world'** including weather extremes (8c). Measurement also shows **'how site conditions can influence the weather'** (8a) and provides evidence to support the following Level 4 criteria:
• **'show their knowledge, understanding and skills ... at more than one scale'**;
• **'describe geographical patterns'**;
• **'appreciate the importance of location'**;
• **'Use a range of geographical skills... and evidence to investigate places and themes'**;
• **'communicate their findings using appropriate vocabulary'**.

While the Level 5 children: 'begin to offer explanations...'.

The study of human features in localities can be viewed progressively by combining the requirements of the programmes of study. The infants **'undertake field work activities in the locality of the school, e.g., observing house types.'** (3b) and study **'how land and buildings... are used'** (5d) and **'become aware... that the places they study exist within [a] broader geographical context, e.g., ...a town'** (1c).

This prepares them for studying differences between settlements (KS2, 9):
• **'that settlements... vary in size and that their characteristics... reflect [different] types of economic activity'** (9a) and
• **'how land in settlements is used in different ways...'** (9b).

The test for attainment can take different styles for each level. Level 1 could be tested by picture recognition of houses and buildings. Level 2 could involve sorting photographs, models or cartoon pictures of places of different size (village, town, city). Level 3 could involve sorting photographs which show character (fishing, seaside resort, market town, industrial town) or making a pictorial/sketch map showing different land uses on the route to school, demonstrating at the same time degrees of skill in mapping (KS2, 3c) on entry into Year 3. The skills, knowledge and understanding required by Level 4 can be tested by comparing aerial photographs and the relevant OS map using grid references, symbols and route descriptions, while those children aspiring to Level 5 would be adding explanations to their descriptions.

## Performance attainments

Performance attainments should not be confused with specific attainments (page 123) which, on the whole, only add to knowledge and give a clue as to the minimum knowledge to be expected at each level. Performance attainments are a declaration that the child has not only reached that level but has also reached a particular stage of maturation which may or may not be coincident with the attainment level. The latter gives some idea of the average stage at which that performance can be reached. For example, both maths and geography follow the same progression in developing a measuring skill – Level 1 comparable vocabulary and Level 2 non-standard measures (for example paces, handspans). However, the National Curriculum for geography allows time for the development of familiarity with maps before requiring specific map measurement. Performance attainment is not always specified in geography, although it is specifically laid down in the programme of study and coincides with statements of attainment in mathematics. The clearest example is that of compass direction. At Key Stage 1, 3c, geography expects children **'to follow directions... north, south, east, west'** while for Mathematics, Shape, Space and Measures (3a), they should understand **'movements in a straight line and of quarter-turns, half-turns, and recognise right angles'** (3b).

At Key Stage 2, both subjects agree again. Geographical work should **'include using coordinates and four-figure references, measuring direction and distance...'** (PoS, 3d). For mathematics, Shape Space and Measures (3), children should understand and use properties of position and movement. At 3b, they should **'use coordinates to specify location, e.g., map references...'** and at 3c **'use right angles, fractions of a turn and later, degrees, to measure rotation, and use the associated language'**. This clearly means understanding what is meant by the eight, then 16 points of the compass.

If you have a large number of Cubs and Brownies in your class you will recognise that the extra practice that these children have in giving and receiving directions puts them at specific performance levels sooner than their peers. This underlines the importance of practice and familiarity.

# Evidence of attainment

The attainment levels require teachers to decide their own criteria for determining if understanding has been achieved. They result from enquiry into a specific area and need a body of knowledge to support a concept. In physical geography, such an enquiry is needed to satisfy KS2, PoS, 7b **'how rivers erode, transport and deposit materials...'**. The evidence may come from river studies, or a day at the beach, or repeated observations of a steep bare slope, such as an old rockery, a scree slope, a disused tip now partially vegetated or just pathways up and down a favourite viewpoint. These studies involve different scales of observation according to the ability of the children as well as the nature of the work undertaken. They can only be tested with allowance for the degree of observation possible during the enquiry.

The localities beyond the home area all require evidence since the scale of comparison will depend upon the variety and depth of information available. The development of economic awareness will be influenced by the amount of help forthcoming from the local community as well as the state of the economy.

The key words in the level criteria are **'show their knowledge, understanding and skills... at more than one scale'**; **'begin to describe... patterns'**; **'recognise... processes'** i.e. children should recognise that building houses on 'spare ground' means a loss of playing space or that a bypass not only brings peace but loss of revenue. This is covered by the criterion: **'begin to show understanding of how these processes can change the features of places'**.

# Other considerations

Having selected the items of attainment which will be tested at a particular point, there are other features to be considered.

- Is the test you have in mind suitable? Will oral questioning really show how much has been observed on the way from school to home or is this tantamount to prompting? If a child finds it difficult to make an accurate freehand drawing because of poor coordination, would the use of information technology, such as *PaintSpa: Colour Painting Program*, help to gain the required evidence of observation?
- Is the assessment manageable, both from the viewpoint of materials and time? Using a photograph to test the children's ability to identify features requires multiple copies. Time has to be set aside to find an acceptable way of doing this (although once done, these sets of photographs will provide a constant for successive tests in later years). Similarly, the same area needs to be used for each child when assessing their skills in mapwork. Here the Ordnance Survey project maps and map extracts are a useful and cheap means of building up a bank of comparable data tests on different features and areas.

These two points do not mean that the only safe test is a pencil and paper test. Examination boards have decades of experience of providing a variety of tests, many of them graphic, many of them used in a cross-curricular fashion. For example, written responses can be open or closed, short or long. They can require one word or several sentences, they can use given language or they can depend entirely upon originality.

Construction and interpretation of maps, diagrams and graphs of all kinds can also be used for tests. Maps can require completion, or can be used as a basis for written work. Analysis of maps or diagrams can be part of a tiered sequence of examination leading to further exercises, such as deciding what is shown by a graph of people's leisure preferences and then applying this knowledge to designing a leisure park. Key Stage 1 children would look at swings, slides, roundabouts and so on, while Key Stage 2 children would set their sights somewhat higher at team sports, adventure activities and so on.

There are many more opportunities within the school for a variety of types of assessment which will remain viable across whole years. Certain structured map programmes (see Chapter six, 'Information technology') lend themselves to using IT for testing. The concept keyboard can be used for its original purpose of testing understanding in non-literate children or merely be used as a pleasant way of linking location to vocabulary.

Where tape recorders are used regularly, oral questioning and activities such as role-play can be recorded and used to check understanding, especially at the end of a long enquiry, as a means of pulling many diverse elements together. This is also a useful way of determining which children have taken the lead and responsibility in group work, which need not necessarily be the same person for each kind of work.

| Year | Age | ASSESSMENT CHECK GRID | | | | | | | | | Key Stage | |
|---|---|---|---|---|---|---|---|---|---|---|---|---|
| Assessment evidence / Topic | ORAL Talking Interviews Questions Discussion | PRACTICAL Models Replicas Collections | GRAPHIC Maps Drawings Diagrams Graphs | NOTES Diaries Research Captions | REPORTS Descriptions Stories | ROLE-PLAY & SIMULATIONS | VIDEO/ AUDIO PRESENTATIONS ASSEMBLIES | TESTS Factual recall | OBSERVATION Fieldwork Classwork | PHOTOS Location Analysis | IT Printouts Problem-solving | |
| | | | | | | | | | | | | |
| | | | | | | | | | | | | |
| | | | | | | | | | | | | |

Figure 1

Fieldwork can also be an area for assessment. Standard record forms facilitate entry of information into data banks but also allow evaluation of competence in dealing with the forms, understanding vocabulary and the subsequent use of the data to make descriptions and analyses of specific features.

## When should we assess?

When the assessment takes place is also of significance. Assessment undertaken at the beginning of a period of study informs the content of the subsequent work, the skills to be reinforced, the knowledge to be added to, the concepts to be extended or built upon. It can take the form of a progress test, to show both pupil and teacher where more effort needs to be applied when a study is in mid-course. At this stage, assessment can also be used to determine the best course of action where there is more than one possible end product, such as either producing a series of maps or making a more ambitious teaching pack for use with a younger age group. The end result could also be used for assessment purposes if the interim assessment did not give sufficient information for immediate records. Figure 1 shows the range of evidence possible. Assessing at different stages, whether final or interim, not only provides useful information for the teacher but also allows pupils to be involved and gain understanding of what is required of them and how improvement can be achieved. However, assessment needs to be considered at the planning stage. Photocopiable page 194 gives help in planning for assessment.

# Assessment and the learning process

There are two areas of assessment which are particular to the study of geography, the use of maps and the use of a geographical vocabulary.

# The use of maps

In Chapter seven of *Educational Assessment of the Primary Child* (1990), Blyth neatly summarises the research undertaken regarding the ways in which children make and interpret maps. He points out that:

'The ways in which children make and interpret maps – an issue on the borderline between geography and psychology because cognitive mapping is involved – has been extensively studied and is well summarised by Catling (1979) ['Maps and cognitive maps: the young child's perception', *Geography* 64,4 pp 288–94] and more generally by Bale (1987) [*Geographical Work in Primary Schools*, Routledge and Kegan Paul]. Most teachers evolve procedures of their own for the assessment of map-making and map reading skills and local groups of schools have developed linked policies, sometimes using guidelines such as those suggested by Catling (1980) in 'For the junior and middle school: map use and objectives for map learning' *Teaching Geography* 5, pp 15–17. As it happens, map skills have been central to studies of spatial perception and understanding, so that this is one aspect of humanities in which standardised testing has been developed, for example in the Richmond Tests of Basic Skills (France and Fraser, 1975) and the Bristol Achievement Tests (Brimer, 1969), both of which qualify for consideration in one of the standard test reviews (Levy and Goldstein, 1986). However, standardisation is necessarily bought at the expense of open-endedness... [and it may be preferred] to adopt instead the kinds of qualitative, intersubjective judgements developed for example by the APU (1982) [Assessment of Performance Unit *Language Performance on Schools 1982: Primary Survey report*, NFER Nelson] in some of its work on written and oral language.'

Catling, in *Outset Geography* and the series *Mapstart*, Renwick and Pick in *Going Places*, the Harrisons in *Into Geography* and subsequent series, such as *Starting Geography* (Scholastic), have all adopted the course of integrating map work with topic work. The emphasis has been to develop the

## THE DEVELOPMENT OF MAP SKILLS

Sequence – read across first, then down

| Level | Using, Reading, Interpreting | Position and orientation | Drawing | Symbols | Perspective (viewpoint) | Scale | Map purpose and style |
|---|---|---|---|---|---|---|---|
| 1 | Talk about own picture maps. Identify local features on aerial photograph. * | Point to places can see. Follow directions - up, down, left, right. * Match pictures on grid. | Draw picture maps with labels of places they know, imagine or from stories. * | Use own symbols. Recognise plan shapes, e.g. feet can be symbols. * | Use models to get different viewpoints. Draw round objects 1:1 to get plan view. | Recognise and name things bigger, smaller, longer, shorter, like, unlike. | Take from and add information to picture maps in story and atlas. Use globes and match with wall maps and pictures. |
| 2 | Follow a route on prepared maps and find information. Find information from aerial photograph. Begin explaining why and how. * | Introduce four cardinal points. Point and draw arrow maps in classroom. Develop locational vocabulary. Introduce simple grids. * | Make a representation of a real or imaginary place. Freehand maps of gardens, watery places, route maps, places in stories. * | Use own and class agreed symbols on maps. Practise plan views to use. Realise need for key. * | Look down on objects to make plan, e.g., on desk, high window to playground. Look at large vertical aerial photographs. * | Draw objects on table or tray to scale using squared paper 1:1 first, then 1:2 and so on. | Use teacher prepared maps, large scale street maps and large scale OS (1:2,500, 1:25,000). Understand purpose of map to show 'where'. Games with maps and globes. |
| 3 | Use large scale map outside. Use maps of other places. Test each other with route maps. Locate photos of features. Use oblique aerial views. * | Use simple grids. Add direction instructions up to eight cardinal points. Practise to improve speed and accuracy. * | Make a map of a short route with features in correct order. Make a map of a small area with features in correct places. * | Give maps a key with standard symbols. Start using OS style symbols. Use plan view regularly. | Look at smaller scale aerial view. Look at view from high place. Use computer program to reinforce. * | Simple scale plan of room with whole numbers, e.g., 1 sq cm = 1 sq m. Use scale bar on atlas maps. Use paces or tape outside. | Start giving maps a title to show purpose. Use thematic maps. Use atlas maps and globe. Move to OS 1:10,000 and 1:25,000 maps. |
| 4 | Relate map to vertical aerial photograph. Relate maps to each other. Follow routes on maps saying what is seen. * | Use four-figure coordinates to locate features. Know directions in neighbourhood. Align map with route. * | Make sketch maps of area using symbols and key. Make plan for garden, play park, with scale. * | Use agreed and OS symbols. Appreciate maps cannot show everything. * | Develop using higher viewpoints up to satellite. Use models to introduce contours and slope. | Use a scale bar on all maps. Use linear scale to measure rivers. * | Use index and contents page of atlas. Use thematic maps for specific purposes. Realise purpose, scale, symbols and style are related. * |
| 5 | Follow route on 1:50,000 OS map. Describe features seen and relate to each other. Interpret relief. * | Use six-figure grid references. Align map. Use latitude and longitude in atlas. * | Design maps from descriptions. Draw thematic maps, e.g., local open spaces. Draw scale plans. | Use standard symbols. Know 1:50,000 symbols and atlas symbols. | Develop understanding of height and slope with map and field work, maps and photographs (contours). * | Read and compare map scales. Draw measured plans, e.g. from field data. * | Appreciate different map projections. Interpret distribution maps and use thematic maps for information. |

\* PoS

Figure 2

concept of side view and plan view first, alongside the use of free-recall maps which call on the cognitive knowledge of the child. Gradually, as understanding of plan view develops in conjunction with the use of symbols, children's maps become more recognisable. With increased experience of the locality, their understanding of direction and distance becomes more accurate.

Sequence develops first and distance is always related to their understanding of scale.

Figure 2 is based upon the chart devised by Catling in *Geographical Work in Primary and Middle Schools* (1988) but with adjustments to take into consideration section 3 of Geographical Skills in the programme of study.

## LOOKING AT SKETCH MAPS: POINTS TO CONSIDER

| Stage | Arrangement | Score | Proportion | Score | Plan view | Score | Map language (use of symbol and label) | Score |
|---|---|---|---|---|---|---|---|---|
| 1 | No logical correspondence between map and subject. | 0 | No realistic proportion. | 0 | No recognisable view. | 0 | No logical correspondence between map and subject. | 0 |
| 2 | Irregular layout but some correspondence if reader knows the subject mapped, e.g. in bunches or lines. | 1 | Proportion right within map but not relative to subject mapped. | 1 | Picture view, i.e. view as seen from front/side. | 1 | Much detail which relates to map drawer, not to the subject, e.g. flowers shown. | 1 |
| 3 | All elements needed drawn but not correctly spaced; rough order. | 2 | Relative size of map objects shows some relationship to subject, e.g., small house, large school. | 2 | Mix of picture, oblique and plan view. | 2 | Much 'photograph-like' detail of specific items, e.g. front of own house, church windows. | 2 |
| 4 | Rough correspondence to subject layout. Correct sequence, two-thirds recognisable. | 3 | Size of objects on map reasonably related to subject. Distance still distorted. | 3 | Consistent viewpoint, oblique or plan view and minor use of picture view. | 3 | Evidence of sorting out irrelevant detail, e.g. showing just roads and houses, no street furniture. | 3 |
| 5 | Sequence logical and spaced realistically. | 4 | Relative size within 10% of reality. Distance improved. | 4 | Consistent plan view with reasonable proportion. | 4 | Greatly simplified map; consistent use of own symbols or standard ones. | 4 |
| 6 | Layout accurate and in proportion (this takes actual time to draw). | 5 | Sizes and distances in proportion. | 5 | Consistent view with good proportion. | 5 | Representation by standard symbol with key. | 5 |

Based on an example in *Geography Teachers' Guide to the Classroom* Fien *et al* (1984, Macmillan)

Figure 3

Alongside the development of map skills, there needs to be some guidance and knowledge of performance rate. Figure 3 shows a simple scoring test which could be used in a pre-test and post-test situation and looks at four elements required in map drawing:
- arrangement;
- proportion;
- plan view;
- use of symbols and labels (map language).

Based upon material by Gerber in *The Geographer's Guide to the Classroom* (1984), it puts into words the summary of Figure 7 in Chapter four, 'Maps and map-making', page 59.

Photocopiable page 195 is a suggestion for a record sheet which can be used as a class profile to aid the inclusion of map work alongside the topic work, both specifically geographical and cross-curricular. It is very rare that a map cannot be drawn for any subject. Make it a personal rule to have a map for every topic.

# Geographical vocabulary

In *Geographical Work in the Primary and Middle School* (1988) John Bentley produced the interesting list of definitions given in Figure 4.

| Geographical term | Definition | Age of child |
|---|---|---|
| Channel | A thing on T.V | 9 |
| Desert | A place with no water surrounded by sand. | 14 |
|  | A very big wide patch of sand. | 8 |
| Estuary | A stray cat or dog | 10 |
| Hill | A bit of land that is bigger than the rest. | 14 |
|  | Quite a big mound of stones | 8 |
| Town | A small amount of houses in the country | 14 |
|  | A busy place with lots of shops and houses | 8 |

Figure 4

So how far are these definitions wrong? Using Chambers Dictionary, we find the following definitions.
Channel:
- the bed of a stream of water;
- a strait or narrow sea;
- a passage for conveying a liquid;
- a groove or furrow;
- a gutter.

Desert:
- a desolate or barren tract;
- a waste;
- a solitude.

Estuary:
- the wide lower tidal part of a river.

Hill:
- a high mass of land less than a mountain;

## Vocabulary at Key Stage 1

### Physical geography
beach cave cliff coast forest highland hill island lake land landscape lowland mountain peak rock sand sand-dune scenery sea valley waterfall pool slope gentle steep flat river stream water headland bay rocks boulders pebbles soil mud sandstone chalk granite clay

### Weather
wet windy dry weather sun cloud rain snow frost ice freezing mild showers cold hot fog autumn spring summer winter pattern snow drifts floods raindrops breeze gale storm water cool dries up cools dew hail sleet forms

### Local places (villages and town, near and far)
address crossing direction flats garden gate home houses landmark local neighbourhood path pavement road route school sign street village surroundings town way shelter doorway park playspace signals library supermarket traffic lights post-box post office minimarket cottage mill church housing estate shop market stalls hotel shopping centre terrace offices motorway city railway bus railway station bus station roundabout street name newsagent chemist greengrocer bridge buildings car park farm tower train open space

### Cities (national and international)
barrier bridge buildings castle cathedral mosque temple city countryside crowds noise large busy modern ancient office block skyscraper shopping centre shopping mall pedestrian precinct street plan settlement shanty town city centre public buildings old buildings museum market place market town factories libraries colleges university flyover ring road main road side street multi-storey carpark departmental store theatre cinema tourists walls underground escalator kiosks boutique

- a mound;
- an incline on a road.

Town:
- a populous place bigger or less rural than a village;
- an urban community.

The first definition under each heading is the meaning nearest to geographical usage. Clearly, each word's everyday use is very close to its geographical meaning, but the teacher should make sure that any language used in geographical description is fully understood by the children. This is particularly so with regard to words used to describe physical geography features which may be used in everyday parlance, but which geographically have a more precise connotation. Thus the use of wordsearches, together with clues suggesting the definition and crosswords to test definition, can reveal much about a child's level of understanding of geographical concepts.

The lists in Figure 5 show the range of vocabulary expected at Key Stage 1. The list is not exhaustive, but includes the words agreed by the current authors of geographical texts. The glossaries found at the back of the best information books will help extend this vocabulary as the Level Three child explores beyond the illustrations of the picture texts.

At Key Stage 2, vocabulary develops to include specific terms. For example, puddles do not just 'dry up', but 'evaporate' and are

---

### Homes (around the world)
brick caravan chalet shanty chimney roof window doorway flats terrace semi-detached detached homes houses hut avenue crescent drive parade road street lane close dwelling cottage apartment walls clay adobe wattle and daub thatch turf wooden frame tools tent felt skins woollen cloth concrete cement tiles slates corrugated iron reed palm leaves stone courtyard shade draught thick warmth space stilts dry damp cool shutters storeys floors bungalow

### People at work (at home and abroad)
factory farm garage jobs kitchen machines office people robot studio television tools workshop work workers equipment services trade industry products craftsman tradesman merchant workman

### Shops and services (in addition to above)
grocer groceries hairdresser fruit vegetables clothes provisions cereals shopper sign telephone parade high street footwear bakery confectionery butcher stationery fishmonger health food shoe repairer hardware florist laundrette café estate agent fast food shop gift shop bank video shop dress shop television shop repair shop cleaners travel agents jewellers charity shop customer delivery van milk float early closing late closing

### Journeys (road, rail, sea, air)
barriers bridge tunnels viaducts route track motorway tanker service area petrol station lorry park freight yard depot coach move transport deliver cargo container dock quay siding warehouse canal

### Environment (near and far)
conservation dust electricity field fumes litter quarry rubbish smoke tip untidy windmill wood mines damage pollution waste ground habitat hedge power station sewage forest fires spraying treatment works refuse junk health waste lumbering mining quarrying fishing change development recycling

### Farming
land rich poor fertile soil harvest desert crop plant chemicals irrigation pests insects cereals wheat barley oats rice maize grain plough sow reap gather collect sort grade store market pasture ditch irrigate wood shelter belt hedge field plot allotment nursery glasshouse roots carrots turnips swedes parsnips potatoes field crops cabbages beans melons millet sugar cane sugar beet plantation estates

### Locational language
left right near to far from turn in front of next to side of nearest further from above looking down opposite views behind underneath back below middle of on top of front side midway compass north east south west direction grid sign point

### The United Kingdom
Northern Ireland Belfast Scotland Edinburgh Wales Cardiff England London capital city country countries flags border boundary sea ocean frontier ferries oil rigs Union Jack France Channel English Scottish Irish Welsh mountains uplands lowlands land river isles islands mainland full address abroad Europe Republic of Ireland coastline

### The wider world
Africa North America Asia South America Australia compass north pole south pole equator continent earth Europe tropics Arctic Antarctica Southern Ocean South Atlantic Pacific North Atlantic Indian climate cold desert distant far dry hot ice oasis plants animals sand stony forests temperature rainforest warm wet polar mild

Figure 5

part of a process known as 'evaporation'. The water that dries up does not just 'cool into clouds', it 'condenses to form droplets and ice crystals'. Patterns of settlement become classified into 'dispersed', 'nucleated' and 'densely populated' areas. Road patterns become networks which are 'linear', 'rectangular', 'regular' or 'irregular'. The use of the land becomes 'landuse' and can be classified.

Many new words will become self-evident as they are associated with classification. Children will begin to encounter the same 'jargon' words in, for example, geography and science. The correct use of these words helps to show how far a concept has been understood and how far the child has moved towards applying the concept to situations beyond the original example used. Figure 6 gives some of the more common geographical terms which it is hoped the Level 4 child will recognise even if they are not used regularly in description and conversation.

## Weather and climate vocabulary

By Key Stage 2, children should be becoming aware that the water cycle encompasses both water over and through the ground as well as water in the air, hence the final terms used under the heading 'Landforms and the hydrosphere' in Figure 6. When testing and teaching the place of water in the environment try to keep the cycle intact. Desert climates are desert because there is no water to evaporate from within the ground except at oases – hence the pleasant micro-climate at oases!

The vocabulary list may seem exhaustive, but it will provide a guide as to further words which are useful geographically for wordsearches, crosswords and cloze work.

## The range of evidence

The range of evidence for assessment bears a close resemblance to the resources for

## Vocabulary at Key Stage 2

### *Landforms and the hydrosphere*
*mountain valley gorge floodplain meander cut offs levees estuary course stream landslips delta springs meadowland ridge gradient range glen summit crags peak snowline glacier tree line avalanche passes coastline glacial valley drowned valley ria fiord scree embankment contour lines scarp source current stream bed channel tributary rapids drainage basin rock layers bedding planes rock beds volcanoes lava cone earthquakes epicentre intensity fault line erupt extinct magma vent columns flow hexagonal cracks joints fossil folds faults hard soft plates 'ring of fire' hazards floods eruptions seismograph tremor hot gas hot spring geyser crater pumice stone ash weathering erosion deposition transport abrasion percolation infiltration evaporation condensation precipitation run off throughflow landscape*

### *Weather*
*meteorological forecast gale breeze storm calm anemometer satellites weather balloons weather ships weather stations blizzard cyclone typhoon hurricane tropical storms monsoon exposure aspect temperature Celsius (C) Fahrenheit (F) Centigrade (C) maximum minimum cloud cover octals humidity chill factor wet and dry thermometer wet season dry season thunderstorm*

*equatorial tropical desert temperate polar Mediterranean depressions anticyclones measurement instruments average weather centre record drought report local climate micro-climate urban climate mountain climate symbol*

### *Settlement*
*rural urban metropolitan industrial agricultural commercial suburban port county regional national inner city new town shanty town garden city conurbation out-of-town shopping centre hypermarket business centre site location dormitory town commuter village grid iron pattern*

### *Transport and communications*
*networks bypass route junction interchange trans-shipment point detour inter-city inter-regional rural urban international infrastructure Customs autoroute toll maps cycle-way commuters ring road traffic jam*

### *Industry*
*resources raw materials product primary extractive secondary manufacturing service export import public utilities assembly line management conveyor belt system production line flow chart manager business plan budget markets*

Figure 6

learning listed in Chapter seven, 'The classroom and resources', and as such should be included in the detailed planning scheme at the beginning of each topic.

## Graphical evidence

The items listed opposite can be used as graphical evidence for assessment. They can be teacher-drawn, needing information adding or use to provide material for written work. Alternatively, they can be pupil-drawn to set specifications or completely original in the selection of every detail, depending upon the degree of competence previously achieved and there can be an element of self- and peer-testing. For example, ask the children each to draw a map of a friend's route to a certain location, such as home, school, the swimming pool and so on. The friends can then be allowed to mark the maps. Alternatively, the children could be asked to make treasure trail maps to be followed by their group, thus also allowing for social skill assessment. The following tools are appropriate for graphical evidence:
- maps;
- drawings;
- diagrams;
- graphs;
- printouts;
- photographs.

## Products

The following products can be used as evidence for assessment.
- Models, for example, showing different house types or the different buildings in a street, a farm layout, the park or a development plan, can be used. Detail, accuracy in scale and layout, as well as social skills, can be assessed.
- Artefacts, such as collections of pebbles, plants, stamps, clothes or foods for specific climates and places, can all be assessed for quality of classification and the use children have made of them in illustrating their work.

## Written evidence

Written evidence could include:
- reports, made with or without the use of information technology;
- notes which can be structured by the teacher or left completely without constraint;
- diaries;
- questionnaires which can also be structured or freestyle, depending upon the teaching requirements;
- stories;
- essays;
- newspaper articles which can be used to provide information or as part of a class newspaper;
- short answer questions, multiple choice questions, comprehension exercises and geographical cloze sentences can be used to monitor skills, knowledge and understanding, where again, groups can devise tests for their peers as part of reinforcement and revision;
- crosswords, wordsearches and word and picture matching can all be used to reinforce vocabulary.

---

*Agriculture*
intensive extensive commercial self-sufficient subsistence plantation ranching arable stock-rearing hill farming dairy farming mixed farming prairie farming land use growing season frost free dry farming irrigation rotation salination pastoralists nomads compounds estancia fertilisers share cropping famine drought overgrazing cash cropping paddy fields weeding bullock tractor cattle station stockyard outback moorland grazing shearing wool auction cattle auction

*Fishing*
plankton shoals grounds quota trawler drifter factory ship inshore offshore international limits over-fishing radar freezing packing exporting fish farming

*Leisure*
holidays recreation theme park national park tourist resorts conservation long distance routes areas of outstanding natural beauty (ANOB) sites of special scientific interest (SSSI) country parks tourism safari park

*Environment*
destruction excavation protection conservation restoration dereliction landscaping afforestation renewable non-renewable degraded preserved balance managed conflict

# Oral evidence

This can be obtained through:
- questioning, either by informal moving from group to group or by formal questioning around the class;
- discussion and interviews – issues such as the environment and conservation, especially in the locality, lend themselves to this approach, discussions between children or interviews with outsiders could be taped;
- sequencing, which could involve giving directions round obstacles or through a maze;
- role-play;
- assemblies and presentations;
- debates;
- tapes and videos of any of the above.

# Evidence from other activities

Other evidence for assessment could include:
- two pieces of work, before and after;
- selected items kept in a personal folder;
- competitions;
- orienteering;
- setting up databases on information technology;
- designing board and card games.

## An overview

Figure 4 on page 157 (Chapter 10) shows how track can be kept of all the evidence and resources for each topic. In other words, if you have a clear plan as to the outcome of each activity when preparing a unit, the assessment can be automatic, as those used to formative assessment will already know.

However, in your planning the following guidelines may be helpful.
- Assessment should not take up too much of your time.
- Assessment should record what a child *can* do – the rest is all to come, no matter how slowly.
- Geographical assessment tasks should test at least one of three elements – skills, areas and themes. Within these elements, knowledge and concepts will be sub-elements. Selection within this framework will be essential. Some items of the programme of study will be visited several times.

Allow a judicious space for development time between each test, for example testing for use of atlas index every other unit. On the other hand, fieldwork on a school journey needs full coverage as soon as possible after the event.
- Assessment can vary in form and timing. It is not always necessary to test at the end of a topic.
- Build in the assessment at the unit planning stage to support resources and objectives.
- Assessment can involve the whole class, with groups working to one combined objective but tested at different times, groups in a carousel timetable and with built-in assessment, and individuals in all these situations looking at personal development.

# Recording

The individual and class profile sheets on photocopiable pages 195 and 196 are intended to aid ongoing teaching. The headings will change as the significance of certain elements becomes clear at various levels. Regular staff consultations and whole-school reviewing of record-keeping is important, as keeping accurate records ensures that a child's progress, or otherwise, is kept in view and can be shown to those immediately concerned, be it parent, headteacher or the next class teacher. There should, moreover, be common criteria and grading.

There is no legal requirement to keep records showing the results of assessment at the level of attainment. However, summative reports have their value in planning. Photocopiable pages 197 to 202 may be useful as a development record to be completed at the end of each term, showing achievement as well as weakness.

# Activity and assessment

Activity sheets given in Figures 7 to 14 could be used for assessment. Similar sheets are to be found in the *Starting Geography* series (Scholastic). Basically aimed at Level 3, the fundamental principle in each can be simplified or made more sophisticated.

Figure 7 shows how the known layout of a neighbourhood can be used to give a fair test for planning routes, recognising plan symbols for dwellings (PoS, 3d) or recognising landforms from contours (Level 5). Figure 8 shows an exercise is using symbols which could also be used for a written comment on the character of the market garden to assess comprehension (KS2, PoS, 9b). This would also apply to English. Figure 9 suggests a layout for a concept keyboard which can be used either to test atlas work (when pressed, the fruits show the country on screen) or sequencing with the growing calendar (KS2, PoS, 3d; 8b). Figure 10 tests north, south, east and west and a route using compass points can be made starting from the home town (KS2, PoS, 3d). Figure 11 also tests map skills (KS2, PoS, 3d), then asks why the particular forms of transport were chosen. It also tests concepts understood on links (KS2, PoS, 5e). Figure 12 is a geographical cloze test. Figure 13 is a straightforward test in map drawing (KS2, PoS, 3c). Figure 14 shows laminated card being made to show the countries of Europe, which is a test in co-ordination and organisation. The initial exercise tests atlas work; further exercises could be capitals and adding symbols to show products.

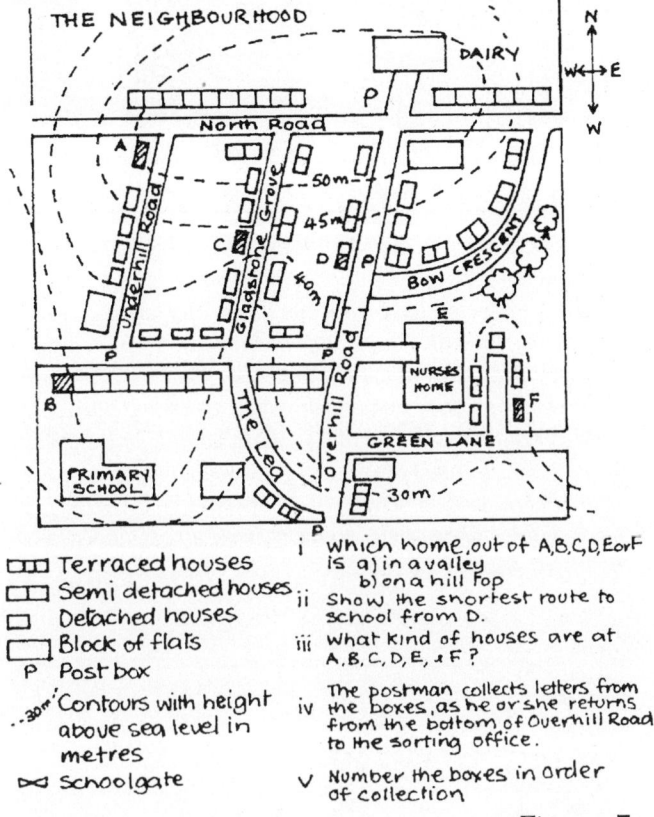

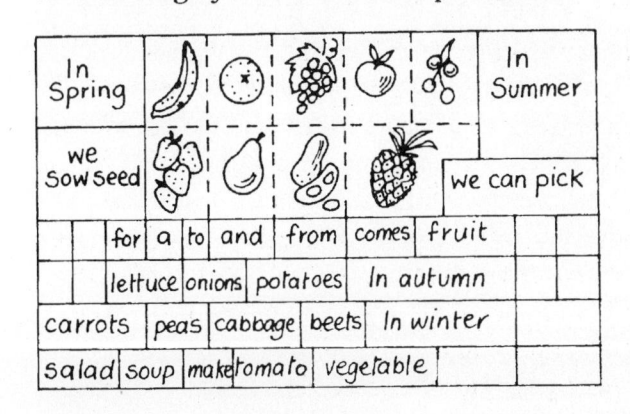

Figure 7

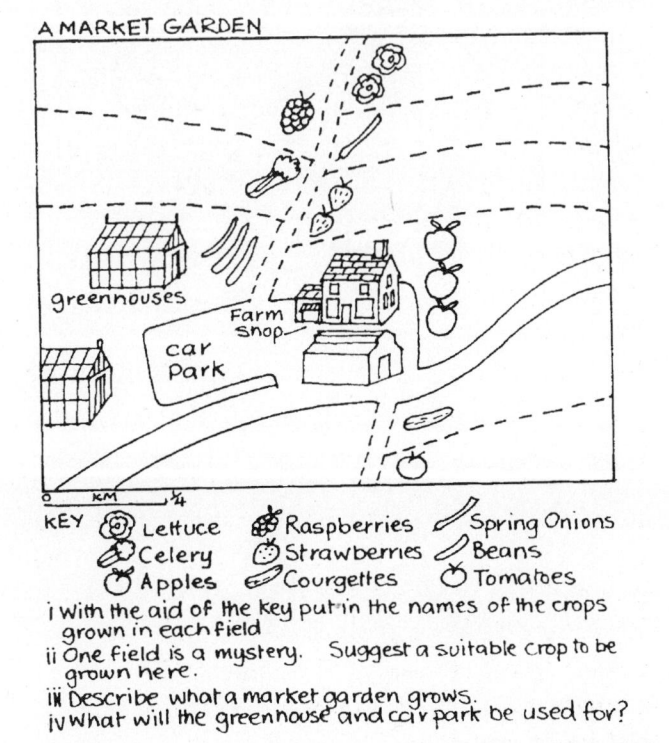

Figure 8

Figure 9

Which way would you go? use compass directions

KEY
- Mountains
- Sandy Beaches
- Castles
- Railways
- Sailing
- Zoos

| TOWN | ACTIVITY |
|---|---|
| From _____ | to _____ |
| From _____ | to _____ |

This could be a wallmap with photographs. By using a motorway map, routes can also be given.

Figure 10

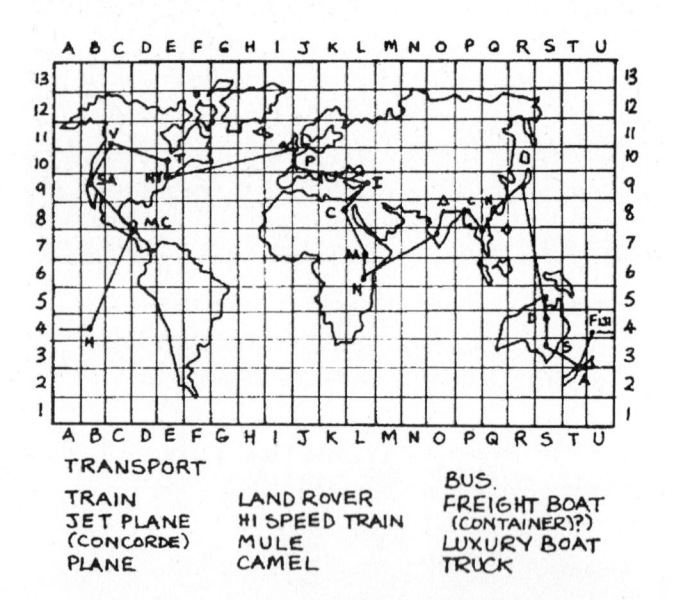

TRANSPORT

TRAIN          LAND ROVER       BUS
JET PLANE      HI SPEED TRAIN   FREIGHT BOAT
(CONCORDE)     MULE             (CONTAINER)?
PLANE          CAMEL            LUXURY BOAT
                                TRUCK

- Name the cities, use an atlas: name the countries
- Give each city a letter/number grid reference.
- For each leg of the journey, choose a form of transport.
- Each form of transport should be different from the one used on the previous leg of the journey
- Give reasons for your choice
- How else could you have travelled?

Figure 11

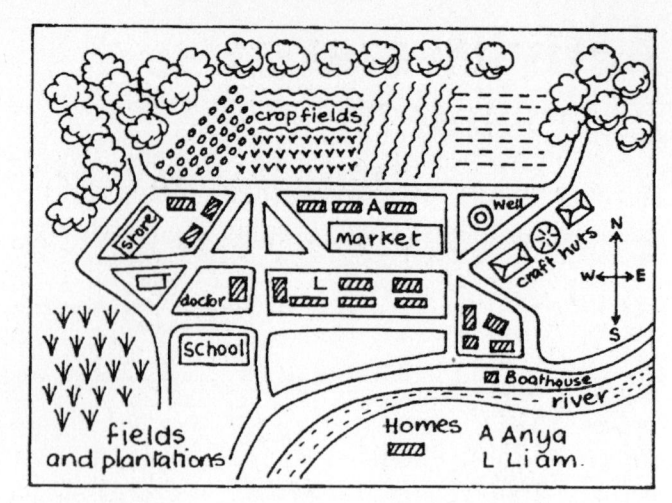

Complete Anya's account of her day by adding the direction she travels (left/right or north/south/east/west):

'Early each morning I leave the house and turn ____ to the well. I carry the water ____ wards back home. Then I cross the road to collect yams in the left field. The sun warms my back as I do this. I go back home then go out again and turn ____ to the crossroads and turn sharp ____ to go to Liam's house. We both go ____ and then ____ to go to school going past the _____'s house. After school, we sometimes go ____ and ____ to watch the craft workers. Sometimes we go ____ and play in the woods near the stores.'

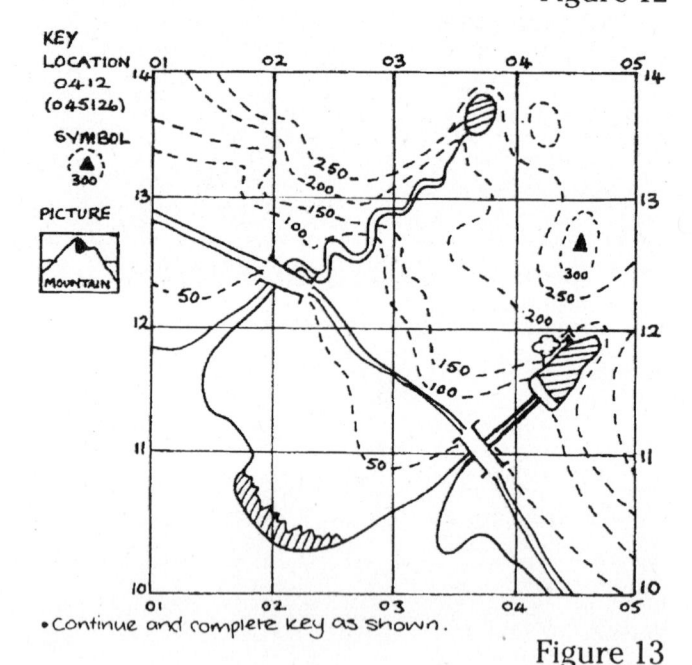

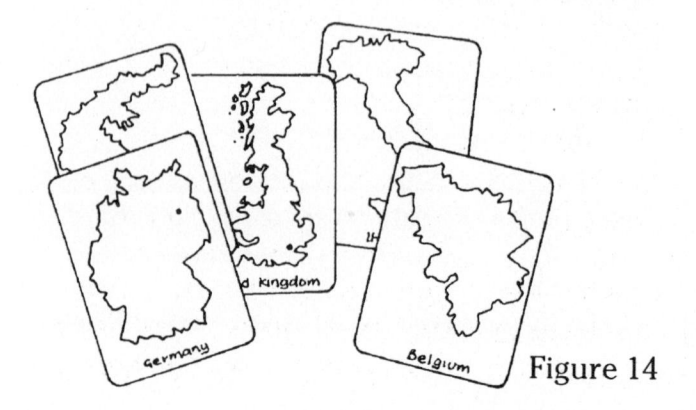

Figure 12

KEY
LOCATION 0412 (045126)
SYMBOL
PICTURE — MOUNTAIN

• Continue and complete key as shown.

Figure 13

Figure 14

# Chapter nine
# Progression in practice

The previous chapters on fieldwork and map skills gave some indication of progression in the development of activities. Jerome Bruner (1963) suggested that there was no subject too difficult to be taught in some form from the earliest ages. This led to the concept of the spiral curriculum. Starting from the basic ideas of the subject (for example, in geography, 'where things are') each successive stage of learning revises, broadens and deepens existing knowledge. Thus a baby's knowledge of where food and warmth can be found develops into a personal geography from which everyday spatial relationships begin to have meaning. These personal daily landmarks grow into a communal appreciation of the locality in which the child and his friends play and go to school. Eventually, a wider world of work and leisure is recognised. Knowledge grows to include features on a regional scale, then to national and international scales. Indeed, the child with relatives on another continent is aware of the wider world in the largest sense from an early age and then has to fit in the rest of the world between the two extremes of the local and the global. It has been recognised that the spiral curriculum provides the necessary structure for a subject which has, in the past, been too easily regarded as a list of localities with certain fixed characteristics. Just to know the location of a place is no preparation for understanding *why* a place is as it is or how it has come to have its own distinctive personality. Yet understanding the character of a place demands skills of searching out the knowledge leading to understanding the factors which have contributed to its development.

137

Figure 1 shows the development of the spiral from the earliest levels and illustrates the progression of ideas, skills and content with reference to features in a locality, together with the child's change in attitude, from considering only his own needs to considering those of others.

The spiral approach is applicable to more than just geography. There are skills common to science, mathematics and to the arts. Each subject has its own simple vocabulary which develops into a more complex language. Each subject requires observation, first of single objects and then of objects in relation to each other, the combinations increasing in complexity with the increasing sophistication of the subject matter. Together, these skills are brought to bear on themes as well as localities, rendering a topic approach an efficient means of reinforcing skills, gathering knowledge and developing attitudes and concepts. This requires that a whole-school approach is employed. In the spiral approach, progression is achieved through developing increasingly difficult concepts and skills both inside the classroom and outside and it is essential that there is agreement upon the increasing complexity, so that progress is even and well-prepared.

There is guidance within the National Curriculum as to how this progression is to be achieved, if the various strands from each level are grouped in sequence. This, however, is a very skeletal framework and, in planning the spiral curriculum, extra steps, often suggested by the programme of study but more often implicit in its assumptions, have to be inserted. The National Curriculum Geography Working Group defined progression as:

- 'gradual extension of content to include different places, environments, human activities and physical processes;
- increasing the scale of the place studies from localities, regions and countries, to international and global;
- increasing complexity of the phenomena studied and the tasks set;
- use of more generalised knowledge and abstract ideas;
- increasing awareness and understanding of social, political and environmental issues involving different attitudes and values.'

(4.1 'Planning for Progression' *Geography Non-Statutory Guidance*, 1991)

| Level | Ideas | Skills | Content | Attitudes |
|---|---|---|---|---|
| 5 | Localities contribute to variety in larger areas. | Reading small scale OS maps. Developing geographical ideas and language. | Other localities in the world, including European regions. | Tolerance of other ways of living and other cultures. |
| 4 | Different places can be classified according to different patterns. | Using geographical language; classifying, measuring, drawing, plans. Using OS maps. | Getting about the home area; finding out about another locality and another economically developing area. | Awareness of similarities and differences between people and other cultures. |
| 3 | Different places have different arrangements. | Using simple geographical language. Neat plans. Sketch routes/places. Simple reference. | Getting about the school and another locality. Localities in other places, including developing countries. | Similarities and differences. |
| 2 | Needs vary in different places. | Drawing round layouts. Sketch plans for imaginary places. | Different houses, schools, villages, towns. | Interest in other people at home and away. |
| 1 | Everyday needs: food, drink, warmth. | Vocabulary models, drawings. | Houses, streets, parks, home. | Need to share. |
| Pre- | Daily happenings. | Talking, exploring, describing. | Immediate environment. Inside & outside. | Looking beyond oneself. |

Adapted from a diagram in *The Study of Places in the Primary School*, ILEA (1981). Figure 1

The following examples of progression show some of the possible teaching sequences.

## Progression in mapwork

Mapping activities involving direction and route following can be used to accommodate increasing complexity of each strand at each level.

### Reception
Ask the children to follow directions (left, right and so on), for example, in the classroom, gym or playground.

### Level 1
Ask the children to follow directions around a larger area (KS1, PoS, 3c) for example to another classroom, feature (e.g. pond) or place (e.g. library), or on a specific journey (e.g. postman's route).

### Level 2
Let the children follow a route using a plan (KS1, PoS, 3e), for example round the school or round a model farm.

### Level 3
The children could be allowed to make a map of a short route showing features in the correct order (KS2, PoS, 3d). They could, for example, show the way home, the route to the shops or the way to the park.

### Level 4
Show how localities are linked (KS2, PoS, 5e).

### Level 5
The children should be able to follow a route on a 1:50,000 or 1:25,000 OS map and describe the features which would be seen (KS3, PoS, 3d).

The programme of study uses the term 'at a variety of scales' (KS2, PoS, 3c, d). The Ordnance Survey makes a distinction between plans and maps. Plans are true to scale and comprise the black and white metric plans at 1:10,000; 1:1,250 and 1:2,500 (Imperial 6", 25" and 50"). Maps are smaller in scale and use colour, for example, blue for water features, green for wood, grey and black for buildings. The 1:25,000 Pathfinder maps are photographically reduced from the 1:10,000 plans and show boundaries to scale but major roads are slightly exaggerated for emphasis. The symbols are very similar to the 1:50,000 Landranger symbols but detail is more easily related to photographs and features on the ground.

Thus at Level 4, the children should continue to make routes but they should relate them to the 1:25,000 maps, make the routes longer and link places further afield, tying in with larger settlements, different places of work, different sizes of roads and routeways. This should be linked with other mapwork, especially work on symbols, to help the development towards being able to describe features on a map without having to relate them to features seen along the route outside first.

Similarly, the programme of study gives guidance upon progression for drawing maps. Although map drawing does not become an identifiable statement of attainment until Level 2 and then at Level 4, it is possible to develop map drawing skills from an early age.

## Progression for developing map drawing

### Reception
Let the children make their own representations of places, both cognitive and imaginary.

## Level 1

Ask the children to draw where they like to play or visit, where it is wet, where it is hilly and so on.

## Level 2

Encourage the children to **'make maps and plans of real and imaginary places using pictures and symbols'** (KS1, PoS, 3d). For example, they could sketch the classroom, a farm or even the Wild Wood from *The Wind in the Willlows*. Show them how to make an arrow map, for example, work places or local woods (Figure 2).

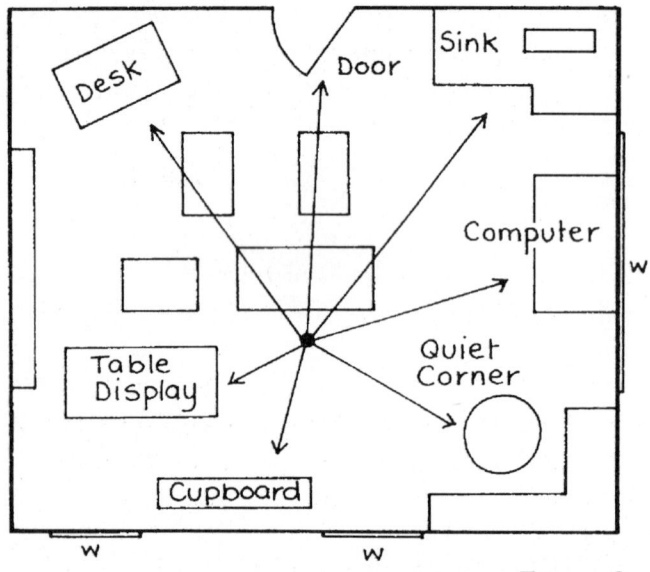

Figure 2

## Level 3

Ask the children to make a sketch map of various places in the neighbourhood. At the same time, let them use a large-scale map to locate their own position (KS1, PoS, 3d, e).

## Level 4

The children should now be able to draw a sketch map using symbols and a key (KS2, PoS, 3c). This could show the landuse of a village, a small estate or a shopping parade. It could show steep and flat places, or show the location of litter bins and other street furniture.

## Level 5

At this level, the sketch map could show the village land use in relation to physical features, or the location of several shopping areas with key features added using OS map information. A small scale sketch map could show holiday places in the UK.

Similar progressions can be constructed for using maps to show position. Reception children can be asked to point to a photograph of their home placed on a map of the neighbourhood. Level 1 children can be asked to do the same without the photograph and also to point out features on an aerial photograph or a photograph taken from a great height. Coordinates can be introduced by playing board games involving matching objects to places. At Level 2, this can be developed into using letter/number grids with picture maps and models, thus preparing for the use of letter/number grids at Level 3 to locate features on maps (KS2, PoS, 3d). At this stage, it is possible to use street maps or 1:10,000 Ordnance Survey plans with suitable border numbers and letters added. From here, the children can progress to the 1:25,000 Ordnance Survey map, using four-figure coordinates to local features such as castles, car parks, quarries (KS2, PoS, 3d), and moving up to six figures for those working towards Level 5.

# Progression in fieldwork

## Places

Recording in the locality starts with the child drawing his or her own front door or a window, progresses to drawing a door and window of another familiar building or house, then an individual building or house in its entirety with labels showing specific features (e.g. roof) and materials (e.g. tiles), followed up with research to find the age of the building.

The next stage is to progress on to group work looking at a specific part of a street or shopping parade, with each member of a group having a specific job. These specific jobs would already be familiar to the children, having been undertaken in isolation in earlier activities. However, when combined with other observations, these tasks would add up to a detailed study of landuse in a small part of the neighbourhood.

With increased confidence, the group work can be extended to cover larger areas or longer routes, such as a park with areas of varied character or a suburban housing estate. The greatest difficulty here will be the necessary adult supervision. One successful study of a planned housing estate was undertaken over a six week period with the help of students from a nearby college, when two classes worked in groups of six to a scheme devised by school staff the previous term.

These developments in fieldwork techniques in and about the locality will take place from Reception to Years 3/4. Other activities will have been taking place outside the classroom, chiefly in the playground but also with visits. The most important of these activities will have been concerned with thematic studies.

# Observation, measurement and recording

Work with weather involves not only observation and recording, but also a degree of measurement of increasing complexity.

## Weather observation

Weather observation is introduced by talking about the weather, developing appropriate vocabulary and noticing changes from day to day. This naturally leads on to asking questions about the way in which the weather changes.
- How much colder is it today than yesterday?
- How much more, or less, cloud is there than yesterday?
- Did it rain heavily in the night?

These questions can be answered by introducing simple equipment in such a way as to make the process of measuring rewarding to the children. For example, they could be asked to catch rain in a wide container and measure it in a narrow, tall container. At this stage, the emphasis should be upon comparison rather than precision. Ensure that the same size containers are used each time the amount of rain collected is compared. For example, use a milkbottle to contain each day's rain and compare the

Figure 3

levels between bottles at the end of the week (Figure 3). With younger children, there is no need to look at everything at once in detail. It makes sense to look at the weather elements separately initially. For example, when investigating the wind the following questions could be asked.
- How do we know it is windy?
- Where is the wind coming from?
- Where is it going to?
- Does this happen every day?
- Does the wind always move things?

Similarly, with the rain a variety of questions could be asked.
- Are there different kinds of rain?
- How do we keep dry?

This initial investigation could gradually be extended in the following way.
- How hot is it?
- How cold is it?
- Is it the same indoors as in the shady areas?
- Where else is it windy? Wet? Cold? Hot? In England? Britain? Europe? The world?

Regularly looking at the daily weather reports in relation to people in various parts of the world helps to develop an appreciation of weather patterns and sequences and the interdependence of people, climate and weather. With older children, the observations can become more precise and sophisticated with the use of maximum and minimum thermometers, and by looking at humidity and chill factors, and making readings for pressure, as well as rain, temperature and wind speed and direction.

## Progression in weather studies

The development of precision in weather observations in relation to the demands of the National Curriculum and the needs of the children is as follows.

### Reception

Talk about the weather regularly and relate it to the children's clothes and everyday activities. Help the children to develop vocabulary in all areas, for example, using vocabulary of the senses (e.g. seeing different clouds, hearing thunder, feeling cold), then grouping the sensations into seasonal words and according to type of element (such as gusty winds). Choose a suitable wet, hot or cold period to find out 'How much ...?'

### Level 1

**'Undertake studies that... are based on direct experience'** (KS1, PoS, 1b). Begin observations of a weather feature over a short period of time. A fortnight usually ensures enough results to be able to make comparisons. By the end of the year wind, rain and temperature reading and recording using simple symbols should be familiar to the children (Figure 4).

### Level 2

**'Undertake fieldwork activities...'** (KS1, PoS, 3b) and make studies on **'the effects of weather on people and their surroundings'** (KS1, PoS, 5c). Encourage the children to record all the features of the weather and make a chart for daily, weekly or monthly changes in each season. Add details of clothes and flowering plants in each season. Put into a simple database for comparison.

Figure 4

### Level 3

The effects of weather (KS1, PoS, 5c) can be extended to support **'how localities may be similar and how they differ'** (KS1, PoS, 5b) using TV or newspaper weather information or a direct fax link. Consolidate the weather observations and increase precision. As before, this can take place with individual elements of the weather but related to specific enquiries. (For example, which is the hottest part of the playground? Where else is it as hot as this?) Start introducing compass directions. Look at the world weather reports. Start using and making a database (Figure 5).

## Level 4

At Key Stage 2 **'opportunities to... develop the ability to recognise patterns'** (PoS, 1c) by collecting and recording evidence (PoS, 2b) and using instruments to make

| Day | | 1 | 2 | 3 | 4 |
|---|---|---|---|---|---|
| Wind Direction N, NE, E, SW, S, SW, W, NW. | a.m. | | | | |
| | p.m. | | | | |
| Wind speed M.p.h. | a.m. | | | | |
| | p.m. | | | | |
| Temperature °C | a.m. | | | | |
| | p.m. | | | | |
| Rain m.m. | | | | | |
| Humidity wet/dry | | W | D | | |

Figure 5

measurements (PoS, 3b) is compounded by studying the three strands in the Weather theme (PoS, 9). Introduce the use of simple equipment for regular observation of rain, air pressure, temperature and wind and let the children enter the results on a database.

Ask the children to make site observations for a database linked to an overlay keyboard showing a map of the school grounds or another suitable site. If possible, use a data logger or a maximum/minimum thermometer and take readings at frequent intervals during the day. Tie this in with environmental decisions such as where to put the guinea pig run or the flower beds. This can then be extended, for example, to considering sites of farms in hilly and mountainous country (PoS, 9a). Regular readings can be maintained on a class rota. Saved to disk, seasons can be compared to each other and year-to-year and seasonal patterns studied (PoS, 9b). The data can be faxed or sent on disk to link schools and world conditions can be compared (PoS, 9c).

## Level 5

In all the levels above the data collected can be used to support and promote work at the same levels for mathematics. In geography, understanding average is essential to understanding the difference between weather and climate. For example, site data can be used to characterise the microclimates found at north facing and south facing playground sites.

Cooperation with the local secondary school may allow access to sophisticated equipment and mutual help on weather projects.

# River observation

Weather recording, especially of rainfall, forms important links with observing the effect of water on the ground and upon difference surfaces. The use of sand tray models to demonstrate the ability of water to move sediment and to shape land is explained in detail in Chapter three. This work can be extended by fieldwork at all levels.

## Progression in investigating rivers

### Reception

Take the children out on a rainy day to look for running water, water standing still, water soaking in and water wetting everything.

Look to see where the water runs to or out of. Where are the drains and gutters (both down from the roof as well as along the side of the path)? Take as many photographs as possible to build up a record of the way water moves and works.

## Level 1

**'Pupils should be given opportunities to investigate the physical... features of their surroundings'** (KS1, PoS, 1a) and to **'use geographical terms... in exploring their surroundings'** (KS1, PoS, 3a). Make a short excursion to see water features in the neighbourhood and find places where rock and soil are found – widening both science and geography experience.

## Level 2

In locality studies, teaching is expected to cover **'the main physical... features that give the localities their character'** (KS1, PoS, 5a). Combine this investigation with the weather observations over the seasons and make maps to show where water, fog, ice and frost are to be found or not at each season. Visit the local stream and/or pond. Notice how the water moves, how dirty it is and so on.

## Level 3

The question 'What is it like?' expects description and comparison of similar features in different places (PoS, 5b), e.g., a pond, stream or other example. Undertake indoor simulations (see Chapter three), followed by fieldwork at a local stream. Find out how many of the features are in the locality. It should be possible to find a stream or ditch carrying running water in any part of the country.

Visit the local stream and begin measurements to see how fast water flows in different parts of the channel. Over the seasons, keep a 'Water watch' in specific places to see the effect of heavy rainfall.

## Level 4

Rivers are expected to be studied for the effect that they have on the landscape (KS2, PoS, 7). Extend the playground experiment (see Chapter three) with increased flow from the hose (erosion increases) and barriers to erosion (a slate layer making a waterfall to show **'how rivers erode, transport and deposit materials, producing particular landscape features'** (PoS, 7b). Encourage questions, observation and description (KS2, PoS, 2a–c) using simple record forms. Extend the investigation to a local stream at different seasons.

Similar small scale work can introduce the idea **'that rivers have sources, channels tributaries and mouths...'**

Follow this by finding the stream investigated on the local map and tracing where it fits with other streams. Then use a smaller scale map to research... **'they receive water from a wide area, and that most eventually flow into a lake or the sea'** (KS2, PoS, 7a).

## Level 5

The studies above will be analysed and the evidence used to draw conclusions about changing river conditions, and a clear description will be made of the overall observations (KS2, PoS, 2a–c).

Progression in the simulations and field observations is given in detail in Chapter three.

# Progression in looking at places

There are several elements to be investigated in each place, such as address, closely followed by building use, landuse, people, economic activities and leisure activities.

To understand the distinctive features that give a place identity, let the children start by looking at the characteristics of personal places, then help them to recognise that although places may have some features in common there are also differences.

Finally, show them how similarities and differences often stem from relationships which are particular to a location.

# Understanding the character of places

## Reception

Ask the children each to consider the following questions.
- Where is my room at home?
- Where is my room at school?
- Where are the different rooms at home?
- Where are the different rooms at school?

Look at different homes and different addresses. Walk round to the nearest homes and let the children draw the doors and label the drawings with the street names and numbers. Encourage the children to say their own address and give addresses for pets and toys, at home and at school.

## Level 1

**'Marking on a map approximately where they live...'** (PoS, 3e). The children should not only be able to say but also to write their addresses. Investigate (house) numbers, together with the concept of odds and evens. Investigate street names. Move on to OS maps and maps of different scales to locate places in the county and country.

## Level 2

**'Locating and naming on a map the constituent countries of the United Kingdom'** (PoS, 3e). Use an atlas and globe to help the children distinguish between the British Isles and the United Kingdom. Use the concept of address to bring in other ideas of place and belonging to community, settlement, locality, region, county and nation. Encourage the children to collect stamps, flags and postcards, and then to locate the appropriate places on a map to give them an 'address'.

## Level 3

**'Identifying major geographical features...'** (KS1, PoS, 3e). Ask the children questions such as the following.
- How do you know where you are?
- What features help to locate places?

## Level 4

**'How the localities are set within a broader geographical context...'** (KS2, PoS, 5e). Discover the places visited for shopping and leisure and plot them on a map. Enclose those places visited most often and discuss this boundary in relation to other uses, such as weather reports.

## Level 5

The aspiring child will give additional examples of features that define locality, area and region, usually related to time, distance and frequency of visits.

# Understanding buildings and land use

Gradually, the emphasis moves away from 'self' and becomes more connected with the spiralling study of place at different levels. The features of a place are often defined by its buildings and the way the buildings and the land about them are used. The sequence could be as follows.

## Reception

Introduce the topic of 'My home'. This could be extended to cover 'Places I know' (e.g. church, playground, shops, school, library).

## Level 1

**'Features that give localities their character'** (KS1, PoS, 5a). This could involve the study of roads, buildings, parks, rivers and street furniture. Study also **'how land**

145

**and buildings... are used'** (PoS, 5d) by comparing buildings of similar size but different uses.

## Level 2

Here **'how land and buildings ... are used'** (PoS, 5d) is applied to areas rather than individual buildings. Ask the children what different places are used for. Let them make maps of eating areas, working areas and play areas at home and at school. Which are large areas? Which are small areas? Organise a short walk to see if any of the uses involve having special buildings or areas outside home and school.

Help the children to be able to distinguish between shops for food, services and other goods, and buildings used as surgeries, offices and so on (Figure 6).

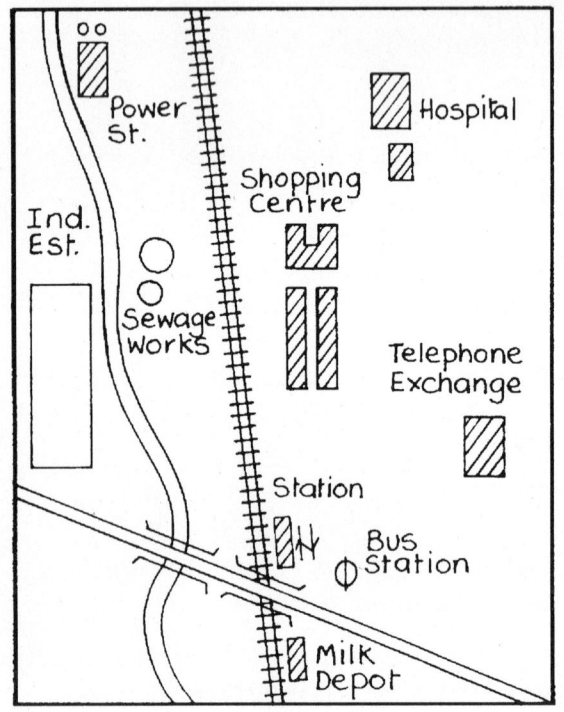

Figure 6

## Level 3

**'Use geographical terms... in exploring their surroundings'** and **'use appropriate geographical vocabulary... to describe... their surroundings'** (KS2, PoS, 3a). Through discussion, identify various centres of activity such as a shopping parade, community centre or a light-industry estate. Explain the relationships between types of landuse, buildings and human activities in the local area and explain why some activities in the local area are located where they are. Ask questions such as the following.
• Why are large shops only on the high street?
• Where are the factories? Are they all in the same area?
• Why is the milk depot near the railway station?

The children can then use this vocabulary to describe their locality to a link school and identify similar features in the contrasting link locality.

## Level 4

Study **'the main... human features... and environmental issues... that give localities their character'** (KS2, PoS, 5a) by using locality maps, photographs and newspaper reports to show the main land uses and pinpoint **'... recent or proposed changes..'** (PoS, 5d). Ask the children to investigate the advantages and disadvantages of replacing the traditional rural landuse of farming with motorway routes, forestry, hypermarket sites and so on. This could be explored through role-play.

## Level 5

At this level, connections are made between changes in land use – for example, links between industrial sites and the road network.

# Understanding the wider world

In the National Curriculum for geography there is an interesting progression in the use of verbs. The necessary verbs start with 'recognise' and 'describe', progress on to 'offer explanations' and 'show an awareness of' before showing understanding for an increasing range of places and themes. These ways of looking at the environment, however, cannot happen until a wealth of knowledge has been developed through looking at the patterns in the home locality and region in many different ways.

These ways of looking and communicating can then be applied to the wider world at each level.

## Reception

Discuss which places the children have talked about within their families. They will also enjoy pointing to specific places on a world map. A child of this age may only be able to recognise one place, but nevertheless that place is part of the world beyond their home area. Whether it is the next country or as far as the opposite side of the globe, the place represents the child's growing awareness of the wider world.

Figure 7

As the programme of study requests a locality either in or beyond the United Kingdom, it makes sense to choose a place with significant differences to complement the similarities which will be found in any two UK localities.

A multicultural school will be spoilt for choice in this respect, while other schools may be located in a twinned town or may be able to make links using business connections. Aim to place the contrasting locality in a broader context, in another region, country or continent.

## Level 1

'Become aware that the world extends beyond their own locality...' (PoS, 1c). In addition to using postcards and photographs, use the globe regularly, together with an uncluttered atlas or wall map of the world. A wall map could also be used as the focus for a display of pictures or artefacts (e.g. toys from other places, Figure 7).

## Level 2

'How localities may be similar and how they may differ' (KS1, PoS, 5b). At this level, the locality for comparison is not large but it must contrast. Children from an upland village need only go to the nearest market town and ask questions. What is this place like? Is it small? Does it have shops? Does the bus come every half hour? Where are the schools? Is it friendly? How is it different to home? How like home is it? A farm visit or a coastal visit could be appropriate here.

## Level 3

'...Describe and make comparisons between the physical and human features of different localities' (AT). Progression implies that the features to be compared at this level should be more specific. Are there mountains or rivers? What do people work at? Where do they work? What are the roads like? What do people do in leisure time?

For infants this could be achieved in their second locality study. For Years 3 and 4 it could be the introduction to a new locality.

## Level 4

Attainment is reached when geographical patterns can be described in the different localities as well as 'how the features of the localities influence the nature and location of human activities within them' (PoS, 5c).

In the context of the wider world, the processes of increasing agricultural production and extending urbanisation can not only be described but some understanding can be shown of the relationship between the processes and the changes which affect the lives and activities of the local people.

The information and the detail for looking at the wider world may come from overseas links or from secondary material giving much more detail in the form of a case study. Packs available from WWF, ActionAid and Oxfam are useful resources (see page 206), but, while usable in part by younger children, still require the maturity of the top junior child to be able to look at several factors at once and do more than just describe. These children should be able to look at a place and recognise that weather or economic agencies have affected its form, be it a plantation or a shanty town, an opencast mine working or a reservoir.

### Level 5

At this level relationships can be identified and explanations offered for a range of processes.

## Progression in looking at human features

### Understanding people

Looking at people, the way they are spread over the earth, how they move about and how they occupy themselves are the basics of geography. Investigating homes develops into investigating communities, which unite into urban hierarchies. Considering the jobs people do about the home develops into consideration of crafts and industries and eventually into economic activities of greater or lesser complexity. Taken together the activities of living form the human features which give character to a locality.

To answer the question 'How did it get like this?' requires an understanding of the importance of work and the effect that different kinds of work have upon a locality. There is a strong link here with history as we recognise how everyday life, work, leisure and culture, which has changed over time, has left its mark on the landscape and human features of each locality. Each school can develop a progression influenced by the resources available locally. The following sequences may be useful.

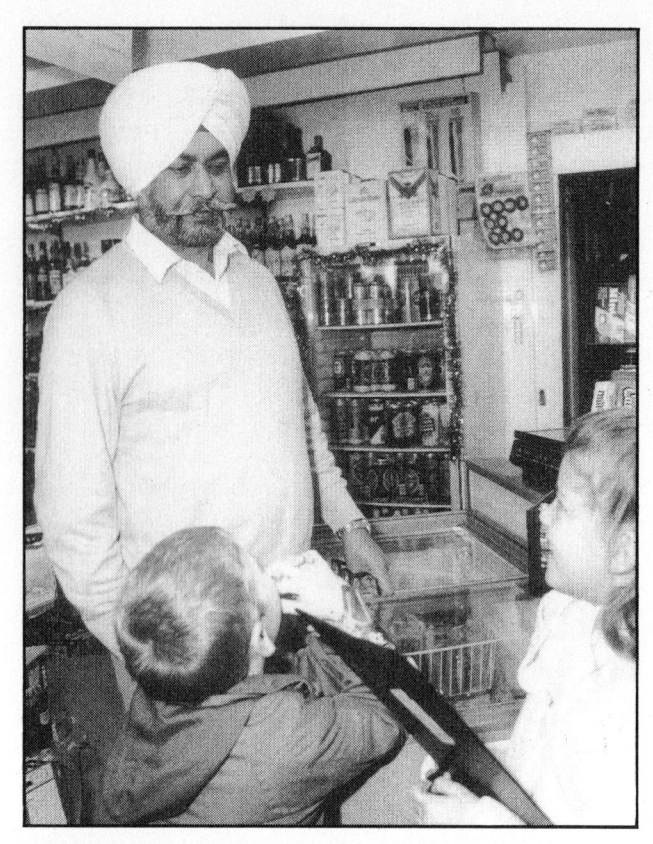

### Reception

Recognise that different people do different jobs in and about the school and that each responsibility and activity deserves a special name and location. These localities can be represented by figures on the school plan.

### Level 1

Develop knowledge and understanding of places (PoS, 1b) by increasing the survey of people who help in school to people who help in the community such as police, milk and post people, drivers and deliverers. Answer the question 'Where?' by making a picture map showing work stations and places visited.

### Level 2

Look at the different jobs done by other people such as relatives and friends and make a picture map of different work places. Develop a vocabulary for work places –

shops, sites, offices, factories, depots, warehouses, garages – and use it to describe their locality and the contrasting locality.

## Level 3

'**Describe and make comparisons between... different localities**' and '**show how localities may be similar and how they may differ**' (KS1, PoS, 5b). Compare local shops with a shopping mall and with the shops used by a link school. Find out the product of a local factory and where it is sold. Compare with one near to the link school. Similarly, compare farms and leisure activities.

## Level 4

'**Recognise and describe human processes**' and study '**how the features of the localities influence the nature and location of human activities within them**' (KS2, PoS, 5c). Contrast the jobs available in a rural area and those in an urban area. Consider the needs of a farming community and of a manufacturing town or the location of old industry near railways and new industries near motorways.

## Level 5

'**Offer explanations for ways in which human activities affect the environment**' (AT) uses the information gathered earlier but relates it to the changes seen in the localities.

# Understanding settlements

Although it is a theme at Key Stage 2, the study of the fabric of settlement begins at Key Stage 1.

## Reception

Encourage the children to talk about their own homes, their animals' homes and other people's homes. Walk round the neighbourhood together and see how many buildings are homes and how many buildings are used for other purposes.

## Level 1

Study '**how land and buildings... are used**' (KS1, PoS, 5d). Make a large scale model of the area and then let the children draw round it to make a plan showing buildings, which the children can then be asked to identify as homes, shops, places of worship or places of work.

## Level 2

'**Become aware... that the places they study exist within [a] broader... context**' (KS1, PoS, 1c). Use photographs, make models and use picture maps to show the differences between villages, towns and cities, in as many parts of the world as possible.

## Level 3

Study how settlements '**...vary in size and that their characteristics... reflect the types of economic activities in the settlement**' (KS2, PoS, 9a). The features investigated could be castles, market crosses, harbours or just boats on the beach, estate villages or just a large number of tractors at the garage, a large clock tower on the most important factory.

## Level 4

Describe '**how land in settlements is used in different ways**' (PoS, 9b). Use the age of buildings or the use of buildings to illustrate areas of different character in a settlement, such as a village, or part of a town or city, such as a suburb or an inner-city area (suburb of the past). Use simple categories at first – houses, shops, industry – before breaking down into discernible sub-groups, such as terrace house, house with gardens, light industry, small shops and so on.

Discuss '**...a particular issue arising from the way the land is used**' (PoS, 9c). Consider the effect new houses or a new supermarket will have on the chosen village or suburb.

## Level 5

Analyse the factors that influence the location and growth of individual settlements and identify the effects of such growth. Where were the first houses? By the bridge? Which is the oldest road? What was built next? This is a good topic for cross-curricular links with history.

Again, the progression is from discrete examples to patterns of distinct features and thence to considering the effect of change.

# Understanding routes

Locality features have links within, as well as between other, localities and it is significant that the examples for the thematic study of the environment at Key Stage 1 are concerned with movement along the links – along the paths, streets and roads.

## Reception

Encourage the children to look at ways of moving about (animals, birds, humans) and how everybody reaches school and by which route.

## Level 1

'**...Express views on the attractive and unattractive features**' of their journeys about the locality (KS1, PoS, 6a). How do people get to school, to the park and to work? How do they travel on holiday? What routes do they take and why?

## Level 2

'**Become aware that the world extends beyond their own locality**' (KS1, PoS, 1c). Investigate the routes people take to get to work both in the home locality and in a contrasting locality. Use road maps or an atlas. Use an atlas and globe to plot the journeys children make to other countries.

## Level 3

'**Become aware of how places fit into a wider geographical context**' (KS2, PoS, 1d). Make a traffic survey at a crossroads at a busy and a quiet time. Note place names from vans and lorries. Ask the children to use the data to make a map and discuss how the goods they buy reach the shops (KS2, PoS, 5e).

## Level 4

Study '**how the features of the localities influence the nature and location of human activities within them**' (KS2, PoS, 5c). Work out the shortest, longest and most level route for a wheelchair between places in school.

Use the sand tray to model the British Isles, complete with upland areas. Put in the motorway routes and intercity rail lines.

Devise a paper and pencil puzzle based on the local road network. Ask the children to try to link five places in the most efficient fashion. Then try to match this route with road patterns, bus routes or milk rounds in the neighbourhood.

## Level 5

'**Investigate how environments change... how people affect the environment**' (KS2, PoS, 10a). This could form useful cross-curricular links with history in showing how the local road and rail pattern has developed and culminating in considering the effect of a by-pass, actual or projected. Both description and explanation is required for the patterns revealed.

# Progression in environmental geography

The term 'environmental geography' covers many aspects which in the past were taught under the heading of resources and landscapes (for example, industrial resources and landscapes). The study of environmental geography has developed partly as a result of seeing the dereliction caused by the abandonment of old industries from the last century and partly through the development of valuing landscape for its own sake. Remember that man has always had an effect on his environment. For example, Neolithic and Bronze Age man cleared a great deal of our upland forest, of which little was able to grow back, and subsequent farmers continued the process.

## Understanding change

### Reception and Level 1

'**Express views on... attractive and unattractive features**' (KS1, PoS, 6a) for example the route to school, the playground and suggest what they would like to change to increase the attractiveness.

### Level 2

'**Express views on the attractive and unattractive features... of the environment of the locality**' (KS1, PoS, 6a) such as the local shopping parade, the park, a wooded area, their own street. In considering improvements (6c), the way it is used by other people should be recognised and the children's own observations used to support their suggestions. Use play people and LEGO to depict the spatial effects of digging pits and quarries in a tray with soil then use mustard and cress to show the effects of landscaping the holes and heaps.

### Level 3

'**The quality of the environment in any locality, either in the United Kingdom or overseas, should be investigated**' (KS1, PoS, 6). This could involve making judgements about places but, at this level, children should also show awareness of similar and different characteristics between places. This in turn will provide information about '**how that environment is changing**' (PoS, 6b). There may be new housing, increased traffic from increased numbers of visitors, or reduced work and increased wasteland from closed industries. This information will guide discussion on '**how the quality of that environment can be sustained and improved**' (PoS, 6c). Look for industrial workings and fields on old maps of the local area and find the same places and their landscape today. Are they hidden? Does anyone remember them from the past? Many places once devastated by industrial

151

workings are now attractions. Thorpe Park was one a gravel workings and the Metrocentre, Newcastle, is built on the site of an iron and steel works.

This work overlaps with initial work at Key Stage 2 where the emphasis becomes more specific **'how people affect the environment'** (PoS, 10a).

## Level 4

At this level, children are expected to **'describe how people can both improve and damage the environment'** (AT). Case studies of places similar to Thorpe Park can be used but useful work can be accomplished by making comparisons – for example, by considering the effect of building reservoirs in their own river basin as well as their chosen overseas locality (KS2, PoS, 10a). Similarly, finding out **how and why people seek to manage and sustain their environment'** (PoS, 10b) can be covered by considering the development of a local country park and the growth of the National Forest (see Resources) as well as by considering the plight of the tropical forests.

## Level 5

At this level, it is expected that the case studies can also provide evidence to explain why the environment was affected in the first place, and that recognition can be made of different ways of management and improvement. In short, this means putting environmental change in context and beginning to understand the effect of change over time.

The progression again follows the pattern of looking at single aspects (Key Stage 1), then putting several aspects in context, whether it is part of maintaining life or part of making life enjoyable. This lends itself to introducing the question of individual responsibility (for example, not wasting paper and reusing aluminium) and of corporate responsibility (for example, returning the land to a usable state. There are also many small topics, such as the importance of sites of special scientific interest (SSSI) and the practice of returning farmland to less intensive use, which can be usefully investigated at this level without trespassing on the larger environmental issues at Key Stage 3.

# Chapter ten
# Programmes of study

'Geography is concerned with the study of places, the human and physical processes which shape them and the people who live on them. It helps pupils make sense of their surroundings and the wider world.' (B1 1.1. *Geography Non-Statutory Guidance*, 1991).

Geography as a subject has kept its identity, despite concerted attempts by both the scientists and the sociologists to hijack various parts of the study of the earth to their domain. There are those who are unable to see the value of wide horizons and prefer to see teaching concentrated upon narrow lines to specific objectives. Geography could be disciplined upon those lines. However, the value of geography is that it can unite several strands together and in so doing illustrates relationships between various processes which work on the earth's surface. One way of looking at these relationships is to take the enquiry approach (see page 154). Another way is to look at distinct issues. Both approaches draw together the different aspects of the programmes of study, both require investigation using geographical skills of observation, recording and analysis and both require real places to be studied to see how human and physical processes affect the environment.

## The nature of the programmes

The programmes of study could be viewed merely as lists of knowledge, skills, and processes with three parts corresponding to: 'skills, places and themes'. However, taken and taught as separate items, the resulting curriculum would be very arid. The places, themes and skills need to be grouped to form units of study. Teachers of geography, however, have freedom to plan their units as they think most suitable for their pupils and school situation.

The attainment target now consists of substantial level descriptions for end-of-key-stage assessment. This clarifies the preparation of unique school plans.

The programmes of study describe what should be taught to help pupils to reach the levels. Planning and teaching National Curriculum geography involves thinking about places and the features which go to make those places distinctive.

In the course of discovering the distinctive features, geographical skills are expected to be developed as an integral part of the study, particularly with map and photographic research. Thematic studies are made in depth, it is hoped, as part of the study of particular places but these can be paired, for instance combining observing the work of a river with weather studies during a particularly long period of high rainfall, or combing settlement study with environmental change particularly over an **'issue arising from the way land is used'**.

Places which are studied in depth have been termed localities to allow some definition of location and size. The **minimum** requirement is two localities at Key Stage 1 and three localities at Key Stage 2. At each stage one locality is the home locality and at Key Stage 1 the other locality should be a contrast within the UK or overseas. In the interests of children's entitlement to wide horizons, a third locality would be preferable in each year. There is no reason why different years should not study different contrasting localities, with each year group reporting back its findings to the whole school. Similarly, at Key Stage 2 the UK locality could alternate between UK regions and the economically developing locality between continents. There is more latitude at this

| CROSS-CURRICULAR LINKS | | | |
| --- | --- | --- | --- |
| **English** | **History** | **Science** | **Mathematics** |
| Stories of different countries and cultures<br>Speaking, listening<br>Reading, writing (descriptions, reports, analyses, imaginative)<br>Interviewing<br>Abstracting and editing from primary and secondary sources | Industrialisation<br>Agriculture<br>Settlement<br>Migration<br>Urbanisation<br>Transport<br>Population<br>Exploration<br>Place in time and space | **Method**<br><br>Enquiry/hypothesis<br>Observation/recording<br>Interpretation<br><br>**Knowledge**<br><br>Climate, weather patterns and processes<br>Water processes and river systems<br>Weathering, erosion, transport, deposition<br>Earth and the Solar System<br>Earth structure and structures<br>Geological time scale<br>Rocks and their properties<br>Soils and vegetation<br>Ecologies | Key concepts shared include:<br><br>Distance<br>Direction<br>Area<br>Density<br>Height<br>Gradient<br>Nodes<br>Links<br>Networks<br>Shape<br>Size<br>Scale |

Figure 1

stage for including a wider range of places studied in depth for the themes of rivers, weather, settlement and environmental change. These can be studied in contexts which include the European Union. With whole school planning (see below) several schools have found this a feasible solution to providing a wide geographical education supported by field work and school links in a variety of places.

At Key Stage 1, the size of locality is necessarily defined as the area within easy access of the school buildings and grounds. At Key Stage 2, the area increases to contain the homes of the majority of pupils in the school. This suits the expanding activities of children with increasing maturity. The definition, however, is a minimum at both stages. Compare the facilities available to the inner city child and the rural child. The former probably has shops, medical care, community centre and local transport to hand but the nearest park is half an hour away by bus. The rural child by contrast has a choice of open play space close at hand but must travel miles for medical care, swimming baths, books, clothes and shoes and must carefully plan that travel. The outer suburban child does not fare much better – the acres of fields being replaced by acres of houses. Yet all are entitled to similar locality experiences and should not be confined by notional definitions of access.

The distinction between the material to be taught at each key stage is bridged by the overlap of levels of attainment and the admonishment **'Each [level] description should be considered in conjunction with the descriptions for adjacent levels'**. This is part of the common requirement that **'material may be selected from earlier or later key stages...to enable individual pupils to progress and demonstrate achievement...in contexts suitable to the pupils' age.'** Good practice in teaching topics in the primary school has always recognised the need to present opportunities for children to proceed at their own pace. This can take place in a variety of ways and not necessarily in a set order. There is no need to feel that the objectives of the higher levels have to be excluded from the teaching of the rest of the key stage. If assessment and record-keeping is maintained upon a whole-school basis and with emphasis on individual development, requirement in the programme of study 'that the children should be taught...' can become the much wider impetus to learn by enquiry.

# The enquiry approach and topics

At the beginning of each programme of study, there is a clear directive to teach by enquiry. **'Pupils should be given opportunities to: b) undertake studies that focus on geographical questions,** *e.g.,* *'What/Where is it? What is it like? How did it get like this?'*.

This is the approach developed in the rest of the chapter.

# The place of geography in the whole-school curriculum

Ascertaining the place of geography in the school curriculum involves agreeing the amount and frequency of time allocated to geography and deciding whether this should be on a specified 'lesson period' allocation or on a broader basis. There has to be a balance between subject-specific teaching and teaching through topic work, while within the topic area each subject should retain its distinctive characteristics. It is useful to consider the cross-curricular links before moving to the overall plan. *Geography for ages 5 to 16* (DES, 1990) consider this overlap which is illustrated in Figure 1.

The high degree of overlap, particularly with science and mathematics, means that there has to be agreement on terminology and the content of basic concepts and when and where they are to be introduced. For example, it could be agreed that the water cycle should be covered in full in all subjects. While it is simple to say that it rains then water runs away into the sea, becomes clouds and then it rains again, it is just as simple to give the full cycle – it rains, soaks in, runs off, dries up, moves away, cools down and rains again. With very young children, this could be introduced by referring to the well in the rhyme 'Jack and Jill' and to the way a hole dug in the sand at the seaside will fill with water. Children can later be introduced to the idea that deserts remain dry because the air is always moving away, taking the moisture with it.

A class investigation into soil might involve the examination of several inches of soil, revealing both vegetative, animal and mineral constituents (science). However, looking at soil from the top of the ground to the rock beneath has to be done *in situ*, and thus falls more into the area of geography. Looking at different places will reveal that soils are the result of the break-up of rocks and that the patterns in the profile, the different layers, are connected with the way water soaks in and dries up (or not) within the ground.

Again, when looking at the local area, the distribution of houses of a certain period can often be resolved by looking at both the sites of the houses (geography) and the position of the houses in relation to the way the land was held by various people, whether church, state, Crown or local landlord (history). Why towns suddenly grew in size (for example, Tonbridge in Kent) can be revealed by looking at both local records (of the craftspeople and the number of boats reaching Tonbridge from the Medway estuary) and the wider world beyond (history). The pace of growth, however, is, recorded in maps and in the age and style of the houses and other buildings that can be seen today (geography).

Links with mathematics are emphasised by the enquiry approach with its requirements for measurement, the use of numerical analysis and data handling techniques. Three essential strands of both mathematics and geography can be developed side by side in the primary classroom:
• the development of the use of coordinates;
• the use of graphs of various kinds;
• the use of models in developing three-dimensional work, whether as part of understanding plan and symbol (for example, using a street of box houses) or as a relief model, built up to help the children understand hills and valleys.

# The planning schedule

It is suggested that the programmes of study be viewed as part of an organised plan. Figure 2 is based on a suggestion in the Curriculum Council for Wales' edition of *Geography in the National Curriculum* 1991.

In a great majority of schools, geographical work has already been taught within the topic framework. The school planning stage will, therefore, consider two strands – what we already know we can do and what is needed to provide the focus at each key stage of the National Curriculum – before

| Stages of planning | Involvement |
| --- | --- |
| Whole-school curriculum plan | Whole staff: establish aims and ethos and out of school work |
| Geography curriculum plan | All staff teaching key stage geography: establish themes, issues, places |
| Scheme of work for key stages | Geography coordinator: overview of resources and expertise |
| Schemes of work for units, large or small 1 2 3 4 5 etc | Small groups/individuals: consider progression, continuity and enquiry |
| Lesson plans for each unit | Individual teachers: activities, resources, outcomes, NC strands |

Figure 2

assessing implications for changes in timing, emphasis, resourcing and staff development.

Figure 3 shows the minimum requirements for both place exploration and thematic investigations at Key Stages 1 and 2. These requirements should then be put alongside what is already happening in your school. Photocopiable page 203 comprises a sheet which can be used for such planning. A filled in example is shown in Figure 4.

| SUMMARY OF MINIMUM REQUIREMENTS FOR EXPLORING PLACES AND INVESTIGATING THEMES AT KS1 AND KS2 | | |
|---|---|---|
| Key Stage | Exploring place | Investigating themes |
| 1<br><br>Levels 1, 2, 3 | Exploration of a small environment familiar to the children. Making maps, labelling and developing vocabulary to use on drawings of and in writing about the school grounds, the pupil's own home, a small park. Following routes and noticing how the land is used and activities in the area.<br><br>Plus knowledge, understanding and awareness of two localities:<br>• Own local area, i.e. a small area that can be covered, e.g. a village, a housing estate.<br>• A contrasting UK locality, e.g., a rural/urban village; lowland/upland village; seaside/inland village.<br>• A locality in a country beyond the UK, e.g. where relatives live or in a school link.<br>• General awareness of other places in the world, e.g., holiday areas, places in the news. | Local scale thematic investigations with an environmental emphasis, e.g. play areas, paths to shops, safer streets, everyday shops, better ways of travelling, different kinds of buildings, more trees, safer water.<br><br>Plus knowledge, understanding and skills:<br>• Developing observation, recording and describing.<br>• Exploring the character of rocks, features in the locality, water and weather.<br>• Noticing the needs of the community as seen in the buildings, kind of work and other activities.<br>• Becoming involved in an environment improvement project, e.g. keep our school tidy, make more green play areas. |
| 2<br><br>Levels 2, 3, 4, 5 | Exploration of at least one locality of similar size, but different character in the UK or overseas by fieldwork and classroom activities. Find out about landscape features, rivers, buildings, patterns of land use, transport, distinctive activities and issues.<br><br>Plus knowledge, understanding and awareness of:<br>• Place localities in context, i.e., the area including the major shopping centres used by the children, short day visits, where their parents work, where the local football team plays, where the changes are happening.<br>• General awareness of other places in the world including regions, e.g. TV regions, water authority regions, counties, and the links between places and different countries. | Local scale thematic investigations with physical, human or environmental emphasis, e.g. microclimate in school; stream studies; a shopping centre, housing estate, landscaping projects, changes in road patterns and access.<br><br>One thematic investigation at regional/city scale with a physical, human or environmental emphasis, e.g. limestone landscapes, new out of town shopping areas, country parks.<br><br>One thematic investigation (physical, human or environmental emphasis) extending to national or international scale, e.g. National parks; areas of outstanding beauty, river basins and reservoirs; changes in work opportunities, fishing and environmental constraints.<br><br>Plus knowledge, understanding and skills:<br>of weather; measurement skills with instruments and maps; rivers and river basins; landforms and how they are shaped by erosion; transport and deposition; environmental quality; population; settlement; land uses; community goods and services; natural resources. |

Adapted from 'Try This Approach', E. Rawlings (Geog Assoc.)

Figure 3

| WHOLE SCHOOL ADJUSTMENTS TO NATIONAL CURRICULUM: GEOGRAPHY | | | | | |
|---|---|---|---|---|---|
| Year | Topics/ Geography already covered | National Curriculum requirements | Changes required | | |
| | | | Topics | Resources | Development |
| R | Myself<br>Homes<br>Shops<br>Water | Local area<br>Contrast area<br>Environment theme | Contrast area<br>Change | Maps<br>Photographs<br>all areas | Use of maps and photographs<br>School links |
| 1 | | | | | |
| | | | | | |

Figure 4

| USING ENQUIRY QUESTIONS FOR SHARING A TOPIC AT KS1 ||
|---|---|
| Geographical enquiry questions related to place Applied to: | A small familiar environment (eg home, school grounds, small park) |
| Where is this place? What is it like? How do people perceive it? What are its main characteristics? | Where is the park from my house (M)? What is a park? Who uses the park (H)(F)? Who works in the park (H)? |
| What are the important physical and human processes operating here? How did it get like this? | How is the land used (H)(M)? What does it grow (P)? Are there buildings (H)? What are the natural features (P)? What have the gardeners done? Has there always been a park (M)? What has been man-made? What has man changed? Do I like the park? Why? What could be improved (E)? What would I show a visitor (F)(M)? |
| How is this place changing? Why? With what consequences? What will happen? | |
| What do people think and feel about it? What do I think and feel about it? | |
| H - Human; P - Physical; E - Environmental theme; M - Map; F - Fieldwork skills ||

Figure 5

# Geographical schemes of work

## Places

Planning should be followed by developing schemes for each unit. Figure 5 shows how enquiry questions can shape a topic on a parks. This is based on questions put forward in E. Rawling's *Programmes of Study: Try This Approach*.

Figure 6 suggests how this can be developed into a scheme and a blank outline scheme form is provided on photocopiable page 204.

| AN OUTLINE SCHEME WHICH COULD BE ADAPTED DEPENDING UPON EMPHASIS FOR EACH YEAR AT KEY STAGE 1 |||||||
|---|---|---|---|---|---|---|
| Week | Questions | Concepts | PoS/knowledge/ skills | Activities/visits | Resources | Outcome Assessment | PoS |
| 1 | Where is the park? What is a park? | There are different uses of land | Study local area Map drawing Map reading Recognise slope, physical features | Take a walk through the park. Read maps. Talk to people in the park, gardeners and visitors. | OS 1,250 map or map from park Tape recorders for interviews Record sheets | Maps and drawings Descriptions on word processor | 1a 3b, 3c 3d 5a |
| 2 | Who uses a park? Who works in a park? How are the different parts used? | Uses of land are influenced by people's needs | Different kinds of users Use geographical language Recognise rock, soil, water | Find out when busy, when open, wheelchair access – counting people, collect samples with permission. Make model using samples. Take photographs, compare with old snaps. Notice signs of wear and tear. Draw up an improvement plan. | Polybags for samples, trowels Camera Old photo album | Observations and labelling of display Mount, label and display favourite features Draw new, improved plan using *Paintspa* | 3a, 3b 5a, 5d 3a, 3b 3d, 5d 3d 5a, 5b |
| 3 | How has it changed? Is the park liked? Could it be improved? | Changes are not always improvements Increased use is not always beneficial | Recognise man-made features, buildings, paths | | | | 6a 6b 6c |

Figure 6

| USING ENQUIRY QUESTIONS TO SHAPE A TOPIC ON PLACE AT KS2 ||
|---|---|
| **Geographical enquiry questions related to place Applied to:** | **An alpine valley – winter scene from travel brochure** |
| Where is this place? What is it like? How do people perceive it? What are its main characteristics? What are the important physical and human processes operating here? How did it get like this? How is this place changing? Why? With what consequences? What will happen? What do people think and feel about it? What do I think and feel about it? | Where is this place from my home? What does it have that is not found here? What is similar to home? How do people get about? What do people do? Where do they work? What kind of buildings are there? Do they have buses or trains? How long does the snow last? Have there always been hotels here? What was here before? Is the change a 'good thing'? What happens if there are too many tourists? |

Figure 7

Figure 7 uses the same enquiry questions for a locality, an Alpine valley, at Key Stage 2. Not only is there a possibility that at least one child in the class knows someone who has been skiing, but resource support is also available from travel brochures, colour supplement travel articles and television coverage of skiing events.

Once the questions have been asked and possibilities for resources and activities have begun to suggest themselves, the scheme can be planned to suit the time available, its place in the overall key stage scheme and in the school scheme. The possible outcomes will not only include the geographical statements of attainment but also core subjects. For example, investigations into ice involve work in science; time, season and compass direction (for aspect and the sun) involve mathematics; technology can be employed in devising ways of keeping roads open and going quickly up steep slopes.

## Themes

Figure 8 applies enquiry questions to topics at Key Stage 1 and Figure 9 does likewise in a broader context for Key Stage 2. Development of these is given in subsequent chapters.

| USING ENQUIRY QUESTIONS TO INVESTIGATE A TOPIC e.g. Water as a stream, Houses as homes |||
|---|---|---|
| **Geographical enquiry questions related to topic Applied to:** | **An investigation at local scale (physical/environmental)** | **An investigation at local scale (human/environmental)** |
| What is the topic or question? Where is it happening? How do people perceive it? How did this situation occur? How did it get like this? What physical and human processes caused it to happen? How is the situation changing? With what consequences? What will happen? What do people think and feel about this? What do I think and feel about it? | What is a stream? Where is there one near school? Can we play there? Are there fish? Does it smell? Why does it move quickly sometimes? What happens when it rains? When it rains a lot? Is this a big stream? Is it always like this? Do I like it? What would make it better? Who else uses it? Do they like it? | What is a housing estate? Are there different kinds of homes here? What makes a home? Why is this estate here? What is it made of? Who made it? Are people making changes? What kind of changes? Why make changes to houses? Do I like the houses? The changes? The estate? What would make it better? |

Figure 8

| Geographical enquiry questions related to thematic topic or issue  Applied to: | A thematic investigation at local scale (physical, human or environmental) | A thematic investigation at regional or city scale (physical, human or environmental) | A thematic investigation extending to national/ international scale (physical, human or environmental) |
|---|---|---|---|
| What is the topic, issue or question? Where is it happening? How do people perceive it?  How did this situation occur? How did it get like this? What physical and human processes caused it to happen?  How is the situation changing? With what consequences? What will happen?  What do people think and feel about this? What do I think and feel about this? | Do some parts of the playground stay wetter and colder than others? Does this affect the way the playground is used? What causes the differences? Can they be changed? Are the differences beneficial? How do we feel about this? Is there room for improvement? | What is chalk downland? Where is it found? What is it like? Does it have high hills? Deep valleys? Do rivers cross it? How is it used? Has it always been like this? How is it changing now, why? What can be done? Do people like the changes? Do we like the changes? | Where do earthquakes happen? What is an earthquake? Are there different kinds of earthquakes? Are people afraid of earthquakes? Do they avoid living in earthquake areas? What causes earthquakes? Do humans cause earthquakes? How do humans protect themselves from earthquakes? What can be done about earthquake disasters? |

Figure 9

The questions need not always be applied in the same order. Asking the question 'Where...?' can be just as important as asking 'What do you do when visiting the seaside? The hills? The mountains?' A question can be used to set a hypothesis, for example, 'Do children in cities travel shorter distances to school than children in rural areas?' Another set of questions can be applied to local and distant places starting with, 'What shall I show a visitor to my home area?' and progressing to, 'What do I want to know about an area I am visiting?' and eventually looking at the question, 'What changes does having visitors make to an area?' The progression from 'doubling-up' with siblings to make room for visitors at home to making space for vast hotel complexes and leisure centres looks at changes which can be explored by role-play, and in so doing emphasises various similarities, as well as differences, within any community.

The important point is to question continually and to avoid falling into the trap of looking at human and physical features with no attempt at understanding them. Questioning is also a way of establishing what false images and perceptions have taken root and can help to dispel preconceived ideas and establish that what may be true of one small part of a country is not necessarily true for the whole country.

# Freedom of choice

The non-statutory guidances and new programmes of study emphasise that the programmes of study can be covered from a thematic and a locality approach.

'Topics covering physical, human or environmental geography enable several localities to be studied at the same time... Topics about one locality allow links to be drawn between aspects of human, physical and environmental geography.' (C5 3.8 *Geography Non-statutory Guidance*, 1991)

'In determining the breadth and depth of the places to be studied, teachers should explore the potential of those places for providing contexts for study in physical, human and environmental geography and for developing geographical skills. Places will be studied in different amounts of detail.' (Page 9 'Knowledge and understanding of places' *Geography Non-Statutory Guidance* CCW, 1991)

**'Pupils should be given opportunities to: become aware that the world extends beyond their own locality, both within and outside the United Kingdom, and that the places they study exist within this broader geographical context...'** (KS1, PoS, 1c).

The teacher is free to choose the character of courses at both Key Stage 1 and Key Stage 2. The minimum requirements allow an emphasis on place studies with thematic knowledge and skill developed in this framework and an emphasis on thematic investigations with knowledge of places developed in this framework.

The teacher is also able to decide how far the course focuses on several major geography-led investigations (the minimum is one thematic at Key Stage 1 and four at Key Stage 2) or uses smaller sequences of enquiry on their own or within work planned for other subjects. In both key stages, the teacher can decide how the balance of skill requirements and locational knowledge requirements are met.

This latter freedom means the temptation to cram certain skills into one short period and to make the children learn locational knowledge by rote must be avoided. Any skill learned has, by its very nature, to be little and often. Similarly, the knowledge of location of place is built up over time by association with other knowledge which acts as a hook on which to fix the locational information. For example, London is famous for the Tower (it has a castle), St Paul's Cathedral (it is one of many cathedral cities) and its location on the River Thames. Furthermore, it is a capital city. Paris also has a castle, a cathedral and is located on the River Seine. It too is a capital city. Both rivers are the major rivers of the country. In the same way, one can go on to ask what distinguishes Berlin, Madrid or Rome. Quizzes and parents can both be used as other learning media, but there is nothing more useful than pointing to where a place is on a map or globe as often as it is referred to in the classroom.

It is said that it takes a fortnight for a habit to be established. Set aside a geography fortnight in which there will be a conscious attempt by everyone in the class, visitors too, to locate every place they mention. The corollary of this is that there have to be maps available on every scale from the locality to the whole world! And, of course, every classroom should have an atlas with a gazetteer – a dictionary of places – alongside the dictionary of words.

# Lesson plans

Once the scheme is set out, whether geography-focused or only including geography, the lessons can be planned. These are very individual pieces of endeavour. Some teachers rely solely upon a small notebook with jottings which are helpful to them but do not necessarily give a clear guide as to how the lesson fits into the larger scheme of things. Detailed planning is fundamental to a child's progress through school and the whole-school approach. Figure 10 overleaf suggests a framework which may be useful for evaluating what was hoped for and what actually succeeded.

Lesson plans should be regarded as recipes, but *not* just the 'great aunt' type of recipe which says, 'Take butter, sugar and ground rice, mix, put with jam in pastry cases and cook in a moderate oven'! In the same way, simply jotting down the word 'houses' as a lesson plan does not tell you *how* or *what* you intend to teach. Noting the precise concepts and knowledge is useful for compiling an overview of what has been covered. The account of activities will similarly encourage a variety of approaches. For resources, remember to note not just the title of a story, but also the author and the ISBN number and publisher of the book in which the story occurs. The story may be tried out using a local library copy or even an inspection copy which has to be returned, but if you intend to purchase it at a later date you will need to know the full details. Similarly, for videos and other media resources, catalogue numbers are invaluable time savers.

| | LESSON PLAN OUTLINE | |
|---|---|---|
| Class | Levels | Key Stage |
| Date/Time | Topic | Lesson No.    /of Total |
| Concept | | |
| Knowledge | | |
| Skills/Vocabulary | | |
| Resources | | |
| Questions | Activities | |
| Assessment | | |
| National Curriculum | | |
| Evaluation | | |

Figure 10

# Chapter eleven
# Topics, projects, places and themes: KS1

'Geography is a good straightforward subject and would be quite easy if it were not so big', Eric Linklater from *The Wind on the Moon* (Canongate, 1986) quoted in *Geography for ages 5 to 16* (DES, 1990).

One of the more repeated complaints from teachers and student teachers grappling with the demands of the National Curriculum has been, 'I've been given this topic to do but I cannot see where the geography fits in.' On one occasion a teacher was complemented upon the good geographical content of a topic and gave the reply, 'But I was only doing shape for maths!' Nonetheless, her reception class had walked round to each other's front doors, had been photographed and had put their addresses under their own photographs. Besides recognising the oblongs, triangles, squares and circles involved, the children also enjoyed saying where each front door was in relation to other front doors '... and that's Rajiv's shop, I get ice-cream there'. There had been no hidden agenda, except perhaps one for safety in learning/reinforcing the idea of address, but an enquiry question ('Where?') had been asked and answered. Direct experience had been used, the child's cognitive map had been reinforced, features had been recognised, both outside and in the classroom, and pride in belonging to a place had been emphasised. There may also have begun the idea of a route! Concepts from the programme of study for geography had all been touched on, as well as work in mathematics being covered.

The HMI report *Aspects of Primary Education: The teaching and learning of history and geography* (HMSO, 1989) was critical of the use of topics as a means of teaching geography. Nonetheless, where geography was well taught, topic work was very often the main feature of the curriculum. Certainly topic work, with contributions from several disciplines, is very often the only way of completing a rounded study with excellence in presentation (art), based upon previous observation, recording and interpretation (science and geography) which initially started from an idea in a story (English). The mechanics of reporting the evidence and analysing the results could be covered by work in IT, while technology and mathematics would also play their part. Thus, the topic of 'Homes' could be introduced with the tale of 'The Three Little Pigs'. Figures 1 and 2 show how this could be developed and extended for classes at Key Stage 1. A map showing regional house styles or a travel game involving holiday in different kinds of home could also be used to introduce other places and to discover the range of knowledge in the class ready for developing future work. These ideas are developed in *Starting Geography: Homes* (Scholastic, 1991).

## Starting points: stories and poems

Many stories and rhymes can be used as starting points for geographical topics, not least because they often use geographical vocabulary. Stories and rhymes also rely upon setting the scene and in so doing provide stimulus for considering different environments.

In *Geographical Work in Primary and Middle Schools* (1988, GA) Alison Tonkin has shown how stories can be used to illustrate basic geographical concepts for young children. For example, 'Little Red Riding Hood' could be a starting point for urban

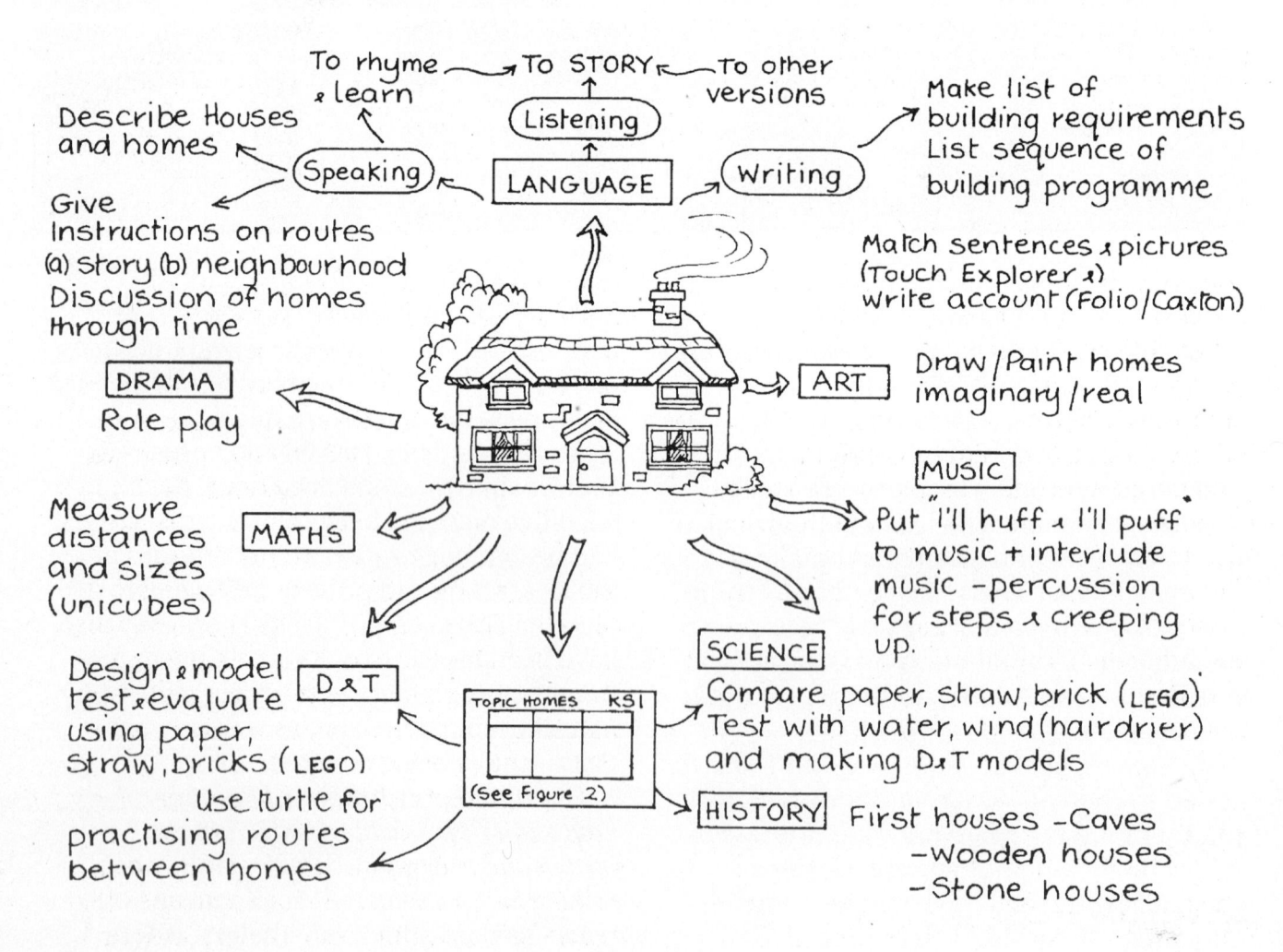

Figure 1

| Geographical questions | Concepts/Skills/PoS | Activities |
|---|---|---|
| How are homes different? Why are they different? Where do the materials come from? | Similarity difference 5b, a | Compare pigs' homes. Compare with own home. Discuss preferences. |
| How can you make a symbol which will remind us of the straw house? Can you make it smaller? | Symbol, scale, communicating 3d | Draw a symbol for each pig's home. Draw the symbol exactly the same but smaller. |
| What does it look like from above? What would a giant see if he looked down on your house? | Space, mapping 3d | Draw a plan of each house and other homes. |
| Which way round shall we put it? Where shall we put the homes? Why? Where are they on the map? N, S, E & W. How is our map different to the world outside (flat/slope, other houses etc.)? | Space/direction, mapping 3c/d | Paint large floor map with paths. Include N, S, E & W. Place the three homes on the map - models or plan shapes. |
| Which way will he go? Is there a quicker way? Which house does he blow down first? Will the pigs be able to see him coming? What will the wolf see on the way? | Scale direction, hypothesising, discussing, planning 3c, 1b | Discuss possible routes for the wolf taking into account the order of the story. |
| How shall we tell him the way? | Direction, giving and following instructions 3a, b Mappings, points of compass 3c, d | Give the wolf instructions on which way to go (left/right, NSEW depending on level). Child or programmable toy takes on the role of the wolf. |
| Although this is an activity for the higher levels of ability, children at lower levels could be asked how the map was different from the floor map. | Space/location, mapping 3e | On a simple 3 x 3 or 4 x 4 grid work sheet draw a map, pictorial or symbolic, of the floor map. Place homes on your map using a simple key. Give letter/number coordinates of the house. Mark the route on the map. |

Based on Figure C3, 'Geography in the National Curriculum : Non Statutory Guidance for Teachers' (1991, CCW)

Figure 2

children in finding out about the character of a wood. Support material could come from other stories, such as *The Tale of Squirrel Nutkin* by Beatrix Potter, and from using picture reference books to find out about the different trees and bushes behind which the wolf could hide and which provide shelter for all the other animals living in the wood. Concepts of distance, direction and location can be illustrated from the route Red Riding Hood takes, imaginary maps can be drawn and a frieze made of the features mentioned in order. This could then be contrasted with a frieze of features passed on a walk familiar to the children.

# Using story for graphicacy

Maps and routes can be drawn from many stories. Roald Dahl's *Fantastic Mr Fox* contains a cognitive map of places which the fox can reach from under the ground. *Rosie's Walk* by Pat Hutchins involves another fox and gives an interesting basis for making a route map or devising a game of route instruction with associated symbols. R. L. Stevenson's *Treasure Island* is well known for its possibilities for map-drawing and developing direction, location and symbols at an imaginative level. The Narnia stories by C. S. Lewis inspired the publishing company, Collins, to produce a poster map of Narnia which could be used as the inspiration for a class poster competition. *The Lion, The Witch and the Wardrobe* especially forms an excellent basis for Level 3 work on winter weather, as well as introducing topography and associated geographical terms for relief features such as hills, mountains, lowlands and so on.

## Story and environment

Environments are beautifully described and illustrated by Helen Cowcher in *Rain Forest* and *Antarctica*. Nigel Gray describes and Jane Ray illustrates the landscapes which *Balloon for Grandad* flies over after it has escaped out of the window, thus providing an ideal introduction to contrasting localities. This book could prove especially useful if any of the children have already been abroad on holiday and need some help in describing what they saw. In *Noah's Ark*, Jane Ray takes the King James' Bible text of Noah and the flood, but starts and finishes the story in a garden, thus highlighting the fact that although floods are hazards they are also beneficial. Other illustrators with a feel for environment are Brian Wildsmith, John Burningham and Janet Ahlberg.

## Others' view of place

Myths, legends, folk and fairy tales around the world provide the background for investigating contrasting localities in both developed and developing countries. Stories such as those about the Caribbean man-spider, Anansi, present a view of a culture very different from that of the northern hemisphere.

## Different environments and everyday life

The stories of Postman Pat, Ivor the Engine, Spot, Mowgli and Thomas the Tank Engine involve situations which can easily be translated to actual happenings. Thomas the Tank Engine slips on leaves on the line and Ivor the Engine has to cope with snowdrifts. Thomas's 'Branch Line Engines' are based on the narrow gauge railways which were used by the slate and other quarry industries in upland Britain to get their products to the customer. These are an excellent introduction to recognising where and how resources are obtained.

In the same way, Postman Pat's delivery round could be used to encourage the children to consider how the post arrives at their own homes. These stories offer ready-made comparisons for looking at why different forms of transport are used for different purposes.

The Resources section, page 206, attempts to indicate how the attainment targets can be enhanced by the use of stories, poems and songs. However, the selection is bound to have omitted someone's favourites. There is, moreover, nothing to beat the instinct of a good teacher for the potential in a story to provide illustration of a particular point in a subject area.

Remember that a Book Week is meant to have themes. Ask for a series of geographical themes. If they run children's reading sessions, the local library staff could prove helpful with advice and supply. Start a card index system or better still a database!

Stories are good stimuli when it is difficult to get outside the classroom, but direct experience should always be the first resource. Very often one can collect so much information from outside the classroom that the topic work becomes diffused and no subject benefits. Many schools are now beginning to have a flexible approach to topic work. Instead of six weeks of fully integrated multi-subject approach, topics are of varying length. Some topics focus entirely upon the subject needs at National Curriculum level, others have a focus which uses two subjects, such as history/geography, science/geography, geography/technology or geography/mathematics, which then use other subjects in a subsidiary fashion to provide final polish (for example, art, IT and English) or reinforcement (for example, PE and music). The subject focus in no way precludes consideration of cross-curricular themes such as safety, health education, economic and industrial understanding, environmental education, education for citizenship and self-awareness.

Indeed, environmental education is enhanced by the geography environment themes, and to read definitions of environmental education is often to read the subject contributions of geography, history and science.

# Schemes

The following schemes attempt to show how units of work may be planned with topics in mind but also built around key questions which lead to the development of learning and understanding thus accomplishing the objectives of the levels of attainment. They are loosely based upon work undertaken by Gloucester Humanities Advisors who trialled history/geography projects for the National Curriculum with 40 schools. The work was subsequently published in ring binder form, as *Another Time, Another Place*.

## Reception: Buildings and roads

Figure 3 shows the first steps in observation, mapping and considering why people make journeys. Although the statements of attainment are noted, this is only an indication of which part of the programme of study has been considered.

## Year one: Around and about

Map work can be combined with written descriptions of villages, as in the 'Village with Three Corners' in the *One, Two, Three and Away!* books by Sheila McCullagh (Collins) or *Shaker Lane* by Provensen and Provensen (Walker Books), around school to recognise buildings and their uses as well as address. Figure 4 overleaf shows how this topic can be approached over the course of six weeks. In Chapter twelve the same topic is approached in a way that is appropriate for ten- to eleven-year-olds, and thus offers a study in progression.

## Year two: Moving house

Another way of looking at houses is through the topic of 'Moving house'. It could also be a useful way of approaching the trauma of moving house in a school which has an unsettled population. As with year 1, the topic incorporates map, photograph and IT

| TOPIC: BUILDINGS AND ROADS | | | YEAR R  4-5 YEARS  LEVEL 1 | | | TERM: | |
|---|---|---|---|---|---|---|---|
| Week | Questions | Concepts | PoS/knowledge/skills KS/Place: theme | Activities/visits Fieldwork Organisation | Resources Starting points | Outcomes Assessment | PoS |
| 1 | How are buildings arranged near school? | Roads are lined with buildings. | Buildings vary. Buildings join on to, or are spaced apart from, each other. They have an order. | View road from playground and school barriers. Questions and answers - pavements, buildings, houses, garages, traffic. Identify and sort photos. Draw picture map. | Immediate local area. Camera. Photographs. | Display sorts, maps and stimulus posters. Sequence photographs along road. | 5a 3b 3a 3d |
| 2 | How can we show the road and buildings? | Buildings and roads make patterns. | Develop location. Understand slope. Recognise plan. | Show the road shape. Put photographs in order down road. Discuss slope - if present. Replace buildings with boxes or LEGO. Draw round. | Photographs. Boxes for models. | Display model and plan made from model. Make key for detail e.g. pavement, garden, lampposts. | 3c 3d 3a 5a |
| 3 | What happens to the road? | Roads are for journeys. | Develop idea of journey. | View road again at several short periods in groups. Tally vehicles seen, locate delivery vehicles on local map. | Local map. Toy vehicles. Touch pad. Map. | Show map + road + depots and own maps drawn with *Paintspa*. | 3e 3d 6a-c |
| Amendments: | | This can extend by walking further from school; adding a cross roads (brings in direction). Make more detailed traffic survey and location map, link with maths. | | | | | |

Adapted from a case study in *Another Time, Another Place* Gloucester County Council

Figure 3

| TOPIC: ROUND AND ABOUT | | | YEAR: KS1  5-6 YEARS  LEVEL 1 | | | TERM: Autumn, 1st half | |
|---|---|---|---|---|---|---|---|
| Week | Questions | Concepts/ ideas Purpose | PoS/knowledge/skills KS/Place: theme | Activities/visits Fieldwork Organisation | Resources Starting points | Outcomes Assessment | PoS |
| 1 | What does it look like? Does it look the same from two viewpoints? | An area can be represented in a variety of ways. | Representation of an area. Use overlay keyboard to make map relating aerial view, photos, route and features. | Walk around and about. Discussion of aerial photo and features seen on ground and from air. Use overlay keyboard to make map. | Camera. Aerial photograph. Photographs of same features on the ground. *Touch Explorer Plus*. | Drawings of favourite buildings. WP labels. Aerial view with photos, pointers, labels. Map of walk (IT). Assess: location and labels. | 3a-f |
| 2 | Why are they like that? | Buildings are different for various reasons. Different homes can vary from place to place. | Buildings have different uses. Towns and villages are different from each other and from imaginary villages. | Discussion and writing. | Photographs of town and village. | Labelled display to show different buildings in each place. Assess: understanding. | 3b 5a, 5b 5d |
| 3 | Where are the buildings? | Plans are not pictures | Relate a settlement from a model to a pictorial map and then a plan. | Class make model of village or town arranged according to pictorial map, in groups. Draw picture and bird's eye view sketch map. | 'Junk' modelling equipment. | Picture maps. Bird's eye view maps. Assess: orientation. | 5b 5d 3d 3e |
| 4 | How did they come to be like that? | Buildings have different shapes. | Buildings of different ages and/or uses have different shapes. Fieldwork: organisation, observation, recording. | Walk in playground to learn outdoor discipline and discuss use of school buildings. Walk near school to record windows, roof shapes, street furniture etc. | Clipboards. Tape recorder. Pencils. | Drawings. Records. Assess: observation. | 5d 3a 3b 3c 3d |
| 5 | How do other people live? | To compare special buildings e.g. church, farm, house types. | Special buildings have special features. Fieldwork: observation, recording and presenting. | Visit to rural/urban village for contrast e.g. farm, church, town hall. Discuss and match to labels on follow-up sheet. Note address of special buildings. | Duplicated drawings of five buildings a) at home b) at place visited. | Detailed drawings. Group display of buildings seen. Assess: recording & presenting. | 5b 5d |
| 6 | How do we know where places are located? | Each place has an address. | Know own address. Work out other addresses. | Use local base map to locate each child's home; games on name/address, etc. | Register. Photographs. Drawings. | Photograph and map display incorporating address. Assess: knowledge. | 3e 3f |
| Amendments: | | | Use 1-6 with Level 2 with more buildings, larger area visited (whole street, whole farm) and more group work. | | | | |

Adapted from a case study in *Another time, Another Place* Gloucester County Council

Figure 4

work. Figure 5 overleaf shows how this topic could be approached over five weeks.

A corollary of this topic could be to look at family geographies. A great-great-grandfather could have come from one country, met up with great-great-grandmother from other county and moved to yet another county in which they and their children and grandchildren have stayed ever since! Meanwhile, other relatives such as cousins, uncles and aunts might have moved from other places to other countries. Plotting the journeys on a map of the British Isles and the world will help increase awareness, as well as indicating where to choose the contrasting localities of most benefit to the class. (PoS, 1c).

## Year 2: A first farm visit

Becoming aware of a world beyond school may only require a short journey to a rural or city farm, or into the suburbs for a market garden. Some children may have visited a working farm while on holiday, others may only keep pets, but these experiments can be sufficient to develop understanding of a farm, its buildings and the land it occupies. Suggestions for development of this topic over five weeks are given in Figure 6 overleaf. (PoS, 5d).

## Year 3: The land

Recognising a familiar feature as geographical often needs persistence. I have not forgotten being told (by a teacher!) that I was joking when I thought to point out that the valley side we had just descended had been constructed by the stream which was being studied. Fortunately, children are more prepared to accept the possibility of enormous consequences of river work over time. Figure 7 on page 171 offers ideas for developing this topic over three weeks (PoS, 5a).

## Year 4: Rivers, soils and water

The science programme of study on materials requires the recognition of rock, rocks and soil – and that they occur naturally. To understand changes in the character of landscape and the pattern of rural land use, the characteristics of rocks and soils should be seen on location and linked to the features developed on them in the locality. Why is it difficult to scramble to the top of the hill? Why does the school field become boggy? What makes Castle Hill? Why is the heath a heath? Why are carrots grown here and only conifers grown there? (PoS, 5a, b; 7b).

## Other topics and themes

### Birthdays

Is there a difference between having a birthday in winter and one in summer? Is party food different between the seasons? Are parties the same in other countries? What do children eat at parties in other parts of the world? What kind of games do they play? Do they have birthday parties at all? (PoS, 5c).

### Ourselves

How similar or different is my day from Rajiv's in India or Sam's in Australia? How different is it from that of other children in other countries?

Let the children draw round their hands and feet to compare sizes and to make 1:1 plans. Hand spans and feet can be used to make measures, although of course, individual hands and feet are different lengths so when using them as units of measurement you might find that any piece of classroom furniture measured appears to keep changing size! Are we all the same height? Do we all have the same colour hair? Is it the same colour as that of children in other countries (PoS, 4 and 5b).

### Toys

Use a world map so show where the children's toys were made. Show various

| TOPIC: MOVING HOUSE | | | YEAR: KS2   6–7 YEARS   LEVEL 2/3 | | | TERM: | |
|---|---|---|---|---|---|---|---|
| Week | Questions | Concepts/ ideas Purpose | PoS/knowledge/skills KS/Place: theme | Activities/visits Fieldwork Organisation | Resources Starting points | Outcomes Assessment | PoS |
| 1 | What makes a garden? | Gardens vary in size and character. | Maps, use of land, production. Houses with and without gardens. | Maps of own gardens. Symbols for planning a vegetable garden. | *Mole Moves House* by E. & G. Buchanan (1989, Macdonald). | Maps, plans. Imaginative map of Mr Carrington's gardens. | 5a 3a-d |
| 2 | What makes a house? | Houses vary in shape and size. | Type of house: bungalow, terrace, flats, semi-detached, etc. Building materials. | Explore Albert's House to determine what is needed in a new house. Observe different types round school. Sort collection and label. | Albert's House software. Use photos or field observation. Collect materials. | Map of Albert's House. Graph of house. Map of types. Mr Carrington's bungalow. | 5a 3f |
| 3 | Why change house? | Change for improvement. | Change for space, pleasure, job, etc. | Visit a local large house. Explore garden. | Estate agents' descriptions. Local map. | Map of visit. Drawing of house and labels. | 6a-c 5d |
| 4 | How do people move? | Journeys are of different types. | People make different journeys. | Investigate how people travel to school, to work and on holiday. Look at delivery vans and classify. | Toy vehicles. Holiday homes and houses. Atlas/map. | Picture maps of journeys. | 5a 3a |
| 5 | Where would you like to move? | Town and country are different. | Contrasting localities and sizes. | Draw map and write about where to move. | *Town and Country Mouse*. | Maps and descriptions. IT. | 5b |

**Amendments:** In an urban area the large house and garden may be the local museum and park. This can move up to Level 3 by starting at week three and using *Town and Country Mouse* as a starting point.

Adapted from a case study in *Another Time, Another Place*, Gloucester County Council, which used the story *Mole Moves House*.

Figure 5

| TOPIC: A FIRST FARM VISIT | | | YEAR : KS1 | | | TERM: | |
|---|---|---|---|---|---|---|---|
| Week | Questions | Concepts | PoS/knowledge/skills KS/Place: theme | Activities/visits Fieldwork Organisation | Resources Starting points | Outcomes Assessment | PoS |
| 1 | What is a farm? | Farms have special buildings and special animals. | Learn that farms are special places. Prepare for visit. | Make a model farm and draw a pictorial map. Use for directional games and farm vocabulary. Make questionnaire. | Model materials and toy animals and vehicles. | Pictorial map. Route directions for a partner. Questions on IT. | 5d 3a-f |
| 2 and 3 | What work is done on a farm? | Farmers grow crops and keep animals. | Learn that farm work is different for different parts of the year. Time and seasons. | Follow programme arranged beforehand with farmer for groups and helpers. Collect samples rocks/soil/ plants. | Tape recorder. Questionnaires. Maps. Camera. | Model of farm visited. Farmer's Year Chart (for example, available from Shell Ed. Service). | 5d 5c 5a 3b |
| 4 | How does the work change? | Farms are affected by weather and land. | Learn that rock, soil, water and light affect plants. | Plant experiments +/– water, light, inside, outside. School garden. See where fields, woods and water are on farm. | Weather records. Seeds. Map of farm. | Put model on map of farm showing land use and where samples taken. | 5c 5a 3a 3d |
| 5 | How different from the home area? | Farms make country. | Look for similarities and differences. | Compare buildings, open spaces, roads, vehicles etc. | Photographs of both places. | Mount display and show whole school. | 5b 3f |

Figure 6

| TOPIC: THE LAND | | | YEAR: KS1 | | | TERM: | |
|---|---|---|---|---|---|---|---|
| Week | Questions | Concepts | PoS/knowledge/skills KS/Place: theme | Activities/visits Fieldwork Organisation | Resources Starting points | Outcomes Assessment | PoS |
| 1 | Is the land about school high or low? | Some places are higher than others. | Understand hill, valley, slope and other vocabulary. | Look for high and low things in the classroom (cover with cloth), in school, in the playground. View from the school. | Local photographs | Drawings. Labels to photographs. | 5a 3a 3f |
| 2 | How do you get from high to low? What is the land made of? | Land slopes down or up hill. Different rocks are found in different places. | Recognise rock, soil and water in the landscape. | Walk in the school locality with map to show where road slopes. Collect rocks or identify local rocks/brought in rocks. | 'Grand Old Duke of York'. Local rocks. Local map. | Labelled rocks on base map of area + hill, etc. Labels. | 3b 3c, 3d 5a |
| 3 | What makes a steep slope? | Slopes vary. | Recognise steep slopes on different scales, e.g. river bank, mountainside. | Experiment with cars and wooden slopes; build gentle and steep slopes in sand and gravel. | Photos of hills and mountains. Toy models. | Model with labels. | 5a 3f |

**Amendments:** If relevant, add an oblique aerial photograph to look at local hills from the air and compare with places on the 1:10,000 OS map.

Figure 7

| TOPIC: ROCKS, SOIL AND WATER | | | YEAR: KS1/2 | | | TERM: | |
|---|---|---|---|---|---|---|---|
| Week | Questions | Concepts | PoS/knowledge/skills KS/Place: theme | Activities/visits Fieldwork Organisation | Resources Starting points | Outcomes Assessment | PoS |
| 1 | What are rocks? Where are they in the locality? | Rocks are compact substances with different characteristics. | Discover differences between rocks. | Walk round school/park, collect rocks and put in bag with label of where collected. Sort and classify on colour, shapes in rock, hardness and roundness. | Start collection with material from building merchants. Make reference collection for school. | Labelled collection - use WP for labels. Map of rock features in locality. | 5a 3a 3b |
| 2 | What is soil? Are there different soils in our area? | Soils are made of different materials. | Discover the characteristics of different soils and how they work with water. Soils = earth. | Walk round school/park, collect soils and label. Sort and test for colour/ holding together with water/dirtying of fingers. Shake and settle with water. | Have set of reference soils from local DIY (up to 12 possible). Set of jars for settling. | Labelled set of soils settled in water. Map of open spaces. | 5a 5d 3a 3b |
| 3 | How do rocks and soil affect the land? | Rocks and soil react differently to water. | Discover what happens to water on rock and soil. | Make plate gardens with rock pieces and soil; shake grass seed over, water with spray. Draw result or make pictorial map. | Old plates or seed trays; grass seed; lid to collect water. | Labelled garden and map. Label map above for water and vegetation. | 3d 3a |

Figure 8

171

famous toy-making regions, for example wooden toys from the Black Forest, musical boxes from Switzerland, kites from Japan, LEGO from Legoland in Denmark and so on. Look at the different materials that are used and help the children to see how some are made from grass and leaves as well as wood and metal, glass and different fabrics. Costume dolls can be used to demonstrate similarities and differences, especially in national dress (PoS, 4 and 5b).

## Wheels

Organise a simple traffic survey, either from the school playground or looking at the children's toy vehicles. Sort them according to size, capacity, number of wheels and length, and then by the kind of work they do. Who do the vehicles help in their work? From this will come service, retail, manufacturing and industries such as farming, quarrying and so on (PoS, 5a).

Where can these vehicles go? Start by looking at cycle ways, then progress through major and minor roads to motorways (PoS, 5a). Look for these routes on the local map and road maps.

Where do the vehicles 'live'? Make plans of car garages, houses with garages (What happens if there is no garage?), parking zones, car parks, bus garages, emergency services garages and depots, repair garages and petrol garages (PoS, 5d).

Where do you or the children's family or friends park their cars on a sunny day to keep them cool? (Direction and shadows (PoS, 3c; 5c)).

What happens when the ground slopes? Is there a limit to how steep a slope a vehicle will climb? Organise a test using model slopes in sand, gravel and wood. If your school is in a hilly area, look for evidence of old tramway and gravity railways from quarries and mines. These are often still shown on the 1:50,000 Ordnance Survey maps, certainly on the older one-inch maps (3e; 5a).

Look at the location of railways and the different kinds of railway. Why do they take the route they do? (3e; 5d).

## Water

This is often regarded as a science-focused subject, but again by applying the questions 'Where?', 'How?' 'What?', 'Why?' and 'When?', the geographical themes are covered and, if applied to the home area and a contrasting locality, the major features of water in the environment are covered. Skills of mapping and measuring are an integral part.

*Starting Geography: Water* (1992, Scholastic) expands upon the possibilities outlined in Figure 9.

## Air

Another topic which is often given a science focus is 'Air'. However, this has many geographical applications. Science tends to look in detail at one spot, whether experimentally or at one place upon the globe. Geography, on the other hand, looks at similarities and differences between locations as well as the overall view of global climate.

A country's climate is its average weather. Britain's climate is very changeable indeed, this is its major feature. By contrast, the equatorial climate is very predictable. Almost to the time of day, the daily thunderstorm occurs. As one moves away from the equator, tropical climates acquire extremes of very dry and very wet seasons and as one moves out of the tropics so the dry seasons get longer and the wet seasons less and less predictable. Raymond Chatlani's poem in *The Green Umbrella* (1991, A & C Black) describes a stream and a desert and captures perfectly the way in which hot winds blow out from the deserts, taking with them moisture from beyond the desert edge. The winds cool on reaching areas beyond the deserts and the moisture falls to form rivers and streams again.

Notice how in temperature latitudes the air changes character from day to day or at least from week to week. Help the children to observe how the direction from which the wind is blowing gives the air its character, such as the summer heatwave with winds

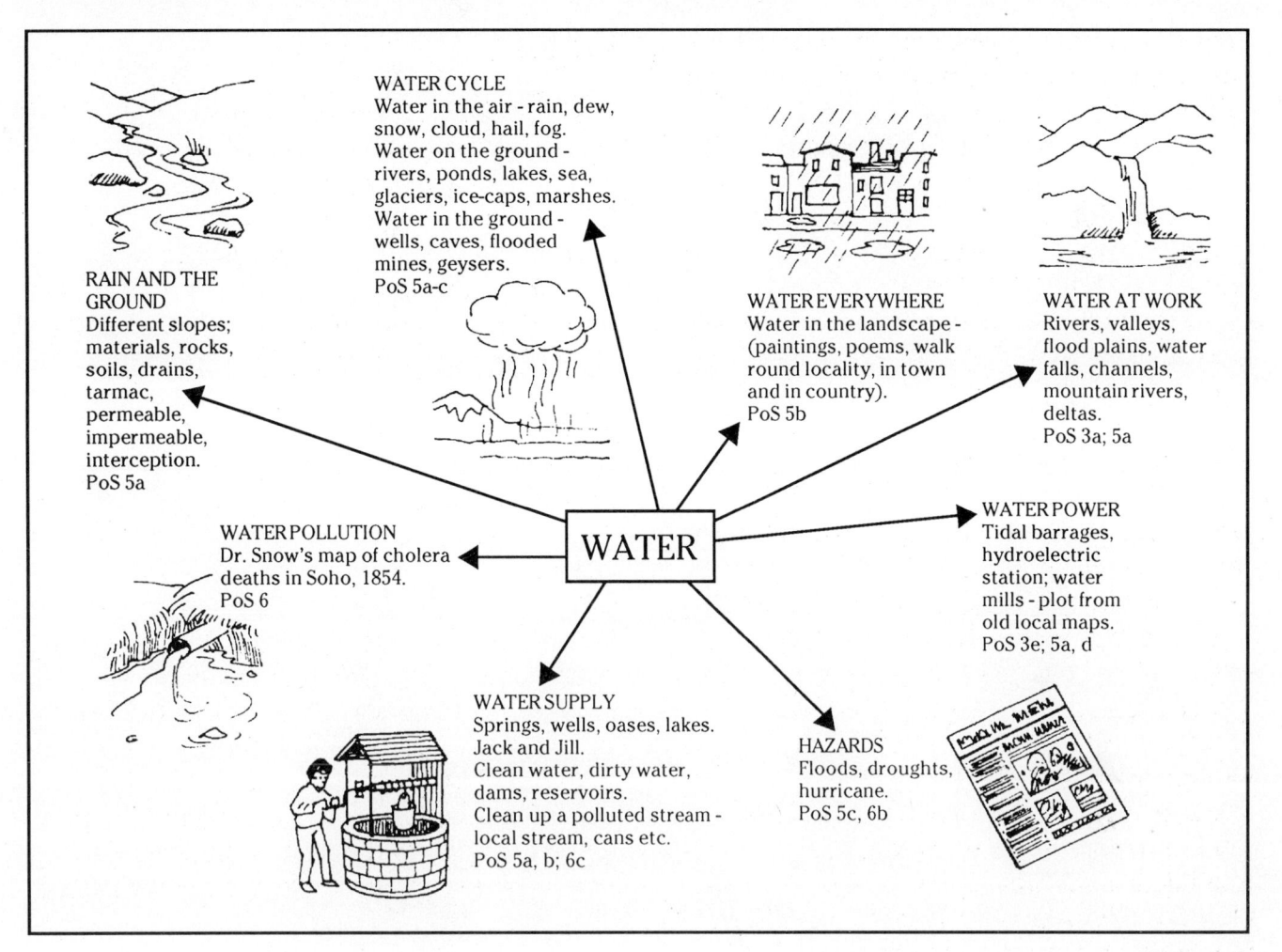

**WATER CYCLE**
Water in the air - rain, dew, snow, cloud, hail, fog.
Water on the ground - rivers, ponds, lakes, sea, glaciers, ice-caps, marshes.
Water in the ground - wells, caves, flooded mines, geysers.
PoS 5a-c

**RAIN AND THE GROUND**
Different slopes; materials, rocks, soils, drains, tarmac, permeable, impermeable, interception.
PoS 5a

**WATER EVERYWHERE**
Water in the landscape - (paintings, poems, walk round locality, in town and in country).
PoS 5b

**WATER AT WORK**
Rivers, valleys, flood plains, water falls, channels, mountain rivers, deltas.
PoS 3a; 5a

**WATER POLLUTION**
Dr. Snow's map of cholera deaths in Soho, 1854.
PoS 6

**WATER POWER**
Tidal barrages, hydroelectric station; water mills - plot from old local maps.
PoS 3e; 5a, d

**WATER SUPPLY**
Springs, wells, oases, lakes. Jack and Jill.
Clean water, dirty water, dams, reservoirs.
Clean up a polluted stream - local stream, cans etc.
PoS 5a, b; 6c

**HAZARDS**
Floods, droughts, hurricane.
PoS 5c, 6b

Figure 9

blowing out from the continent from the east to the west, already hot and dry; the winter snow coming from the polar regions due to the north wind; the mild wet weather brought by lows generated over the Gulf Stream in the mid-Atlantic and moving in from the south west; the Gulf Stream itself moving from the warm equatorial regions to bring warmth to the cooler latitudes; and those very warm, humid days characterised by winds from the south bringing tropical air direct from the Azores. Science supplies the criteria for describing these parcels of air as they arrive at the weather station, while geography explains the reasons for the variations between the masses of air.

'Adopt' cities in other countries and let groups of children record the weather and compare it with the local weather. With younger children, comparisons can be made by thinking about the clothes that are worn and the food that is eaten, while older children can compare data and look at the average figures for the place as given in an atlas. Thus the term 'continental temperate' and 'maritime temperature' may begin to mean something when London's cool summer is compared with Moscow's oven-like temperatures.

Figure 10 overleaf shows how air can be harnessed to provide energy. Again, science and technology provide the precise knowledge but maximum benefit can only be achieved by using geographical skills to find the best site for any wind generator. This need not always be in the windiest place in the locality for siting megawatt wind farm. Many farmers have a wind generator often adjacent to their buildings, which provides power for specific packing or processing enterprises and which still manages to provide some surplus for the national grid system. Look at the work of windmills. Are they always used for grinding corn? Can they be used for pumping water away from the fields (for example, in the fens and

**PRESSURE**
Global climate; continental highs and lows, air masses. 'The stream and the desert', Raymond Chatlani in *The Green Umbrella* (1991, A & C Black).
PoS 1c; 3f; 5c

**WIND POWER**
Windmills, wind farms. Yachts/Explorers tall ships.
PoS 1c; 3f; 5a

**RISING AIR**
Air transport. Gliding, balloons.
PoS 6a-c

**TEMPERATURE**
Seasons/day and night changes, weathering, wind chill, altitude.
PoS 1e; 3f; 5c

**AIR**

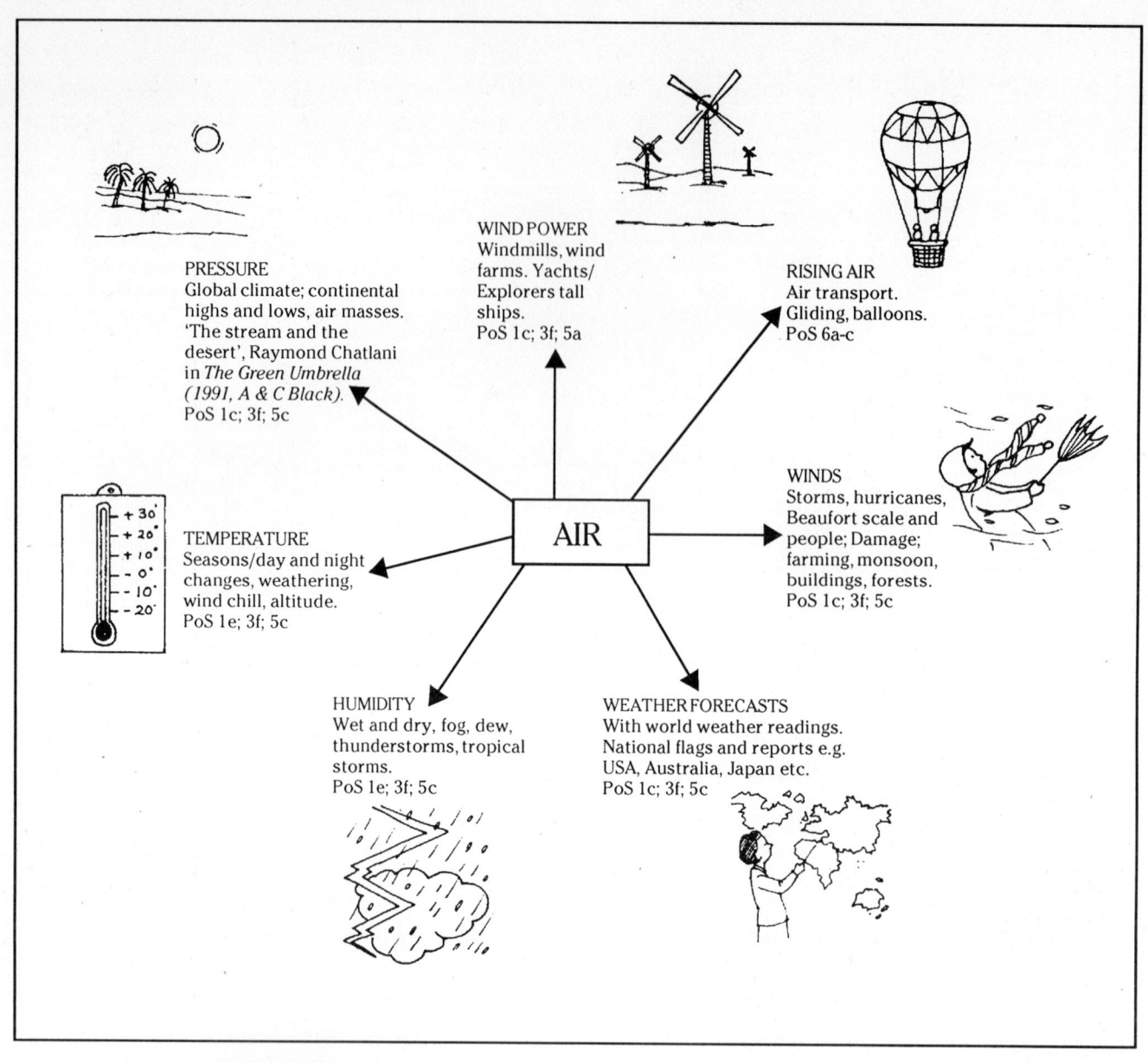

**WINDS**
Storms, hurricanes, Beaufort scale and people; Damage; farming, monsoon, buildings, forests.
PoS 1c; 3f; 5c

**HUMIDITY**
Wet and dry, fog, dew, thunderstorms, tropical storms.
PoS 1e; 3f; 5c

**WEATHER FORECASTS**
With world weather readings. National flags and reports e.g. USA, Australia, Japan etc.
PoS 1c; 3f; 5c

Figure 10

lowlands)? Why do yachts and tall ships follow certain well-defined routes? What is a harmattan? Where does it blow? When does it blow? Is it liked?

# The whole-school curriculum

Planning the whole-school curriculum and the geography element within it has already been outlined in Chapter 10. Figures 11 and 12 on pages 175 and 176 gives an outline for the geographical content for each term of the year. This includes a range of possibilities and titles and covers both Key Stages 1 and 2. The planning of each key stage should not be done in isolation; Key Stage 1 is the foundation for work undertaken in Key Stage 2. Planning both together will allow for a widening of the scale of study, a return to key ideas at higher levels (the spiral curriculum), the introduction of greater precision and the developing and refining of skills.

Photocopiable page 204 comprises a scheme planning sheet which may be useful both from transferring current topics and planning future topics.

Finally, there are several topics which have yet to be touched upon, for example 'Food', 'People' and 'Places'. These will be considered in Chapter 12 under the umbrella of Key Stage 2.

## Key Stage course: outline planner
## KEY STAGE 1

Specific objectives for geographical education at this KS:
- The local area
- A contrasting locality in the United Kingdom or a locality overseas
- Larger geographical areas

Specific emphases (place exploration/thematic investigation; scale emphases, etc.) by Year:
- R: Home, another building, an open space
- 1: Several homes, journeys (routes), streets, shops, farms
- 2: Villages, land use, locality sizes, rivers, factories

| Year | Term 1 | Term 2 | Term 3 | Opportunities for cross-curricular themes |
|---|---|---|---|---|
| R<br>Age 4/5 | All about me<br>Ourselves<br>School<br>Special days | Toys<br>Seasons<br>People who help us | New life: plants and animals<br>Journeys/roads<br>The farm | Just outside<br>Out and about |
| | Fieldwork in locality in short and group visits | | Longer visit to community building | Sensory trail |
| 1<br>Age 5/6 | Where we live<br>Shopping | Moving around<br>Keeping safe | Our school<br>Mini-beasts<br>Weather<br>The farm | Homes and settlements |
| | Double period work outdoors involving observation and recording | | Farm visit | Following pathways in the locality |
| 2<br>Age 6/7 | Wind and sun<br>Other lands<br>Party time | Under control<br>Wheels<br>People and work | Treasure island<br>The countryside<br>The land | Food and celebrations |
| | Mapping and observation of specific landscape features | | Larger scale investigation – combined with history, maths, science | |
| | Weather observations | ↑ | School garden | ↑<br>On going activities throughout school |
| | Rock Collecting | ↑ | | |

Figure 11

## Key Stage course: outline planner
## KEY STAGE 2

Specific objectives for geographical education at this KS:
- Own local area
- Contrasting UK locality
- Economically developing country
- The home region, other countries

Specific emphases (place exploration/thematic investigation; scale emphases, etc.) by Year:
- 3: Local scale, microclimate, shopping.
- 4: Regional scale, shopping centres, work areas, river basin.
- 5: National scale, getting around the UK and another country.
- 6: International scale, weather hazards, development, conservation.

| Year | Term 1 | Term 2 | Term 3 | Opportunities for cross-curricular themes |
|---|---|---|---|---|
| 3 Age 7/8 | Ground level Rocks and soil Managing waste | Our place Buildings Direction Round and about | Holidays Europe Another farm | Our local community |
| | Investigate specific features in the locality including business and a second visit to a farm | | | Environmental work |
| 4 Age 8/9 | Exploration The forest Paper and print Resources | Supermarkets Food and farming Mountains Lowlands | Up and away Here and there Energy | Water in the landscape |
| | Investigate hypotheses, link observations to cause and effect: school journey to a contrasting locality | | | United work in contrasting locality |
| 5 | Survival Nowhere to play | Did you hear that... Hazards around the world | Beyond... The British Isles | Rocks, resources and rivers |
| Age 9/10 | Follow physical investigation | Half term investigation e.g. shopping, farming overseas and landscape | School journey week; own region Consolidate, and develop previous fieldwork | Use school garden for conservation and irrigation experiments |
| 6 | Moving New worlds New environments | Energy How did that get there? | Conserving or supplying Do we need that? | Our overseas friends Islands |
| Age 10/11 | Research – regional scale topics: floods, sewage, waste. | Depots; housing and industrial development | School journey week: contrasting region | Research and make a trail for visitors |

Figure 12

# Chapter twelve
# Topics, projects, places and themes: KS2

At Key Stage 2, it is still possible to approach teaching geography from the child-centred, integrated topic, particularly when considering the local environment. On the other hand, by Key Stage 2 the geographical emphasis is going beyond the neighbourhood, looking at the immediate is being succeeded by considering several distinct aspects both of the locality and of contrasting localities which are becoming increasingly distant. Figure 1 overleaf gives a summary of the programme of study by level. If traced across the table, the change of focus with increasing maturity becomes apparent. Descriptions of single elements develop into descriptions of grouped elements and then to reasons for the location and the size of those elements. Homes give way to settlements, villages grow into towns and cities and crafts become industries which compete for land and sites from and to which they can distribute their products quickly. In order to cope with this increasing complexity, some school have chosen to treat geography in a more compartmentalised way. Yet even when compartmentalised, other curriculum subjects still use geographical examples to illustrate certain concepts or skills. This is especially true of history and science when dealing with the environment. (For example, consider the sites of the Saxon shore forts or the location of the habitats of different species.) Similarly, the geographer will often need to use mathematics and technology to process the data and simulate the fieldwork processes which require analysis and explanation in the classroom. English skills are vital for clarity of description and analysis, while reading stories, poems and descriptive accounts plays no less a part at Key Stage 2 than at Key Stage 1. This strong two-way partnership should be maintained at all costs.

## Role play

One way of developing understanding is to put the children into situations which model the lives of people in different environments.

| | A DESCRIPTION OF THE PROGRAMME OF STUDY BY LEVEL SHOWING PROGRESSION KEY STAGE TWO | | | | |
|---|---|---|---|---|---|
| PoS Theme | Level 2 | Level 3 | Level 4 | Level 5 |
| Geographical skills | Enquiry should take place outside and inside classrooms based on fieldwork and other activities. Observation should include measurement and involve the use of IT. Further information should come from a variety of sources and skills developed in using photographs, videos, visitors accounts, maps, globes, TV and radio programmes, computer databases, books, newspapers, CD-ROM. | | | | |
| | • Use tape measures, clinometers, stop-watches, rain gauges, thermometers, vanes and wind gauges.<br>• Measure and record weather observations.<br>• Develop a geographical vocabulary to aid description from pictures, photographs and other sources.<br>• Make representations of real or imaginary places.<br>• Draw sketch maps using symbols and key.<br>• Follow a route; make a map of a short route; use symbols with keys.<br>• Interpret symbols, measure direction and distance and follow routes.<br>• Determine the straight line distance between two points on a plan/map.<br>• Use letter and number coordinates; use four-figure grid references to locate features; locate their position on a large scale map.<br>• Relate features from a vertical aerial photograph to a map.<br>• Use maps to find locations; use atlases including the index and contents additional to the maps.<br>• Use IT to obtain information, handle, classify, and present data. | | | • Interpret maps showing relationships.<br>• Follow a route on an OS map and describe what would be seen.<br>• Use conventional 1:50,000 or 1:25,000 OS map symbols with the aid of a key.<br>• Use six-figure grid references. |
| Places | • Investigate the use of buildings and land in the local area. | • Use correct geographical vocabulary to identify local landscape features and industrial and leisure activities. | • Know the geographical features of the home region.<br>• Know that own locality is part of a region. | • Study the main features of the home region and how they are inter-related. |
| Localities:<br><br>UK contrast<br><br>Economically developing country (EDC) | • Describe the homes, buildings, services and types of work in the local area. | • Describe features and occupations of other localities and compare with local area (UK, EDC). | • Examine the effect of landscape, climate and wealth on the lives of people in a locality in an EDC. | • Understand how occupational land use and settlement in patterns of an EDC are related to the area's environment and locality.<br>• Understand how occupational land use and settlement patterns in an EC locality are related to the area's environment and locality. |
| | • Investigate features of other localities and how these affect other people's lives (UK or overseas).<br>• Identify and describe similarities and differences between local and other areas (UK or overseas). | • Observe and suggest reasons for relationships between land use, building and activities, e.g. shops and homes.<br>• Suggest reasons for location and presence of specific economic activities in local area. | • Understand how localities have been changed by human actions (UK and EDC).<br>• Investigate recent or proposed changes in a locality (UK and EDC). | |
| Regions:<br><br>Home and beyond | • Know that their country is part of the UK (England, Scotland, Wales and N Ireland). | • Locate on a map the UK countries.<br>• Mark home location on BI map. | • Identify on globes and maps the places specified on maps A, B and C. | • Identify on a globe and map the places specified on maps D, E and F. |

Figure 1

| | A DESCRIPTION OF THE PROGRAMME OF STUDY BY LEVEL SHOWING PROGRESSION KEY STAGE TWO | | | |
|---|---|---|---|---|
| PoS Theme | Level 2 | Level 3 | Level 4 | Level 5 |
| Rivers | • Identify water in different forms. | • Recognise what happens to rainwater when it falls on different surfaces, slopes and runs over the ground.<br>• Identify and describe landscape features including river, hill, valley, lake, beach. | • Perceive that rivers erode, transport and deposit materials.<br>• Know that rivers have sources, channels, tributaries and mouths, and that they receive water from a wide area (drainage basin). | • Recognise the causes and effects of river floods and methods used to reduce flood risk.<br>• Perceive the effects of frost action, chemical and biological weathering. |
| Weather | • Investigate the different effects of weather on people and the environment.<br>• Recognise seasonal weather patterns. | • Appreciate weather conditions in different parts of the world. | • Recognise how site conditions can influence surface temperatures, affect wind speed and direction. | • Know the difference between weather and climate.<br>• Recognise the seasonal patterns of temperature and rainfall over the British Isles. |
| Settlement | • Recognise that homes and other buildings are part of settlements of different sizes. | • Recognise that buildings and other features can show how and why settlements began and grow/function. | • Study the layout and function of a small settlement or part of a larger settlement and evaluate the effect of current or recent change. | • Recognise the reasons for the location and growth of individual settlements and the benefits and problems of growth. |
| Settlement | • Recognise how goods and services needed in the community are provided. | • Recognise that work and buildings require land to be used in different ways and in different amounts. | • Understand the reasons for different land uses and for location of different types of work. | • Understand why economic activities may develop in particular locations. |
| Settlement | | | • Study an issue which demonstrates how conflict can arise over competition for land use. | • Investigate types and patterns of land use in farming, manufacturing and retail industries. |
| Environmental change | • Identify activities which have changed or are changing the environment.<br>• Consider ways in which they can improve own environment. | • Recognise how extraction of natural resources affects the environment.<br>• Recognise activities intended to improve the local environment. | • Recognise damaged environments can be restored and damage prevented. | • Understand why rivers, lakes and seas are vulnerable to pollution. |
| Environmental change | | | • Know ways of improving the environment and of the need to give special protection for some types of environment. | • Investigate ways of preventing pollution. |

Figure 1 *(continued)*

Role-play is a development from the shop and house play of the younger child. Characters have to be assumed, then attitudes and perceptions can be challenged, as more than one point of view is presented.

In the National Curriculum Working Party final report (June 1990), the aims of geographical education are stated to be to:
- stimulate pupils' interests in their surroundings and in the variety of physical and human conditions on the Earth's surface;
- foster their sense of wonder at the beauty of the world about them;
- help them to develop an informed concern about the quality of the environment and the future of the human habitat;
- enhance their sense of responsibility for the care of the Earth and its peoples.

One way of achieving this is to put children in the position of thinking about the basic requirements of human beings. The urban child could perhaps be asked to imagine being stranded out in the countryside. How would they survive? This question of survival involves an interesting combination of science and geography skills.

Some years ago a young doctor and a museum curator set out to walk from Scarborough to Southport, eating only what they could find in the hedgerows, fields and woods on the way. It was summer and hedgehogs were still plentiful, but they were defeated by the enticing smell of bacon and eggs halfway across Lancashire!

The children could be asked to plan a similar venture. Mapwork would be needed for finding out how England could be crossed from east to west. (What terrain would be crossed? How could the towns be avoided?) Science skills would be needed to find out what would be the edible and easily gathered foodstuffs from the habitats which would be encountered.

Survival is a theme which stimulates imagination and creative capacities and can involve children in considering distant environments. (What would happen if they were survivors of a plane crash in the jungle, a desert, a polar ice cap or the highest part of the Andes?) The programme of study requests that children should be taught **'how the features of localities influence the nature and location of human activities within them.'**

With sufficient guidance and resource material, children should be able to use the survival theme to accomplish this request, with the added bonus of recognising what remarkable achievements of self-help and adaptability are made by local people. This can be emphasised by reading extracts from James Vance Marshall's *Walkabout* (1980, Penguin) in which an Aborigine boy meets two American children lost in the Australian desert and finds them 'amazingly helpless; untaught, unskilled, utterly incapable of fending for themselves; perhaps the last survivors of some peculiarly backward race'.

Role-play is basically a classroom debate, so it is important for the teacher to prepare it well beforehand to ensure that the parameters are clear regarding both the characters and concepts to be discussed. What are 'basic needs'? Who will provide them? How will they be provided? What will be the consequences? Use photographs, descriptions and a worksheet stating the situation, perhaps in the form of a question, for example:
- Fairs to come to the Heath in summer as well as Bank Holidays – should this happen?
- Winter Olympics for the Cairngorms?
- New irrigation schemes and villages for the pastoralists (who previously had followed their herds for food and water)?

About six or seven characters, such as the local resident, the occasional visitor, the regular visitor, the commercial concern, the government and so on will cover most interests in the problem. *The Green Umbrella* (1991, A & C Black) provides some interesting starting points. Initially produced for use in assemblies, it looks at how we should care for water, air and other elements of our environment.

# The place of role-play in a scheme

The use of role play could be tied to a specific scheme, for example, ActionAid's

*Pampagrande: a Peruvian village* study (see Resources, page 206).

Introduce the role-play by telling the children who their characters are and where they live. For example, 'You are six (or nine or eleven – whatever the age of your class). You live in _____ village in the country of _____'. Enquiry questions which could then be raised could include:
• What will we expect to find there? (Are their perceptions stereotyped?)
• What is it really like? (Collect information from a variety of sources.)
• Why is it as it is? (Encourage the children to make connections between factors, such as weather and climate in relation to farming; location in relation to people and communications.)
• How is it changing? (Use news media and simulations.)

Let the children work in pairs or groups, considering the viewpoints of the different characters so that all sides of the arguments can be presented. Then ask one spokesperson for each character to put their view to a simulated meeting of the local community. Different perceptions will emerge and the teacher must act as chairperson and final arbitrator in the debate. Alternatively a vote could be taken.

Outcomes could be presented as a newspaper report or a display of photographs of the children with bubbles of their statements of each viewpoint presented from the platform could be made. At the same time, the following questions should be explored:
• Do different lifestyles damage the environment?
• Can we learn from other people's lifestyles?
• How are traditional ways of life changing? Is this a good thing?
• Are modern improvements useful in difficult environments (for example, snow mobiles, tractors instead of dog sledges and bullocks)? Where does the energy come from?

Form links with technology by asking the children to build working models of shadufs or a shanty town (complete with water and power). Let them construct a model tropical grassland village using traditional materials and then introduce the concept of 'intermediate technology' and consideration of an economically developing country.

Further suggestions and sources of information are given in the Resources section on page 206.

Figures 11 and 12 in Chapter eleven, pages 175/6, suggest the topic areas which could be covered geographically.

# Landscape evaluation

Evaluation of a landscape is a useful way of developing children's skills in the observation of detail and encouraging them to go beyond superficial appreciation. Figure 2 offers a scheme which is not apparently demanding but which would, however, benefit from being discussed beforehand or at the first viewpoint to ensure the individual parameters have some semblance of

| Assessment scheme A (Simple) | |
| --- | --- |
| Very pleasant/very attractive | 5 |
| Pleasant/quite attractive | 4 |
| Acceptable/reasonable | 3 |
| Not very pleasant | 2 |
| Unpleasant/unattractive | 1 |
| Nothing to recommend | 0 |

Figure 2

agreement. By nature, evaluation has various idiosyncratic approaches which can be adopted. This is no bad thing but some corporate agreement is helpful, if only to guide the indecisive as to what is being looked for!

This scheme can be used initially for looking at wide views of a landscape, applying the scale first to the foreground, then the middle distance, then to the far distance. If necessary, divide each distance view into left, centre and right regions. Use squared paper to make a simple sketch view on which each area has its appropriate code,

| Assessment section B (landscape elements) | Code | Score |
|---|---|---|
| • Water character | | |
| Clear, fast flowing, rapids/falls | A | 10 |
| Clear, slow, pools, no pollution | B | 7 |
| Water muddy, no pollution | C | 3 |
| Organic decomposition, some pollution | D | 1 |
| • River channel character | | |
| Incised channel in rock | a | 10 |
| Incised channel in loose deposits | b | 8 |
| Eroding channel with slumping | c | 4 |
| Poorly defined shallow channel | d | 2 |
| Channel difficult to define | e | 0 |
| • River channel margins | | |
| Trees lining bank, penetrable | t | 5 |
| Grass lined channel | u | 4 |
| Trees and shrubs, impenetrable | v | 2 |
| Houses, boundaries, e.g. walls | w | 1 |
| Regulated channel (concrete, etc) | x | 2 |
| Rubbish present | y | 1 |
| Rubbish very evident | z | 0 |

Figure 3

then correct the areas with an appropriate map.

More detailed evaluation can be made along a trail, such as a stream valley. Similar criteria could be established for following a main road which moves from an inner city area, through basic nineteenth century housing, nineteenth century mansions with twentieth century infill, public housing and private estates and finally to the open land at the edge of town.

Assessment scheme B (Landscape elements; for example, stream channel and valley) allows for sophisticated assessment with many categories, although the five point scale may be found more manageable for some children. However the technique stays the same. Examples of assessment using Figure 3 could be as follows:
• Tree lined, eroding channel with slumping on its banks and muddy water with high sediment content = Ccu and score 12.
• A stable, incised channel, eroded in loose deposit with rapidly flowing clear water and some trees = Abt and score 22.
The most degraded and derelict landscapes should have the lowest scores. The point score could also be made into a colour code, e.g. greens through yellows to orange and red as the landscape deteriorates from rural to industrial/urban.

# Schemes for Key Stage 2

## Holidays

The topic of holidays can be used successfully with Year 3 children, as it is appropriate to any age or stage of development. The elements shown in Figure 4 opposite can be taken in sequence as a half-term project or as units on their own to fit in with other geographical themes. For example, week 2 could include looking at the theme of settlements and how they have distinctive buildings which reveal the function of the settlement (for example in holiday resorts). Week 3 could involve seeing how transport routes are not always the most direct route between places.

## A contrasting UK locality

Another area of overlap between Key Stages 1 and 2 is the contrasting areas in the United Kingdom. Many urban or lowland children will not be familiar with upland areas and vice versa. Figure 5 opposite shows how this topic can either fit in with pictorial or video information or can be used with the older children as a follow up for a residential school journey.

## An urban environment

This topic offers children a chance to investigate the use of buildings, use correct geographical vocabulary and use maps and photographs to find out where features are located and where the children are themselves. It allows observation of how land is used in different ways and encourages the children to observe and explain the relationships between landuse, buildings and human activity.

Figure 6 on page 185 shows how this topic can be used for identifying how an environment has been changed, especially if using a series of aerial photographs taken at different times, a series of maps of a similar scale (e.g. 1:2,500) and a set of trade

| TOPIC: HOLIDAY PLACES | | | | YEAR : KS1/2 | | | TERM: |
|---|---|---|---|---|---|---|---|
| Week | Questions | Concepts | PoS/knowledge/skills KS/Place: theme | Activities/visits Fieldwork Organisation | Resources Starting points | Outcomes Assessment | PoS |
| 1 | Where have you been? | Holiday places are in many landscapes. | Learn about highland, lowland, coast, mountain, islands, cities, theme parks, National Parks, different environments. | Locate postcards. Sort into environments. Describe each environment. Graph kinds of holiday places. | Postcard from children. Map of UK and Europe or world. John Burningham's *80 Days Round the World* (Collins). | Display of map and cards and paintings. Chart of kinds of holiday places. | 4 5b 3f |
| 2 | Why go to holiday places? | Holiday places have special features. | Building functions. Need for car parks. Leisure needs. Attractions. | Discuss the different buildings at a holiday place. List - draw in groups. Plan an ideal resort, including the beach. Compare with home. | Select one place or use a big book photograph. | Likes and dislikes about a holiday place. WP writing. | 5d 6a 3f |
| 3 | How to get to holiday places in the UK? | People use different transport for different reasons. | Cover delivery and speed of transport needs. | On overlay mark in routes to different places where class have holidayed. Role-play transporting ice-cream, a sick child, a large family, etc. | UK map showing motorways, railways and ferries. | Print out of maps showing routes to different places plus keys and labels. | 3a 3e 5d 6b |
| 4 | How to get to foreign holiday places. What to see? | Different transports take different routes. Different weather. | Time zones; changing points; ports, airports, railway and bus stations. | Follow, in groups, the routes taken by a lorry driver, John Burningham or Phineas Fogg/ Jules Verne, Michael Palin. | World map, atlas. Globe. Orange peel. Photographs. | Maps of routes - if possible on different projections. Make travel presentation with IT. | 3a, 3e 1d, 8 5d, 6a-c |

Figure 4

| TOPIC: CONTRAST LOCALITY | | | | YEAR : KS1/2 | | | TERM: |
|---|---|---|---|---|---|---|---|
| Week | Questions | Concepts | PoS/knowledge/skills KS/Place: theme | Activities/visits Fieldwork Organisation | Resources Starting points | Outcomes Assessment | PoS |
| 1 | Where is this place? What is it like? | Rocks, slopes and open space are important features of upland areas. Tall buildings, narrow streets of some urban areas. | Understand the difference between hills and mountains, rivers and valleys, steep and gentle slopes. Relationship of moor, wood, field, marsh to open space; or park, housing estate, office block. | Listen, watch and discuss. Make models in the sand tray or with papier mâché and relate to photo or map. | Regional descriptions, e.g. *James Herriot's Yorkshire* or John Hillaby's *London Photographs*. Video of, e.g. *One Man and his Dog* or *Eastenders*. | Make a display, and photo and labels. | 5a, 5b 3e, 3f 3a |
| 2 and 3 | What do people do here? | The countryside is a workplace or the office block or the industrial estate. | Tourism and farming are economic activities or office, industrial and service industries. | Role-play a farmer's day with a disastrous interruption of a gate left open, or a traffic jam preventing deliveries. Look at the role of litter. | Use one of the many farming stories or city tales. Relate to photograph and map + above. | Prepare an assembly on other people's work. | 5a–e |
| 4 | How has it changed? | Tourists cause changes in both localities. | Characteristics of tourist facilities and activities in both areas. | Either put symbols on a base map of activities and discuss, or in groups plot information on base map of accommodation activities. CP's and protected land. | 1:50,000 OS map + view-points and car parks and roads + tourist information for either area. | Design a poster for the country code or make a plan for keeping traffic moving. | 1d 6 or 10 |

Figure 5

directories. Usually one or all of these resources can be located at the borough reference or local history library. Failing that, your county hall or the country record office should have material covering the main local urban areas.

The historical element of this topic could be used to develop a whole-school project involving a local neighbourhood study.

## The tropical rain forest

Many explorers in history travelled to the equatorial lands, so this unit could be part of a larger cross-curricular topic on 'Exploration'. It could stand in its own right as part of work on an economically developing country or could be part of looking at 'different cultures and different lives'. The resources for this area are at the moment limited, but it is worth approaching the Commonwealth Institute as well as the various aid agencies. There are also radio and television programmes which concentrate on this area, so it is worth checking the schedules regularly for material to record. Figure 7 gives a breakdown of this topic area.

## Regional country parks

Country parks provide locations for studying contrasting localities, environments which have undergone change and environments which are having to cope with increased visitor use. There is also potential for a strong element of economic awareness to be developed. Extractive industries have affected a large part of both lowland and upland Britain. This in turn raises the question of restoration of damaged land and evaluation of land for conservation, farming and other uses. Consider using the land evaluation keys given on pages 181 and 182 to quantify observations.

This study could be part of a school journey week or just a school journey day. Figure 8 on page 186 gives a more detailed breakdown of this topic area.

## Open space

This topic can be covered by investigating the idea of finding somewhere to play. There is a strong element of environmental geography here and the landscape evaluation keys would be relevant. Remember the Bangladeshi child who has no play space because every scrap of land is needed to grow food (page 120).

This topic could focus on an economically developing country, such as Venezuela, whose urban centres are growing faster than the planners can make provision for. One of the characteristics of the tropical shanty town is that it is possible for someone to move there without having any prior family or job connections with the area and find space upon which to put shelter. Figure 9 on page 186 shows how this topic can be developed.

## Islands

Islands, for all their size, can provide a thematic focus for several geographical topics:
• regional and global transport networks;
• volcanoes;
• tropical habitats including coral reefs;
• island economies (for example, the Harris tweed industry, the Shetland oil service industry, the Channel Island flower and vegetable industry and the wine industry of Cyprus).

However, it should be kept in mind that islands are also communities which need educational, financial and medical services. Figure 10 on page 187 offers potential development areas.

| TOPIC: AN URBAN LOCALITY | | | | YEAR : KS2 | | | TERM: |
|---|---|---|---|---|---|---|---|
| Week | Questions | Concepts | PoS/knowledge/skills KS/Place: theme | Activities/visits Fieldwork Organisation | Resources Starting points | Outcomes Assessment | PoS |
| 1 | What is it like? | Roads are a collection of land uses. | Recognise the variety in building type, age, materials. Recognise variety in land use. | PREPARATION Observation and naming of features; discussion of similarities and differences. Determine questions of enquiry. | Photographs of locality to be looked at. | List of investigations. Questionnaires and worksheets made using WP and graphic programme. | 1 2 5 |
| 2 | Can we compare two roads? | Maps and record sheets can produce data from fieldwork. | Look at detail for buildings, shops, houses, to find out age, use, function, street features, street activity. | FIELDWORK In small groups: Relate photographs to map to locality. Map street furniture. Log pedestrians and traffic. Tally building types. Describe/sketch specific buildings. Log shop types. Complete ticksheets for labels, etc. | Maps. Clipboards. Questionnaires. Worksheets. | Completed record sheets. Data for entering on data sheet on return and for use with touch pad. | 3a, 3b 3e, 3f 9a, 9b |
| 3 | What is happening in the two roads? | Some roads are busier than others. Some roads have specific land uses. | Recognise different land uses. Learning about safety. Recognise different buildings. | FOLLOW-UP In groups: Complete picture maps and outlines. Complete street plans. Draw up bar charts by hand or using IT. Picture poster for safety. Relate photographs and building survey. | Data sheets. Maps. *Our Facts* or *Data Show*. | Maps. Description of differences. Graphs according to differentiation. Display of specific buildings and detail. | 9b 10a |
| 4 | Has there been change? | Change can be recognised in the environment. Records provide evidence of past geography. | Use of photographs and documents to provide evidence of past geography. | GROUP WORK on maps, photographs, directories to find out changes in buildings, activities (industry, farms), roads, open spaces. | Old (aerial) photographs. Old map. Local street directories, c.1850, for 1900,1930,1950. | Maps and diagrams. Identifying and listing of features. | 5c, 5d 9b, 9c 10 |
| Amendments: | 1. The fieldwork could be undertaken on two separate occasions by two classes, or one class, or during a school journey. 2. Extra adult help is required (see Chapter 3). 3. Evidence of change in Bermondsey is given in 'Field Excursions in the London area', Vol. 9 *Field Studies for Schools* Ed. D. G. Mills, Chapter 9 'Bermondsey' (Rivingtons, 1972). | | | | | | |

Figure 6

| TOPIC: TROPICAL RAIN FOREST | | | | YEARS: 3/6 8–11 YEARS  KS2  LEVEL 3/5 | | | TERM: Half-term |
|---|---|---|---|---|---|---|---|
| Week | Questions | Concepts | PoS/knowledge/skills KS/Place: theme | Activities/visits Fieldwork Organisation | Resources Starting points | Outcomes Assessment | PoS |
| 1 | What is 'jungle'? | Character of tropical rainforest. | Character of tropical vegetation and natural life. | 1. Sketch their own idea. 2. Watch video and notice special features. 3. Complete sketch with labelled features. | Video and picture pack. | Sketches and descriptions. | 1, 2 5a 3a, 3e |
| 2 | Where is the tropical rainforest? What is the weather like? | Equator and tropics global position. | Latitude, equatorial areas. Tropical climate. | 1. Put Equator and tropics on world map. 2. Shade in forest areas. 3. Show cities. | Globe; Atlas; Equal area map (Eckhert). Atlas climate data or newspaper. Local weather data. | Distribution map and labels. Climate graphs. | 3d 8 5b |
| 3–5 | What do people do? | a) Conserving traditional life. b) Exploring plantation life. | Traditional village living or plantation and urban life. | Use pictures in groups to answer series of questions asked by class and teacher. | Video or picture pack. | Drawings. Labelled models. Labelled maps. | 3e-f 5c, 5e 9c |
| 6 | What is happening? | a) Changes to tradition. b) Changes to products. | Threats to tradition. Commercial production. | Research Amazon Highway. Research other crops. | Media descriptions, e.g. BBC Radio 4. | | 9c 10a 10b |
| Amendments: | Videos: *Jungle...*, YTV *Two-Way Ticket* series; *Go Bananas*, Oxfam; *Yanomami: Song of the Jungle*, WWF Picture packs: *Rain Forest Child*, Lyle and Roberts, Greenlight Publications; *Focus on Castries, St Lucia* photopack, Geographical Association, CWDE + *World Studies 8-13*, Fisher & Hicks (O & B, 1985) BBC Radio 4 programmes on Developing Brazil (Bristol) | | | | | | |

Figure 7

| TOPIC: VISIT TO REGIONAL COUNTRY PARK | | | YEAR: 5/6  9–11 YEARS  KS2 | | | | TERM: |
|---|---|---|---|---|---|---|---|
| Week | Questions | Concepts | PoS/knowledge/skills KS/Place: theme | Activities/visits Fieldwork Organisation | Resources Starting points | Outcomes Assessment | PoS |
| 1 | How do we get there? | Journeys do not always take the shortest route. | OS and aerial photograph reading. Home or other region. | Use journey data sheet to mark on landmarks and distances; on return identify on OS map. | Data sheet. OS maps 1:25,000, 1:50,000. Aerial photograph. | Maps of routes with symbols and landmarks in correct order. Assess. | 3e 1b |
| 2 | What is to be seen from one place? | Landscape contains evidence of use and past history. | Different land uses. Different recording techniques. | Complete sketch diagrams; maps or tally chart from same viewpoint – crops, grass, arable, rough, woodland, park. Note building and road use. | Data sheets. OS maps, old and new 1:25,000. | Sketches. Maps. Graphs entered on database with other areas. Assess for accuracy. | 3a, b e, f 5a, 10a |
| 3 | What is to be seen from several places? | Change can be seen over a wide area. | Transport networks. Environmental quality. | Follow a trail. Stop at significant points for evaluation work in groups. | Route map and data sheet. Landscape evaluation sheet. Information boards and sheets. | Series of data sheets for use in class. Assess for recording. | 5c 3c, 3f 10a |
| 4 | How did this landscape get like this? | The British landscape is man-made. | Natural resources and their extraction. How localities have changed as a result of human actions. How land is used in different ways. Ways in which damaged landscapes can be restored. Reasons for location of work. | Use secondary sources to support analysis of maps made from field data. Research local history and maps to see changes in boundaries, quarries and roads/paths. | Geological Survey maps. Historical records. Land Use Survey map (2nd edition). County plan. | Series of maps of distributions and changes by different groups and reports by individuals using IT. | 3c, 3e 3f 5d, 5e 9b, 9f 10a, 10b |
| 5 | What is the quality of the landscape? | Is the current use the best use? | Synthesis of above knowledge to provide reasoned arguments. | Set up a debate or role-play the various people involved in the creation and maintenance of the Country Park. | Visitor from CP or industry (e.g. quarry) or craft. | Short report plus map and photos showing where improvements could be made. | 10 9c |
| Amendments: | Always prepare route well first; take photographs at viewpoints in order to facilitate accurate base sketch maps. Order OS maps/copies from LEA, and note industrial/environmental intrusions and see if visits can be arranged or visitors to present PR views of presence in park. | | | | | | |

Figure 8

| TOPIC: OPEN SPACE | | | YEAR: 5/6  9–11 YEARS  LEVEL 4/5 | | | | TERM: |
|---|---|---|---|---|---|---|---|
| Week | Questions | Concepts/ ideas Purposes | PoS/knowledge/skills KS/Place: theme | Activities/visits Fieldwork Organisation | Resources Starting points | Outcomes Assessment | PoS |
| 1 and 2 | Where is it? What is it like? | Places are different in shape and climate. | Location: Venezuela. Modelling and begin relief and contours. Find out about weather. | Look in atlas for location. Look at local map and UK for location. Model Venezuela relief and local or British relief. | *Nowhere to Play* by Kurusa (A & C Black). Weather data, atlases. | Model. Climate graphs. | 3d, 3e 4 5a, 5b |
| 3 and 4 | How did it happen? | Town populations grow quickly for various reasons and services are last to come. | Economically developing country. Urban growth and jobs. Urban growth and space. | Study new housing estate – note services (drains) and other infrastructure; building materials; facilities access; buses, bins' day, electricity and telephone supply. Make model of shanty town. | Research books on Venezuela from County Library and embassy information. | Make maps. Compare with maps of San José shanty town. | 1c 5a, 5b 3 9 |
| 5 and 6 | What might happen? What can be done? | Issue of sanitation. Issue of play space. | Water supply and sanitation problems. Distribution of open space within town. Community issues. | Look at local water supply and rubbish disposal. Group work: Identify local open spaces and playground sites. Plan and design adventure ground, map layout. Prepare report on use. Visit from planner. | Maps. Council information. Yellow Pages for makers of equipment (carpenters, tube-makers). | Maps to show recycling, rubbish and sewage works. IT for report. Plan of playground. Visitor survey and graph. | 9 10 3 |
| Amendments: | This could also be used as a bridge between primary and secondary school, especially on the playground development. Picture packs from Action Aid *Peru* and Trocaire/CAFOD *Fala Favela*. | | | | | | |

Adapted from a case study in *Another Time, Another Place*, Gloucester County Council

Figure 9

# Round and about

Using the spiral curriculum approach, topics can be returned to in successive years. The topic of 'Round and about' is related to the similarly named topic suggested for Key Stage 1 in Chapter eleven. If this topic is undertaken alongside work on the urban environment, progression can be seen in the study of a settlement, especially in the amount of recorded data required at the higher level of study. Figure 11 overleaf shows how this topic can be developed.

# Localities in other countries

Some schools prefer to work on one large topic, with each class taking a different part. Europe could be treated with each class looking at a different country, although this approach might be better suited for a scheme between a secondary school and the top classes of its feeder schools in their last term before moving up.

The Caribbean Islands are a suitable focus for such an approach, as are countries of West and East Africa. Figure 12 on page 189 outlines the enquiry questions, the concepts, skills, approaches, resources and outcomes which should be expected from this kind of investigation.

# Economic and industrial understanding (EIU)

Cross-curricular topics which have a geographical focus are appropriate to the field of economic awareness or economic and industrial understanding (EIU). So, a topic on 'Clothes' can deal not only with **'how people affect the environment'** (PoS, 10a) by producing cotton or wool for manufacture in city factories but also the

| TOPIC: ISLANDS | | | | YEAR : 5/6   9–11 YEARS   LEVEL 4/5 | | TERM: | |
|---|---|---|---|---|---|---|---|
| Week | Questions | Concepts | PoS/knowledge/skills KS/Place: theme | Activities/visits Fieldwork Organisation | Resources Starting points | Outcomes Assessment | PoS |
| 1 | What is an island? | Islands are lands completely surrounded by water. | Range of size of islands. Location of British Isles. Location of Caribbean islands (or others). | Draw imaginary island plus symbols and key. Discuss islands known (IoW, IoM). | *Treasure Island* or map of ferries to British Isles. Atlas. | Maps plus symbols and key, assess. Labelled map of UK to show islands. | 1 3 |
| 2 | How are islands made? | Islands are part of the continents. | Volcanic islands. Coral islands. Flooded landscape islands (BI). | Shape islands with two hills and a valley. Flood-mark contours either as filling or emptying. Build up volcanic islands with Plasticine and sand for lava and ash. Build coral islands with shaped polystyrene. | Model material. Water tank. Research material on volcanoes and coral reefs. | Labelled models. Map of contours. | 5a 3e |
| 3 | What are islands like? *1 Temperate* | Islands have similar features to the mainland. Islands rely on communication. | Islands depend upon air and sea transport; have special economics, e.g. tourism, fishing. | Compare journeys, farming and jobs of Scottish and English islands. Group work: use newspaper weather statistics. | Ferry timetables. Pictures of Scottish Isles, IoW and IoM from Tourist Offices. | Graphs of journey times. Length of day. Weather descriptions. | 5b 8 |
| 4 | What are islands like? *2 Tropical* | Islands have similar needs all over the world. | See above. | Use timetables to plan a journey to a group of islands in tropics. Compare weather data with school. | Old Air and Shipping timetables from reference library. Time Zone map. Weather data. | Map of route. Itinerary by time. Climate graphs or daily chart. | 5b 3, 8 |
| 5 | How do people live? | Similarities and differences. | Evidence of economic and cultural contrast. | Visit a tropical glasshouse to appreciate physical contrasts and all year round cultivation. Group work on features in each area. | Photopacks. Videos. | Graphs. Maps. Descriptions. | 5c 8 |
| 6 | How are things changing? | Landscapes change with man-made features. | Effect of oil-rigs or reduction of fishing. Effect of tourism or collapse of export markets. | Research: role-play. Consider work opportunities and schooling needs. Plan brochures for: a) industrialists; b) tourists; c) young people. | Library research books. Photopacks. | Brochures with maps for: a) industrialists; b) tourists; c) young people. | 10 |
| Amendments: | | | There are various videos and photopacks, e.g. *St. Lucia, Jungle Child, YTV Two-way Ticket, Hebridean Child*. Travel bureaux provide pictures and details of ferries and air connections. | | | | |

Figure 10

| | | | PoS/knowledge/skills | Activities/visits Fieldwork | Resources Starting | Outcomes | |
|---|---|---|---|---|---|---|---|
| Week | Questions | Concepts | KS/Place: theme | Organisation | points | Assessment | PoS |
| 1 | What is it like? | Different parts of a settlement have different ages and uses. | Combined history and geography. Recording on maps. Working in groups on house type, age, use, materials, size. | Transect across more than one land use area, e.g. housing estate to main road to central shops. | Maps. Clipboards. Age of buildings. Keys. | Field maps. ASSESS FOR NEATNESS! | 9a 3a 3b |
| 2 and 3 | How has it changed? | Uses change over time. | Buildings of different ages have different uses over time. | Groups take areas or streets, relate observations to maps and enumeration returns. | 1851, 1871, 1901 enumeration returns. 1st and 2nd edition OS maps. Current plans. | Wall display 1851 buildings and details, people. Description of change of a selected building. | 9a–c 3d-f |
| 4 and 5 | Why has it changed? | Changes in settlements reflect regional changes. | Research along student-determined lines looking at land use, building of routes, jobs. | Visit from local historian, knowledgeable retired person. Interviews. Look at jobs and birth places in census. | Tape recorder. Newspaper. Archives. | Wall display of current use and changes. Map plus photo and labels. | 9a–c 10a 3 |
| 6 | How have the changes affected the area? | Changes can be regretted but become accepted. | | Interview local people (parents, teachers, neighbours). Make trail of notable places. | Survey of people's feelings on the changes. | Map and booklet using IT on 'notable' places in the locality. Bar chart. | 5c 9c 10 |
| Amendments and notes: | The census returns will need to be typed and checked for errors. The maps will be available at the library/local history archive. IT can be used to devise survey forms and questionnaires as well as a database. | | | | | | |

TOPIC: ROUND AND ABOUT  YEAR: 6  10–11 YEARS  LEVEL 4  TERM: Autumn – First Half

Figure 11

consequences of changes in the clothing trade: **'how localities are set within a broader geographical context ... and are linked with other places'** (PoS, 5e). Figure 13 shows how this can be developed.

## Cross-curricular topics

The topic of 'Food' can be approached through science and technology by looking at content and processing. However, there are also geographical applications. Figure 14 on page 190 shows some of the geographical activities, knowledge, resources and issues involved. World development geography should be seriously considered in this context. This is not just the question of drought and desertification, but of food export to the detriment of subsistence farming for an increasing population.

Similarly, the topics of 'Journeys' and 'Transport' work well with history, science and technology. Figure 15 on page 190 shows the contribution of geography and the application to the geography attainment targets. This topic should involve not only the recognition of a hierarchy of routeways in this country, but also that other countries' networks are nowhere near as complex as the ones we are used to in the UK and Europe. One is aware of the vast gaps in desert areas and the 'romantic' salt and silk routes which cross them. It is the casual mention of the northerly route *or* the southerly route for crossing Canada which makes one turn to the atlas and realise that geography has a ready-made focus here on the theme of accessibility. Doing this under a thematic title helps to make appreciation of the difficulties and differences between localities in studies of smaller regions possible, since the considerations on a countrywide scale would be made beside those on a local scale. A blank topic planning sheet is given on page 205.

| TOPIC: OTHER LOCALITY, EC AND EDC COUNTRIES IN A CONTINENT OR PARTS OF A CONTINENT | | | YEAR: KS2 | | | TERM: | |
|---|---|---|---|---|---|---|---|
| Week | Questions | Concepts | PoS/knowledge/skills KS/Place: theme | Activities/visits Fieldwork Organisation | Resources Starting points | Outcomes Assessment | PoS |
| | What is it? Where is it? What is it like? What is it about? How did it get like this? How and why did it happen? What made it like this? What will happen in the future? What will be the effect of changes? What do people think about this? What do we think about it? | Distance Direction Scale Location Distribution Relationships Changes Awareness of bias Respect for differences | Mapwork Graphicacy Visual interpretation Comparison Observation Recording Interpreting Communicating Using IT Collecting of all kinds of information and artefacts | Group work and pair work Presentations Role-play for decision-making Debates to compare attitudes Simulations Discussions of evidence Investigation of processes Planning of developments Journeys Industrial activity Conservation Link information of own area | Videos Photographs Radio broadcasts Stories Reference books Atlases Slides Worksheets Artefacts and maps of countries concerned Visitors Visits Holidays TV programmes Link information | Maps linking evidence Models Programmes Displays Assemblies Booklets Overlay programme for KS1 Newspaper/magazine articles Tourist brochures Posters, stamps Then and now sequences Pack a suitcase Imaginative writing Research industries Weather forecasts | 1 2 3 4 5 6 7 8 9 10 |

Figure 12

| TOPIC: ENTERPRISE AWARENESS | | | YEAR: 4   8–9 YEARS   KS2   LEVEL 3–5 | | | TERM: | |
|---|---|---|---|---|---|---|---|
| Week | Questions | Concepts | PoS/knowledge/skills KS/Place: theme | Activities/visits Fieldwork Organisation | Resources Starting points | Outcomes Assessment | PoS |
| 1 | Why clothes? | Clothes needed for different occasions and different work. | Clothing worn by different groups at different times. | Investigate clothes worn by different ethnic groups. Different jobs, in and out of school. Different historic times. Different seasons. | Photographs. Items of uniforms. | Drawings of specific uniforms and clothes in season. | 5b 3d-f |
| 2 | Where do we find clothes? | Clothes are found in different shops. | Clothes are sold for different ages, budgets, activities. | High street survey of shops which sell clothes. | Maps. Clipboards. Tally charts. | Bar charts. Time chart linking clothes to age and need. | 2 3a-c |
| 3 | How do clothes reach the shops? How are clothes made? | Clothes are made in special areas. Clothes are made in factories or by individuals. | Research on UK locations. World locations. Work processes, e.g. from sheep to woollen cloth. | Investigate labels. Investigate processes for wool and cotton. Interview visitor. | Make lists of places found on labels. Tape-recorder. Invite local tailor or other worker in cloth. | Map of localities. Taped interview. | 3d-f 5e |
| 4 | How many people does it take to make an item of clothing? | Jobs can be divided vertically or horizontally. | Understand about a production line. | Set up a production line from spinning through weaving/knitting, sewing and making simple items for school funds. | Wool Information Bureau material, etc. | Products to sell! | 3f 5c |
| 5 | What changes have influenced the clothing trade? | Old areas based on energy production have been replaced by areas which can make economies with cheap labour. | Appreciate the value of technology. Recognise the needs of developing countries. | From knowledge of production line set up more economical production plan. Discussion with local firm on management and/or unions. | Flow diagrams. Spread sheet. IT. | Display of industrial sequence. Producing countries. | 3e-f 5e |

**Amendments:** With younger children this sequence could be done for cakes; with all ages for making hand-made paper as a school project. Many similar projects have been developed from a teacher undertaking a 'work shadow' week with a local firm (see PNL 'Primary Enterprise Pack').

Figure 13

## FOOD

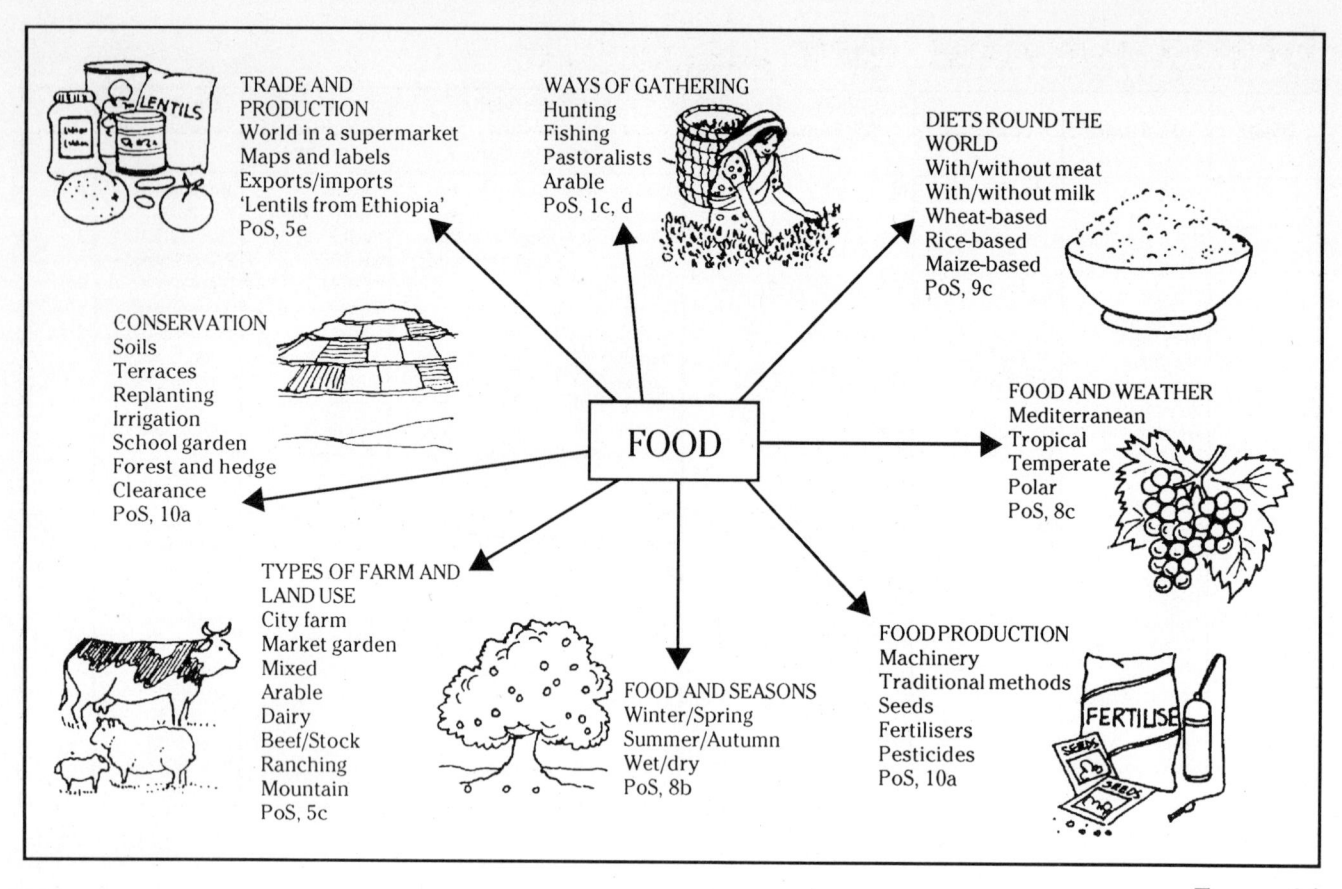

**TRADE AND PRODUCTION**
World in a supermarket
Maps and labels
Exports/imports
'Lentils from Ethiopia'
PoS, 5e

**WAYS OF GATHERING**
Hunting
Fishing
Pastoralists
Arable
PoS, 1c, d

**DIETS ROUND THE WORLD**
With/without meat
With/without milk
Wheat-based
Rice-based
Maize-based
PoS, 9c

**CONSERVATION**
Soils
Terraces
Replanting
Irrigation
School garden
Forest and hedge
Clearance
PoS, 10a

**FOOD AND WEATHER**
Mediterranean
Tropical
Temperate
Polar
PoS, 8c

**TYPES OF FARM AND LAND USE**
City farm
Market garden
Mixed
Arable
Dairy
Beef/Stock
Ranching
Mountain
PoS, 5c

**FOOD AND SEASONS**
Winter/Spring
Summer/Autumn
Wet/dry
PoS, 8b

**FOOD PRODUCTION**
Machinery
Traditional methods
Seeds
Fertilisers
Pesticides
PoS, 10a

Figure 14

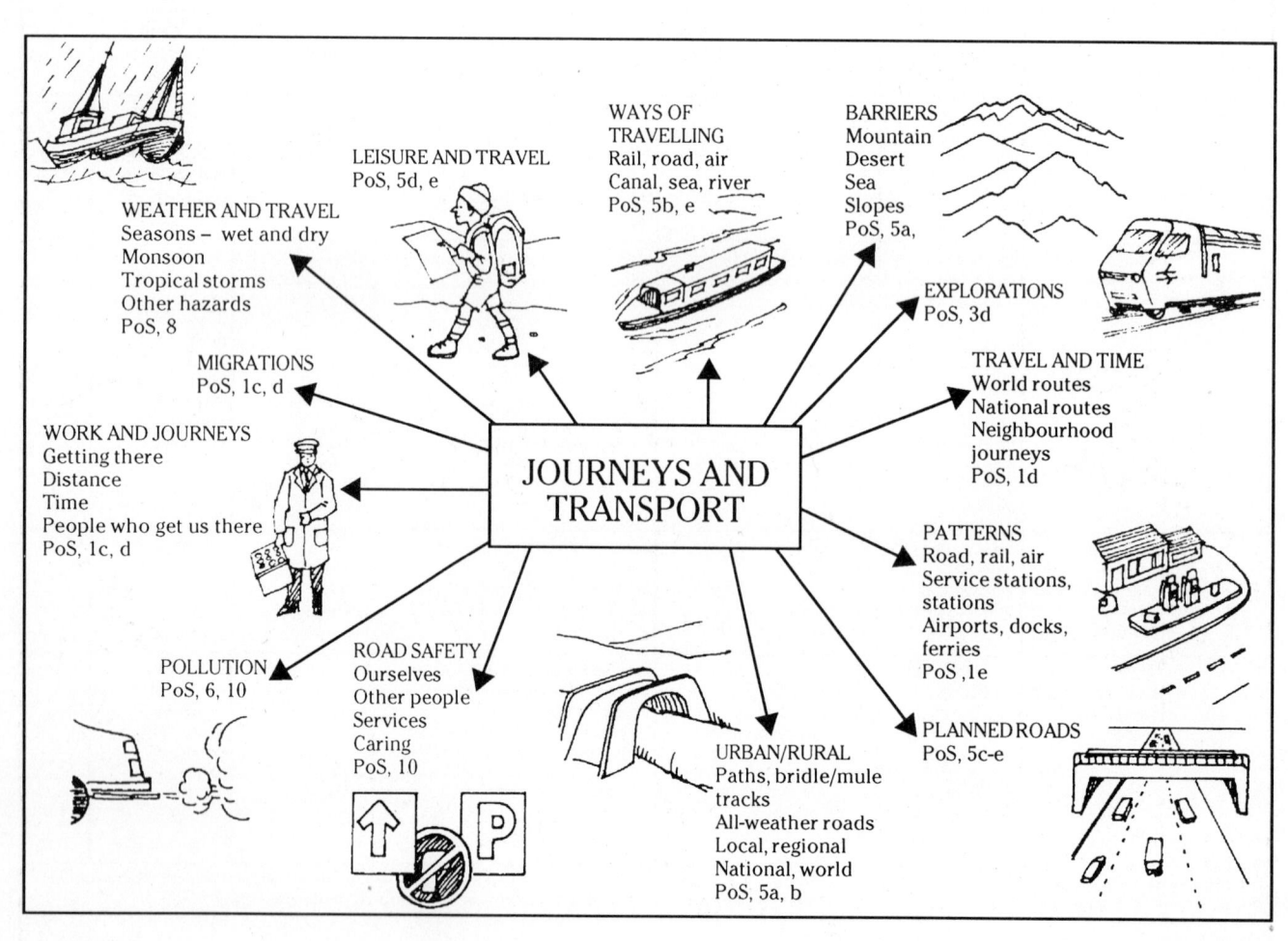

## JOURNEYS AND TRANSPORT

**WEATHER AND TRAVEL**
Seasons – wet and dry
Monsoon
Tropical storms
Other hazards
PoS, 8

**LEISURE AND TRAVEL**
PoS, 5d, e

**WAYS OF TRAVELLING**
Rail, road, air
Canal, sea, river
PoS, 5b, e

**BARRIERS**
Mountain
Desert
Sea
Slopes
PoS, 5a,

**EXPLORATIONS**
PoS, 3d

**MIGRATIONS**
PoS, 1c, d

**TRAVEL AND TIME**
World routes
National routes
Neighbourhood journeys
PoS, 1d

**WORK AND JOURNEYS**
Getting there
Distance
Time
People who get us there
PoS, 1c, d

**PATTERNS**
Road, rail, air
Service stations, stations
Airports, docks, ferries
PoS, 1e

**POLLUTION**
PoS, 6, 10

**ROAD SAFETY**
Ourselves
Other people
Services
Caring
PoS, 10

**URBAN/RURAL**
Paths, bridle/mule tracks
All-weather roads
Local, regional
National, world
PoS, 5a, b

**PLANNED ROADS**
PoS, 5c-e

Figure 15

# Blank outline, see page 118

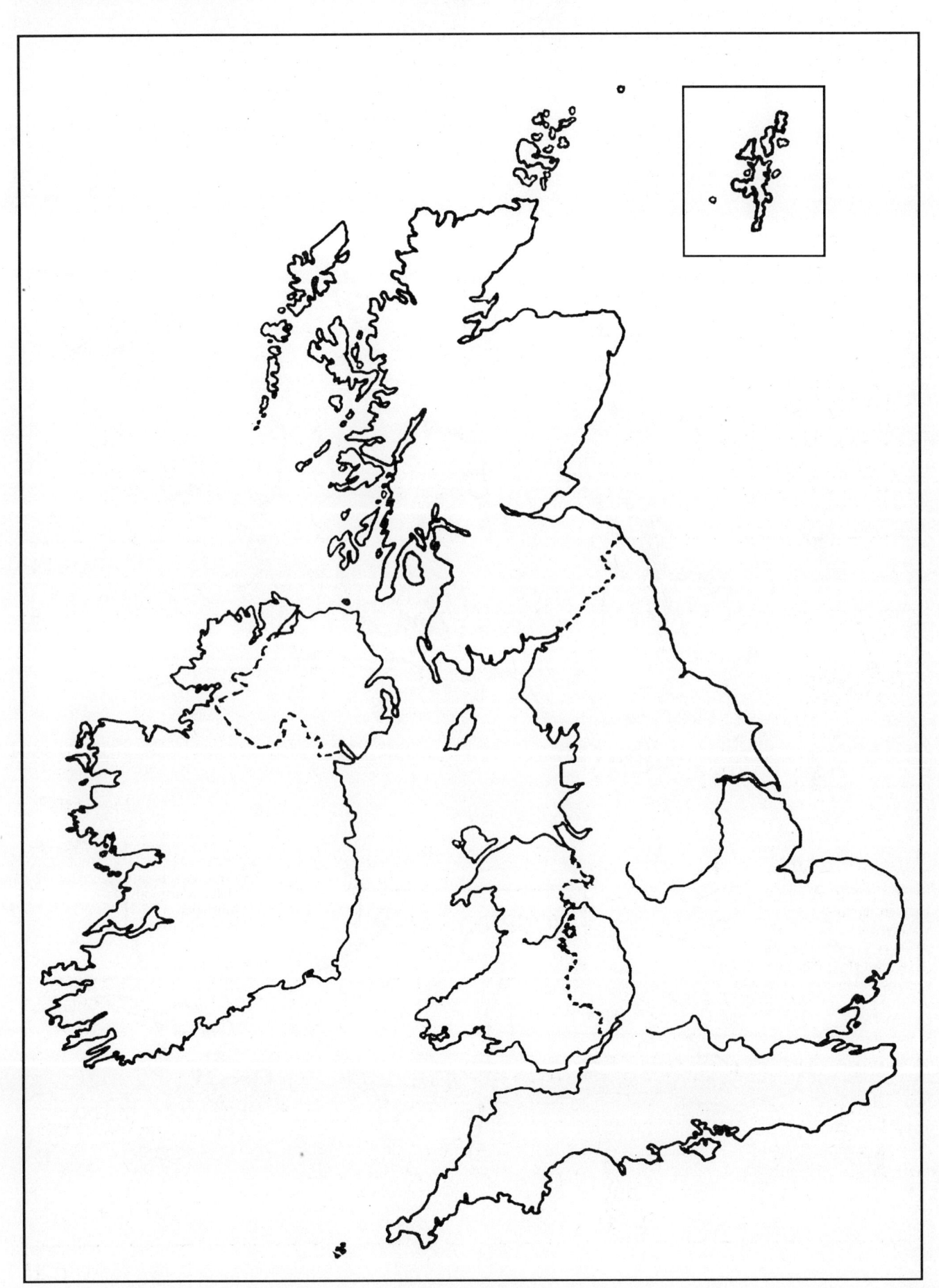

# Blank outline, see page 118

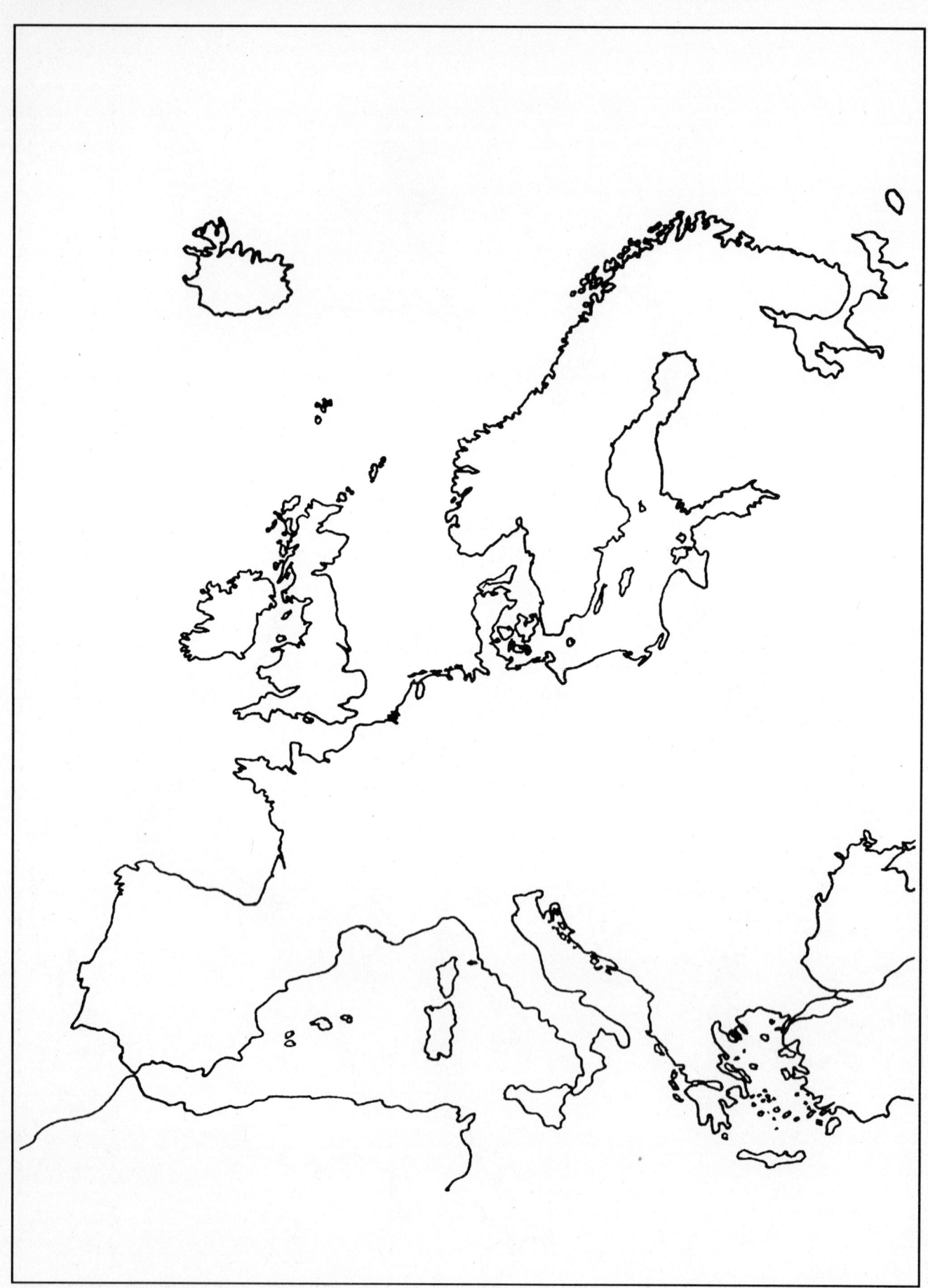

# Blank outline, see page 118

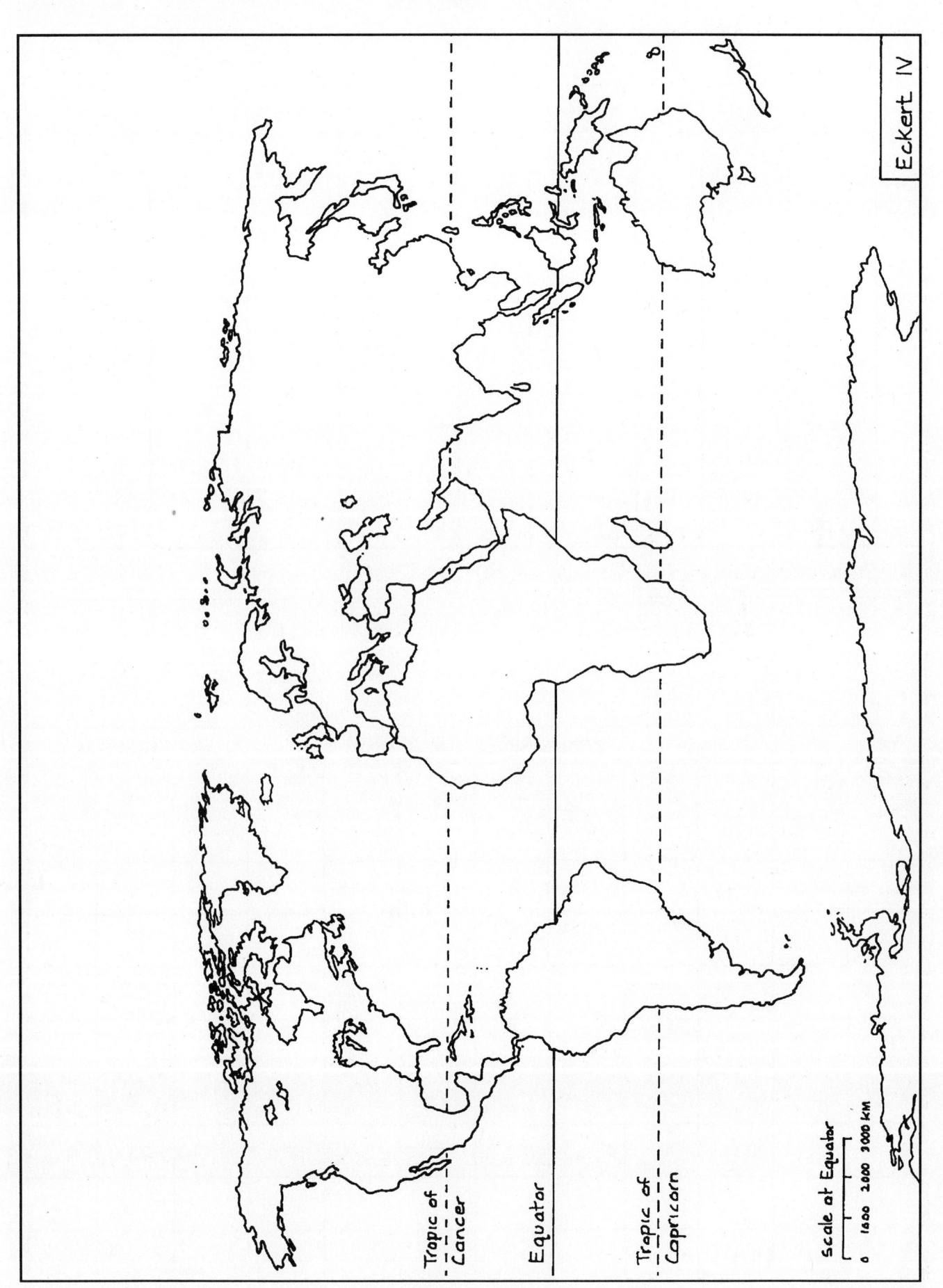

# Assessment charts, page 127

| Topic/unit: | | | | | KS | Class | | | Time | |
|---|---|---|---|---|---|---|---|---|---|---|
| Stage | Enquiry | Concept | Skills | Knowledge | AT/PoS | Activity/Visits | Resources | Outcomes | | Assessment |
|  |  |  |  |  |  |  |  |  |  |  |
| NC Cross-curricular: | | | | | | | | | | |

| Year  Age | | | | ASSESSMENT CHECK GRID | | | | | | Key Stage | |
|---|---|---|---|---|---|---|---|---|---|---|---|
| Assessment evidence  /  Topic | ORAL Talking Interviews Questions Discussion | PRACTICAL Models Replicas Collections | GRAPHIC Maps Drawings Diagrams Graphs | NOTES Diaries Research Captions | REPORTS Descriptions Stories | ROLE-PLAY & SIMULATIONS | VIDEO/ AUDIO PRESENTATIONS ASSEMBLIES | TESTS Factual recall | OBSERVATION Fieldwork Classwork | PHOTOS Location Analysis | IT Printouts Problem-solving |
|  |  |  |  |  |  |  |  |  |  |  |  |
|  |  |  |  |  |  |  |  |  |  |  |  |
|  |  |  |  |  |  |  |  |  |  |  |  |
|  |  |  |  |  |  |  |  |  |  |  |  |
|  |  |  |  |  |  |  |  |  |  |  |  |
|  |  |  |  |  |  |  |  |  |  |  |  |
|  |  |  |  |  |  |  |  |  |  |  |  |
|  |  |  |  |  |  |  |  |  |  |  |  |

# Class recording sheet for topic work, page 134

| Class Names | Map skills | Other skills | Local area | Other areas | Human, physical & environmental |
|---|---|---|---|---|---|
| | | | | | |

# Individual recording sheet, page 134

Name _____ Class _____ Topic _____

Activity  1. _____   2. _____   3. _____   4. _____   5. _____

## Map skills

| | 1 | 2 | 3 | 4 | 5 | Comment |
|---|---|---|---|---|---|---|
| Drawing free recall/scale plan | | | | | | |
| Scale/distance | | | | | | |
| Symbol/key | | | | | | |
| Direction/compass | | | | | | |
| Location/orientation | | | | | | |
| Plan view/relief | | | | | | |
| Knows purpose/devises purpose | | | | | | |
| Use prepared/OS | | | | | | |
| Reading (related to features) | | | | | | |
| Interpreting (describing from map) | | | | | | |

## Other skills

Photograph/pictures
Graphs/charts
Books/videos
Atlas/globe
Equipment
Fieldwork

{ Enquires
  Observes
  Understands
  Interprets
  Uses with other elements
  Uses correct vocabulary }

## Local area

Topical elements

{ Enquires
  Observes & records
  Describes
  Understands
  Uses correct vocabulary }

## Other areas

Physical
Human
Environmental

**Grading criteria:** 1=unable to work without any help; 2=erratic achievement, less confidence; 3=needs practice and consolidation; 4=completes exercises in allotted time; 5=excellent, completes quickly, needs extra work.

# Record wheel, geography skills, page 134

Name _____ Date of birth _____

| R | Y1 | Y2 | Y3 | Y4 | Y5 | Y6 |
|---|----|----|----|----|----|----|
| 4-5 | 5-6 | 6-7 | 7-8 | 8-9 | 9-10 | 10-11 |

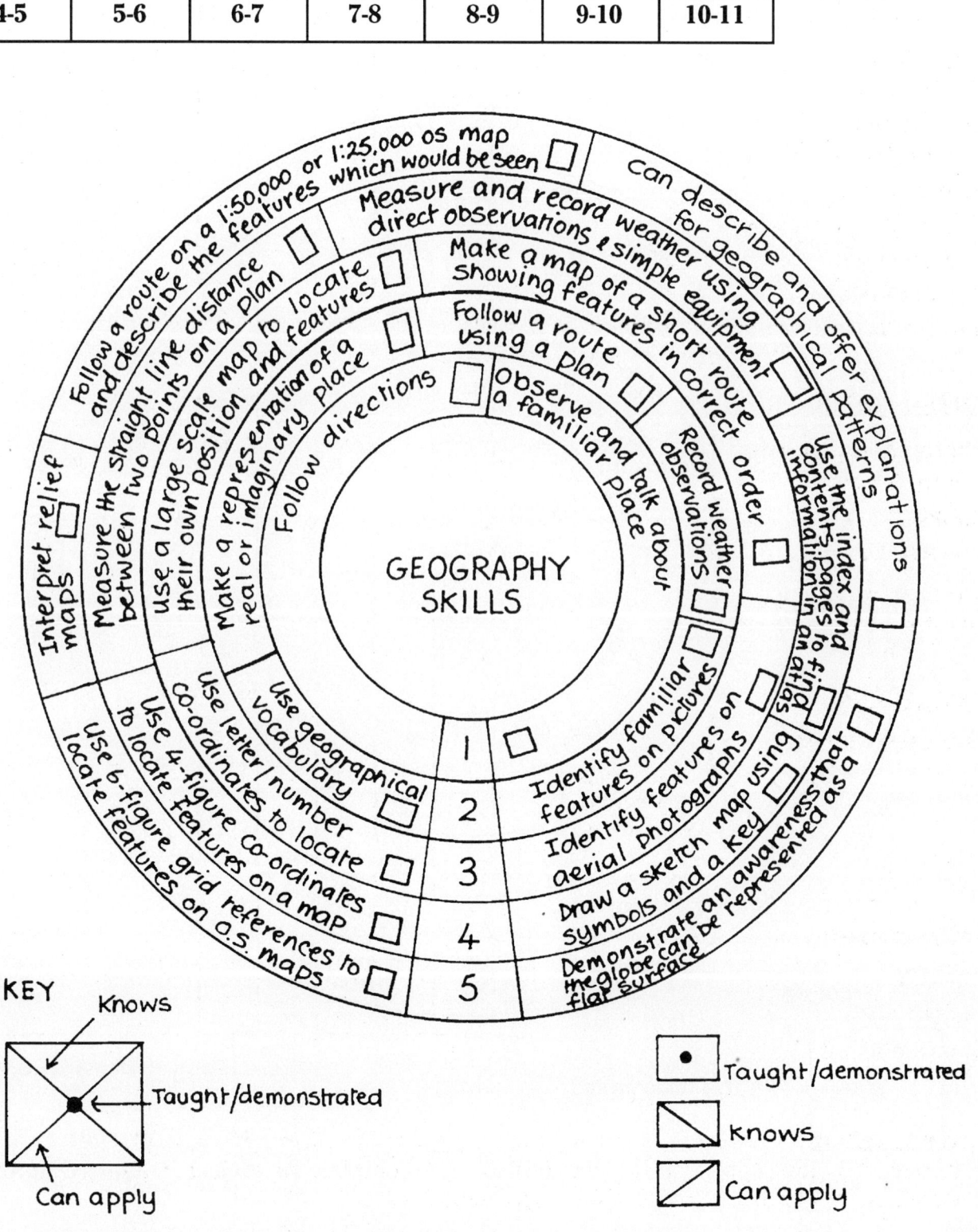

Tick age

## GEOGRAPHY SKILLS (Record Wheel)

Outer ring skills:
- Follow a route on a 1:50,000 or 1:25,000 OS map and describe the features which would be seen
- Measure and record weather using direct observations & simple equipment
- Can describe and offer explanations for geographical patterns
- Use the index and contents pages to find information in an atlas
- Identify familiar features on pictures
- Identify features on aerial photographs
- Draw a sketch map using symbols and a key
- Demonstrate an awareness that the globe can be represented as a flat surface
- Use 6-figure grid references to locate features on O.S. maps
- Use 4-figure co-ordinates to locate features on a map
- Use letter/number co-ordinates to locate
- Use geographical vocabulary
- Measure the straight line distance between two points on a plan
- Use a large scale map to locate their own position and features
- Make a representation of a real or imaginary place
- Follow directions
- Observe and talk about a familiar place
- Follow a route using a plan
- Record weather observations
- Make a map of a short route showing features in correct order
- Interpret relief maps

Inner levels: 1, 2, 3, 4, 5

### KEY

Knows — top-left triangle
Taught/demonstrated — centre dot
Can apply — bottom-right triangle

- •  Taught/demonstrated
- ◨  Knows
- ◪  Can apply

# Record wheel, places, page 134

Name _____ Date of birth _____

| R | Y1 | Y2 | Y3 | Y4 | Y5 | Y6 |
|---|----|----|----|----|----|----|
| 4-5 | 5-6 | 6-7 | 7-8 | 8-9 | 9-10 | 10-11 |

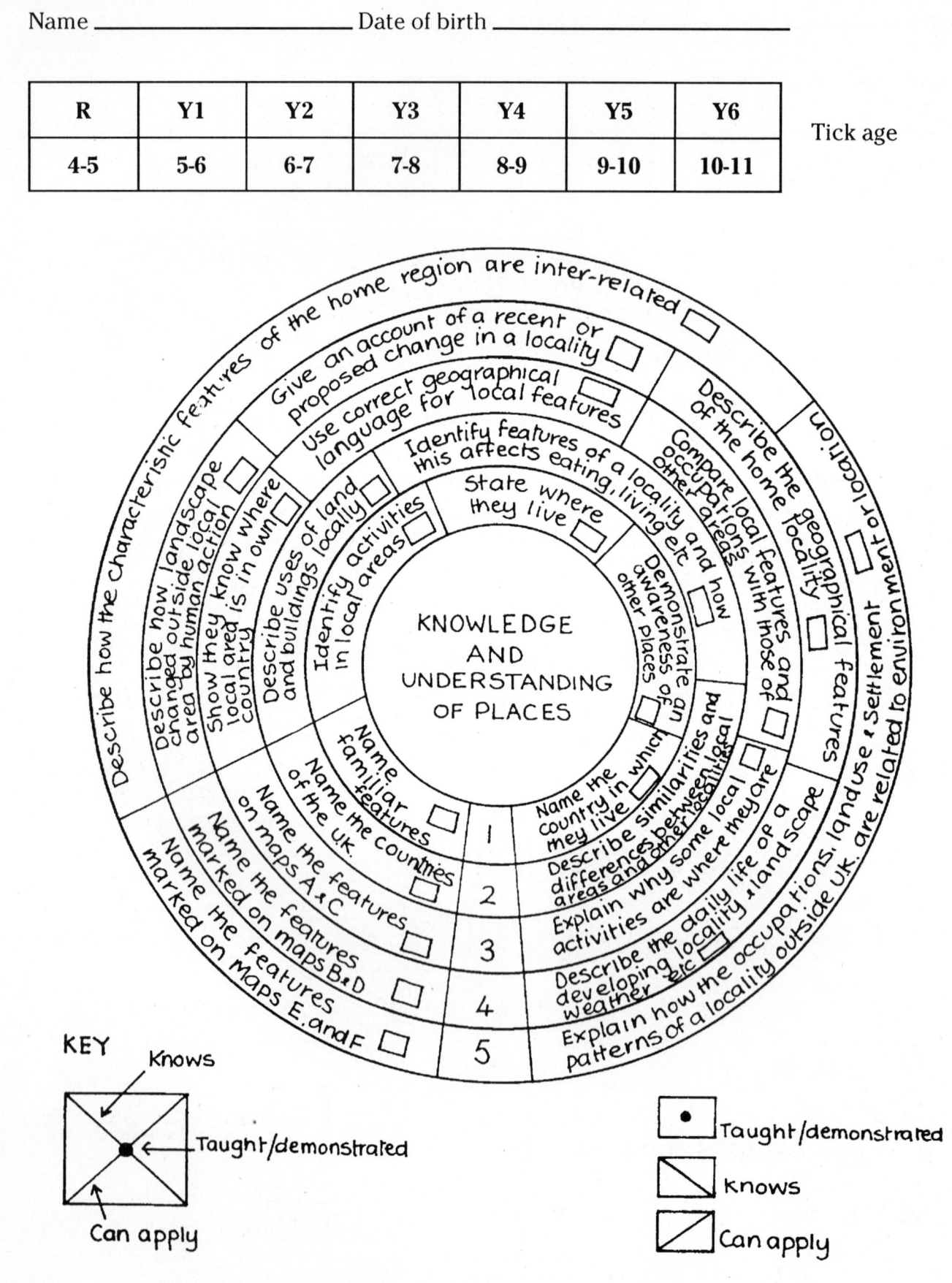

Tick age

## KNOWLEDGE AND UNDERSTANDING OF PLACES

Outer ring:
- Describe how the characteristic features of the home region are inter-related
- Give an account of a recent or proposed change in a locality
- Use correct geographical language for local features
- Describe the geographical features of the home locality
- Compare local features and occupations with those of other areas
- Describe how geographical features are related to environment or location
- Explain how the occupations, land use, settlement patterns of a locality outside UK are related to environment or location
- Describe the daily life of a developing locality – landscape, weather etc
- Explain why some local activities are where they are
- Describe similarities and differences between local areas and other localities
- Name the country in which they live
- Name familiar features of the UK
- Name the countries of the UK
- Name the features marked on maps A & C
- Name the features marked on maps B & D
- Name the features marked on maps E and F
- Describe how landscape changed outside local area by human action
- Show they know where local area is in own country
- Describe uses of land and buildings locally
- Identify activities in local areas
- State where they live
- Identify features of a locality this affects eating, living etc
- Demonstrate an awareness of other places

Inner numbers: 1, 2, 3, 4, 5

**KEY**
- Knows
- Taught/demonstrated
- Can apply

- • Taught/demonstrated
- ◻ (diagonal) Knows
- ◻ (crossed) Can apply

# Record wheel, physical features, page 134

Name _____ Date of birth _____

| R | Y1 | Y2 | Y3 | Y4 | Y5 | Y6 |
|---|----|----|----|----|----|----|
| 4-5 | 5-6 | 6-7 | 7-8 | 8-9 | 9-10 | 10-11 |

Tick age

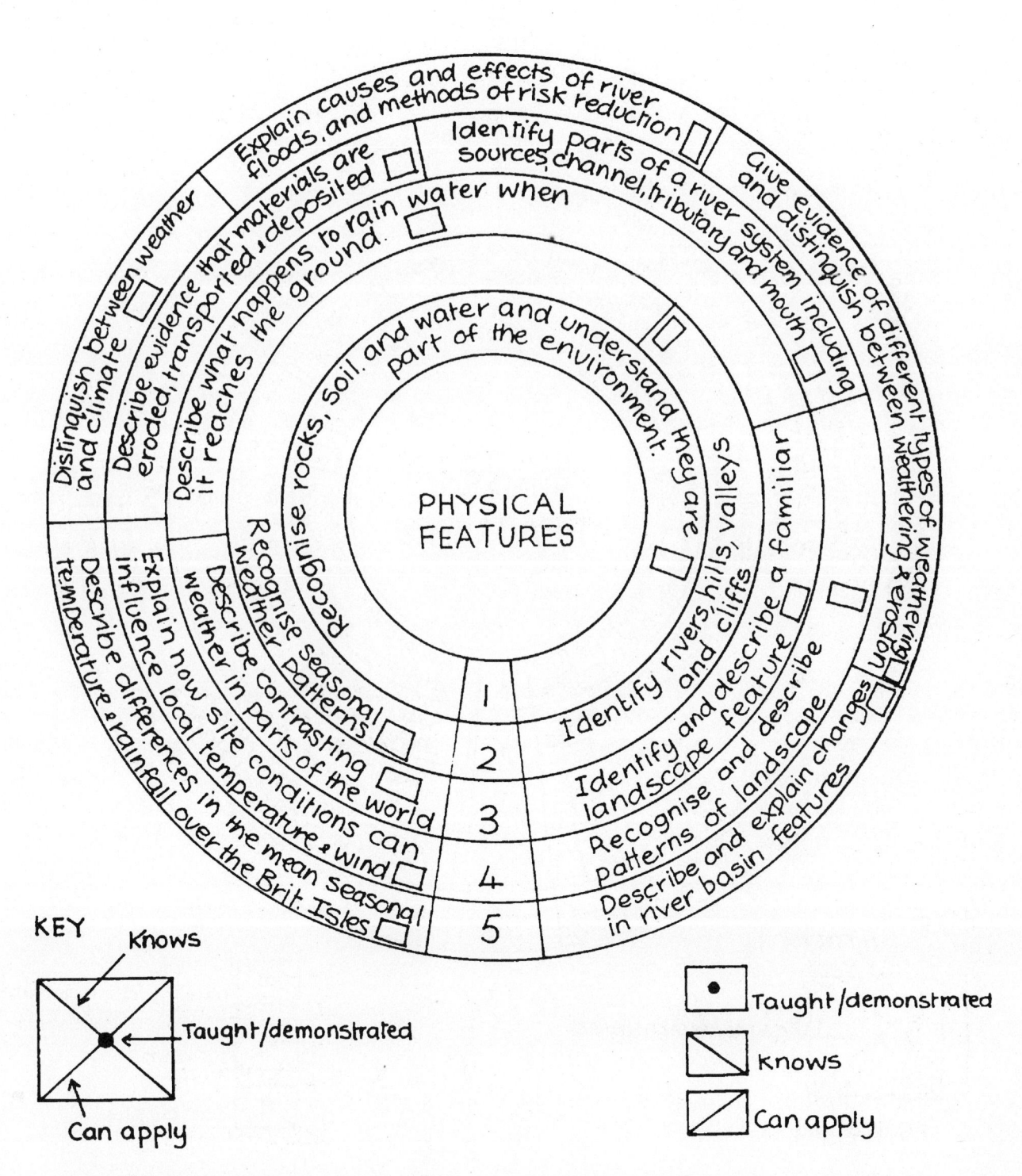

**PHYSICAL FEATURES**

Outer ring:
- Explain causes and effects of river floods, and methods of risk reduction
- Identify parts of a river system, including sources, channel, tributary and mouth
- Give evidence of different types of weathering and distinguish between weathering & erosion
- Describe and explain changes in river basin features
- Recognise and describe patterns of landscape
- Identify and describe a familiar landscape feature
- Identify rivers, hills, valleys and cliffs
- Describe contrasting weather in parts of the world
- Explain how site conditions can influence local temperature & wind
- Describe differences in the mean seasonal temperature & rainfall over the Brit. Isles
- Describe what happens to rain water when it reaches the ground
- Describe evidence that materials are eroded, transported & deposited
- Distinguish between weather and climate

Inner ring:
- Recognise rocks, soil and water and understand they are part of the environment.
- Recognise seasonal weather patterns

Segments numbered 1, 2, 3, 4, 5

**KEY**
- Knows
- Taught/demonstrated
- Can apply

- • Taught/demonstrated
- ◻ Knows
- ◨ Can apply

This page may be photocopied for use in the classroom and should not be declared in any return in respect of any photocopying licence

# Record wheel, human features, page 134

Name _____ Date of birth _____

| R | Y1 | Y2 | Y3 | Y4 | Y5 | Y6 |
|---|----|----|----|----|----|----|
| 4-5 | 5-6 | 6-7 | 7-8 | 8-9 | 9-10 | 10-11 |

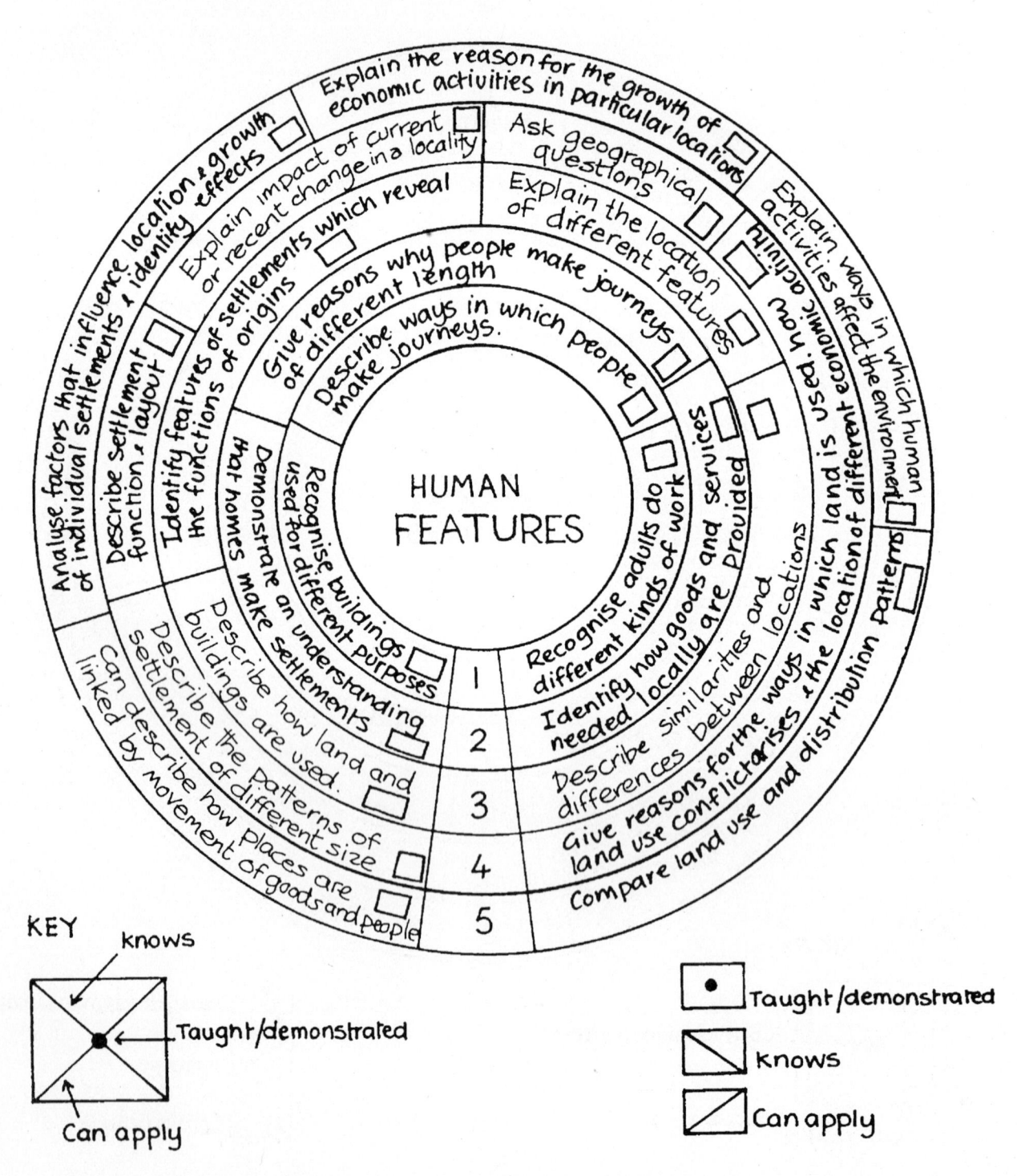

Tick age

## HUMAN FEATURES (record wheel)

Inner ring (level 1):
- Recognise buildings used for different purposes
- Recognise adults do different kinds of work
- Demonstrate an understanding that homes make settlements
- Describe ways in which people make journeys

Level 2:
- Describe how land and buildings are used
- Identify how goods and services needed locally are provided
- Give reasons why people make journeys of different length
- Identify features of settlements which reveal the functions of origins

Level 3:
- Describe the patterns of settlement of different size
- Describe similarities and differences between locations
- Explain the location of different features
- Describe settlement function & layout

Level 4:
- Can describe how places are linked by movement of goods and people
- Give reasons for the ways in which land use conflicts & the location of different economic activity
- Ask geographical questions
- Explain impact of current or recent change in a locality

Level 5:
- Compare land use and distribution patterns
- Explain ways in which human activities affect the environment
- Explain the reason for the growth of economic activities in particular locations
- Analyse factors that influence location & growth of individual settlements & identify effects

## KEY

Square divided by X with:
- top: knows
- centre dot: Taught/demonstrated
- bottom: Can apply

- ☐ (dot) Taught/demonstrated
- ◨ (one diagonal) Knows
- ⊠ (cross) Can apply

This page may be photocopied for use in the classroom and should not be declared in any return in respect of any photocopying licence

# Record wheel, environmental change, page 134

Name _____ Date of birth _____

| R | Y1 | Y2 | Y3 | Y4 | Y5 | Y6 | |
|---|---|---|---|---|---|---|---|
| 4-5 | 5-6 | 6-7 | 7-8 | 8-9 | 9-10 | 10-11 | Tick age |

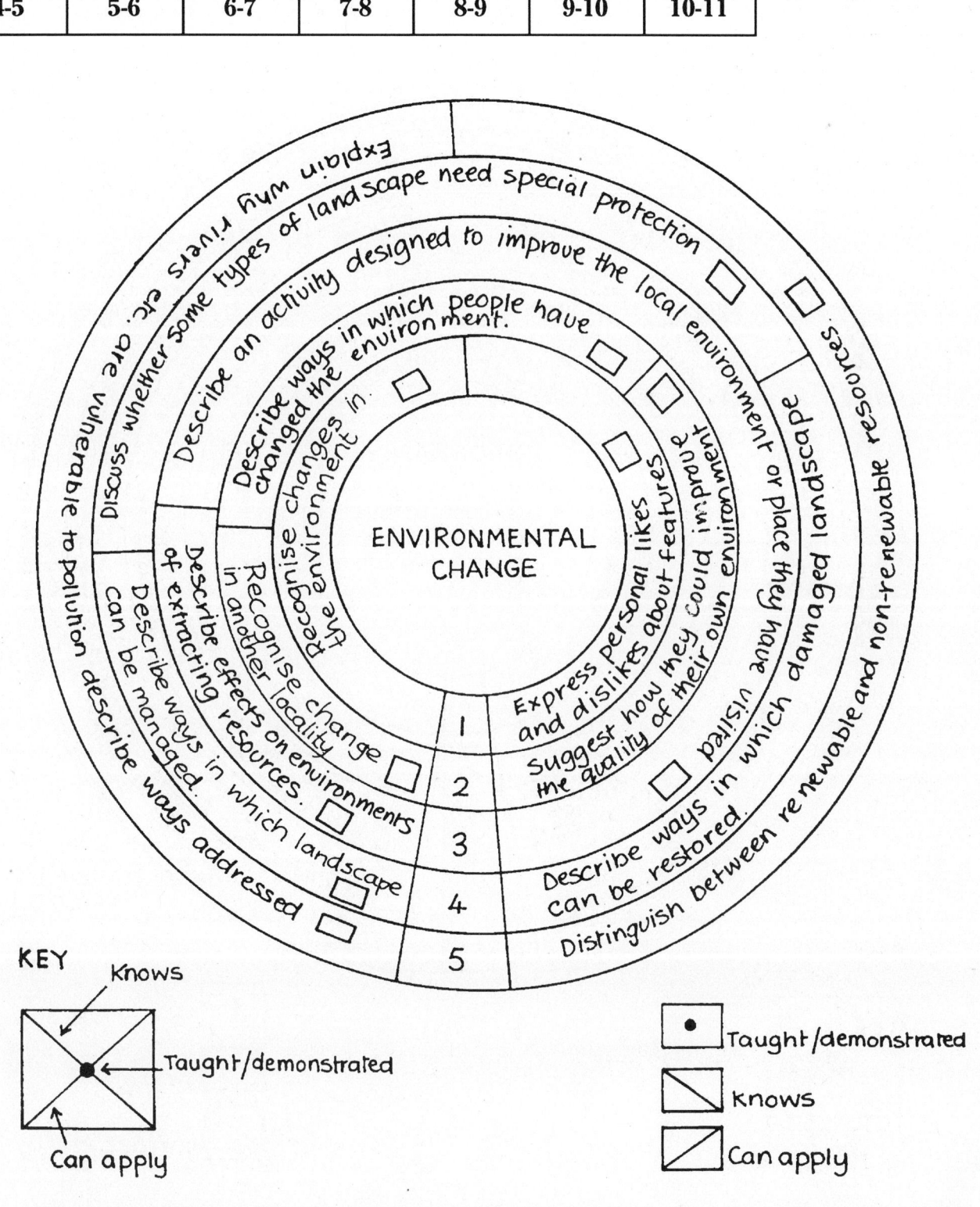

**ENVIRONMENTAL CHANGE**

Segments (numbered 1–5) around the wheel:

1. Express personal likes and dislikes about features of the environment.
2. Recognise change in the environment.
3. Describe changes in another locality.
4. Describe ways in which people have changed the environment.
5. Describe an activity designed to improve the local environment.

Outer ring:
- Suggest how they could improve the quality of their own environment or place they have visited.
- Describe ways in which damaged landscape can be restored.
- Distinguish between renewable and non-renewable resources.
- Describe ways in which landscape can be managed.
- Describe effects on environments of extracting resources.
- Discuss whether some types of landscape need special protection.
- Explain why rivers etc. are vulnerable to pollution describe ways addressed.

**KEY**

Square with X through it, dot in centre:
- Knows
- Taught/demonstrated
- Can apply

- • Taught/demonstrated
- ◸ Knows
- ◿ Can apply

This page may be photocopied for use in the classroom and should not be declared in any return in respect of any photocopying licence

# Record wheel, geography and information technology, page 134

Name _____ Date of birth _____

| R | Y1 | Y2 | Y3 | Y4 | Y5 | Y6 | |
|---|----|----|----|----|----|----|---|
| 4-5 | 5-6 | 6-7 | 7-8 | 8-9 | 9-10 | 10-11 | Tick age |

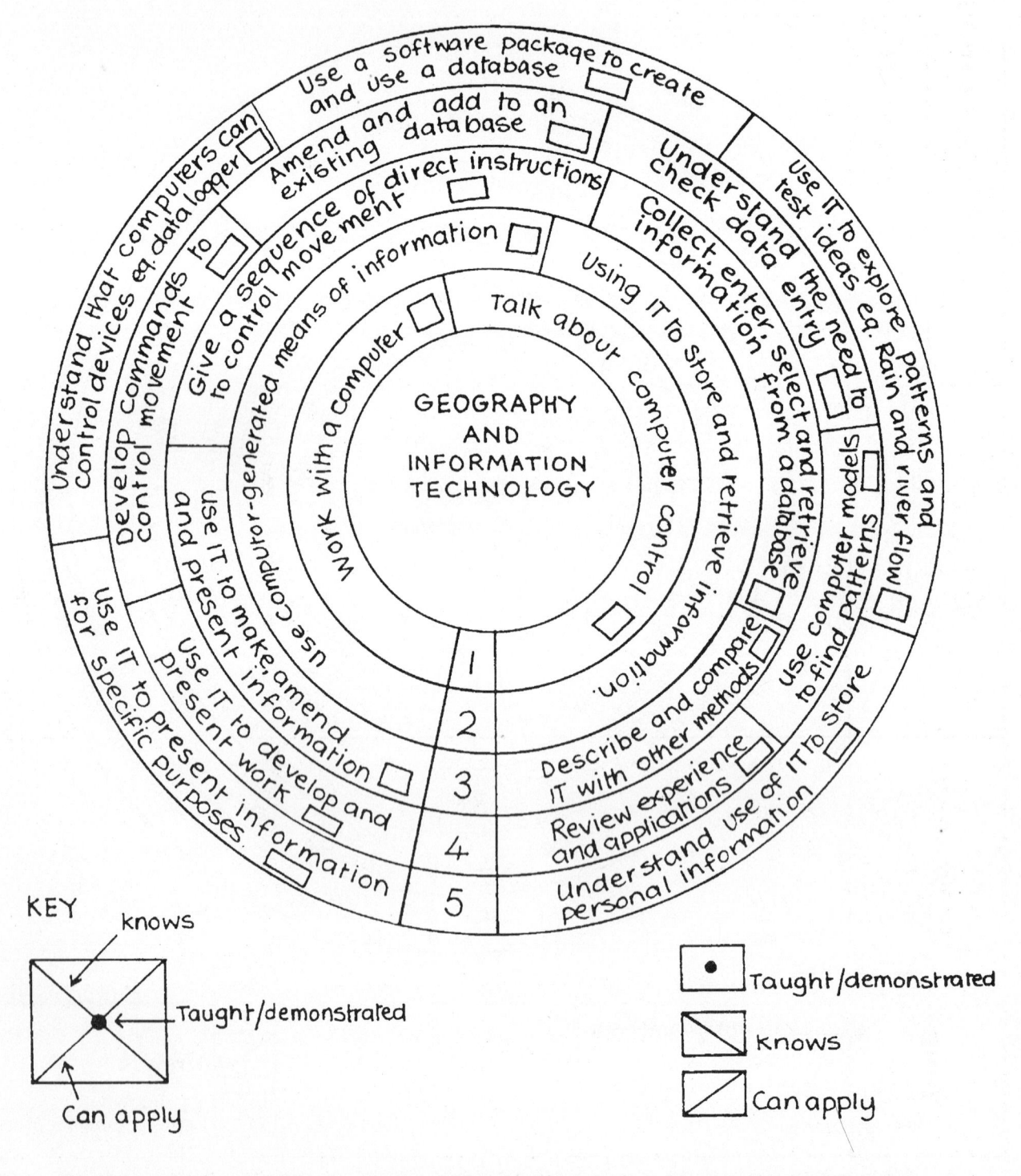

**Centre:** GEOGRAPHY AND INFORMATION TECHNOLOGY

**Inner ring:**
- Work with a computer
- Talk about Using IT to store and retrieve information
- Use computer-generated means of information
- Use IT to make, amend and present information
- Use IT to present information for specific purposes
- Describe and compare IT with other methods
- Review experience and applications
- Understand use of IT to store personal information

**Middle ring:**
- Give a sequence of direct instructions
- Collect, enter, select and retrieve information from a database
- Develop commands to control movement
- Understand the need to check data entry
- Use IT to develop and present work
- Use computer models to find patterns

**Outer ring:**
- Use a software package to create and use a database
- Amend and add to an existing database
- Understand that computers can control devices eg. datalogger
- Use IT to explore patterns and test ideas eg. Rain and river flow

**Levels:** 1, 2, 3, 4, 5

KEY
- knows
- Taught/demonstrated
- Can apply

- ● Taught/demonstrated
- ◻ Knows
- ◻ Can apply

# Whole-school adjustments to National Curriculum Geography, page 157

| Year | Topics/ geography already covered | National Curriculum requirements | Changes required |||
|---|---|---|---|---|---|
| | | | Topics | Resources | Development |
| | | | | | |

# Outline scheme sheet, page 174

| | |
|---|---|
| PoS | |
| Outcomes/ Assessment | |
| Resources | |
| Activities/ Visits | |
| PoS/ Knowledge/ Skills | |
| Concepts | |
| Questions | |

# Topic planning sheet, page 188

| TOPIC: | | YEAR: | | TERM: | | |
|---|---|---|---|---|---|---|
| | Week | | | | | |
| | Questions | | | | | |
| | Concepts | | | | | |
| | PoS/Knowledge/ Skills/KS/Place/ Theme | | | | | |
| | Activities/Visits/ Fieldwork organisation | | | | | |
| | Resources/ Starting points | | | | | |
| | Outcomes/ Assessment | | | | | |
| | PoS | | | | | |

This page may be photocopied for use in the classroom and should not be declared in any return in respect of any photocopying licence

# Resources
## Useful addresses

### Maps and aerial photographs
**Aerofilms Limited**, (see Chas Goad)
**Cambridge Publishing Services**, PO Box 62, Cambridge CP3 9NA: inflatable globes.
**Chas Goad Limited, (Mapping Division)**, 8–12 Salisbury Square, Old Hatfield, Hertfordshire AL9 5BJ; agent for all Aerofilms * photographs and posters, OS maps and plans.
**National Map Centre**, 22–24 Caxton Street, London SW1H OQU: class sets of OS map extracts, foreign maps, OS agent.
**National Remote Sensing Centre Limited (Air Photo Group)\***, Arthur Street, Barwell, Leicester LE9 8GZ: aerial photographs on disk, *Discovering Aerial Photographs I & II, Discover Godstone*.
**Ordnance Survey\*** The Education Team, Room C454 Ordnance Survey, Romsey Road, Southampton SO16 4GU.
*\*When ordering photographs give the school address, and six-figure grid reference from a local 1:50,000 Land Ranger sheet.*

### Fieldwork and equipment
Educational suppliers: **NES/Arnold; Hope Education; Philip & Tacey**
**British Orienteering Federation**, Riversdale, Dale Road North, Darley Dale, Matlock, Derbyshire DE4 2HX
**Field Studies Council**, Preston Montford, Montford Bridge, Shrewsbury SY4 1HW
**The Geological Museum**, Exhibition Road, London SW7 2DE
**Geo Supplies Limited**, 16 Station Road, Chapeltown, Sheffield S30 4XH: soil samples and workcards.
**National Rivers Authority**, Rivers House, Waterside Drive Aztec West, Almondsbury, Bristol BS12 4UD: *Riverworks* pack.

### Slides, videos and filmstrips
**BBC Educational Publishing**, PO Box 234, Wetherby, West Yorkshire LS23 7EU: BBC education videos. Further information from:
**BBC Education Information**, White City, 201 Wood Lane, London W12 7TS
**Central ITV plc** resources available from:
**Educational Television Company**, Leah House, 10a Great Titchfield Street, London W1P 7AA
**Drake Educational Productions**, 89 St. Fagan's Road, Fairwater, Cardiff CF5 3AE: also posters.
**DS Limited**, National Audio Visual Aids Library, Normal College, Siliwen Road, Bangor, Gwynedd LL57 2PZ
**The Slide Centre**, 17 Broderick Road, London SW17 7DZ
**Viewtech Film and Video**, 161 Winchester Road, Brislington, Bristol BS4 3NJ

### Posters
**PCET (Pictorial Charts Educational Trust)**, 27 Kirchen Road, London W13 0UD
**Shell Educational Service**, Shell-Mex House, Strand, London WC2R 0DX

### Software
**AUCE (The Advisory Unit: Computers in Education)**, 126 Great North Road, Hatfield, Hertfordshire AL9 5JZ: *Aegis 2 Primary*.
**AVP**, School Hill Centre, Chepstow, Gwent NP6 5PH: resumé in catalogue of programs available for primary schools, supply software, e.g. *Project HIT* (Longman).
**Hoddle, Doyle and Meadows Limited**, Old Mead Road, Elsengham, Bishop Stortford, Hertfordshire CM22 6JN: *Our Facts/Touch Explorer Plus* (MESU/NCET).
**Keydata**, Longman Resources Unit, 62 Hallfield Road, Layerthorpe, York YO3 7XQ: *Keydata/Key Plus*.
**MAPE**, Newman College, Bartley Green, Birmingham B32 3NT
**NCET (National Council for Educational Technology)**, University of Warwick Science Park, Sir William Lyons Road, Coventry CV4 7AL
**RESOURCE**, Albert House, Exeter Road, Doncaster DN2 4PY
**Sherstone Software**, Swan Barton, Sherstone, Malmsbury, Wiltshire SN16 0LH: *Map Venture*.
**SPA Limited**, 'Paintspa', PO Box 59, Leamington Spa CV31 3QA: Paintspa.

### Localities, Themes, Wider World
**ActionAid**, Education Resources, The Old Church House, Church Steps, Frome, Somerset BA11 1PL: *Pampegrande; Chembakolli* and other packs.
**Centre for European Education**, Central Bureau for Educational Visits and Exchanges, Seymour Mews House, Seymour Mews, London W1H 9PE
**Centre for Global Education**, York University, Heslington, York YO1 5DD
**Friends of the Earth**, 56–58 Alma Street, Luton LU1 2PH
**Christian Aid**, PO Box 100, 35 Lower Marsh, London SE1 7RL
**The Commonwealth Institute**, 230 Kensington High Street, London W8 6NQ: artefacts and information.
**The Council for Environmental Education**, School of Education, University of Reading, London Road, Reading RG1 5AQ
**Curriculum Council of Wales**, Castle Buildings, Womanby Street, Cardiff CF1 9SX
**Department of Trade and Industry**, The Environment Division, 3.063, 151 Buckingham Palace Road, London SW1W 9SS
**Development Education Centre**, Gillett Centre, 998 Bristol Road, Selly Oak, Birmingham B29 6LE
**The Geographical Association**, 343 Fulwood Road, Sheffield S10 3BP: UK & overseas packs, satellite photograph pack.
**HMSO**, PO Box 276, London SW8 5DT
**Mini-Enterprise in Schools Project/Schools Curriculum Industry Partnership**, Centre for Education & Industry, University of Warwick, Coventry CV4 7AL
**Learning through Landscapes**, 3rd Floor, Southside Offices, The Law Courts, Winchester, Hampshire SO23 9DL: *Directory*.
**National Association for Environmental Education**, University of Wolverhampton, Walsall Campus, Gorway Road, Walsall, West Midlands WS1 3BD
**National Trust Education Manager**, 36 Queen Anne's Gate, London SW14 9AS
**Oxfam**, 274 Banbury Road, Oxford OX2 7GZ: e.g. *Arctic Child, Rainforest Child* and *Go Bananas* photopacks.
**Scholastic Limited**, Westfield Road, Southam, Leamington Spa CV33 0JH
**Survival International**, 310 Edgeware Road, London W2 1DY: *Doorways* and *Homes* (photopacks of homes around the world), and *Dream Flight* (video).
**UNICEF-UK**, 55 Lincoln's Inn Fields, London WC2A 3NB
**Worldaware**, 1 Catton Street, London WC1R 4AB: photopacks on health, and trees, around the world, *The Water Game* (software simulation); resources for *St Lucia* plus nine other locality packs.
**World Wide Fund for Nature-UK**, Panda House, Weyside Park, Catteshall Lane, Godalming, Surrey GU7 1XRL: UK and overseas resource packs and videos.

# Reference for teachers
## Magazines and books
Corporate or individual membership of the 'Geographical Association' includes subscription to *Primary Geographer*. The October 1992 edition has an analysis of **atlases**: major publishers are Collins/Longman, Schofield Sims, Heinemann/Philips, Folens, Kingfisher, Usborne, Wayland and O.U.P., e.g., *New Oxford School Atlas* (OUP) and *Keystart* (series).

Catling, S. (January 1978) 'Cognitive Mapping' *Teaching Geography* Vol.3 No.3 Geographical Association
Catling, S. (1979) 'Maps and Cognitive Maps: the young child's perception' *Geographical Magazine* Vol.64 No.4
Catling, S. (1980) 'For the Junior and Middle School: Map use and objectives for map learning' *Teaching Geography* No.5
Long, M. (1962) 'Research in Picture Study' *Geography* Vol.46 Geographical Association
*Geographical* The Royal Geographical Society
Parker, C. (1991) 'Geography and Information Technology' *Micro-scope 32* (MAPE)

*Another Time, Another Place* (1991, Gloucestershire County Council Humanities Advisers)
*Aspects of Primary Education: the teaching and learning of History and Geography* HMI (1989, HMSO)
*Bright Ideas: Geography/Environmental Studies/The Green School* (Scholastic)
*Curriculum Guidance 7: Environmental Education* (1990, NCC)
*Curriculum Matters 15: Information technology from 5–16* (1991, DES)
*Down to Earth* S. Nortcliffe (1984, Leicester Museums)
*Educational Assessment of the Primary Child* J. R. Beech/L. Harding (eds.) (1990, NFER/Nelson)
*Environmental Education in the Primary School* P. Neal/J. Palmer (1990, Blackwell)
*An Eye on the Environment* H. B. Joicey (1986, Bell & Hyman)
*Explorations: a guide to fieldwork in the primary school* S. Wass (*Primary Bookshelf*, Hodder & Stoughton 1990)
*Focus on IT* (1991, NCET)
*Geographical Fieldwork* J. Frew (1986, Macmillan Educational)
*Geographical Work in Primary and Middle Schools* D. Mills (ed.) (1988, Geographical Association)
*Geography and History through stories* A. Gadsden (1991, Geographical Association/Cheshire County Council)
*Geography in the National Curriculum* DES (1991, NCC)
*Geography in the National Curriculum: Non-statutory guidance for teachers* (1991, CCW)
*Geography Non-Statutory Guidance* (1991, CCW)
*Geography outside the Classroom* (1989, Geographical Association)
*Geography Through Topics in Primary and Middle Schools* (1989, NCET/Geographical Association)
*Geography Work in Primary Schools* J. Bale (1987, Routledge & Keegan Paul)
*The Green Umbrella* WWF-UK (1991, A&C Black)
*Groundwork: Practical ways of learning about soils* M. Jarman (1984, Leicester Museums)
*Making Global Connections* D. Hicks et al (1989, Oliver & Boyd)
*National Curriculum Working Party on Geography Final Report* (June 1990)
*Place: a practical guide to teaching about places* (1992, Geographical Association)
*Place and Time with Children Aged 5 to 9* J. Blyth (1990, Routledge & Keegan Paul)
*Places in the Primary School* P. Wiegand (1992, Falmer)
*Planning for Geography for pupils with learning difficulties* J. Sebba (1991, Geographical Association)
*Primary Geography* M. Foley/J. Janikoun (1992, Stanley Thornes)
*Primary Humanities and IT in the National Curriculum* (1990, NCET)
*Primary Matters: Children using computers* A. Sraker (1989, Simon & Schuster)
*Primary Schools, Geography and the National Curriculum* M. Naish (1992, Geographical Association)
*Programmes of Study: Try this approach* E. Rawling (1992, Geography Association)
*Safety in Outdoor Education* (1989, DES)
*School Links International* R. Beddis/C. Mares (1991, Tidy Britain Group/WWF-UK)
*Teaching children through the Environment* P. Mayes (1985, Hodder & Stoughton)
*Teaching Economic Understanding through Geography* G. Corney (1992, Geographical Association)
*Using Information Technology Across the National Curriculum* S. Senior (1989, Owlet Books)
*The Weather Book for Primary Teachers* S. Harrison/F. Havard (1992, Simon & Schuster)
*World Studies 8–15* S. Fisher/D. Hicks (1989, Oliver & Boyd)

## Series
*Blueprints National Curriculum Geography* (Stanley Thornes)
*Europe/Into Europe* (series) (Wayland)
*Fieldwork Investigations* (series) S. Warn (1991, Nelson) (1885, Arnold Wheaton)
*Ginn Geography* W. Chambers/W. Morgan (Ginn)
*Into Geography* (series) P. and S. Harrison/M. Pearson (Nelson): National Curriculum editions available
*Mapstart* (series) and *OS Mapstart* S. Catling (Collins Educational)
*Mapwork with Ordnance Survey* (series) P. and S. Harrison (Holmes McDougall)
*Oliver & Boyd Geography* (series) W. E. Marsden et al (1992, Oliver & Boyd)
*Outset Geography* (series) S. Catling et al (4 books) (Oliver & Boyd)
*Oxford New Geography* (series) G. Elliot/K. Martin (O.U.P.)
*Primary Geography Matters* (Geographical Association)
*School Base Geography* (KS2 copymaster and teacher's books) S. Scoffham et al (1986, Schofield and Sims)
*Science 5–13 Teachers Resources* (series) (Simon & Schuster Young Books)
*Spotter's Guides* (KS2 series) (Usborne)
*Starting Geography* (series) R. Bowles (Scholastic)
*Time and Place* P. & S. Harrison (series) (Simon & Schuster
*The Young Geographer Investigates* T. Jennings (series) (Oxford University Press)
The **children's reference series** published by Franklin Watts, Simon & Schuster, Wayland and A & C Black are clearly described in their catalogues.

# Fiction for children

## Landscape and places
*Bears Who Went to the Seaside* S. Gretz (1988, A & C Black)
*The Chronicles of Narnia* C. S. Lewis (1980, Armada Lions)
*Coral Island* R. M. Ballantyne (1986, Puffin Classics)
*Dear Daddy* P. Dupasquier (1986, Picture Puffin)
*Fantastic Mr Fox* R. Dahl (1982, Young Puffin)
*Katie Morag* (series) M. Hedderwick (1988, Picture Lions)
*Our Village* J. Yeomen (1988, Walker Books)
*Rewards and Fairies* R. Kipling (1965, Macmillan)
*Ride to the Rescue* J. Crebbin (1990, Young Puffin)
*The Secret Garden* F. H. Burnett (1982, Puffin Classics)
*Shaker Lane* A. and M. Provensen (1991, Walker Books)
*The Tale of Peter Rabbit* B. Potter (1987, Warne)
*Treasure Island* R. L. Stevenson (1989, Armada)
*We're Going on a Bear Hunt* M. Rosen (1989, Walker)
*Where the Forest Meets the Sea* J. Baker (1989, Walker)
*Wilberforce...* (series) M. Gordon (Picture Puffin)

## Directions, Follow a route, Journeys
*A balloon for Grandad* N. Gray/J. Ray 1990, Picture Lions)
*Gerry's Seaside Journey* M. Cartlidge (1990, Little Mammoth)
*The Hobbit* J. R. R. Tolkien (1969, Longman)
*The House at Pooh Corner* A. A. Milne (1928, Methuen): see map of Hundred Acre Wood
*I'm Going on a Gorilla Hunt* M. Jones (1989, Picture Puffin)
*The Journey Home* J. Plindall (1990, Walker Books)
*Jyoti's Journey* H. Ganly (1986, André Deutsch)
*The Little Explorer* M. Joy (1990, Young Puffin Books)
*A Nice Walk in the Jungle* N. Bodsworth (1991, Picture Puffin series)
*Noah's Ark* J. Ray (1990, Orchard Books)
*Rosie's Walk* P. Hutchins (1992, Julia MacRae)
*Spot's First Walk* E. Hill (1986, Picture Puffin series)
*Tikatoo's Journey* A. Loverseed (1990, Blackie)
*The Wheels on the Bus* P. O. Zelinsky (1990, Orchard Books)

## Other places
*A Thief in the Village* J. Berry (Puffin)
*Around the World in Eighty Days* J. Verne (1990, Puffin Classics)
*Anno's Journey* M. Anno (Bodley)
*Babar's Travels* J. de Brunhoff (1991, Methuen Children's Books)
*Nazrul's Kite* R. Warner (Black)
*Oh Kojo! How Could You!* V. Aardema (Macmillan)
*Poems from around the world* (anthology) (Simon & Schuster)
*The China Coin* A. Baillie (1991, Blackie)
*The Drum* C. Achebe (series) (Heinemann)
*The Owl and the Pussy Cat* E. Lear (1991, Simon & Schuster)
*Under the Storyteller's Spell* (Puffin)

## Land use, buildings and settlements
*Better Move On, Frog!* R. Maris (1982, Julia MacRae)
*Bridget and William* and *Horse* J. Gardam (1984, Young Puffin Books)
*Dick Whittington* F. Hunia (1978, Ladybird Books)
*Going Shopping* S. Garland (1985, Picture Puffin)
*A House is a House for Me* M. A. Hobermann (1982, Picture Puffin)

*The Lighthouse Keeper's Lunch and Other Tales* R. and D. Armitage (1980, Picture Puffin)
*Little Pete Stories* L. Berg (1952, Methuen)
*The Mice and the Clockwork Bus* R. Peppe (1988, Picture Puffin)
*The Pied Piper of Hamelin* R. Browning; S. & S. Corrin (eds.) (1990, Picture Puffin series)
*Postman Pat* (series) J. Cunliffe (Hippo)
*The Village of Round and Square Houses* A. Grifalconi (1989, Macmillan Children's Books)

## Activities
*Amoko and the Party* S. Appiah (1991, André Deutsch)
*Anancy the Spider Man* P. Sherlock (1983, Macmillan Children's Books)
*Charlie and the Chocolate Factory* R. Dahl (1979, Puffin Books)
*Growing Vegetable Soup* L. Ehlert (1990, Gollancz)
*Happy Families* (series) A. Ahlberg (Young Puffin Books)
*The Jolly Postman: Or other people's letters* J. and A. Ahlberg (1986, Heinemann)
*Meg's Veg* H. Nicoll/J. Pienkowski (1982, Picture Puffin)
*The Very Hungry Caterpillar* E. Carle (1974, Picture Puffin)
*The Wishing Tree* U. Bahl (1988, Deutsch)

## Weather and seasons
*The Adventures of Huckleberry Finn* M. Twain (1981, Puffin Classics)
*Anna, Grandpa and the Big Storm* C. Stevens (1985, Young Puffin Books)
*Antarctica* H. Cowcher (1990, André Deutsch)
*Bringing the Rain to Kapiti Plain* V. Aardema (1986, Macmillan Children's Books)
*The First Rains* P. Bonnici (1988, Mantra): India
*Flames in the Forest* and *Getting Granny's Glasses* R. Bond (1988, Young Puffin Books): rural India
*Ivor the Engine and the Snow Drifts* O. Postgate/P. Firmin (1977, Picture Lions)
*Legends of Earth, Fire and Water* E. and T. Hadley (1985, CUP)
*Not so fast Songololo* N. Daly (1987, Picture Puffin) South Africa
*Storm* K. Crossley-Holland (1985, Heinemann)
*Thank You for a Drink of Water* P. and V. Smeltzer (1980, Armada Lions)
*Tiddalick: The Frog who caused a Flood* R. Roennfeldt (1981, Picture Puffin series)
*Walkabout* J. V. Marshall (1980, Puffin Books)
*What-a-Mess in Spring* (etc) F. Muir (1986, A & C Black)

## Likes and dislikes
*Daisy* B. Wildsmith (1991, OUP)
*Father Gander's Nursery Rhymes for the Nineteen Nineties or the Alternative Mother Goose* (1989, Oleander Press)
*Mysteries of the Seals* R. Kerven (1989, Puffin Books)
*Oh! The Places You'll Go* Dr. Suess (1991, Harper Collins)
*One World* M. Foreman (1990, Andersen Press)
*Rainforest* H. Cowcher (1990, Picture Corgi)
*Stig of the Dump* C. King (1970, Puffin Books)
*There's a Troll at the Bottom of My Garden* A. Jungman (1991, Viking Children's Books)
*The Wind in the Willows* K. Grahame (1961, Methuen Children's Books
*The World that Jack Built* R. Brown (1990, Andersen Press)